TO THE LAST
CARTRIDGE

TO THE LAST CARTRIDGE

ROBERT BARR SMITH

AVON BOOKS ◆ NEW YORK

TO THE LAST CARTRIDGE is an original publication of Avon Books. This work has never before appeared in book form.

The following chapters were previously published in magazine form: *Cushing's Battery at Gettysburg,* December 1991; *Pursuit of the Altmark,* July 1988; *Dien Bien Phu,* April 1992; *Disaster on the R.C.4,* February 1990; *Fight at Adobe Walls,* April 1992; Black Hawk War, April 1991; *Doniphan's March,* June 1991; *Invasion of Madagascar,* March 1991; *General Walther Wenck at Stalingrad,* November 1990; *Pierre's Hole,* June 1992; all copyright© Empire Press. *To Die Alone in Silence,* October 1992© Vietnam Magazine.

AVON BOOKS
A division of
The Hearst Corporation
1350 Avenue of the Americas
New York, New York 10019

Library of Congress Cataloging in Publication Data:
Smith, Robert B. (Robert Barr), 1933-
    To the last cartridge / Robert Barr Smith.
        p. cm.
    1. Military history. I. Title.
D25.S555 1994   93-28664
355'.009—dc20   CIP

First Avon Books Trade Printing: February 1994

AVON TRADEMARK REG. U.S. PAT. OFF. AND IN OTHER COUNTRIES, MARCA REGISTRADA, HECHO EN U.S.A.

Printed in the U.S.A.

OPM   10 9 8 7 6 5 4 3 2

To my wife, my best critic and best friend

and to the three men who taught me what being
an officer is all about:

General George S. Blanchard
Major General Willard Latham
Major General William L. Webb

My thanks to Empire Press and its fine publications,
Military History, World War II, Vietnam, and *Wild West,*
for their gracious permission to reprint chapters that first
saw the light of day as articles in their magazines;
and to the United States Naval Institute
and its fine periodicals, *Proceedings* and *War at Sea*
for the same kindness.

CONTENTS

———— ⌁ ————

PREFACE

This book is about men at war. The soldiers come from many different countries and many different times. What they share is uncommon heroism and devotion. Each chapter deals with a separate feat of arms, usually a fight against long odds, sometimes hopeless ones. Whether these soldiers won or lost, they left behind a flash of dignity and courage to light a little the lives of men and women who appreciate self-lessness.

Every soldier knows that war is not glamorous. Every soldier knows it is full of agony and loss and pain. But every soldier also knows that in war ordinary men rise up to do extraordinary things, and good men become even better.

Nobody ever described this phenomenon better than one of the finest soldiers who ever walked, a lean Maine preacher called Joshua Chamberlain. Chamberlain commanded the 20th Maine Volunteer Regiment in an extraordinary fight at Gettysburg—you can read about it in the chapter called "Bayonet!". Chamberlain knew war as well as any man ever has, and this is what he had to say about it:

> In the privations and sufferings . . . as well as in . . . battle, some of the highest qualities of manhood are called forth— courage, self-command, sacrifice of self for the sake of something held higher . . . fortitude, patience, warmth of comradeship . . .

So while this book does not seek to glorify the agony of war, it does try to say something about the good and valuable things that come out of it—the wonderful qualities that sleep inside ordinary people.

Those qualities, fostered by fine leadership, have often won fights that logically should have been lost, like the desperate battle on a soggy Belgian hillside in 1815.

"A damned close-run thing," the Duke of Wellington called it. "The nearest thing you ever saw in your life."

The Iron Duke spoke of Waterloo, his last and greatest victory, and he spoke the simple truth. It *had* been a close-run thing. All day the French infantry of the line, and then the heavy cavalry, had hurled themselves on those steady lines of British infantry. And when the great clouds of white smoke had blown away, the British had not moved a step.

Finally, as the dreary afternoon wore on towards night, the Old Guard, the bravest of them all, had tried, only to reel back, bloodied and defeated. And when at last that long line of British bayonets started down off Mont St. Jean, an empire died in that gloomy evening. The sun of Austerlitz had sunk forever.

Those granite lines of ferocious red infantry gave all that soldiers could give, and a measure more, and it was enough to beat the most famous soldier of all time and change the course of European history. This book is about that kind of fighting man. It is about that same kind of do-or-die, fight-to-the-last-man spirit that wins impossible victories against impossible odds.

That same spirit also makes men die well in bad places, in fights they have no real hope of winning, to leave this world with honesty, at least, if not with victory. That spirit breeds stories of amazing loyalty and courage unto death, tales that motivate other men in later times to do as well.

The soldiers and sailors I've written about come from many countries and many times. They are American frontier scouts, British colonial infantrymen, French paratroopers, and Spanish military cadets. But they have in common high courage and immense determination in fights against odds. Some lived and some died; some won and some did not. All fought exceedingly well.

The chapters are about individuals and small units, mostly battalions or smaller. Large units have suffered as badly and performed as heroically; many larger units have taken dreadful casualties, sometimes much greater in total numbers than the units I've written about. But tragedy and suffering—and even courage—are somehow not as impressive in multitudes as they are in small bands, where we can almost feel the fear and the bravery and the hopelessness. We need to see the faces of individual soldiers to really live their fights, to think their last thoughts, to feel with their fingers the last cartridge in the pouch.

Their stories are interspersed with short vignettes of the soldiering breed, some serious, some a little comic. They are meant to inform and amuse, and maybe emphasize the intense humanity of the fighting men who inhabit these pages. For they were all fond of life, and not at all anxious to die in pain in some dirty place far from home. That humanity makes all the more wonderful their courage and loyalty and perfect willingness to fight, as the German army says, "to the last cartridge."

FOREWORD

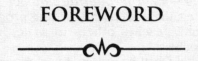

The author notes in his preface that this book, *To the Last Cartridge,* is about "men at war"—not the agony, despair, or horror always to be found, but the *men.* The span of history, the complexity of some engagements and the simplicity and poignancy of others, and the ability to draw pictures with words all show that we have here an important work by an unusually talented writer. His ability to turn a phrase is apparent from the outset as he describes Simon, Earl of Leicester, who awaited death at the hands of his attackers by the waters of the Avon in 1265: "The tall earl sat in his saddle wearily, watching doom riding slowly toward him."

Robert Barr Smith earned undergraduate history and graduate law degrees from Stanford and served for over two decades in war and peace as an officer in the United States Army. For nearly twenty years I have known Bob Smith, serving directly with him during tours in Germany. He proved himself a superb soldier—strong leader; senior parachutist, trim of body and hair; model of decorum and fitness; German interpreter; and lawyer without equal. And he was more: an intelligent and caring officer who was articulate in oral and written expression; persuasive, yet not dogmatic, in case discussions; and a gentleman, a genuinely nice person, and a dedicated family leader. *To the Last Cartridge* reflects Colonel Bob Smith on every page as he tells of these events he knew through his historical research, cast against the background of his own long service in the United States, Europe, and Vietnam, and filled with admirable images.

After army retirement, Professor Bob Smith joined the University of Oklahoma as professor of law and director of legal writing in the School of Law, and as adjunct professor of military science. Thus he is doing today what he loves: teaching and inspiring young students in law, writing, and history. Through multiple awards the university has recognized his leadership of Sooner students in their winning performances in moot court and "best brief" intercollegiate competitions. His book *The Literate Lawyer* has improved the university's legal research and writing programs. Professor Smith not only teaches others to write, but also does, well, what he teaches.

In addition to how well he writes, the rich contents of "Colonel the Professor" Smith's tales merit a few random samplings.

SWEEP OF HISTORY—in 1452–53, the fall to Turkish siege of Constantinople, ending a thousand years of rule by emperors; and in 1877–78, the fall to Russian siege of a Turkish stronghold at Plevna in Bulgaria, slowing Russian forces as they attempted to move toward that same Constantinople. In the last century, engagements by British colonial soldiers as they fought battles far from home and support, often with loyal native troops, as in Afghanistan in 1838–42. In 1940, brave deeds at sea, the night boarding of the German ship *Altmark* in "neutral" waters of Norway and the freeing of British seamen captured by the *Graf Spee* before its earlier sinking. In the last century and this, tales of the French Foreign Legion: the 1863 death of the legendary Captain Danjou in Mexico—giving the Legion its most sacred relic, his wooden hand, and its "high holy day" of April 30, Camerone Day; to the heroic fighting in Indochina some four decades ago, and the celebration of Camerone Day a week before the fall in 1954 of Dien Bien Phu.

AMERICAN MILITIA AND THE CITIZEN SOLDIER— In 1814, the battle at Bladensburg Bridge in Maryland when, at the approach of regular British troops, American militia left their positions defending the bridge and ran, leaving that approach to Washington open to the following burning of the capital. In 1846–47, the march of eight hundred tough Missouri volunteers led by their elected commander, Colonel Doniphan, on a long, difficult march to Mexico to contribute to victory in war with that country. In 1863, the critical action of the 20th Maine under its brave, scholarly former professor from Bowdoin in holding Little Round Top on the second desperate day of fighting at Gettysburg.

PATHOS—In February 1891 in New York City, the picture of General Joseph E. Johnston, then eighty-four, standing bareheaded in bitter weather at the funeral of his old foe in the late war and his friend, General William T. Sherman, only to contract pneumonia and die himself a short time later. In 1936, the terrible choice of a besieged commander in Spain when told by telephone to surrender his fortress or his son would die, and his son was on the phone; the commander told his son that there would be no surrender and that he should die like a patriot. The son was shot.

HUMOR—In 1868 in Colorado, the account of two scouts sent dismounted from a cornered cavalry unit through Indian territory to bring help, hidden in a "shallow buffalo wallow" when a large party of hostile Indians halted a few yards away, reduced to using their only silent weapon to drive off a rattlesnake that attempted to share their tenuous hiding place—repeated sousing of the snake with tobacco juice. Before World War II, the story of a young British subaltern posted to command Gurkha troops in India who showed great poise: After leaving a party with the hostess's daughter for amorous pursuits nearby, he was interrupted by his passing Gurkha band, which, of course, recognized him and saluted. Though "out of uniform," he rose and returned the salute.

PERSONAL HEROISM—In 1862, the discipline and courage of British troops who stood in ranks as their ship with too few lifeboats slowly sank and women and children were evacuated. In 1945 on Okinawa, the feats of an Army medic in an infantry unit as he crawled again and again into the teeth of Japanese fire to drag to safety his wounded comrades, until his own shattered limbs stopped him. In 1968, an account of action at a fire base in Vietnam under heavy attacks by fire and waves of enemy, and of Lieutenant Colonel Charles Rogers as he rallied troops repeatedly and successfully, even when he could no longer stand because of multiple wounds. (This account brought to mind personal memories of this rare soldier, who later retired as a major general and entered the ministry in Germany. I recently saw him laid to rest at too young an age in Arlington National Cemetery. Years after that bitter fight in Vietnam, Charles

Rogers responded characteristically when asked if he had been afraid. "No," he said. "I was too busy worrying about my men.")

This excellent selection of stories shows that Bob Smith shares that concern for and admiration of the brave deeds of men in battle. Readers will enjoy the author's depictions of their willingness through history to serve leader, cause, and country and to fight, often *To the Last Cartridge.*

William L. Webb, Jr.
Major General U.S. Army (Retired)
Vienna, Virginia
September 1992

THE GENTLE WATERS OF AVON

The tall earl sat in his saddle wearily, watching doom riding slowly toward him. Trapped in a deep bend of the River Avon below the little town of Evesham, he was outnumbered two to one. Down the gentle slopes of Green Hill to his front flowed a forest of glittering steel and fluttering lance-pennons. There was no way out, for the orderly ranks before him stretched clear across the gap between the two arms of the river that hemmed him in. Simon de Montfort, Earl of Leicester, knew he was about to die.

At first he had thought the approaching force was the army commanded by his son, Simon the Younger. Indeed, borne before it was a cluster of banners that belonged to units of his son's host. However, a sharp-eyed barber of Evesham, peering from a church tower, soon recognized the oncoming troops as hostile. The banners had been captured from Simon the Younger's men, and the old earl's heart must have sunk when he heard the news. There would be no help.

There would be no escape across the Avon either, for the Bengeworth Bridge crossing, the road toward the south and Evesham village, was also held against him. And the mass of his enemies closing in gave no opening to Simon's military genius. The royalists were well arrayed, and kept well in hand. Somewhere out there, he knew, was his sometime charge and pupil, Edward, Prince of England. Simon could not restrain his admiration . . . and his pride: "By the arm of Saint James," he said, "they come on well! It was from me he learned it!"

Simon turned his big body in the saddle with a scrape and clink of mail. Behind him, in armor unmarked by any badge

or device, rode his prisoner, King Henry III of England, his
enemy of twenty years. Let the feckless king be led into the
battle—perhaps he would take a spear-thrust meant for one
of Simon's men. The Earl did not care. His eyes found his
sons Henry and Guy, who sat their horses near him in silence. "May God have mercy on our souls," said their warrior
father, "for our bodies are theirs."

Simon was a very old man for his time, at least sixty-five,
at an age when other men sought little more than a warm
fireside, a joint of beef, and the tumbling affection of their
grandchildren. For Simon those homely pleasures were
never to be. For him there was only hardship, grinding responsibility, and bloody war—not rest, but ever fresh treachery and new enemies. He was tired now, terribly tired, but
still hardy and tough, able to ride all day in full armor and
fight at the end of the ride.

And he still harbored a tiny spark of hope. For off to the
northeast his son Simon should be coming, hurrying to his
aid with a strong force of men-at-arms. He could not, Simon
the elder reasoned, be more than ten miles away at Alcester,
at the juncture of the Alne and Arrow rivers. If the earl could
win through to Alcester, he might join with his son, and the
two together might turn on Edward's royal host and rout
them yet.

It was August 4, 1265, a dismal day of ominous and frightful portents. As Simon and his men watched their deaths
ride toward them across the lovely and fertile vale of
Evesham, even the heavens seemed to mourn. For above
Green Hill there appeared an ugly and unseasonable cloud,
evil black wrack scudding across the face of the sun, blotting
it out, turning the bright morning into baleful twilight.

Thunder hammered and boomed above the placid Avon,
and spiteful tongues of lightning flickered toward the earth.
Only a few drops of rain fell. But still the thunder rumbled
and muttered, and the day grew darker and darker. In the
Abbey of Evesham, only a few hundred yards away, the darkness was so profound that the monks in their chapel could
not read the words of the litany before them.

To the men waiting for hopeless battle—men of a profoundly religious and superstitious age—this dreadful gloom
was a sign of sure calamity. The monk Robert of Gloucester,

only some thirty miles away at the time of the battle, described the fear and horror inspired by the storm:

> In the north-west a dark storm there arose
> Suddenly swart enough, that many a man agros.
> And it overcast all the land that men might scarce see,
> A grislier weather than it was might not on earth be.

Behind Simon and his sons waited 160 knights, tough veterans, loyal and able, bearing on their surcoats the white cross they had worn during their victory at Lewes, just fifteen months before. Behind them stood ranks of English infantry and some Welsh bowmen. They were all tired, horse and foot alike, animals and men, but perhaps with one last desperate effort . . . and Simon called to his men.

Without a miracle, a dream was about to die here in the sleepy, lush vale of Evesham. A dream, an ideal, the germ of representative government, had been born and grown to flower with the Earl of Leicester. It had been a bright promise while it lasted, but now it was about to fade and wither. England had been traveling the long, bloody road to Evesham for almost twenty years.

Henry III was a feckless, frivolous man, devout always, kind usually, generous—with the public treasury—often. He was no soldier, although he persisted in trying to act like one. Henry was badly beaten by the enemies of England in both France and Wales, to the vast disgust of most of the English baronage.

He dipped deep into the coffers of England in a truly silly attempt to buy for his son Edmund the throne of Sicily, and to support his brother Richard of Cornwall as Holy Roman Emperor. Even worse, his court was infested with a plague of rapacious foreigners, anathema to native-born Englishmen and even to that part of the nobility who still had one foot in their continental possessions. Queen Eleanor's Savoyard relatives flocked to England for money, appointments, lands, and castles. Henry even made one of them Archbishop of Canterbury.

The wave of Savoyards followed close on a pestilence of grasping adventurers from Poitou, all brought in by a Poitivin favorite of the king. One of these at one time held the post of sheriff in sixteen shires, and ended up treasurer of

England. Busily competing with these parasites for appointments and lands was an invasion of Italian churchmen. These aliens, as grasping as the rest, had been sent by the pope, relying on the grant of England as a fief of Rome, made by Henry's worthless father, John. The best of the English churchmen were ready to back a strong man who would stand for the rights of the English Church against foreign influences.

As if all this were not enough, Henry also provided with open hands for another avaricious swarm of foreigners, his Lusignan half brothers, sons of his mother's second marriage to a French noble. These foreigners also partook of Henry's incredible generosity, skimming much of the cream of the lands and offices of the realm. They and the others even received grants of royal castles.

On top of that, the king gave presents to virtually everybody he met, spent lavishly on food and wine, started menageries, and built extensively. His masterpiece was lovely Westminster Abbey, but that beauty cost much money too.

There had been steady resistance to Henry's preference for foreigners over native-born Englishmen. The justiciar, Hubert de Burgh, led the resistance until Henry dismissed him in disgrace. Much of the English clergy resisted the king's subservience to Rome, led by Robert Grosseteste, Bishop of Lincoln. Three times the resistance forced Henry to reissue Magna Carta; three times he ignored it.

And so, by 1258, the baronage had had enough of Henry's waste and incompetence. When Henry went back to Parliament to ask for more money to feed his projects and provide for his insatiable relatives and favorites, Parliament refused. Instead, the king was required to sign a compact called the Provisions of Oxford. The key provision was the establishment of a Council of Fifteen, who would fill offices and otherwise guide the country. Leading the barons and churchmen was the king's own brother-in-law, Simon de Montfort, Earl of Leicester.

The council began by insisting that all royal castles be returned to the king. When his Lusignan relatives arrogantly refused to disgorge their holdings, they were deported. A mob of Londoners threw rocks and offal at Queen Eleanor, hated because of the rapacity of her relatives, an insult Henry would never forget. Perhaps inevitably, the conflict be-

tween king and barons came to open war. Both sides buck-
led on their armor and prepared.

The issue was decided on the fourteenth of May, 1264, outside the little town of Lewes, on the edge of the Sussex
Downs. After a success at Northampton, and much harrying
of opponents' lands, the king and his son Edward had
moved south against the vital Cinque Ports. After receiving
the surrender of Winchelsea, they were now encamped before Lewes, knowing Simon and the baronial army must be
near. In fact, the earl was only nine miles away. His exact location remained unknown to the royalists, even when he
sent a deputation to make one last try for peace. They were
scornfully received, the offer rejected out of hand.

Except for a vedette, or picket, the king left unoccupied the
high ground overlooking Lewes. The picket, probably only a
single soldier, was left on Offham Hill, from which a man
could watch for trouble coming down the roads from the
north. Down in the town there seems to have been a good
deal of roistering by the royalist forces.

> Long and loud were the cheeres theye rais'd
> And the wine cup circled free
> No care had theye for the coming fraye,
> No thoughte of eternitye.

There is evidence that the royal army was doing more than
drinking, as well. One chronicle mentions the useful services
of "seven hundred whores," although it is not recorded how
all these ladies came to be in tiny Lewes at such an oppor-
tune time.

In any case, good soldier Simon, having heard mass, was
moving swiftly through the night while the royal forces drank
Lewes dry and pursued such other sports as caught their
fancy. Simon's leading elements surprised the picket, sound
asleep on his hilltop, and when morning broke the royalists
looked out their windows to find Simon's army lining the
slope of the hill above the town. The royalists armed themselves desperately, and tried to form for battle.

In both foot soldiers and armored cavalry, the royalist
forces outnumbered by two to one Simon's small force, a
mix of men-at-arms, Kentish bowmen, and a contingent from
London, townsmen enthusiastic but wholly untrained. In the

green Londoners lay Simon's weakness, and in the end his salvation.

For Edward the prince charged with his knights headlong into the Londoners, who panicked and scattered and took to their heels. Edward, not yet the seasoned soldier, pursued, cutting down the luckless amateurs as they ran. It may be he pursued so viciously because he remembered the taunts and filth hurled at his mother the year before. In any case, he pursued too far, at least four miles, and then took time out to cut up Simon's baggage-train.

While he was away, Simon closed on the royal army, probably while it was still milling about trying to form up outside the town. Simon had the advantage of having his men formed and ready, and could launch them in a downhill charge. He struck Henry's army with a shattering charge of heavy cavalry, and drove the royalists in disorder back into the town. As Henry's men began to waver, Simon threw in his cavalry reserve, striking an exposed flank, and the royal army began to come apart.

The inoffensive little town caught fire during the fighting, and through the leaping flames and lowering smoke, hand-to-hand fighting swirled through the narrow streets. As Simon's men pressed deeper into the town, surviving royal men-at-arms began to surrender or run. The king surrendered, and his brother the emperor also fell into Simon's hands. Edward, returning late, his horses blown, was deserted by many of his men. He, too, would surrender, to spend the next months in honorable restraint as Simon's prisoner.

In the fifteen months that followed, Simon struggled to rule England, keeping up the pretense that the king still ruled, deferring to Henry, and showing him every honor. And it was during these fifteen short months that the hope was born. It was not just the widely shared belief that England should be for Englishmen, not foreigners, a first glimmering of real national spirit.

More than that, ordinary people saw in Simon's rule their chance to be part of government, to have some say in the future of England. Their hope was celebrated in "The Song of Lewes," a thirteenth-century Latin poem written by some unknown churchman.

So now God bless
Sir Simon, with his army and his sons!
Courageously they ran the risk of death,
And fought with might and main, for they had felt
Such sorrow at the lamentable plight
Of those who lived in England at that time.

For in March 1265, Simon summoned Parliament to carry on the business of government, a sort of Parliament no man had seen before. This time he included not only knights— that had been done before—but summoned representatives from various cities and boroughs. For the first time, the people had some voice in government. For the first time, the real heart and strength of England had a hand in guiding their own future.

The dream did not last, of course. Within a year many of Simon's supporters fell away, some wooed by the royalist party, some jealous of Simon's power, others disappointed of rewards. Edward managed a spectacular escape from his guards, an escape apparently engineered by the beautiful Maude Mortimer, in whose castle the prince quickly took refuge. So it was to be war again.

Simon took the field, moving west across the Severn to attack the bases of royal strength on the Welsh marches. But while he was west of the river, he learned of Edward's escape. Immediately he started to double back, only to find all boats destroyed or taken by the royalists. His son Simon, who should have been marching from the east to join him, was nowhere to be seen. In fact, he was still at Kenilworth Castle, some thirty miles away.

And Edward knew it. He had been brought word by a mysterious figure, an attractive woman known to history only as Margot the Spy. Whoever she was, this daring woman handed young Edward the key to victory. She also told the prince that Simon the Younger was encamped outside the castle walls at Kenilworth, apparently with little or no security. And so Edward turned his back on Simon, stranded across the Severn, and marched hard from Worcester on the unready baronial forces at Kenilworth.

He struck them in the darkness, having covered thirty-four miles in just twelve or thirteen hours, a lightning march for the time. A butchery followed, with much of the baronial party cut down unarmored, even naked, as they fled their tents in panic. Many others scattered into the night, never to re-form. Simon the Younger made the castle, and the castle held, but his force was badly diminished at little cost to Edward.

Meanwhile, Earl Simon and his tired little army had finally found a few boats at a place called Kempsey, just four miles from Worcester, and laboriously crossed the river. Since the royal pickets had been withdrawn, Simon must have suspected that Edward had gone after his son. But he could not have known of the disaster at Kenilworth. Had he known, he would have marched hard for London, his main source of strength, avoiding contact with Edward's superior force if he could. Instead, fatally, he moved east along the gentle Avon. Toward Evesham.

And now, as heavy rain began to fall in the bend of the Avon, Lewes was yesteryear, and that victory, so fair and promising for better times, was ashes in Earl's Simon's mouth. Now it was time to die, or, if God willed, perhaps to break through with at least a few of his faithful men. Simon knew how deep ran the hatred of the king and his supporters. There would be no magnanimity from Harry of Winchester. And Simon de Montfort would never crawl and beg, not even for life itself.

He formed his cavalry into a wedge, a solid arrowhead of horseflesh, iron, and steel, the infantry and archers to follow close behind. Overhead flapped the de Montfort standard, the silver fork-tailed lion. At last, when the royalist lines were close enough, Simon waved his men forward. The lance-points swung down, and the big horses began to gain speed. They would strike toward their right front, in the direction of Alcester, and the tremendous shock of that steel wedge just might rupture the royal lines and open the way. Edward could not be equally strong everywhere.

It almost worked. The mailed wedge of veterans smashed deep into Edward's ranks, long swords slashing their enemies from the saddle, axes and maces crushing helmets and mail to reach the flesh beneath. Deeper they drove and deeper, and the royal line recoiled and sagged before them. But it would not break.

And now the lines of Edward's knights pressed in on both sides of the wedge, and Simon's men began to go down. King

Richard cried out desperately, "By God's head, I am Henry the old king of England! I am Harry of Winchester, your king! Do not kill me! Do not hit me, I am too old to fight." And a royalist knight heard him, pulled off his helm to confirm his identity, and led the frightened monarch out of harm's way.

As the fighting centered on Simon's banner, and the little knot of devoted men around it, Simon's son, Guy, fell badly wounded beneath the horses' hoofs. Soon after, Henry, his eldest son, was down and dying, and the father spurred into the ranks of his enemies.

"It is time for me to die!" he roared, and drove into the mass of men around him, red sword rising and falling, until his war-horse fell beneath him. Still the tall old man fought on, wounded now, fighting on foot against a circling mob of enemies. And at last a man-at-arms lifted de Montfort's mail from behind and stabbed deep into his back.

"God's grace," cried the earl, and went down at last, falling under the hammer-blows of many men now, until the life was beaten out of him, his armor torn and bloodied. And with him fell all but twelve of his 160 knights and perhaps 4,000 common soldiers, for no quarter was given by the royal forces. The foot soldiers were cut down like rabbits as they tried to stand, or to hide in the lush cornfields of the Vale of Evesham. More died as they ran desperately for the Avon. The placid river flowed a dirty crimson, and men died miserably in the mud of its banks, or sank into its waters forever.

For this was no ordinary fight. It was normally knightly custom to take prisoners, at least of other knights, to let ransom substitute for blood once victory was assured. But not this awful day, for this was war to the knife. There had been far too much blood shed, too many hot words exchanged; there had been too much treachery, too much double-dealing and oath-breaking. And now it would all be washed out in bloody vengeance, murderous, primitive and purging.

Even Simon's death did not content his enemies. His corpse was stripped of its armor as it lay in the dust, the gray head cut off, the arms and legs chopped from the body. And last, the ultimate indignity, Simon's genitals were cut away. The leader of this ugliness, Roger de Mortimer, still not content, would send head, hands, and genitals to his castle of Wigmore on the Welsh marches. There his fury of a wife would admire and gloat over them. Maud Mortimer was at prayer when the remains were brought to her, but she received them nonetheless, in her chapel, and in full view of the congregation.

"Such was the murder of Evesham," wrote Robert of Gloucester, "for battle none it was." Even some men initially made prisoners were cut down in the general vengeful celebration after the fight.

And while the final butchery was still going on, the earl's son, Simon the Younger, appeared with his army not far from the battlefield. He was close enough, at least, to see, or learn from his scouts, what had happened there, and know his father's gray head now decorated the point of a lance.

"Feebly have I gone!" he cried, and indeed he had. For he had been at Alcester—only ten miles away—*the night before*, but had halted for dinner and a comfortable sleep. Worse, he had taken time for breakfast before leaving Alcester this morning. Had he come on the night before, or even marched at daybreak, he would have reached his father over a clear road, still unblocked by royal troops. Together they could have fought with some sort of parity; perhaps, with the earl's acknowledged leadership ability, they might have turned defeat into victory. Now there was only shame and retreat. Young Simon turned back, riding quickly for the castle of Kenilworth and safety.

Young prince Edward had won. What remained of the baronial party lay amongst the cornfields, its leader hacked and mutilated, its hopes shattered. And that was the moment, perhaps, when Edward the prince started to become Edward the monarch. For he was touched by the bloodied corpses of men he knew.

He wept over the body of Henry de Montfort, who had been not only his cousin, but also his first playmate. He allowed the Benedictine monks of Evesham to collect the pitiful pieces of the earl's shattered body, and he himself went to the abbey to watch the monks bury before the high altar of the abbey church all that was left of Simon de Montfort.

The Barons' War was over. There would be more fighting before the last sparks were extinguished. Kenilworth Castle would hold out gallantly for many months still. But in the end, the castle was forced to surrender, and Simon the Younger made good his escape to the continent.

And there were other pockets of devoted resistance still to stamp out. Even while the fighting continued, Edward did much more than campaigning to wash away the hatred and blood of the revolt. At Whitsun of the next year, down in the Berkshire wood of Alton, he cornered the famous young commoner Adam Gurdon and his small band of retainers. And there, as their men-at-arms watched, the two tall young men in mail fought it out single-handed, until at last Adam could fight no more.

Edward saw to it that his gallant young enemy was cared for, and the two rode together to the castle of Guildford, where Adam was well and honorably treated. Edward was becoming distinctly kinglike now, deeply concerned with healing the country's dreadful wounds, putting vengeance and strife behind him. Adam Gurdon would remain his friend in later days, fighting for Edward the king in the Welsh wars to come.

It was well for England that Edward was determined to bury the past. For many of his supporters, and most of all his father, were determined on extracting the last measure of vengeance from all their surviving enemies. In the end, most of the defeated were allowed to retain their estates on payment of a sum of money, usually based on the estimated yearly rents from their lands.

The great earl's tremendous influence on the course of England lived on long after his death. He had started something, this novel business of including ordinary men in the decisions of government. He was no democrat, this wise, formidable man, but he had the vision to see the advantages of the rule of law, and he accepted the astonishing idea that Parliament could meet, and act, whether the king willed it or not.

And that lesson was not lost on his nephew, now Edward I. In 1282, at Shrewsbury, he would convene a Parliament that included representatives from twenty boroughs and towns. And at Westminster, in 1293, members sat who represented the commons, along with the nobility and princes of the church. The Model Parliament, it was called, and it might never have existed without that first pioneering effort by the old Earl of Leicester.

The common people certainly idolized Simon. He was

their champion, whatever his own motives might have been. A chronicler of the time spoke for ordinary Englishmen:

> Wanne king Henry hadde the victori at Evesham, and Simonde the erle was y-sley . . . thatt was grete harm to the comens of Englonde, that so gode man was destroiedde, ffor he was dede for the common profite of the same ffolke, and therefore God hathe schewed off him many grete miracules to diverse ffolkes of her maladies and revawnce, werefore thei have be heledde.

The story spread that when Maud Mortimer brought the hacked pieces of his body into the chapel at Wigmore, the whole congregation saw Simon's hands rise and clasp in prayer. And it is true that the chatelaine of Wigmore did not keep the hands, but sent them back to Evesham.

And for many years after the battle, ordinary people came on pilgrimage to Evesham. They would gather at a small pool near which Simon died. The pilgrims believed that the little mere—still called de Montfort's well—turned blood-red before their eyes. It was said that when Simon's enemies dismembered him he did not bleed, and that his innermost garment was found to be the hairshirt of the penitent.

Stories multiplied of miraculous cures for the sick and crippled who knelt to pray before the great earl's tomb in the abbey. People came from London and Canterbury, from as far away as Newcastle in the north, and more than two hundred miracles were attributed to the spirit of the dead Simon. Many of these were attested to by witnesses, one at least by the population of a whole Berkshire village.

Simon began to be called a saint, his name revered like that of Thomas à Becket, martyr of Canterbury. There would never be a serious attempt at canonization, because the pope of the time was entirely supportive of Richard. But in the minds of the ordinary people he would be Saint Simon for years to come.

To this day Simon is remembered at Evesham. In 1918 a memorial cross was erected in the abbey ruins above his grave. And there, on the Sunday closest to the anniversary of Simon's death, the rector of Evesham holds a service in his memory. It is a touching tradition. But Earl Simon's real monument is up in bustling London, overlooking the

Thames. In the corridors of Parliament sons and daughters of laborers and millionaires, shopkeepers and knights, rub elbows, talk and argue, and carry on the business of government. It is not the institution Simon de Montfort envisioned, but in a very real way he was its father.

STIFF UPPER LIP

By and large, the British army has been very well led over the years. If its higher command has sometimes been fusty and slow to learn, its junior leaders have a well-deserved reputation for daring and cold courage. And to the general surprise of foreign observers, the British officer corps has also kept a devil of humor and humanity quite at odds with its reputation for staid conservatism. Nowhere was that devil more active than in the British Indian army. And nowhere in the Army of the Raj did the imp laugh and caper more often than among the officers of Gurkha units.

As every good soldier knows, the Gurkhas are wiry little men from Nepal, that misty kingdom up on the Roof of the World. Long ago they fought the British. Out of that sanguinary introduction came a long friendship, a brotherhood nurtured in blood from Delhi during the Indian Mutiny to the Falklands War with Argentina. Even today the British army maintains Gurkha battalions, and it is considered a great honor among Nepalese hillmen to be accepted as a long-service soldier of Her Britannic Majesty. The competition for a space on the muster-roll is fierce.

The Gurkha's reputation as a warrior has been earned on a hundred battlefields. He is a little lion in action, cheery, reliable, profoundly conscious of the history of his unit and the obligation that goes with the uniform. He has earned more than his share of Victoria Crosses.

He is a modern soldier, adept with all modern weapons. But he also carries inside him a strain of aboriginal, almost mystic courage. And when he closes with the enemy, he will do hideous destruction hand to hand with his ancestral weapon. It is a wicked reverse-curve chopping blade called a kukri, and it can remove a foeman's head with a single stroke. And has.

A British officer who commands Gurkhas must be a special man. He is hand-picked, and serves a probationary period before he is fully accepted. He must speak Gurkhali, although his men are also taught some English. He knows his soldiers intimately. They are his children. He knows their thoughts and emotions like his own, and joins them in the dances of their celebrations. He is expected to demonstrate a special aplomb, a coolness special even among his largely unflappable brethren.

John Masters, whose books are the best ever written about soldiers, told this anecdote about one such officer, a subaltern in a Gurkha unit in India prior to World War II.

The occasion was a party at the bungalow of a Eurasian lady, given on a regimental guest night. The party was attended by a group of officers and the lady's daughter, a nubile lass with eyes for one of the young officers. By common consent the pair edged away from the party, moved by a desire to culminate their mutual passion. But where to go? There was no private place to be had in or out of doors.

At last, using that initiative for which Gurkha officers are famous, the subaltern chose the concrete platform supporting a war-trophy cannon, away from the house, close to the dark and empty road. And on that wretched couch the officer and the lady fell avidly to satisfying their hearts' desire.

For a little time the road remained dark and empty, until, in the midst of the couple's transports of ecstasy, there appeared around a corner the unit's bagpipe band, en route to play at the guest night. The Gurkha pipe major was surprised, not to say astonished, at finding one of the battalion's lieutenants in extreme undress uniform by the side of the road. Good soldier that he was, however, he did the only correct thing, and gravely ordered, "Eyes right!" And the band,

with impassive mien, marched smartly past the gun platform.

It is not recorded whether the young subaltern entirely
stopped what he was doing. What he did do was also the only
correct thing. He raised his head and smartly returned the
salute. Masters recalled that the lieutenant became a general
in later years. One hopes so. Such men are hard to find.

THE END OF A THOUSAND YEARS
THE CANNON OF THE PROPHET AT CONSTANTINOPLE

Great Byzantium was dying. Constantinople, pillar of eastern Christendom, was crumbling, wasting away, losing its
people, losing its strength, losing everything but its pride.
And its magic.

For a thousand years the sumptuous city by the Sea of
Marmara had commanded the Bosphorus, the narrow gut
that connected Mediterranean to Black Sea, West to East.
For all those long centuries she had dominated Eastern
trade, held the line against the barbarian infidel, ruled in incredible magnificence a Christian empire in Asia.

She had been adored as the jewel in the crown of orthodox
Christianity, coveted for her incredible wealth and power, re-
viled for her wickedness as the Whore of the Bosphorus.
Time out of mind, she had been locked in acrimonious dis-
putation with Western Catholicism over the terms of reunion
between the two churches. Theologians East and West argued angrily over differences in doctrine that seem minuscule to modern people.

In the fifteenth century, however, they were anything but
minuscule. Though the fresh winds of the Renaissance blew
across much of the Western world, men still quarreled bit-
terly, unforgivingly, over matters of faith. Most of their dis-

putes were inconsequential; modern people would call them petty. Petty they certainly were, but in 1453 they would bring down an ancient empire.

Now in the mid-fifteenth century, Constantinople was surely in deep decline, only a shell of what she had been, but still a powerful symbol to the faithful. Denuded of population, full of empty houses and silent squares, she was still the center of life for every Orthodox Catholic, and now she was menaced by the very Antichrist, the heathen Turk.

The heathen Turk in this case was Mehmet II, called Mohammed in the West. He was only twenty-three, but he was farsighted, ruthless, shrewd, and very able indeed. He had in his hand an extraordinary military machine, proven in battle, and a complex political apparatus that answered only, and instantly, to him. And this young absolute ruler wanted one thing from life, one thing above all others: He wanted Constantinople.

Mehmet was very much a traditionalist, an orthodox Moslem and a believer in the absolute right of the sultanate. He had, after all, indulged on his accession in the time-honored practice of having his brother strangled, to insure he would have no rival.

But for all his cruelty and suspicion, Mehmet also cultivated both science and art. And he was open to things new, when they suited him, and one of the things that suited him was artillery. Mehmet had already ordered his own foundries to explore the casting of bigger and better cannon. He also paid quadruple the going rate to employ a talented Hungarian cannon-founder called Urban. Urban hired on in the summer of 1452, after his services had been turned down by the Byzantines.

Urban told the sultan he could make a cannon that would batter down the walls of Babylon, if need be, and Mehmet believed him. Within three months the Hungarian had indeed cast a gun that sank a Venetian ship in the Bosphorus, when the vessel refused to heed a Turkish command to heave to. Between the range of the gun and the fate of the crew—they were decapitated or impaled—Eastern Christians must have trembled. The sultan, delighted, ordered Urban to produce a cannon twice as big.

Urban promptly did so. By the next January there appeared at Adrianople a monstrous thirty-two-inch gun firing a thirteen-hundred-pound stone ball more than five hundred yards. It was a gigantic piece, this cannon. It took fifty yoke of oxen and four or five hundred men to move, and that very slowly indeed.

It required many more men to mount and level and serve it, and all that took time, too. But once it was finally in position, it did horrible things to ancient masonry walls, walls like those of Byzantium. Mehmet ordered the monster hitched up and started southeast . . . toward Constantinople.

Nor was this the only cannon Mehmet's troops possessed. His train of artillery was ultramodern for the time, an age in which torsion-powered ballistae and catapults were still widely used in siegecraft. His superb artillery fitted well with the rest of his forces, which included some of the most dangerous infantry in the world.

Mehmet, like his predecessor, employed several sorts of troops. There was cavalry, of course, once the traditional Moslem arm. There were also irregulars, Bashi-Bazouks, men whose job it was to skirmish and forage. They were of little use in a stand-up fight, but were widely feared for their fondness for rapine, loot, and indiscriminate killing.

But Mehmet's main strength was in two kinds of trained infantry. The first were Anatolian Turks, tough, disciplined, well armed and protected. They were formidable enough, but the real strength of any Turkish army of the day was the contingent of Janizaries.

The Janizaries came largely from Christian families, men from the four points of the compass, taken as children by the sultan's agents and raised as Moslem soldiers. They lived a monastic sort of life in their own barracks, forbidden to marry. The faith and the sultan were wife and parents to them. They knew no other allegiance.

In the mid-fifteenth century they were about twelve thousand strong, professional fighting men in the purest sense, highly trained and without other purpose. They were the sultan's shock troops, fanatic, ascetic, ruthless. Assured of a place in paradise as Moslems fighting for the faith, they feared death not at all.

No other Turkish troops were quite like them. Uniformed in blue, with large white felt hats, they were the highly paid elite of the realm. Even their rank titles were different: noncommissioned officers were called, curiously, "head cooks" and "water carriers"; one officer rank translated literally as "soup kitchen." They were well led and equipped with the best of arms and armor.

Even as Mehmet began to stretch out his talons toward Constantinople, even though men of the West knew something of his avarice and power, few thought the great city was in any real danger. Her walls, after all, were legendary.

The Greeks of Constantinople were not so sure. To them, the Turkish host looked as numerous as the stars in the sky. Some said that the city was assailed by three or four hundred thousand of the infidel. In fact, although the Turkish army was surely large, it is unlikely to have much exceeded one hundred thousand men. In addition to the hard core, the Janizaries, there were perhaps seventy thousand more excellent infantry, and about twenty thousand Bashi-Bazouks. They were an impressive sight, this Turkish host, all color and noise, standards and trumpets and great drums, but the great city was just as formidable.

Even against an attacker with artillery, the walls of Constantinople were daunting. The city was a rough triangle, its seven-mile-long eastern side fronting on the Sea of Marmara, its shorter northern side on the Golden Horn, the inlet that was the major harbor of the city. Its land side, the most vulnerable part of the defenses, was five miles long, and was protected by immensely strong double walls, reinforced with fifty towers. The walls were old, but they could hold a long time, manned by enough determined defenders.

And that was the problem. The garrison was terribly outnumbered. Even if the old fortifications held together, the defenders were stretched so thin that one man had to cover eighteen feet of wall. Some use could be made of carefully hoarded reserves, rushed to any threatened point. Still, especially in view of the inevitable losses, there were too few men to defend everything. And no part of the wall could be left undefended.

Such troops as the emperor had were effective soldiers. There were some Greek soldiers, good enough men, but the cream of the defenders were Italian. They were volunteers mostly, with some mercenaries, all determined to hold this bastion of Christianity against the Moslem menace. They came from Venice, Pisa, and Genoa for the most part, and the cream of them were seven hundred Genoese, commanded by an able and magnetic soldier called John Giustiniani.

They were a pitiful few to hold this vast expanse of walls. They were so few, as it happened, because of the perpetual quarreling between the Western and Eastern churches. At a church conference some years before, an agreement of union had been hammered out between Rome and Constantinople. It was still a practical nullity, however, because bitter doctrinal haggling continued, and unscrupulous politicians exploited centuries-old religious prejudice to inflame much of both West and East against the pact of union.

As a result, when Emperor Constantine XI appealed to the West for aid, he got a lot of sanctimonious rhetoric and very little practical support. The pope, to his credit, tried to raise support for the Eastern Church, although he still had profound reservations about the depth of Eastern adherence to the union agreement. He reached into his own skimpy treasury to buy and send a shipload of supplies to the East. And, following papal urging, dedicated fighting Christians like Giustiniani responded.

Otherwise, sadly, there was little help forthcoming. The maritime merchant states of Italy all tried to straddle the fence, sending fulsome messages and a few soldiers while keeping intact their lucrative trade arrangements with and through the Moslem world. Either Venice or Genoa might have raised twenty thousand men and a hundred ships in defense of the Eastern church.

But neither did. Venice, for example, made a great show of repudiating the sultan. At the same time, however, she ordered her captains to protect the Eastern Christians—but not to attack or provoke the sultan's men. How that feat was to be achieved was left unclear. It was an order guaranteed to produce terminal timidity in the sea dogs of the republic. Venice also voted to send ships and men to help the city. That measure sounded positive, but it was accompanied by endless foot dragging, delay that insured the promised reinforcements would not arrive in time to help.

Genoa had a special problem. She actually occupied, as a trading depot, an area just across the Golden Horn from Constantinople, a place called Pera. The Genoese leader there was told to make the best arrangement he could with Mehmet. Ordinary Genoese might join the defense of the city, as Giustiniani did. Otherwise, there would be no help for the Eastern Christians.

Mehmet had no problems with indecision or disunity. He knew what he wanted, and within the sultanate, what Mehmet wanted was all that really mattered. Through the last days of 1452 he finalized his plans, brushing aside the objections of his longtime counselor and vizier. "Only one thing I want," he told the old man. "Give me Constantinople!" And his armies began to gather as the year turned.

As the days of March passed, Turkish contingents converged on the city. Mehmet's troops were enthusiastic, well equipped, tightly disciplined, full of talk about words of the Prophet that predicted the city's fall. In the Sea of Marmara a cloud of sails appeared, Turkish warships cruising that very water that once was a Byzantine lake.

Inside Constantinople there was fear, cold fear of those baleful galleys offshore, fear of the apparently limitless hordes gathering before the walls, fear above all of the coming of the Antichrist. There was no lack of frightening signs, a couple of small earthquakes and a thunderous rain.

Nevertheless, the city rallied and went to work. Everyone turned out to repair the walls, arms were collected and distributed, and a great store of provisions was collected and inventoried. And a few at a time, fighting men arrived from other lands, many of them hardened professionals.

John Giustiniani brought his seven hundred troops into Constantinople in late January. He also brought a reputation for defending fortified places, so the emperor charged him with command of the vulnerable western wall. Included in his responsibility was the crumbling Blachernae Palace, which held the vital northwest corner of the city's defenses.

Giustiniani was a born leader. Men responded to him, even many of the Venetians, to whom the ordinary Genoese was little better than a Turk. He was able to work closely with the Venetian ship captain Gabriele Trevisano, who, with eight other of the republic's commanders, stayed on with his vessel, giving the defense some much-needed strength afloat in the Golden Horn. Counting the hardy Trevisano, the Christian fighting fleet in the Golden Horn numbered just twenty-six. They were terribly outnumbered.

There were other volunteers. From Genoa came Maurizio Cattanaeo, the Langasco brothers, and three Bocchiardis, who brought their own company of troops with them. And there were Catalans, devout residents of Pera across the Golden Horn; there was a Castilian grandee, Don Francisco de Toledo; there was an engineer named Grant, perhaps a Scot very far from home; and there were Cretans, Provencals, and a scattering of Moslem supporters of Orhan, pretender to the sultanate.

Altogether, they were a mixed bag, but one thing they had in common: Every soldier knew there would be no leaving the city once the Turkish ring closed. After that, he must win. To lose was unthinkable: If you lost, you died miserably, or you became a slave. And it was infinitely better to die than to live as a Turkish slave, chained to a galley oar for endless dreary years.

Some men there were who could not face death, or castration, or a life shackled to a Turkish oar. Toward the end of February seven ships, mostly from Crete, fled from the Golden Horn at night. On board were some seven hundred Italians. Their shameful flight diminished the strength of the city, although stout hearts like Giustiniani doubtless felt better off without such jackals near them.

The emperor might have fled, as well. There were still imperial cities to which he could have sailed, and any Christian state would have made him welcome. But Constantine was no coward, and would share the fate of his city. He was an able soldier himself, and had the patience and understanding to heal quarrels between disputing churchmen and bitter rivalry between the Italian contingents. His people genuinely loved him.

So the stage was set. The old walls were as well repaired as might be. The city was provisioned. The populace was mobilized. The tragic lack was men: There were just under five thousand Greek fighters and about two thousand foreign volunteers. Together they had to cover fourteen miles of walls.

The experienced Christian soldiers knew full well where the worst of the danger lay. The Old Blachernae Palace was an obviously vulnerable point, exposed as it was to attack from both west and north. The greatest danger, though, would surely come along the valley of the River Lycus, which entered the city through a conduit in the western wall. The walls in this area were called the Mesoteichion. They had been flooded with blood in past sieges; now they would be reddened again.

When Sultan Murad had attacked the city in 1422, the city's defenders had stopped the Turks at the outer of the two walls. Giustiniani elected to defend it again; he had too few men to fully man both fortifications, and precious few to constitute any kind of useful reserve.

On the fifth of April an enormous fanfare and celebration burst out in the Turkish lines. The garrison of the city lined the walls, listening to the blare of trumpets and thunder of drums from the camps of their besiegers. The sultan had come. Now it was beginning.

The garrison filed to its stations. The west wall near the Lycus Valley—the Mesoteichion—was defended by the emperor himself, at the head of the best of the Greek troops. Shoulder to shoulder with him were Giustiniani and his men. To their north stood the Bocchiardi brothers' detachment. The Venetian leader, Minotto, held the critical Blachernae Palace.

Along the seawall, the garrison was more thinly spread. One quiet sector was even held by Greek monks. In that way, two pitifully small detachments were formed as reserves. Across the mouth of the Golden Horn, from Seraglio Point north to Pera, the defenders stretched an enormous boom to shut out the Turkish warships.

The defenders could clearly see the brilliant red-and-gold tent of the sultan himself, pitched a bare quarter of a mile from the Mesoteichion. With him were the Janizaries, the cutting edge of the Turkish army. The deadly stroke would come here, the defenders knew. Whatever happened elsewhere along the walls, the mortal danger would come over against the valley of the little Lycus.

To add to the shortage of trained manpower, the defenders lacked artillery. There was a reasonable supply of hand weapons, javelins, arrows, and the like. There were plenty of stones to drop on the heads of assaulting infantry. There were even a few torsion-powered catapults and similar weapons. What few cannon Constantinople possessed, however, were short of powder; worse, their recoil threatened to tear down the crumbling fire steps of the old walls. There could be no reply to Mehmet's modern guns.

The Turks set to digging immediately, and soon a ditch

surrounded the city, a ditch backed with an earth rampart. A wooden palisade rimmed the rampart, which was pierced by sally ports. The saltwater approaches to the city were ringed with Turkish ships, many of them carrying heavy artillery. To completely isolate the garrison, two small forts outside the walls were overrun, their survivors dying the singularly ugly and lingering death of impalement. The Constantinople garrison watched their death agony, and knew what the future held. The city was alone.

Mehmet's great guns opened fire on the wall near one of the city gates on the sixth of April, after a ritual surrender-summons had been rejected. By the end of the next day a breach had been made, but the defenders had it filled by the next dawn. The sultan's guns then fell silent until the eleventh, when they began the bombardment that would go on constantly for the next six weeks.

Some of the Turkish guns—including Urban's monstrous cannon—were so ponderous that they could be fired but seven times each day. Many pieces shifted as their wood-and-rubble platforms settled in the spring mud; these had to be laboriously relaid between shots. The hammering went slowly, but it never stopped, and the old walls could not stand up to its cumulative effect.

The Greek and Italian defenders did what they could. In some places bales of wool and leather sheets were hung over the wall to shield it, but they did little good. Within a week the outer wall along the Lycus Valley was crumbling badly, much of the rubble sliding down to fill the ditch before the wall. Each night soldiers and civilians, men and women, worked through the darkness to fill the breaches with sacks of dirt, baulks of wood, anything to keep the wall intact. A stockade was built to back up the fragile wall, and still the cannonade went on.

There was one bright spot. On April 12 the Christian ships routed a Turkish attack on the boom protecting the Golden Horn, hammering the Turkish ships with rock-throwing machines. The defenders were even able to pursue the defeated Turks outside the great boom. The Christians' rejoicing was short-lived, however. The sultan brought a big gun up near enough to bear on the ships guarding the boom. When the cannon's second shot sank a Christian ship, the boom-guard was forced to withdraw out of range, and hover thereafter inside the boom.

The first land assault came on the night of April 18, predictably along the Mesoteichion. Mehmet's men came shouting out of the darkness, making the night hideous with the glare of flares, the thunder of drums, and the clang of cymbals. They charged across the useless ditch, through the remnants of the crumbled wall, and hurled themselves at the stockade. The screaming Turks hurled torches at the wooden walls, tore at the barrels of earth atop it with hooks on the end of their lances, pushed up the face of the stockade in tremendous numbers.

They achieved nothing. Giustiniani's men met them head-on under a shower of arrows and javelins, and hurled them back in confusion. The Westerners' armor was much superior to the puny equipment of the Turks, and Turkish bodies piled up along the foot of the stockade.

The attack lasted four hours. And when the clanging of weapons and the horns and drums and cymbals were at last silent, at least two hundred Turkish dead lay before the city. The defenders had not had a single man killed. The garrison was jubilant, and there was more good news to come.

Two days later the wind turned to the south, and on the twentieth of April sails appeared in the Sea of Marmara. They were Christian sails, the wings of three Genoese galleys full of supplies, hired and loaded by the Pope. With them was a big Greek cargo vessel loaded with precious Sicilian corn, and they were all pushing hard for the city, driven by the providential south wind.

The Turkish ships poured into the Marmara, rowing-galleys mostly, not dependent on the wind for power. A cloud of them surrounded the Christian vessels, but they could not close with the tall ships, which showered them with missiles from their rigging and high gunwales. But then, just as it appeared nothing could stop the Christian vessels from gaining the Golden Horn, the vital wind died away, and the precious relief ships rocked and pitched in a strong south-flowing current, their sails limp, surrounded by Turkish galleys.

The Turks smelled blood and closed to board, dozens of their vessels crowded tightly against the four Christian ships, which lashed themselves together at last to fight as a unit. The Genoese were well armed and armored, swinging axes at the heads and arms of desperate boarders. The Byzantine crew drenched their attackers with the terrible Greek fire, the liquid death that spurted from nozzles down onto the smaller Turkish ships and their screaming crews.

All afternoon the Christian crews fought on against odds, panting and tired, assailed by relays of fresh Turkish boarding parties as more of the sultan's ships joined the fray. And then, as the sun began to sink into the Thracian highlands behind the city, the south wind returned, the sails filled, and the beleaguered big ships bulled their way through their tormentors to safety. By dark they were through the boom, and all of Constantinople rejoiced.

Sultan Mehmet did not. Although his admiral had done everything a commander could do with the forces the sultan provided, his master broke him, beat him, banished him in impoverished disgrace. And the sultan's temper was not improved next day, when a large tower collapsed along the Lycus, carrying the wall with it. Opportunity beckoned, but there was no assault, and by next morning the Christian ants had filled the breach.

By now, however, the sultan's agile brain had come up with an answer to the problem of the boom and its tenacious defenders. One of his advisors seem to have been an ingenious Italian, who told the sultan how ships might be transported overland. So, said the sultan, if I cannot break through the boom, I will go around it.

And he did. At dawn on April 22, as Constantinople celebrated the Sabbath, the sultan's fleet began to move. One by one the ships were hoisted onto wooden cradles, pulled from the Sea of Marmara, then laboriously dragged cross-country north of Pera. Covered by constant cannon-fire, huge teams of oxen and units of men heaved and tugged to the Golden Horn dozens of ships. Five long miles they moved on a sea of greased wooden rollers, their crews on board, their sails hoisted, drums and trumpets playing as they came. Now there was another vast expanse of wall to worry about.

An attempt was made to attack the new Turkish fleet with fire ships a little before dawn on the twenty-eighth. The attempt failed miserably, however, thanks largely to the delay encountered when the Genoese insisted the Venetians include them in the enterprise. As the Genoese prepared a ship, word of the desperate enterprise leaked out, and the

Turks were waiting. The operation misfired amidst desperate fighting, during which the Christians lost ninety seamen
and a galley, in exchange for only one of the swarm of Turkish vessels.

Anxiety mounted within the city. Now Turkish guns on
pontoons opened on the ancient Blachernae corner of the
fortifications, Turkish ships feinted at the Golden Horn's
walls, and the incessant cannonade went on along the Lycus.
Hunger was becoming a factor, too, as supplies diminished.
Help was desperately needed, and a swift Venetian galley ran
the blockade to seek help.

Everybody in the city expected help from the West. Back in
January, the Venetian ambassador had written the republic,
asking for help. There had been no answer. Back in Venice a
fleet had indeed been made ready, but it had not sailed until
mid-April. Even then, it was hedged about with complex instructions that practically insured a delay of many months
before any effective help could reach the desperate city. In
fairness to the Venetians, deeply concerned about their Eastern trade network, they probably did not begin to realize
how dangerous the situation in Constantinople actually was.

Constantinople could not wait. The shortages grew, there
was petty bickering between Genoese and Venetians, between
Western and Eastern churchmen, and the Turks attacked
again. In the darkness of May 7 another Turkish storming
party struck a section of ruined Mesoteichion wall, running
in over the clogged ditch to attack the patched-up defenses.
In spite of their ardor and their numbers, the Turks were
again repelled in bitter hand-to-hand fighting, in the course
of which the sultan's standard-bearer was bisected by a
Greek soldier.

A few days later the Turks struck the Blachernae corner
about midnight. Again they were thrown back in hours of
close fighting, this time with the help of Venetian sailors
landed from galleys in the Golden Horn. Although the Turks
made no headway, the sultan was stepping up the tempo.
And he was deciding on the point at which he would throw
the final, deciding assault. By mid-May he had reinforced the
batteries along the Lycus Valley.

And the sultan now tried a new wrinkle, one more menace
to try the tired defenders. Now, far beneath the ground supporting the city walls, the garrison began to hear the unmis-

takable sounds of digging. Among the sultan's troops were a
number of silver miners from the lodes of Serbia, and these
experienced men were now burrowing beneath the city's
walls.

Now began a deadly game of underground cat and mouse.
The defenders countermined, setting fire to the Turkish tim-
bers to collapse their tunnels and crush their miners,
drowning the diggers with floods of water from the city's cis-
terns. Men grappled and died in subterranean gloom, dying
miserably far below the light of day.

As if this horror were not enough, the sultan's engineers
produced monstrous wheeled towers to menace the Mesoteichion. These huge structures were covered with hide to
fend off missiles, and their top story was level with the top of
the city wall.

The first of these towers covered Turkish laborers filling in
the ditch; with that task done, the next step would be to
push the tower against the ruined wall, onto which the tower
would disgorge a horde of assault troops. A night sally by the
defenders ended this threat, however, as the attacking party
pushed barrels of powder against the tower's base and
touched them off. The tower collapsed in a column of fire,
and the defense had bought a few days more of life.

On May 23 the defense won an enormous victory, one that
vastly boosted morale throughout the encircled city. This
day, at the Blachernae, the defenders turned back yet another Turkish mine. This time, however, they took some
prisoners, and among them was a senior Turkish engineer.
The careful application of torture produced the location of
all the remaining Turkish tunnels, and Grant tracked down
and destroyed them all. It was the end to any serious threat
from below ground.

But the cannon never stopped. As a Greek historian of the
time wrote, "The cannons decided the whole issue." The battered walls crumbled further and further, and inside the city
supplies were growing terribly short. Everybody was tired
and hungry, and many men were wounded. On top of the
strain and the fatigue came dreadful news from outside. The
little boat that had escaped to seek Venetian help was back,
running daringly in to the boom under cover of darkness.
There was no Venetian fleet, the crew said. In twenty days
they had seen no friendly sail.

There would be no help.

Morale was not improved by the occurrence of an eclipse on the night after the Venetian boat returned, nor by the resurrection of any number of dire prophecies about the fall of the city. But it would not be omens or predictions or even isolation that would kill great Constantinople. It would be the cannon, the murderous cannon and the final merciless, ceaseless storm, and now it was coming.

On the night of Sunday, May 27, the Turkish camp glared with torchlight as relays of laborers poured still more filler into what was left of the city ditch. There was much noise, as well, exultant singing and loud music. And then, at midnight, there was suddenly darkness and silence.

The sultan had decreed a day of rest and contemplation on Monday. He himself spent the day moving through his camps, inspecting and exhorting. He instructed his officers clearly: Tomorrow the assault would go in and continue, no matter the cost, until the defenders were exhausted and worn down. There would be assaults everywhere, to stretch the garrison as thin as possible; but the main attack would go in up the Lycus Valley. There would be no failure.

The exhausted garrison prepared as best it could. The tiny cannon reserve was moved to the Mesoteichion; what final repairs were possible were made to the shattered walls. A huge religious procession snaked singing through the city's streets, and all the church bells of the city rang out. East and West so far buried their quarrels that Greek and Italian worshiped together, and priests of the two churches served at the altar side by side.

On the night of the twenty-eighth of May, the Christian leaders attended services at St. Sophia's; Constantine himself prayed in a chapel alone, sharing with his God the last hours of the last Byzantine emperor. As his officers crowded around him, he asked forgiveness of any man he might have wronged. Then, his soul at peace, he rode back to the Lycus Valley walls to abide the assault he knew was coming. The city, about to die, was united.

Then the garrison stood to their posts. Once the remnants of the outer wall were manned, the gates to the inner wall were closed and locked behind them. There would be no falling back; the Christians would stand or die.

The storm broke just after midnight on the twenty-ninth of

May. With a tremendous shout, with clashing cymbals and bleating trumpets and thundering drums, masses of Turkish infantry ran in out of the night and hurled themselves at the battered city wall. This time the attack came all along the wall; there could be no movement of men from one threatened place to another. Women, including nuns, worked to shore up the crumbling walls and stockade. Those who could not help at the walls crowded into the churches—if they could not fight or bolster the defenses, they could at least pray.

The first waves of Turkish attackers were Bashi-Bazouks, the irregular infantry of hideous reputation, drawn from the dregs of the sultanate, from Christian lands as well as Moslem ones. To be sure this riffraff stood to its work, Mehmet placed Turkish military police behind them. If any man faltered, he was whipped back to his duty; who ran, died.

For two hours the Bashi-Bazouks assaulted the outer wall all along its length, pressing especially hard against the critical fortifications in the Lycus Valley. They died in hundreds, cut down by the keen steel of the defenders, pushed from their scaling ladders, brained with rocks, shot down by the primitive arquebuses concentrated along the Lycus walls.

At the end of two hours of hand-to-hand slaughter, Mehmet called away the remains of the Bashi-Bazouks. They had not penetrated the Christian defense anywhere, but they had served to badly tire the defenders and deplete their supply of missiles. Now, running in under the cannonade, came Turkish infantry out of the Anatolian homeland, better armed, better armored, better disciplined. And, above all, fresh.

The Christians met them with the fury of despair, fighting in a nightmare world of gloom, lit only by muzzle-flashes, the flare of torches, and a sinister moon that veiled its light behind scudding clouds. Amid a terrible din of roaring cannon and banging arquebuses, cheers, prayers, and screams of agony, the defenders fought on in a cloud of powder-smoke and dust.

A little before dawn, a ball from Urban's big gun struck the stockade flush, flattening a large section of it, and the Anatolians, howling in triumph, rushed into the breach. Giustiniani met them head-on with his exhausted Italians and Greeks. In the stygian gloom their weary sword arms

rose and fell, killing and killing until the remains of the Anatolians broke and ran for their lives. The Lycus wall had
held again.

So had the rest of the line. Along the Marmara a party of
Greek monks had repulsed Turkish landing parties, and
there had been a ferocious struggle for the Blachernae walls
before the Venetians and the Bocchiardi brothers had
cleared the walls of attackers. The city was still secure.

But the worst was yet to come. Quickly, before the weary
defenders could catch their breath, Mehmet waved in his
elite infantry, his Janizaries, hurling them at the battered
stockade in what everybody knew was the ultimate assault.
Mehmet himself stood at the edge of the city ditch, urging his
shock troops on. These soldiers, Mehmet's best, were tightly
disciplined and excellently equipped; the fighting along the
Lycus Valley was hand to hand and ferocious. The defenders
knew they must hold here; if they failed, it was better to die
at the wall.

For an hour they held, throwing back assault after assault
as a wan, sickly dawn broke over the suffering city. And then
the tide turned abruptly, not for lack of courage in the defense, but for lack of care. For tucked away where the
Blachernae walls joined those leading down to the Lycus was
a little sally port, used by the defenders to counterattack into
the flank of the Turkish advance.

And the little port, called the Kirkoporta, had somehow
been left unlocked, and through it charged about fifty enter-
prising Janizaries. A nearby Christian unit retook the gate,
leaving the Turks isolated inside the city; they might have
been wiped out easily. But before anybody could exterminate
this handful of invaders, catastrophe struck on the walls.

Giustiniani was down, the heart and spirit of the defense.
A musket-ball had driven through his breastplate, and he
could fight no more. He was in great pain, and asked his
men to take him from the wall. When they sought out the
Emperor Constantine to ask for a key to a little gate into the
inner city, the emperor pleaded with Giustiniani to stay on at
the wall, no matter how badly hurt he was.

The gallant Genoese refused; he was dying, and in too
much pain to understand or care what his departure might
do to the defense, already hanging by a thread. And as he
was carried through the little gate to the inner city, the heart

went out of many of his exhausted men: Some of them followed their mortally wounded leader back, away from the outer wall.

And the city died in that moment. Now there was no holding the Turkish attack, which foamed over the outer wall, beat down the remaining defenders, and forced its way through the inner wall, into the heart of Constantinople. Many more poured through the Kirkoporta, brushing aside the Bocchiardis' handful of weary men. The emperor himself rode among the remnants of his men along the Lycus wall. Even he could not rally them; they were exhausted, most of them were wounded, and they would not stand.

For a little time the emperor, Don Francisco of Toledo, and two others held the gate through which Giustiniani had been carried, but the flood of fugitives and the press of victorious Janizaries was too strong to resist. Constantine decided. He would not survive the fall of his city to be a trophy for a heathen conqueror. "The city has been taken," he shouted, "and I am still alive!"

And so, with the others at his back, the last Byzantine emperor threw away his imperial regalia and pressed forward into the throngs of Janizaries, sword in hand. He was never seen again.

Two of the three Bocchiardis cut their way to the Golden Horn, and made their way across it to Pera. Most of the other leaders died in the desperate fighting in the streets, or fell captive to Mehmet's men. Many other Italians fought through the tumult in the streets to reach their ships, set sail, and reached the great boom, picking up swimming fugitives as they went. They scattered the Turkish fleet, most of whose sailors were already in the city looting, cut the lashings of the boom, and won free into the Sea of Marmara. There they picked up a strong north wind—"a Christian wind"—and sailed rapidly south to safety.

Within the city there was no safety. Blood ran down the gutters of the streets as the Turks killed everything that moved. Turkish law allowed three days of pillage in a conquered city, and the rampaging troops broke in everywhere to loot and destroy, rape and kill. Gradually, as the bloodlust subsided, they began to take captives: The young and able-bodied, at least, had real value in the slave market.

Palaces, convents, churches, none were spared. By day's

end, there was little left to steal, and the tumult in the fallen city began to quiet down. The sultan now proclaimed an end to pillage, and his men began to sort out their captives. There were about fifty thousand of them all told. Only five hundred were fighting men; except for the few who had fled by sea, the rest had died fighting.

Mehmet reserved many of the choicest young women—and young men—for his own seraglio, then supervised the division of the rest. He also kept for himself the Byzantine aristocracy and those government officials who survived. Many of these he freed.

Not so the Italians. Many were executed, and with them died Orhan, pretender to the sultanate. Others, more fortunate, were ransomed by Pera merchants. A cardinal of the Roman church survived after trading his churchly robes for a beggar's clothing. The beggar died in his new finery; the cardinal, unrecognized, was ransomed.

Some of the ordinary Greek citizens were allowed to return to their homes. Others passed into slavery, including hundreds of children sent as presents to the Moslem rulers of Spain, Egypt, and Tunis. Others were killed outright.

Toward the end of June the sultan left the city for Adrianople. There was still some normal life in a few sectors of Constantinople that had yielded instantly to the sultan's troops; the conqueror had even agreed to reserve one of the largest churches for the use of his Christian subjects.

Otherwise, Mehmet the Conqueror left a ruined, ghostly city, a shadow of the glory that had been, largely depopulated and desolate. The Moslem call to prayer echoed through the empty, weeping streets of ancient Byzantium. Where a thousand years of emperors had walked, there were now only shades of the past, ghosts who moved without sound, and vanished with the coming of the day.

MAN OF FEW WORDS

Arthur Wellesley, the Duke of Wellington, is arguably the greatest commander ever to lead troops. Famous for his concern for his soldiers and his astonishing coolness under fire, he also won a small measure of renown for his terse speech.

Wellington had the gift of saying much in very few words, as he did when asked if he enjoyed music.

"I only know two melodies," he replied. "One of them is 'God Save the King' . . . and one of them isn't."

His talent for spare speech remained with him even in times of greatest stress. At Waterloo, after hours of the bloodiest imaginable fighting, he sat his horse beside Lord Uxbridge, his second-in-command. As the tide turned and Napoleon's army began to break before the thin line of redcoats, a cannonball moaned in past the neck of Wellington's horse and smashed Uxbridge's knee into bloody junk.

Uxbridge looked down. And then, the essential Regency officer, he remarked almost casually to the duke: "By God, I've lost my leg."

The duke, equally cool, glanced over at Uxbridge. "Have you, by God!"

And he had. So the duke dismounted in the carnage and helped Uxbridge down and then returned to the desperate business of beating the French. After the battle this iron man would break into tears over the terrible losses among his troops. For now, however, there was the job to do, and the less said, the better, even about a friend's dreadful wound.

NO SURRENDER
SIR RICHARD GRENVILLE IN THE AZORES

> I adore war. I have never felt so well, or so happy, or enjoyed
> anything so much . . . It just suits my stolid health, and stolid
> nerves, and barbaric disposition. One loves one's fellow-man
> so much more when one is bent on killing him.

So wrote young Julian Grenfell from Flanders, before his
death in World War I. His philosophy is not hard to understand when his bloodline is considered. For young Julian—
and his brother, also killed fighting his king's enemies—were
descendants of a remarkable line of fighting men and daring
sailors, the West Country Grenvilles.

These tough young men came of the same stock as the
toughest of all the sea dogs, Sir Richard Grenville, captain of
Revenge, aptly called in England "the Spaniards' terror." Sir
Richard was a veteran of war, fighting as a young volunteer
against the Turks in Hungary, serving repeatedly against
Spain at sea. Just three years after the destruction of the
Spanish Armada, Sir Richard fell, still defiant, still hammering his sovereign's enemies, nearly three hundred years before young Julian died for his country in Flanders. His story
is one of the classic tales of courage and defiance.

The year was 1591, the place the Azores Islands. England
had embarked on a program designed to keep mortal enemy
Spain in relative poverty, by cutting off from the mother
country the vital treasure flotas from the New World. Without
the gold and silver from the Indies, aggressive, avaricious
Spain would have to stay home; the menace to England and
Protestant western Europe would be much diminished.

The British plan was to cruise the waters between the

Azores and Spain with a squadron of six fighting ships and their logistic support, called "victualers." These watchdogs would be regularly relieved by other battle groups. The theory was that Spain had lost so many ships in the Armada disaster, that she would be unable to mount a fleet large enough to break through the tiny English flotillas.

The British government had miscalculated badly. To begin with, it proved more difficult than expected to regularly relieve the watchdogs east of the Azores. As the months passed on station in the Atlantic, both hulls and ballast became foul, food spoiled, water ran low.

Worse still, Spain was rapidly rebuilding her fleet in both her own home ports and in Portugal, and was even contracting with other nations for ships. Phillip II of Spain lost no time in laying down more huge galleons—one group of them to be called "The Twelve Apostles." In 1590 he hired another dozen galleons from the town of Ragusa (modern-day Dubrovnik, in the former Yugoslavia). The gold of the New World financed an enormous spate of shipbuilding, and Spain was rearming far faster than England thought she could.

Even so, the Spanish treasury was rapidly shrinking. While one fleet got through in 1589, containing ships from both the New World and the Indies, Martin Frobisher captured two rich prizes off Portugal. More ships managed to avoid the English pickets in 1590, but the high seas were still terribly hazardous for Spanish seamen. That summer an English captain struck near Havana, capturing two galleons of the treasure fleet from New Spain. The main fleet, Spain's critical imperial funding, would have to wait until her forces were stronger.

The chance came in 1591. It had to be done this year or never. A monstrous flota would gather on the western rim of the broad Atlantic, taking safety in their numbers. A second fighting fleet under Admiral Bazan would meet them at the Azores, and together they could push through any of the tiny English squadrons. The treasure fleet would sail from Havana later in the year, in the hope that the English would exhaust their supplies and leave the Atlantic open.

Lord Thomas Howard was at sea with a small fleet late in the spring, battling bad weather that drove him back into port. Grenville, with him as vice admiral, kept to sea, riding out the gale, and as a result capturing a large Lübeck merchantman, laden with masts and timber desperately needed by the Spanish building program. In the wake of the storm, the little fleet rallied, and Howard set a course for the Azores.

Back in England, intelligence of the great Spanish rebuilding project was beginning, to prompt reaction. Reinforcements were hurriedly gathered to defend the island, and a few ships were sent west to join Howard. Even reinforced, Howard's little flotilla was small enough, its fighting strength concentrated in the queen's ships *Defiance, Revenge, Bonaventure, Lion, Foresight,* and *Crane.* The first four were midsize fighting galleons; the last two were warships of much smaller size.

But no Spanish fleet appeared. Out in the Azores, Howard and his captains cruised and waited, but found nothing. As the hulls gradually fouled and more and more men went down ill, Howard fumed, "almost famished for want of prey, or rather like a bear robbed of her whelps." Steaming August came to the Azores, bringing still more sickness, and still no sails cut the skyline.

Howard correctly reasoned that the Spanish were waiting to sail until the year was dying, willing to chance the gales of autumn on the thesis that the British would give up and go home before the Spanish reached European waters. And so Howard took a necessary chance, anchored off Flores, and set many of his healthy men to work on critical maintenance tasks.

It was water he needed, water and a thorough cleaning for his ships, and rest for his men, for his ships were rotten with sickness after four months on station. Nobody is certain today exactly where Howard anchored, but it seems most probable that he lay in a little bay off the north tip of the island of Flores, while parties went ashore to fill water casks and haul out fresh rock for ballast. Others dumped overboard the old ballast, stinking with the slops and waste of the ships, and set to scrubbing and fumigating with vinegar.

Howard must have thought he had time for these essential tasks, although he took the precaution of posting a pinnace west of the islands to warn of any Spanish sail. If Howard expected the flota still to be at least days away, so indeed it was. The Spanish fleets of Mexico, Santa Domingo, and elsewhere had not collected and sailed from Havana until the end of July. Although they had already lost a number of ships to English privateers, they still numbered more than seventy sail.

What Howard did not expect, and could not predict, was the huge Spanish fleet bearing down on him from the *east,* coming from El Ferrol in northwest Spain. For Don Alonso de Bazan was already in the Azores with a fleet of some fifty-five vessels, including about thirty fighting ships, some of them the great Apostles. On board were some seven thousand infantry.

Bazan had anchored briefly at Terceira, the Spanish headquarters in the islands, and there he had learned where Howard's ships were. He knew their strength as well, and identified their commander, Howard, "an inexperienced man and not a sailor," and vice admiral, Grenville, "a great corsair and of great estimation among them." The Spanish knew Grenville well, for he had hurt them again and again. No Spanish captain could have forgotten Grenville's capture of a Spanish treasure ship by boarding her from a raft made of pieces of wooden chest, a raft that disintegrated as Grenville and his men fought their way up the Spaniard's side.

On August 31 Bazan sailed to attack. Terceira lies to the east of Flores, and Bazan laid his plans to reach Flores early in the morning, when the wind was fresh, and to surround the island so that no English ship could escape. In the event, he was delayed by damage to one of his ships, and could not raise Flores until about five in the evening. The delay may have saved Howard.

For a bold British captain called Middleton had shadowed Bazan in his pinnace *Moonshine,* and on the thirty-first managed to reached the Flores anchorage with his news. He was only just in time. Even as Howard began to recall his men from ashore, the Spanish fleet appeared over the skyline in four divisions, cleared for action and coming hard with the winds at their backs. By five o'clock firing had already begun, as the British ships clawed desperately for sailing room, some of them slipping their cables to clear the anchorage.

Howard had given the only sensible command, refuse action and run for the open sea. He was terribly outnumbered, and his crews were decimated by sickness. If he stayed to fight—always the first reaction of the Elizabethan sea dog—he could lose his whole fleet. And so his captains cracked on sail and cleared Flores, getting the weather gauge of the Spaniards in the nick of time.

Except *Revenge*. Nobody knows to this day why Grenville did not do all he could to obey his admiral's order and run. There is some suggestion that he stayed too late to recover some sailors still ashore. Sir Walter Raleigh wrote that Grenville simply scorned to run from his country's enemies. He chose rather to fight his way through them. And he turned *Revenge* in to the heart of the Spanish fleet, and some of them fell back from his daring rush. But then, as more and more tall ships loomed up around him, he lost his wind because of their huge bulk.

> The great *San Philip* being in the wind of him, and coming towards him, becalmed his sails in such sort, as the ship could neither weigh nor feel the helm: so huge and high carged was the Spanish ship . . .

And so Grenville and his *Revenge* stood and fought, fought against enormous odds for fifteen desperate hours through the night.

Revenge was a hardy ship, a veteran of the Spanish wars, and Drake's flagship during the rout of the Armada in 1588. She was classified in England as a second-rate battleship, ninety-two feet long and thirty-two at the beam, drawing fifteen feet. But she was dwarfed by Spanish warships that towered above her, heavily armed behemoths three times her size.

For *Revenge* was a small ship by Spanish standards. She was 441 tons, and carried forty-two bronze guns of various sizes and a crew of about two hundred men. None of these men were soldiers like the Spanish shipboard infantry, and many of them were too ill to fight.

She was grappled and boarded first by *San Felipe*, one of the great Apostles, which packed a thirty-three-gun broadside, and carried a sizable complement of infantry. Four other Spanish vessels joined the action, and made repeated attempts to board *Revenge* throughout the afternoon and evening. Again and again Grenville's seamen and "gentlemen volunteers" closed hand-to-hand with the Spanish infantry, with pistol, boarding pike, sword, and hand grenade on decks slippery with blood. Again and again they threw the Spanish back, leaving the deck and the greedy sea littered with dead.

Meanwhile *Revenge* and her enemies kept up a ceaseless series of broadsides, and *Revenge* was soon dismasted, her rigging a hopeless tangle. She was holed again and again, her deck a wilderness of flying splinters and grapeshot, hideous with the cries of hurt and dying men. On she fought, as darkness fell over the Azores.

At one point little *George Noble,* a victualer, sailed through a hail of Spanish shot, closing *Revenge* to offer her slight help. But Grenville waved her off with thanks; she could only die with *Revenge,* and there was no point in losing still another ship. *Foresight* also tried to help, but Grenville ordered her away as well. At one point, Howard and his ships tried a feint to draw off the Spanish vessels. But Bazan would not take the bait, and in time the rest of the English had to draw off to save themselves.

By three in the morning, *Revenge* had been attacked in relays by fifteen of the Spanish warships. Grenville had been badly wounded in the body a little before midnight. His surgeon had been killed while dressing the wound, and Grenville hit again, this time in the head. But still he stayed in command, tough and fiery and still full of fight, and the battle went on.

And by morning *Revenge* was still fighting, even though she had by now taken so many broadsides that her upper works had been shot away to deck level. She was a charnel house, "her masts all beaten overboard . . . in effect evened she was with the water, but the very foundation or bottom of a ship . . . filled with blood and the bodies of dead and wounded men." By Raleigh's account, stout little *Revenge* had been hit eight hundred times.

But *Revenge* had made the Spanish pay. The fighting galleon *Ascension* had gone to the bottom during the night, and a second warship was sinking as the sun rose. Another man-of-war would sink later, and still another would be run ashore to save her crew. Many of the others had been badly battered by Grenville's guns, including the mighty Apostle

San Felipe, leaking badly, her hull smashed by a volley of English bar-shot. The Spanish had lost over four hundred men in dead alone.

By dawn's light the survivors of *Revenge*'s crew and their fierce captain could look on the terrible vengeance they had taken for their ship:

> *And the night went down, and the sun smiled*
> *out far over the summer sea,*
> *And the Spanish fleet, with broken sides*
> *lay round us all in a ring.*

Defiant *Revenge* still was, but almost helpless, too. For, as Raleigh wrote,

> *All the powder . . . to the last barrel was spent,*
> *all her pikes broken,*
> *fortie of her best men slaine,*
> *and the most part of the rest hurt.*

Revenge could fight no more, but Grenville would not hear of surrender. Terribly wounded, he called his exhausted crew together, urging them "to yield themselves to God, and to the mercy of none else." And then he turned to his master gunner and commanded him to collect what powder he could find, and "split and sink the ship."

The master gunner, an eagle of the same stamp as his commander, was ready to obey. But other officers asked Grenville to reconsider. *Revenge* already had six feet of water in her; she was too badly hurt to survive and would never be a Spanish prize. Some of her crew still lived, many of them badly hurt. They had fought with wonderful courage all through the bloody night, but now they had nothing left to fight with. It was time to save the crew, who might still live to serve queen and country again.

Grenville, desperately hurt, still would not listen, and the doughty master gunner had to be locked in a cabin to keep him from falling on his own sword. Grenville's officers at last took matters into their own hands and opened negotiations with the Spanish. The Spanish, for their part, had had quite enough of this astonishing little ship and her murderous gunfire. A compact was quickly reached.

And so the firing stopped and the sea air was clean of powder-smoke for the first time in fifteen hours. The Spanish sent boats to *Revenge* and took possession of what was left of her. They brought away her surviving crew and her wounded, including Grenville, so badly hurt that he passed out during his transfer to Bazan's flagship. Before he did, he called to his sorrowing crew, asking them to pray for him.

To Bazan's great credit, he treated Grenville with the utmost respect. A surgeon was sent to attend him, and he was made as comfortable as possible even though he was, in their eyes, "the admiral of the great sailors and corsairs of England, a great heretic and persecutor of Catholics."

A Dutch observer wrote later that Bazan himself refused to visit Grenville, but that the other Spanish captains came to see him on *San Pablo*, to "comfort him in his hard fortune, wondering at his courage and stout heart, for that he showed not any sign of faintness nor changing of colour." They doubtless were also impressed by Grenville's after-dinner snack of three or four glasses of wine, which he would drink, and then

> take the glasses betweene his teeth and crash them in peeces and swallow them downe, so that often times the blood ran out of his mouth without any harme at all unto him.

But even Grenville's spirit could not prevail over his many wounds, and he knew it. He lingered several days, and then slipped away. No record of his burial remains, so he may well have been buried at sea. The Dutchman Linschoten left his account of his last words, perhaps apocryphal, but typical of the man:

> Here die I Richard Grenville, with a joyful and quiet mind, for that I have ended my life as a true soldier ought to do, that hath fought for his country, Queen, religion and honour, whereby my soul most joyfully departeth out of this body.

And so for Grenville the pain and struggling was over. But not for the Spanish. Bazan stayed on in the Azores for another two weeks, gathering in convoys from the New World as they arrived until some 140 Spanish ships lay together off

Corvo Island. The treasure fleets had already lost some 70 ships to storms and English warships. Worse was to come.

For before the great fleet could sail for Spain, the Azores were struck by a cyclone of astonishing violence, leaving as many as half the fleet sinking or driven ashore. Among them was *Revenge,* smashed on shore at Terceira with all her crew and some English prisoners. The destruction was so great, and the storm so violent, that the islanders believed that Grenville the mighty heretic had returned from hell, "where he raised up all the devils to the revenge of his death."

What remained of the Spanish fleet was scattered over hundreds of miles of stormy Atlantic. Still at sea, in spite of the storm, Howard and other British commanders snapped up still more of the struggling Spanish ships. It was, as many men said, a disaster worse than that of the Armada, and strict orders were given not to discuss the extent of the Spanish losses.

Nevertheless, the Spanish celebrated the capture of one of their great enemy's famous warships—it was, after all, both their first and last such capture of the war. One of the Apostles, *St. Andrew,* sailed into Lisbon hung all over with flags and pennants, firing salutes in honor of her part in the victory.

St. Andrew's triumph would return to haunt her. For in 1596 Sir Walter Raleigh descended on Cádiz with vengeance on his mind, boarded and captured *St. Andrew* and another Apostle, and brought them in triumph back to England. Among the Spanish ships left burning behind him in Cádiz harbor were two more Apostles, including *San Felipe,* the first ship to board *Revenge.*

Revenge was deeply mourned in England, and controversy raged over whether Grenville disobeyed his commander in an attempt to provoke Howard to stand and fight. Tempers ran so high that Howard was accused of favoring the Spanish, and there is some indication that Raleigh challenged him to a duel.

At least some of *Revenge*'s men came home, a few at a time. The government paid six months' pay to the widows of men who had died in her. And in the hearts of Englishmen, she and her crew and her captain secured a permanent place in history. Bacon would call it:

that memorable fight of an English ship call the Revenge . . .
memorable (I say) even beyond credit, and to the height of
some historical fable.

And the Grenvilles went on serving their country. Grenville's son, John, was a sea dog after his father's heart, serving against the Spanish and dying finally on Raleigh's
expedition to Guiana. His grandson, Bevil, was a mainstay of
the Royalist cause during the English Civil War, killed in action finally at Lansdown. A second grandson, Richard, also
served the king with distinction, although his foul temper
made him "a caricature of his grandfather," and universally
detested.

Bevil's own son, John, only sixteen, also fought with great
distinction, and was badly wounded. An unrepentant Royalist, he was ennobled when Charles II came into his own
again. In later years the family lost the title, but never took
off their swords. A Grenville fought against the Turks threatening Austria and Hungary, and became a count of the Holy
Roman Empire. Others fought England's wars in Flanders
under Marlborough.

Sir Richard Grenville's direct line became extinct, but the
family itself—the name now Grenfell—continued, with the
same spirit that commanded *Revenge*. Before he died, Julian Grenfell wrote a poem that pretty well summed up the
family's indomitable spirit:

> And when the burning moment breaks,
> And all things else are out of mind,
> And only joy of battle takes
> Him by the throat, and makes him blind,
> The thundering line of battle stands,
> And in the air death moans and sings,
> But Day shall clasp him with strong hands,
> And Night shall fold him in soft wings.

THE REDOUBTABLE MS. PITCHER

"Molly Pitcher" was a common nickname during the Revolutionary War, a good-natured complimentary term for any women who carried water to men in combat—in a pitcher or otherwise. There were therefore a number of "Molly Pitchers." At least one of them, though, won a permanent place in American history in 1778, on the bloody field of Monmouth, New Jersey.

This Molly was Mary Ludwig Hays, wife to cannoneer John Hays, and sometime assistant gunner to her husband. In the desperate fighting at Monmouth Molly carried water to the struggling soldiers until John Hays collapsed behind his gun, perhaps wounded, more probably simply exhausted from the heat.

Molly sprang to nurse her husband, then took over his place serving the cannon. In the end she served the piece alone, sponging the barrel after each round, then loading, laying, and firing the gun. Through it all she kept an eye on her husband, and kept her sense of humor as well. As she stretched to pick up a fresh cartridge, an enemy round-shot hummed between her legs, tearing off part of her petticoat but doing no other damage. Molly didn't miss a beat, remarking only that had the round been a little higher, it might have carried away something else.

Molly was presented to General Washington, the story goes, who gave her a gold coin and promoted her to sergeant on the spot. She was called "Captain Molly" after that, and it is said that allied French troops, ever gallant, filled Molly's hat with silver coins. It is a pleasant story, and even if it isn't true, it is a small measure of recognition for all the women who followed their husbands through the war. The young country's hard-won victory was theirs as well.

Later on, Molly Pitcher Hays at least got a half-pay pension for the rest of her life. And she got something more enduring as well, a statue in her honor in a Carlisle, Pennsylvania, cemetery, with her country's thanks carved permanently in the stone.

> O'er Monmouth's field of carnage drear
> With cooling drink and words of cheer
> A woman passed who knew no fear
> The wife of Hays, the gunner . . .
> From the ranks this woman came
> By the cannon won her fame.
> 'Tis true she could not write her name
> But freedom's hand hath carved it.

A TRIAL OF SOULS
CHRISTMAS MORNING AT TRENTON

> These are the times that try men's souls.
> The summer soldier and the sunshine patriot
> will, in this time of crisis,
> shrink from the service of his country.

So wrote Tom Paine, deep in the dismal winter of 1776. The year that had begun with the shining dream of a young, free America was turning into a nightmare of defeat and disloyalty. There had been a few bright spots, but for George Washington's ragged army, the autumn had been a dreary time of unrelieved disaster.

For Washington and his green army had been well and truly whipped by General William Howe and an efficient army of British and German regulars. Howe was an able soldier, even if he sometimes seemed less interested in war than in politics and the pleasures of the flesh.

Howe wasted most of a month in New York, but when he moved at last, he moved quickly. Confronted by Washington's army on Manhattan Island, Howe sent the Royal Navy thundering up the Hudson, shooting their way past Fort Washington on Manhattan itself, and Fort Lee on the Jersey shore. Howe himself moved up the East River with most of his force.

Washington fell back up Manhattan, leaving garrisons in Forts Lee and Washington, and going into camp himself at White Plains. There he was attacked by Howe at the end of October, and driven back to North Castle, behind the Groton River.

Now Howe, contrary to Washington's expectations, moved to attack Fort Washington, left isolated by the American retreat. On November 16 waves of British infantry and blue-coated Hessians went cheering in through heavy American fire, pushing on implacably across abatis made of felled trees with their branches cropped and sharpened. The American musketry cut down the attackers in dozens, but there was no holding the fury of the storming parties. Swept by fire from a man o' war in the Hudson, hemmed in by those terrible bayonets, the garrison surrendered, three thousand men Washington could not afford to lose.

Before the defense caved in, the American muskets had taken a particularly heavy toll of the Hessian infantry attacking the north side of Fort Washington. The Germans were angered by their losses, and had to be held back from bayoneting American prisoners.

Among the commanders of the veteran Germans was an experienced officer named Johann Gottlieb Rall. He was a distinguished soldier, who had fought through the Seven Years War and volunteered to serve with the Russian army against the Turks. He was a professional. Like his men, he had performed well this day, and we will meet him again.

Howe now moved with uncharacteristic speed. At his orders Lord Cornwallis quickly crossed the Hudson, and the Fort Lee garrison abandoned its fortifications in unseemly haste. Behind them they left desperately needed ordnance and supplies, having time only to remove their stores of gunpowder. General Nathaniel Green, commanding at Fort Washington, got clear in the nick of time, leaving more than a hundred prisoners in the hands of the pursuing British.

By this time Washington had taken a detachment of his army back to the hamlet of Hackensack, New Jersey, and Greene joined him there. It was no place to make a stand. There was no decent defensive terrain, and Washington could not even dig in. His picks and shovels were mostly British now, lost along with the rest of the supplies at Fort Washington. Worse still, his little army, now down to three thousand or so, was cold, hungry, and depressed.

Rain fell in torrents, freezing rain that soaked ragged, ill-equipped soldiers short of everything, even blankets. There were a few tents. Those, too, had been part of the precious stores in Fort Washington. Worst of all, Washington's repeated orders could not move jealous, arrogant General Charles Lee to join him with the main body from North Castle.

And so Washington fell back across New Jersey, his ragged men slogging down roads turned to ribbons of glutinous mud. His little army melted away as men simply walked off, turned for home with a bellyful of wet and cold, of hunger and defeat and misery. Some of them fell victim to a disorder euphemistically called "barrel fever," a malady incurred from an overdose of firewater, which in turn produced a plague of quarrels, black eyes, and bloody noses.

Step by step the tiny army fell back across New Jersey, the Delaware Line marching as rear guard to the wretched column of shivering men. Out behind the rear guard rode the general himself, supervising a party of sappers as they destroyed bridges and felled trees across the road.

All around the little army Jersey Tories got ready to welcome Howe. Everywhere "sunshine patriots" turned their coats and prepared their protestations of loyalty to the Crown. The Continental Congress, ever fearful, ever penurious, packed up to flee from Philadelphia to Baltimore.

At the last, Washington had a little luck. The British, healthier, better fed, flushed with victory, might have cut Washington's tired men off from escape. With any one of a dozen junior British officers leading the British pursuit, the

Revolution might have ended before the turning of the year. But Howe commanded now, and as usual, he moved with glacial speed.

And so Washington and his men made the Delaware River at Trenton ahead of the pursuit. They swept up all the boats they could find on the north shore, and crossed to safety in Pennsylvania, just as the leading elements of Howe's force came into view. At last the Continental army, what was left of it, had room to breathe a little.

Washington continued bombarding the stubborn Lee with letters, but still that worthy dawdled. By December 13 he had moved south only as far as Basking Ridge, New Jersey. At that place, comfortably ensconced in a tavern some miles away from his army, he was whiling away the morning at his favorite occupation, scribbling off a letter attacking General Washington. "Between us," he wrote to the equally arrogant General Gates, "Entre nous, a certain great man is most damnably deficient."

Lee meant Washington, of course, but at that moment the words fit Lee himself precisely. For just as Lee signed his poisonous letter, the quiet morning was shattered by pistol-shots and the clash of sabers outside the tavern. If Lee had been unconcerned with the war, the British had not, and Lee was the prisoner of a hard-eyed dragoon lieutenant colonel named William Harcourt.

It was all the more embarrassing because Lee—once of the British army—had been an officer of this self-same dragoon regiment. Worst of all, Harcourt had served under Lee in Portugal years before. Lee departed into captivity clad in slippers and a scowl.

So, thanks to the enterprise of Colonel Harcourt and his dragoons, Washington had yet another small piece of luck. Now Lee's troops made their way to join Washington, minus the major irritant of Lee himself. Washington could count on six thousand men, at least for a little while.

But Washington was still surrounded by troubles. In only a few weeks most of his men's enlistments would expire, and few of his soldiers showed much inclination to reenlist. If they went home—and Washington could not hold them against their will—the Revolution was finished, and so was the new nation.

His army was short of all kinds of supplies as well, and illness pulled men down on every side. A strength report for that dismal December listed a little over 6,000 men "present fit for duty." The same document reported 600 men sick in camp, and another 2,580 "sick absent." And that dismal report did not count the devoted men limping and coughing, but too proud to leave their comrades.

Washington pondered and prayed, groping alone in that terrible dark time for some way to stop the inevitable. Now, in the midst of crisis, he again had a little help from the lack-adaisical Howe. Instead of forcing the river—with some decent planning, his excellent troops could have managed it—Howe went into winter quarters. He left a string of posts to hold New Jersey, and he himself returned to New York.

Sound tactician that he was, Howe nevertheless turned to interests other than martial. There lived in New York in those days a ravishing blue-eyed blonde, wife to one Joshua Loring, commissary of prisoners for the British forces. Loring, oblivious to much of anything but money and influence, seemed more than content to tolerate Howe's intimate attentions to Mrs. Loring.

The general's cavortings with the lady were common knowledge, and produced a bit of clever doggerel, which reflected the disgust felt by many of the British officers.

> *Awake arouse, Sir Billy.*
> *There's forage in the plain.*
> *Ah, leave your little filly,*
> *And open the campaign.*
>
> *Heed not a woman's prattle*
> *Which tickles in the ear,*
> *But give the word for battle*
> *And grasp the warlike spear.*

But "Sir Billy" had plainly put away the warlike spear for the season. There would be no offensive action until the spring. Howe was a Whig in any case, of that party that felt considerable sympathy for the colonists and thought they might by concession be induced to return to the imperial fold. And by spring, after all, the wretched Americans might dissolve of their own accord, without fighting or bloodshed on either side.

Indeed they might. If Sir Billy could afford to do nothing, Washington could not. If he waited, his army would melt away from discouragement and expired enlistments. If he waited, the Delaware would freeze, and then, surely, even the inert Howe would cross and destroy the remnants of the Continental Army. Washington's plan was a piece of astonishing audacity, but audacity was all he had. Attack it would be, and Washington made his plans.

On December 23 Washington paraded his troops, and had read to them part of Tom Paine's latest pamphlet, *The Crisis*, "These are the times that try men's souls . . ." The words rang like a bugle through the icy day, and they moved the tired, beaten men who listened to them. Paine had been one of them this dreadful year, carrying a musket all through the terrible retreat, and he spoke for them all.

Now Washington laid his plans. He would carry the war to the enemy, crossing the swollen river to strike part of the Hessian garrison that held the Jersey bank. On both sides of Trenton, New Jersey, the Delaware River runs generally from northwest to southeast. Into the Delaware, just east of Trenton, Assunpink Creek falls in from the north. It was bridged close to its confluence with the Delaware, but otherwise it cut the village off from Bordentown, downstream to the southeast.

The Hessians—about three thousand of them under an officer called von Donop—were spread out to cover some six miles of river between Trenton and Bordentown. About half of them were in Trenton, a village of perhaps a hundred houses, plus a stone barracks dating back to the French wars. Washington chose this quiet village as the target for his last-chance attack, the assault that would make or break the infant Revolution.

Washington's plan was complicated for green soldiers to execute, especially in darkness and bad weather. Brigadier General James Ewing was given nine hundred men, and told to cross the Delaware and establish a block east of Trenton. He was to cut off any chance of escape by its Hessian garrison. Lieutenant Colonel John Cadwalader's mission was to cross downstream of Trenton. With two thousand men, he would neutralize the Hessian garrison at Bordentown, preventing reinforcement for the Germans at Trenton.

Washington would lead the main effort. He would cross the Delaware upstream of Trenton with twenty-four hundred troops and some artillery, marching down the north bank of the river to strike Trenton in the numbing cold and darkness just before dawn. He chose the time of his attack well; his choice of the day was inspired.

For Washington chose Christmas eve for his crossing, with the attack set for dawn the next morning. If ever his quarry would be unwary, that would be the hour. His Hessian opponents were used to continental campaigning, spending the coldest months of winter snug in quarters. They were also, in the German tradition, dedicated celebrators of the yuletide. Maybe, just maybe, what with the darkness and the cold and the festive evening, Washington's men might surprise their veteran enemies.

On the twenty-third Washington issued orders to cook rations for three days, a certain sign that the regiments were about to move. Each man was issued forty rounds of ammunition as well, and the army knew it was on the way to another fight. Washington chose a significant countersign for the attack itself: "Victory or death" it was, and it pretty well described the desperate nature of the assault on Trenton. If the men survived a failure at Christmas, the new nation almost certainly would not.

Mother Nature was as formidable an obstacle as the Hessians posted on the far shore, and a whole lot less predictable. As grim, icy Christmas eve day wore on toward evening, frigid rain turned to sleet, driven by an arctic wind. Great cakes of drifting ice scudded down the swollen Delaware. It would be achievement enough just getting across the greedy, hostile water, let alone tackling experienced veterans on the other side. At the crossing place, McConkey's Ferry, the Delaware was a little less than a thousand yards across. Like the night, the river was in a foul mood.

The men Washington was going to attack were none other than Colonel Johann Rall's stout infantry, three Hesse-Kassel regiments named for their commanders, Rall, Knyphausen, and Lossberg. They were about as popular as the flu with the residents of New Jersey, being given to looting and vandalism on the grand scale. As one anguished Trenton resident wrote,

No house nor home, no woman nor child
was safe from their wanton cruelty . . .
They pillaged and destroyed as they chose,
only stopping short of absolute murder.

In addition to these unendearing traits, the Hessian soldiers were inordinately fond of the grape and of warm hearthsides, especially during the feast of Christmas.

These professionals were part of the large German contingent raised in several German states and committed by treaties between their rulers and Britain for service in America. At full strength—at which they seldom were—a German regiment numbered about six hundred men. They included, like British regiments, an elite grenadier company. They all wore the usual German dark blue uniform coat, with cuffs, lapels, and coat-skirts of contrasting color, orange for the Lossbergs, red for the Ralls, black for the Knyphausens. Like the British and most Americans, their weapon was the smoothbore musket, a brass-fitted .75-caliber flintlock of little use outside about eighty yards. All of them carried a long socket-bayonet, and most had a short sword as well.

If they were not popular with American civilians, they were nevertheless experienced soldiers, well fed, well trained, and generally well led. As Washington's men had learned to their cost at Fort Washington and elsewhere, the Hessians were a tough proposition for any army to tackle, most any time.

But this was not most any time; it was Christmas. Across the river from Washington's shivering men, Colonel Rall arose late, as was his wont, and addressed himself to the congenial business of celebrating the season. He had been at it for some time, neglecting the most elementary defense of the town, and collecting all the artillery uselessly in front of his quarters.

Lieutenant Andreas Widerhold, a disgusted Hessian officer, painted his commander in dreary colors:

He enjoyed himself until the small hours of the
night, went quickly to bed, slept until nine,
and when we would go to his quarters between 10
and 11 o'clock for the parade, he would some
times still be in his bath . . .

* * *

Colonel Rall's chief pleasure seems to have been the music of his regimental band, which played daily during the changing of the guard.

On Christmas eve Rall was entertained at the home of a Trenton merchant named Hunt. After a sumptuous dinner there was a card game, and repeated libations of wine. All of this continued far into the frigid night, until dawn was almost ready to fight its way through the clouds and swirling sleet. What, after all, was there to fear from these ragtag, bobtail Americans?

There was a great deal to fear, and most of it came about through Rall's own grievous mistakes. First of all, contemptuous of these *vedammt* rebels, he had not built earthworks, the defenses ordered by his superior, von Donop. Second, he had not insisted on the regular patrolling his men usually carried out regardless of the weather, rain or shine, winter or summer.

Last, and most damaging, he had failed even to read a note passed to him during the jovial Christmas Eve card game. It had come from a Tory farmer out of Bucks County, Pennsylvania. This loyal man had fought his way through the terrible night with news of the enemy. He was rewarded by being refused admittance, turned away again into the gloom and cold.

The best he could do was scribble Rall a note, hard, accurate information that the Americans were coming, coming this very night. Rall rammed the note into his pocket, unread, and returned to his wine and cards.

The farmer's note was not the only warning the Hessians had. There had been a series of alarms and excursions, none of them seeming to amount to much more than a bickering of outposts. There had been rumors of an impending American attack, but Rall had brushed them off as "old women's talk." Even as Washington was preparing to get his men on the road to Trenton, Rall was ridiculing an officer's suggestion that some simple steps be taken to lighten the detachment in case it had to fight.

"Fiddlesticks," snapped Rall. "These clodhoppers will not attack us, and should they do so, we will simply fall on them and rout them!"

The alert commander of a Highland regiment had warned of American concentrations as far back as the twenty-second. In response to his report, von Donop made a sortie on the next day, marching off toward the town of Mount Holly, eighteen miles from Trenton. A trumpery skirmish with an American detachment followed.

Nobody much got hurt on either side, although both commanders claimed victory. The real importance of the Mount Holly affair seems to have been von Donop's meeting with an attractive widow of Mount Holly, from which were removed "all the women . . . except one widow . . ."

Apparently von Donop was entranced by this one remaining lady, enough, at least, to stay on at her Mount Holly home. He was still there, taking his ease and whatever else, as Christmas eve came and went. He was, as one of his officers said, "extremely devoted to the fair sex," a devotion that took him completely out of the action about to explode at Trenton.

There is evidence that the American demonstration at Mount Holly was a carefully contrived feint, intended to achieve exactly what it did, misleading von Donop out of any chance to react to the Trenton attack. It is pleasant to suppose that the comely young widow gave whatever she gave out of purest patriotism, committing her fair body to the success of Washington's desperate crossing. We shall never know.

Meanwhile, the despised Americans were crossing, ice-crusted boats full of ragged soldiers and a few guns, ferried across without loss by the genius of Colonel John Glover and his men. Glover's soldiers were fishermen, master small-boat handlers from Marblehead, Massachusetts—after the terrors of the gray Atlantic rollers, the ice-clogged Delaware held little fear for them. Glover's men got Washington's strike force across without a single casualty, unless you count the commander of the Delaware Line, who complained that he fell into the Delaware and "have been suffering from piles ever since."

They battled through the ice floes in heavy craft called Durham boats, which would each carry thirty troops, with half a dozen Marblehead men laboring to move them. The Durham boats were the children of the local iron industry, for these sturdy craft were designed to haul both ore and pig iron, and were accordingly very tough indeed. They were forty to sixty feet long, looked a little like huge canoes, and would carry fifteen tons.

Best of all, the Durham boats drew only thirty inches of water fully loaded. That made them ideal for crossing the shallow Delaware, and their tough construction made them virtually impervious to drifting ice. Each one of them would move a lot of soldiers and horses . . . and they would move artillery as well. Eighteen guns they carried this night, the artillery that would make all the difference once battle was joined.

The Durham boats bore no resemblance to the overloaded little cockleshell shown in the famous painting of Washington crossing the Delaware. Nor, surely, did the general, an experienced soldier and woodsman, stand upright in the boat, smugly staring across the river during the crossing.

What the general did was supervise an orderly, professional military operation. He got a brigade across to provide security at the landing place, then got himself, his little staff, and his horse over to begin organizing things on the Jersey shore. It was a miserably slow process. Washington had hoped to have everybody across and formed up by midnight, but the appalling weather slowed the troops down so far that they did not get on the road to Trenton until between 3:00 and 4:00 A.M.

As they pushed through the darkness toward their target, the weather turned even worse. Now, however much misery it caused the slogging troops, it dropped a friendly veil about their advance. They remained undiscovered, although they were already three hours behind schedule. Rain poured down from a glowering black sky, and the savage cold reduced everything to slow motion.

Now Washington split his advance into two columns. He would take an inner road, about two miles from the riverbank. General John Sullivan would lead his troops down the river road straight at the town. He would strike the town from its front, while Washington broke in the back door. If everything worked as planned, Sullivan would drive the Hessians through Trenton, and Washington's men would cut off their retreat eastward across the Assunpink.

The night was hideous, a pitch-dark maelstrom of swirling rain now turning to sleet. The tattered Americans, soaked and shivering, quickly began to leave crimson splotches on the snowy road, but they trudged on still. Men with split boots, men with cracked shoes, men with their feet wrapped in sodden rags, all leaned doggedly forward into the sleet and pushed ahead.

In the morning the track of the army would be clearly marked by their own blood, but just now no amount of cold and jagged ice was going to stop them. Nobody knew better than they about trying men's souls, but there was a sense of purpose driving this little army through the screaming night.

Washington rode up and down the shadowy column, tireless, urgent, driving. "Press on, boys, press on!" he called, and his officers moved through the gloom, keeping the men moving. The cold was dreadful, and much of the road was slick with ice. Here and there a lantern shed a dim, bobbing corpse-light across the stooped, shuffling column, and an occasional torch flared from a creaking artillery carriage. Otherwise, there was only the rattle and clink of harness and equipment, and the crunch of tired feet on the icy road. The men were soaked through, trying as best they could to keep their musket priming dry under their coattails, or with a handkerchief wrapped about the pan of the weapon.

There was an occasional brief halt, but even rest was dangerous. In spite of all the officers and NCOs could do, it was hard to get exhausted men up and going again. Two soldiers fell into deep sleep during one halt in the bitter cold. They would not waken ever again. The only safety in this miserable night was in movement, and Washington and his officers ordered and pushed and cajoled: "Soldiers, keep by your officers, for God's sake, keep by your officers!"

Sullivan, pushing on through the blackness, sent a message to Washington, advising his commander of what the general surely knew already: The horrible weather had thoroughly wet the priming of nearly every musket. There would be precious little chance to reprime in the soaking night. Washington was as grimly purposeful as his shivering men: "Tell General Sullivan to use the bayonet. I am resolved to take Trenton."

Washington's task had been made somewhat easier by Rall's own headquarters. The Hessians were good soldiers, and accordingly sent out strong patrols about dawn each day. This ugly morning, however, the dawn patrols had been canceled by the field officer of the day, apparently out of consideration for the men who would have to trudge through that bone-chilling weather. The Hessian garrison would pay dearly for that little kindness.

On the edge of that sleepy village stood the shop of cooper Richard Howell, and in it were a couple of dozen Hessians serving as an outpost for the main body. The senior officer was an active, intelligent lieutenant called Andreas Wiederhold, and he had done his duty, Christmas eve or not. He had sent out his own patrols into the swirling sleet, without result. Now, about dawn, still another patrol had trudged in out of the bitter dawn to report that all was quiet.

Wiederhold, a good officer, well knew the age-old propensity of tired, cold soldiers to prefer a warm fire to an extended hike in miserable weather. And so he took a look outside himself, and he was horrified at what he saw. For coming at a trot out of the woods to his north was a column of ragged men—they were armed, they meant business, and they were surely Americans.

Wiederhold roared his orders and fell in his handful of men. When the attackers were close enough, he gave the order to fire, and his men cranked off a volley into the storm blowing into their faces. By now, however, there seemed to be Americans everywhere Wiederhold looked, and the young lieutenant quickly realized that this isolated house was not a happy place for twenty-odd German soldiers. He quickly pulled his men back from the cooper's house, attaching his little band to a company of the Lossberg regiment.

Washington's column saw the houses of Trenton begin to loom up out of the gloom about the time Wiederhold saw his first Americans. It was almost eight o'clock when a pallid, anemic daylight revealed Wiederhold's astonished Hessian picket tumbling out of a house on the edge of the village. "Turn out!" roared men of the German outpost. "Turn out, the enemy! *Heraus, heraus, der feind!*"

As a spattering of shots from Washington's men brushed the Germans back, off to Washington's right the thump of artillery announced the beginning of Sullivan's attack along the river road. At the head of Sullivan's advance, a party of the brand-new New Jersey Continentals struck the first Hessian picket at a house called The Hermitage, just outside Trenton.

The German outpost, a detachment of rifle-armed jaegers, managed one volley before the Americans were on them with fixed bayonets. Having no bayonets of their own, the jaegers sensibly decamped. After one more attempt to make a stand in the town, most of them ran for it, and did not stop until they had crossed Assunpink Creek to safety.

Against all hope, the attack of Washington's two separated columns had been perfectly coordinated, in spite of the gloom and sleet and rain. Rall had been caught flat-footed, and his hungover soldiers scrambled desperately into the streets to form. It was too late.

Already American grapeshot was humming down the streets of Trenton. A pair of six-pounder cannon under a slim, boyish gunner captain called Alexander Hamilton swung into action at the intersection of Trenton's two major arteries, King and Queen streets. Together with other guns, Hamilton's pieces poured their fire down both streets, firing grapeshot, roundshot, and explosive shells that bounded evilly through the snow until they burst with a roar and a flash of crimson.

Rall's own men were the "regiment de jour," the quick-reaction unit. They had been required to sleep in their uniforms with weapons to hand, and had run quickly into King Street to form up. Their attempt was gallant but already futile, as load after load of grapeshot and shell whirred down the street and dropped blue-coated soldiers writhing in the snow.

Everywhere Hessian soldiers poured out of their warm houses in confusion, trying desperately to rally in spite of the scythe of grapeshot whistling down the streets. As Rall's own men struggled to form on King Street, the von Lossberg regiment tried bravely to fall in on Queen.

The third Hessian regiment, Knyphausen's black-uniformed fusiliers, already had its hands full nearer the river road, trying to cope with Sullivan's onrushing men. Out in front was tough, ornery John Stark, colonel of the First New Hampshire Regiment, and his men were coming on so fast that the Knyphausens never really got set to meet them. The Knyphausens recoiled, still firing, trying to maintain some sort of order in the face of the rapid American advance. Like their sister regiments, they began to take fire from fences and buildings all around them. Their enemy was everywhere.

When the shooting started, Colonel Rall was still fast

asleep in his headquarters on King Street. Characteristically he had been hard to rouse, even when the first shots were fired at the town's edge. His adjutant, Lieutenant Piel, at last shook the general awake, then rushed into the street to help rally Rall's confused men. When Rall did not appear, Piel ran back into the building, only to find his befuddled commander still in his nightshirt, asking vaguely what the matter was.

Finally Piel was able to make Rall comprehend that the town was swarming with Americans, and that a battle was in full swing under his very windows. That astonishing news seemed to jerk the colonel awake, and at last he threw on his clothes and ran to do his duty. Once up, he rushed into the street, shouting to his milling men to form up and advance. If Rall's sense of caution had been sadly lacking, there was nothing wrong with his courage.

As the Hessians fell back in confusion through the town, Washington's shouting men were driving hard around the north edge of Trenton. They smashed aside what resistance there was, capturing two more German guns on the way and pushing on down Assunpink Creek toward its mouth. Down along the Delaware, Glover's Marbleheaders carried the vital Assunpink bridge toward Bordentown. The trap had closed.

Near Rall's headquarters two Hessian guns were overrun before they could fire, captured by a regiment led by a tavern-keeper nicknamed Joe Gourd, so-called for the receptacle in which he was wont to serve his customers rum punch in happier times. Just now Joe Gourd was proving to be a better than adequate commander, pushing fast and hard into the village streets.

His leading element, the daredevils who charged the Hessian guns, were led by an eighteen-year-old lieutenant called James Monroe. Monroe quickly went down with a serious shoulder wound, but he would survive, of course. One day he would rise to greater heights, surely, but he would never do anything for his country more important than the capture of these two deadly guns.

Meanwhile, Rall was doing his level best to rally his men. He was mounted, his sword drawn, shouting orders to his milling soldiers. From time to time he still seemed perplexed, uncertain about what had actually happened to his peaceful garrison town. At one point he even seemed confused by the crack of American rifles; "Lord, lord, what is it?" he mumbled.

American infantry went down parallel streets at the double, and some of them took shelter in buildings to replace the wet priming of their muskets. Now their fire began to pull down Hessian officers trying to rally their men, and two of their bullets tore into Rall himself, mounted and shouting encouragement by his troops. He was carried to a church in the village, desperately wounded and out of the fight for good. With their commander down and grapeshot shrieking around their ears, the heart now quickly went out of many of the Hessians.

Those of the Germans who went on fighting were gradually penned into an apple orchard on the eastern edge of the village. A few managed to break for the fords of the Assunpink and escape through the icy water. But most did not, and many of the remnants of the Ralls and Lossbergs surrendered there, faced by increasing numbers of American infantry and by those deadly cannons, manhandled down from the other end of the town.

The Knyphausens stuck it out a little longer, losing more men in an attempt to escape across the Assunpink Bridge. But soon they, too, seeing their comrades calling it quits in the orchard, laid down their arms, the ubiquitous Wiederhold interpreting the surrender terms. There was a great rolling cheer from the American troops, and those who had hats threw them in the air. It was over.

It was over for poor Rall as well, for he was dying. For all his arrogance about the despised Americans, for all his sloth, he had done what he could to lead his men, and had died trying. Quite in character, one of his last acts was to plead with his conquerors for kindness to his men, a favor Washington was ready to grant in any case.

Rall lay down to die at his Trenton headquarters, and in his vest pocket somebody found the warning note passed to him on Christmas eve by the Tory farmer . . . the note poor Rall had put aside unread. It had cost him his life, and he knew it. "If I had read this . . . I would not be here," he said quietly, and so it was.

The victory had not been perfect. General Ewing had not crossed to carry and hold the bridge across Assunpink Creek. Some four hundred Hessians had escaped that way, and a few more elsewhere. Cadwalader's crossing had misfired as well. Still, in less than an hour Rall's veterans had ceased to exist as a military force, and the magnitude of the American success was astonishing.

In addition to over a hundred casualties—about a quarter of them killed—more than nine hundred Hessian troops were prisoners. Also, the Americans had captured six cannon, more than a thousand precious muskets, and four colors.

The price had been ridiculous. While two Americans had frozen to death during the advance, nobody at all had been killed in the battle. Even more surprising, there were only four wounded, including Monroe and another officer who had charged with him to capture the Hessian guns. Another three exhausted Americans would freeze to death in the boats during the bitter retreat, but they were the last payment for the astonishing victory at Trenton.

Rall's errors had contributed much to Washington's amazing victory. So had the very heavy Hessian loss in officers, which had quickly sowed confusion in their ranks. But in the end it was Washington's triumph. His enterprise and daring had won it, his leadership and inspiration which had sent his tired men into the town at the double, in an irresistible charge.

Washington and his officers debated whether to press their victory, to drive on through the sleet to attack Princeton, or maybe even Brunswick. A few officers urged their general to press on—they had the initiative, they should keep it. Most of Washington's leaders, and Washington himself, saw things rather more clearly. His scrappy little army was exhausted, hungry, ill-shod. Some of it was drunk, too, having liberated a considerable amount of Hessian rum in Trenton. There were, moreover, a good many unwhipped enemies nearby. It was time to go.

It was, and the army moved quickly to retire across the Delaware. Washington was jubilant. He had been outgeneraled on Long Island and Manhattan and had suffered terribly from the snide jealousy of Lee and the perennial shortage of everything, especially men. But now, in spite of his detractors, in spite of terrible odds, in spite of sleet and snow and shivering men with broken shoes, he had destroyed three veteran enemy regiments.

"This is a glorious day for our country," he said as the shooting died away, and he was even righter than he knew. For now his destitute men would remain with the colors, almost to a man. Now wavering civilians would hesitate before declaring their allegiance to King George. Now the Tories of New Jersey, and there were lots of them, would lie low yet awhile.

Washington got his men and his prisoners and booty safely back over the threatening Delaware, and got clean away. To add insult to injury, he not only evaded a vigorous pursuit by Cornwallis, but bloodied that officer's rear guard in the process. Washington pushed his exhausted men hard, deep into New Jersey, while the ragged Continental army chuckled at the frustrated British pursuit, "in a most infernal sweat, running, puffing and blowing and swearing at being so outwitted."

It was as well that Washington had chosen to retire. He had evaded the British pursuit by the narrowest of margins, and the day after Trenton, more than one thousand of his men were reported unfit for duty.

Washington's Hessian prisoners were paraded through the streets of Philadelphia, and the whole town turned out to see them. The Hessian band, poor Rall's pride and joy, was a special hit in Philadelphia, and remained in that pleasant town many weeks to cheer and comfort the citizenry. While Philadelphia rejoiced, word of this winter miracle spread quickly through the struggling new country.

The great British victory, which yesterday had seemed but a matter of weeks or months, was suddenly not nearly so certain. The British professionals recognized the change in their ragtag opponents. Harcourt, the tough dragoon who had captured General Lee, paid Washington's men the finest kind of soldier's compliment:

> *Though it was once the fashion of this army*
> *to treat them in the most contemptible light,*
> *they are now become a formidable enemy.*

Indeed they were. This Washington and his ragged ruffians were suddenly much more than they had seemed to be— perhaps they were winter soldiers after all.

It was going to be a long war.

"TAKE A POSITION LESS EXPOSED"
THE BLADENSBURG RACES

It happened during the War of 1812, a silly little border squabble that never should have been fought at all. America was miserably unprepared for war with Britain, or with anybody else, for that matter. The United States Army was microscopic, thanks to a parsimonious Congress, and for a while the nation's quarrels would have to be fought mostly by militia units. But militia were a weak reed at the best of times, often poorly trained, usually miserably led. A lot of purple prose was written, then and later, about minutemen springing from their plows to repel the invader. In real life, however, the minuteman generally did a lot better sticking to his plow and leaving war to the professionals.

Now, with the right kind of training, Americans make fine soldiers; they always have. In the War of 1812 Winfield Scott's regulars showed just how good well-schooled American infantry could be. Oliver Perry and Andrew Jackson achieved prodigies with ordinary, ornery, individualistic citizens.

But occasionally even the most martial of peoples fail in combat with a capable enemy. This is especially likely to happen when untrained enthusiasts go off to make war against professional troops. Once in a great while, a day of failure is so bad that it is downright embarrassing, a source of national shame. For a young, proud United States of America, that shame was the day called the Bladensburg Races.

It was the Summer of 1814, and the British were coming again. There weren't very many of them, only about four thousand, but they were regulars, the red-coated hardcases who had whipped the best of Napoleon's commanders. Worse still, they were in Chesapeake Bay, covered by a small fleet, and right in America's backyard.

By the middle of August, the British were headed for America's capital. John Armstrong, the Secretary of War, was obsessed with the invasion of Canada, and had done little to prepare for operations at home. His local commander was an incompetent named Winder, notable for very little besides being the brother of the governor of Maryland, a fact of some political importance.

There were virtually no regular troops to be had, and so Armstrong and Winder had to make do with militia. As it gathered, Washington collapsed in panic, and the roads out of town were crowded with wagons full of furniture, government documents, and frightened people.

The British, meanwhile, were marching north without anybody getting in their way. They were on their way to Bladensburg, Maryland, from which a good road led west to the national capital. After a good deal of dithering, Winder managed to get to Bladensburg ahead of the British. There he lined up his troops, such as they were, on the west bank of the Anacostia River, by a bridge the British would have to use.

Winder needed all the professional help he could get. As it was, though, he had a lot of amateur assistance he did not need. Up above the bridge with the sweating militia was President James Madison himself, accompanied by his cabinet. Secretary of State James Monroe even seems to have taken it upon himself to alter the position of some of the American troops. He did not do very well at it either, but then, neither did anybody else this broiling day.

By now the Americans had about six thousand men up to oppose the British. That ought to have been enough to hold any bridge, but the redcoats were not impressed. There were light infantrymen out in front of the British column, and they did not stop. Under fire, and taking casualties, the redcoats dropped their packs and came on in open order, bayonets winking wickedly in the sun.

So far, the militiamen had stood their ground reasonably well, but now trails of flame began to issue from the British lines. With a prodigious whooshing, fiery thunderbolts came arching in on the quaking militia. These hideous apparitions were Congreve rockets, mostly sound and fury and precious little explosion, and they hit nobody at all.

They did not have to. All this hissing and banging was too much for the militia, most of whom turned and bolted in panic before those deadly bayonets got anywhere close to them. And so began the Bladensburg Races, in which the American army departed in indecent haste, standing not upon the order of its going. With it went its commander, the presidential cabinet, and a lot of militiamen who would have fought had somebody stayed to help them. The only casualty of this astonishing rout was an officer who killed himself running.

With this fleet-footed mob went also the President of the United States, who intelligently remarked to Armstrong that it would be sensible to "take a position less exposed," and did so. The whole rabble went streaming back to Washington and beyond, the president and his sweating cabinet ending up a full sixteen miles past the capital.

The British re-formed and came marching inexorably on down the road. About a mile west of Bladensburg they ran into a buzzsaw, tough Navy Commodore Joshua Barney and an outnumbered contingent of American sailors and marines. Barney's musketry and heavy naval guns cost the British a substantial number of casualties, until the red infantry got around behind Barney's cannon, and in among the crews with bayonets. The redoubtable Barney went down wounded, and his surviving men spiked their guns and joined the retreat.

And so a foreign enemy came to Washington. British troops found dinner for forty ready at the White House, and sensibly decided not to waste it. Unchallenged, they then burned the White House and some other public buildings, stayed on a day through a tornado and a torrential rain to burn some more, and departed.

The damage to Washington was not as bad as it might have been; many of the fires were put out by the rain and the tornado. The damage to American pride ran far deeper. The country had been treated to an astonishingly feckless performance by its government, and people were angry and ashamed. For a while, at least, there was some show of unity, although that did not stop American contractors in New England from selling tons of supplies to the British in Canada that very autumn.

In time this stupid little war would be settled by negotiators from both nations, settled intelligently by leaving everybody exactly where they were when war broke out. The peace that followed was remarkable in its permanence—it is still going strong, and the two antagonists have since fought repeatedly as allies.

Nothing can erase the shame of a farce like the Bladensburg Races, but thoughtful soldiers and statesmen learned from its memory. That memory helped to build a better army, in time a regular army, the army of Saint-Mihiel, Bastogne, and Pork Chop Hill, Dak To, Hue, and the Persian Gulf. A little humility is not an altogether bad thing.

PIERRE'S HOLE

The 1832 Rendezvous was in full swing. The Mountain Men had come together from all across the wild Rockies to do their trading and sow a few wild oats. For a little while they left behind the hardship and mortal danger of the high mountains for the peace and quiet of a jewellike valley of deep grass and plentiful game.

This lovely valley was called Pierre's Hole. It lay north-to-south, about twenty miles long and perhaps two miles wide. Through its lush mountain meadows, flanked by stands of timber, ran the south fork of the Teton River, headed north for its own rendezvous with the Snake. For a few days, at least, they could enjoy plenty of raw whiskey and compliant Indian women and, as the saying went, "sleep with both eyes shut." The valley might be full of rattlesnakes, but no Indian war party would dare disturb so many armed men.

Pierre's Hole lay west of the Teton Range in what is now Teton County, Idaho. Today this beautiful spot is called Teton Basin. To the west and southwest the valley was sheltered by the Big Hole range; to the south loomed the Palisades. Through a gap in the Palisades a trappers' trail wound into the valley, branching up from the well-used route between Green River and the Snake.

Across the guardian peaks of the Tetons, through Teton Pass, lay a similar oasis, Jackson's Hole, named, like Pierre's, for an early trapper. Pierre, in this case, was one "le grand Pierre" Tivanitagon, who flourished in this wild country until the implacable Blackfeet cut him down in the winter of 1828.

And so, beginning in late June, the trappers rested and waited to begin trading, told tales of isolation and hardship and comrades dead in last season's Indian fights. And at noon on the eighth of July, the popping of rifle shots announced the arrival of the 180-mule supply caravan of the Rocky Mountain Fur Company. At the column's head was its "booshway" (bourgeois, or boss), veteran trapper-turned-trader, scar-faced Bill Sublette, followed by more than one hundred of his men.

Tagging along for safety was a party of seventeen Eastern tenderfeet, led by Nathaniel Wyeth of Cambridge, Massachusetts. Wyeth was a tough-minded Yankee entrepreneur, a former ice merchant with a nose for opportunity. He had his eyes fixed on Oregon, on what he perceived as a golden opportunity for trade in furs and salmon.

And so he had started west with his men and a conglomeration of trade goods and equipment. He even dragged along three incredibly clumsy boats on wheels, the better to ford western rivers. Some of his men lost heart and turned back, and Wyeth dumped the boats in St. Louis, but with some of his goods and men he was still westbound, enthusiasm unabated.

Sublette had won his race with arch-competitor American Fur Company, some eighteen hundred miles of tough trail from St. Louis. American's caravan, led by Lucien Fontenelle, was still far away to the north, up in the Big Horn Valley. Sublette's column traveled military-style, camping in hollow square, changing their night guards every four hours, standing to before dawn each morning. Even so, and even though they had beaten Fontenelle, it had not been an easy trip.

First, they had repulsed a nighttime Blackfoot horse raid in the Wind River country. They lost about ten horses, but the raiders did not charge home, and nobody was hurt on either side. Next, famous trapper Broken Hand Fitzpatrick, sent from Pierre's Hole to hurry them on, had been cut off by Blackfeet on the return trip, lost his horses, lost his weapons, and nearly lost his hair. After days alone, on foot, he at last fell in with two friendly Iroquois and was brought to Pierre's Hole. He was exhausted and emaciated, and his hair had turned snow white. He was a grim reminder of the death that lurked everywhere out in the primeval wilderness.

Sublette's column had brought the necessary, and now both celebration and trading could begin. Sublette would have first crack at the bales of fine fur brought in by his own men, by the "free"—unaffiliated—trappers, and by the several hundred Indians in the basin: some Flatheads, about 120 lodges of Nez Percés, and a handful of Iroquois and Delawares. Altogether, counting men from the American and Rocky Mountain companies, the free trappers, the Indians, and some men recently employed by a bankrupt fur company, there were almost one thousand men at Rendezvous.

The trading and roistering went on for over a week. The trappers exchanged their precious beaver plews for powder and ball, knives, hatchets, kettles, blankets, and the bright trade goods beloved of the Indian women. They traded for fresh horses as well. The Nez Percés bred a particularly fine pony called the Pelous horse, ancestor of today's Appaloosa. The name of the neighboring Cayuse tribe provided the western generic term for horse.

The mountain men did not seem to mind that everything was marked up as much as 2,000 percent over St. Louis prices. Life in the mountains was an uncertain thing at best. They could not know that this was the last great harvest of the beaver trade, but they did know it was better to take life as it came, enjoy it while you could. And they did.

The trappers and Indians partook copiously of Sublette's little square kegs of pure alcohol. Because it was unlawful to give or sell liquor to Indians, Sublette had gotten a "passport" in St. Louis to carry up to 450 gallons of whiskey "for the special use of his boatmen." That was purest nonsense, of course, since Sublette came overland and had no boat-men. At Rendezvous, however, nobody cared how the alcohol got to Pierre's Hole. Most of the men present simply enjoyed it, got gloriously drunk, and found cooperative Indian women.

And then, the whiskey drunk, their furs gone, the moun-tain men began to pack for the high country and the beaver streams, for the Green, the Yellowstone, the Snake, and the Humboldt. Rendezvous began to break up on July 17, as Bill Sublette's brother Milton led thirteen of his men southwest-ward out of Pierre's Hole.

With them were Wyeth and ten of his people, the rest hav-ing decided western adventure was not for them. Wyeth intended to accompany Milton Sublette to the lower Snake until he cleared Blackfoot country, then strike for the Colum-bia. Also with Sublette were fifteen free trappers under vet-eran Alexander Sinclair. A few Flathead braves tagged along; there was safety in numbers in this perilous land.

They did not get far, perhaps from too much celebration, and camped eight miles south of Pierre's Hole. Perhaps they were just cautious, wary from experience, from the horse raid on Bill Sublette's column, and from Broken Hand's ter-rible experience. It was well they were careful, for trouble was not far away.

Next morning, breaking camp, the remains of their holiday mood vanished and they reached for their long rifles. Drop-ping down from the Palisade range to the south wound a long column of Indians, perhaps as many as two hundred of them, displaying a British flag. The mountain men sent a couple of trappers clattering back to Rendezvous for rein-forcements, looked to their priming, made a barricade of their packs, and waited. Now, as the trappers watched, most of the Indian women and children returned to the moun-tains, an ominous sign. The braves came on, and the trap-pers thumbed back their hammers, for these were Gros Ventres.

All mountain men knew the Big Bellies, so called for their insatiable appetites, capable of wearing out anybody's hospi-tality. Even their kinsmen, the Arapaho, called them spong-ers. American trappers simply called them "Blackfeet," lumping them together with that much stronger nation, whose language they often spoke, and with whom they often allied against the white man. The Gros Ventres were, however, a distinct tribe, not only acquisitive but very tough indeed.

This group was returning from a visit to the Arapaho, a vacation taken at least in part to escape the wrath of the British Hudson's Bay Company, to whom the Big Bellies had been a perpetual plague and menace. In fact, this Gros Ventre party had stolen their British colors from a Hudson's Bay Company party they had recently ambushed.

Perhaps as a ruse, perhaps sincerely, the Gros Ventres sent forward an unarmed war chief, Baihoh. He carried a red blanket and a medicine pipe, a holy article with a green soapstone bowl and long, decorated wooden stem. It may be that Baihoh thought he was dealing with Fontenelle's men, who he knew should be in that area; the Gros Ventres were then at peace with the American Fur Company. As the Arapaho said later, Baihoh would never have advanced alone and unarmed if he knew he was dealing with his enemies, the Rocky Mountain Company men.

Milton Sublette was too old a dog to wholly trust the Big Belly envoy, but he was willing to parley. He chose, however, the wrong men to talk peace. He sent a half-breed Iroquois named Antoine Godin, one of the men who had rescued Broken Hand. Beside him rode a Flathead, whose tribe had been repeatedly savaged by both Blackfoot and Gros Ventre war parties.

Godin had cause to detest the Blackfeet, for they had killed his father up on Big Lost River two years before. And this chief, in Godin's eyes, was just another Blackfoot. And so, as the Gros Ventre extended his hand, Godin gripped it hard and shouted to the Flathead, "Fire!" The Flathead's rifle roared, Baihoh toppled from his horse, and before the Gros Ventres could react, Godin and the Flathead were galloping back to the trappers' barricade, whooping and waving the red blanket . . . and the chief's scalp.

A roar of rage erupted from the Gros Ventres, and the fight was on. The Big Bellies quickly took cover in a wooded swampy area, fortifying their refuge with logs, branches, and trenches dug furiously by some of their women. Both sides filled the air with lead, but there was little movement until Bill Sublette arrived with white and Indian reinforcements.

He had brought, by frontier standards, a whole army. Behind him rode some two hundred white trappers, plus about two hundred Flatheads and three hundred Nez Percé warriors, all eager to fall on the hated Big Bellies. Taking command, Bill Sublette got Wyeth's greenhorns out of the line of fire, then led a force of some sixty volunteers into the willow-shaded swamp. With Sublette was veteran frontiersman Robert Campbell, with whom Sublette exchanged oral wills as they moved into combat.

Now the fighting turned to a murderous point-blank hail of arrows and rifle-balls, and the Indian barricade proved a tough nut to crack. Sinclair went down, mortally wounded, and was carried out of the line of fire. Sublette nailed one Gros Ventre brave peering through a chink in his barricade, but it was difficult for the besiegers to get a clear shot.

The Big Bellies were shooting well—veteran trapper Henry Fraeb lost a lock of hair to a well-aimed ball. Even under such circumstances, as Zenas Leonard wrote,

> . . . any man not evincing the greatest degree of courage . . . is treated as a coward; and the person who advances first, furthest and fastest, and makes the greatest display of animal courage, soon rises in the estimation of his companions. According with the hope of gaining a little *glory* . . .

Leonard, the Sublettes, and others pressed ahead into the fire.

Bill Sublette, standing behind a tree reloading, was hit in the shoulder by a ball that went on to strike another trapper in the head. Although Sublette remained in command for a time, the shoulder was broken, and he was losing blood. He finally collapsed and was carried back to safety.

Other trappers and Indian allies fell under the Big Bellies' accurate fire. One boozy white man wobbled into the open, climbed on the logs of the Indian barricade, and promptly took two bullets in the head. There was considerable confusion, and the attackers recoiled. A flanking party led by Milton Sublette also failed to gain any ground from the Gros Ventres.

Even the bravest of the trappers were glad to fall back. One of them, the indestructible Zenas Leonard, later wrote that he was delighted to carry away a wounded trapper. It gave him a chance to fall back without anybody questioning his courage, and he lost no time in packing his companion out of the fight.

The trappers had now managed to cover two sides of the Gros Ventre position, but in doing so, were shooting at each other as well as their enemies. It was desperate work at close quarters, and some of the trappers began to lose any enthusiasm they might have begun with. Wyeth, in the thick of the fight, observed dryly:

> The idea of a barbed arrow sticking in a man's body, as we had observed it in the deer and other animals, was appalling to us all, and it is no wonder that some of our men recoiled from it.

Nevertheless, the attackers worked in closer and closer to the Gros Ventre line, both sides screaming insults at one another.

As the day wore on, however, ammunition began to run low, so low, in fact, that after the fight the trappers would have to return to the battlefield to dig lead from the trees. Finally the attackers decided to burn the Big Bellies out, and began to gather dry wood and brush. The Indian allies were not happy with the idea—fire would destroy the booty they hoped to gain—but they need not have worried.

For before any fire was laid, the Gros Ventres shouted that they would be avenged, that four hundred lodges of their tribe were near and would exterminate the white men utterly. Somehow this threat got mistranslated into a warning that a multitude of Gros Ventres were even now plundering the trappers' main camp back at Rendezvous. Leaving only a small guard to watch the Gros Ventres, most of the trappers immediately raced off north to save their possessions.

Other besiegers heard only "Blackfeet comin', heap Blackfeet, heap big fight!" According to one account of the fight, this was enough to convince them that the unseen Gros Ventre reinforcements were about to attack them directly, and many of them ran for their lives. It did not take these heroes long to realize that no hostile reinforcements were nearby, and some returned to continue the siege of the Big Belly breastworks.

The trappers who had raced off to defend their camp did not return until after dark. They had found their possessions intact; no Gros Ventre warriors had ever come near the camp. Now they waited out the long night, and with the dawn began again to close in on the Gros Ventre stronghold. Closer and closer they crept, and no shot was fired. Finally they mounted a charge, up and over the logs and branches, to find . . . nothing.

Sometime during the darkness the Gros Ventres had skillfully withdrawn, taking their wounded with them. Inside their defensive position lay twenty or thirty dead horses, but only nine Indian corpses. A few more Gros Ventre bodies turned up as the trappers fruitlessly followed blood trails into the woods. The trappers also found a few forgotten white men, a wounded mountain man who soon died, and a wounded Gros Ventre squaw whom the Flatheads murdered forthwith.

The fight was over. As Wyeth somewhat melodramatically wrote:

> The din of arms was now changed into the noise of the vulture and the howling of masterless dogs.

And that was all, all, at least, except to bury the dead and collect the booty. There was lots of that, blankets and other personal possessions and a herd of several dozen horses, including the treasured pony Broken Hand had lost during his escape from the Blackfeet.

The Gros Ventre body-count rose to sixteen, and the Big Bellies admitted twenty-six of their people had been killed. Since Indians customarily understated their losses, this was probably substantially below their actual casualties. Of the fur company men, five were dead and six wounded. Seven friendly Indians had been killed, and seven more hurt.

The Gros Ventres had fought well, against great odds. Leonard honestly wrote that the Big Bellies had shown themselves to be both smarter and braver than their attackers. They had, he thought, deserved to win.

There would be more trouble to come. Although the trappers returned to Pierre's Hole for a few days, giving Sublette time to heal a little, there were beaver to trap and many miles to cover, and the mountain men began to filter off toward the far rivers. Almost immediately one small party lost three dead to the Gros Ventres on the slopes of Jackson's Hole. Others were picked off by ones and twos that year and later, out in the merciless wilderness. Ironically, a veteran leader of American Fur Company trappers was among those ambushed and murdered by the Gros Ventres before the year was out.

Bill Sublette, on his way east with 168 packs of precious beaver, ran head-on into the main Gros Ventre body, angry and painted for war. But the Indians were short of powder, and from long experience they were a little reluctant to tangle with "Cut-face," as they called Sublette. Sublette avoided a fight, mixing a judicious combination of ready rifles and a gift of twenty-five pounds of tobacco. He could afford the present: His pelts were worth eighty-five thousand dollars.

And so Sublette came out of the high country in safety, his animals laden with the last great beaver harvest. Washington Irving, out on the frontier with a government commission, watched Sublette lead his men home:

> Their long cavalcade stretched in single file for nearly half a mile. Sublette still wore his arm in a sling. The mountaineers in their rude hunting dresses armed with rifles and roughly mounted . . . looked like banditti returning with plunder.

Bad as Pierre's Hold had been for the defeated Gros Ventres, the worst was yet to come. Continuing their travel home, they now moved east of the Continental Divide . . . into the Absaroka Mountains, heartland of their bitter hereditary enemies, the Crows. At least forty Big Bellies left their bones in Crow country. And many of those who did get home did not survive long. Only two years after the Pierre's Hole fight, deadly smallpox swept through the Gros Ventres, killing most members of the bands who had fought so well against Sublette's men. It was a sad end for a tough, proud people.

GOING FOR THEM BALDHEADED

"Who," tourists ask, "was the Marquess of Granby, and why are so many pubs named after him?" The answer to their question lies far back in the mists of the year 1760 and the extraordinary charge at Warburg.

It all started in 1759, the year it "rained victories" on British arms. That was the year of Wolfe's triumph at Quebec, the year of Admiral Hawke's destruction of the French fleet at Quiberon Bay, and the year of Minden, in north Germany.

Minden had added another chapter to the glorious history of the British infantry, for it was there that some forty-four hundred English foot—six regiments—not only drove off a charge of massed French cavalry, but counterattacked, driving horse, foot, and guns before them off the battlefield. The British regiments that fought at Minden picked roses on their way into the cannon's mouth, wearing them in their hats during the action. They wear them to this day on the first day of August, the anniversary of their astonishing victory.

But the British cavalry did not share the glory of Minden. Champing at the bit for action, they nevertheless saw none, held out of the battle by their commander, the incredibly inept George Sackville. Although he was repeatedly ordered to charge, Sackville refused to move, pleading that his orders were not clear.

Sackville was cashiered for his disobedience, but he would return to again disgrace his country years afterward, now as Lord Germain. Risen to be a favorite of King George III, and Secretary of State for North America, he would exercise all his considerable stupidity and insensitivity to help Britain lose her American colonies. For it was Sackville's bungling leadership that led to the surrender of Gentleman Johnny Burgoyne, abandoned and unsupported by other British forces.

But that was in the future, and in 1760 the British cavalry thirsted for a chance to prove what they could do without Sackville, now gone and unlamented. They got the chance on July 31 at Warburg in Hanover, as part of a badly outnumbered British-German army facing a French force half again their size.

This time the British cavalry were commanded by a real leader, Lieutenant General Sir John Granby, and it was he who led the hell-for-leather charge that broke the French and captured ten of their guns. No British cavalryman would ever forget the sight of Sir John, galloping in front of his roaring squadrons, his hat and wig blown away and trampled by the frantic horses, his bald dome glittering in the sun. And from that day on, "going for them baldheaded" would be synonymous with flat-out reckless derring-do.

Granby would win both honor and a marquisate for his courage and leadership that day. But it was afterward that Britain learned the real measure of the man. For Granby reached into his own pocket to set up as publicans a number of his sergeants disabled at Warburg; good officer that he was, he did not forget who had made the victory possible.

And to the grateful NCOs, what finer name could there be for a new public house than The Marquess of Granby . . . and what finer signboard than a galloping officer, bald head shining as a beacon to his men?

DIE HARD
THE 44TH FOOT AT GANDAMACK

The Great Game. Through all the years of the British Raj in India, the lion and the Russian bear scowled at one another over the high passes of the Himalayas. Both sides courted the Afghans, trying to keep a friend in control at the court of Kabul. The British—the East India Company in those days—were content to hold what they had; the Czarist Empire sought ever more territory. To complicate matters, the Persians also sought pieces of Afghan territory, and with Russian encouragement tried to take the Afghan city of Herat.

By 1838 the situation was critical. The company's political agent, a daring Scot named Alexander Burnes, had been rebuffed in an attempt to reach an arrangement with the Afghan emir, Dost Mohammed. The emir wanted an alliance that would help him against the Sikhs, with whom he was embroiled in a territorial squabble. Since the Sikh leader, Ranjit Singh, was already a company ally, Burnes could offer no satisfaction, and returned to India. Dost Mohammed then entertained a Russian envoy, who would promise anything. Calcutta looked around for an alternative.

The company found it in Shah Shuja, the fat, elderly ex-emir of Afghanistan, overthrown by Dost Mohammed in one of the endemic civil wars that plagued that benighted land. The head of the company's political arm, John Hay Macnaghten, decided that old Shuja would make the ideal emir, quiet, pro-British, and quite malleable. He was not impressed with the fact that Shuja was also extremely unpopular with his countrymen.

From that point on, things became increasingly unreal. On

the curious notion that the Afghans would welcome back an unpopular ex-emir, and enjoy occupation by a British army to save them from a Russian or a Persian one, the company decided to intervene directly, to invade. Before Macnaghten could do much about his scheme, the political situation improved. The Persian attempt on Herat came unstuck. Better still, from the standpoint of John Company, St. Petersburg was forced to repudiate the doings of their Kabul envoy, who promptly shot himself. Nevertheless, the temptation to install a semipermanent solution to the Afghan problem was overwhelming, and the company began to gather troops.

The guts of the army were company soldiers, mostly Indian with a stiffening of British troops. Shah Shuja raised a number of levies of his own, and the whole force approached fifteen thousand men. There should have been some Sikhs as well, ferocious fighting men always welcome as allies. But ungrateful Ranjit Singh reneged on his agreement to help, and even denied the expedition passage through his lands below the Khyber Pass.

Worse still, the army towed along a monstrous tail of camp followers, some thirty-eight thousand of them, and an endless baggage train of thirty thousand camels. This multitude pushed off in December 1838, forced by Ranjit Singh's recalcitrance to circle the long way through Baluchistan and the Bolan Pass.

This aggregation was called, curiously, the Army of the Indus, even though the first thing it did was leave that storied river behind. And at first things went well. The passage through Baluchistan was smooth enough, and the army took the considerable city of Khandahar with only minor skirmishing. Shah Shuja was delighted.

The next sizable place was Ghazni, and it was a different animal altogether. Ghazni Fort was old beyond the knowledge of men. It had thick walls of mud brick, and a garrison of some three thousand Afghans. A straightforward attack by escalade, storming the walls, would have cost much blood. The British had no artillery, but they did have Shah Shuja. One of his agents learned that one of the entrances to the fort—the Kabul Gate—was not strongly held. And so, on the night of July 22, British sappers blew in the gate, and the 13th Light Infrantry—later the Somerset Light Infantry—went through. In the wild melee that followed, the

Afghans lost the whole garrison—some 1,200 of them killed—against company casualties of 17 dead and 160 wounded. The campaign had begun well.

It continued well, as the column entered Kabul a little more than two weeks later. Shah Shuja was back on his throne, although it was soon plain that his subjects were not enthralled. Mopping up went on apace, as the British scattered Afghan resistance and reduced mud forts. And at last, in August, Dost Mohammed came in and surrendered.

As time went by, however, it became clear that only British troops were keeping Shuja on his throne. The occupation looked like a permanent thing, as prices rose in the bazaars and British officers brought their wives to Kabul. Macnaghten and Burnes, the political arm of the occupation, were convinced that all was going well. Some of the European troops were released to return to India, including the invaluable 13th Light Infantry.

The occupation stretched into two years, and the unrest in Afghanistan grew worse. There was violence and rumors of revolt, murders of soldiers in the streets. As full-scale riot loomed, many officers suggested the British should occupy the Bala Hissar, the great fortress that dominated the city. Instead, the army was moved to an area outside the city, poorly situated on low ground and surrounded by groves and gardens that restricted the defenders' fields of fire. The magazine was even outside the ditch and low wall of the place, which was overlooked by old Afghan forts on the high ground.

If this were not bad enough, Macnaghten now committed the ultimate blunder. Pinching the company's pennies, he cut in half the traditional subsidy to the wild hill tribes, including those who controlled the high ground around the passes into India. The result was anarchy along the border, and the choking off of his supplies. At the same time, he sent more troops back to India, just as the storm broke.

It erupted on November 1, 1841, when a mob attacked Burnes's house. Held off by the fire of a handful of British troops inside, the mob contented itself with butchering Burnes and his brother as they tried to escape in disguise. There was much worse to come.

Company personnel found in the city were chased and murdered, and it was soon apparent that Shah Shuja had lost what little control he had ever had. The British commander, General William Elphinstone, was old and sick and did nothing. The country fell apart around him in a welter of killing, fire, and looting, and he did not act.

At last his second-in-command, Brigadier John Shelton, led a sortie that reached the Bala Hissar. Its only effect was to rescue the useless Shuja, and the column soon returned to its virtually indefensible cantonment. Now the Afghans occupied the heights overlooking the British camp, and the British 44th Foot had to go up and throw them off. But the Afghans and their guns were back on the high ground a week later, and this time they could not be moved. It was clearly time to get out.

In fairness to Elphinstone, there were no good options. He could surrender, negotiate, or retreat. Surrender, he would not, and retreat was a last resort. He had some forty-five hundred men, but only some seven hundred of these were British. He was also saddled with at least twelve thousand camp followers and a whole zoo of commissariat animals. So it would be negotiation, and Macnaghten would do the talking.

From early December until Christmas, Macnaghten talked. The Afghan leader was now Akbar Khan, Dost Mohammed's son, a leader of real talent. And at last the best Macnaghten could gain was a promise to provide food, fuel against the winter cold, and safe conduct to the border. Under the circumstances, it was not a bad bargain, but Macnaghten blundered again.

For Akbar Khan tested him, suggesting a secret agreement by which the British would remain in Afghanistan, and the other chiefs would be betrayed. Macnaghten agreed to it, and at the next session a mob closed in on him and his tiny escort. Macnaghten was murdered on the spot, his body dismembered and exhibited through the city.

It was the last straw for Elphinstone. He agreed to Akbar's terms, and on January 6, 1942, the remnants of the Army of the Indus started east for Jellalabad, about sixty miles as the crow flies. It was followed by its long trail of miserable camp followers. The cold was piercing, and Akbar's promises of food and fuel were never kept. And then, little by little, the tribes began to strike at the long column, butchering the helpless civilians and cutting out the supply animals.

The soldiers' agony was the worse because the tribesmen's rifled jezails outranged the company's muskets, and shot straighter to boot.

Now the wake of the column was littered with corpses, many murdered by the Afghans with all the hideous refinements of slow cutting up, others simply dead of exhaustion or the cold. The Indian sepoys began to desert in greater and greater numbers, and were joined by what remained of Shuja's Afghan levies. Little was now left but the hard core of the column, the 44th Foot—later the West Essex Regiment.

Shelton now began to assert himself and, with the 44th in front, began to open the road, repeatedly clearing narrow gorges of roadblocks with the bayonet. The 44th suffered terrible casualties, but charged grimly again and again, uphill through the snow.

On the eighth of January the pitiful column pushed into the Kurd-Kabul Pass, a narrow hell five miles long, and lined with tribesmen thirsting after the infidels' blood. The army left some three thousand dead behind in this ghastly place, but the survivors staggered on. At this point, surprisingly, Akbar Khan offered protection to the married European officers and their wives—and he kept his promise this time, sheltering seven officers, ten women, and thirteen children. And on the eleventh, at Jugdulluck Pass, Elphinstone went to parley with Akbar, and remained a prisoner. Now Shelton was in full command, as he had been in fact for days.

But it was too late. Shelton's men cleared Jugdulluck Pass at horrible cost, but there was no column to follow them. There were only corpses behind them in the pass, as the Afghans closed in to kill and loot. And when the 44th cleared the mouth of the gorge, only twenty officers and forty-five soldiers remained. A few were still mounted; most were on foot.

The end came on a little knoll outside the village of Gandamack. The few mounted men had pushed on, hoping to outrun pursuit. The remnants of the 44th would run no more. Firing their last round or two, they set themselves back to back on the little rise and fought with cold steel and musket butt until they were submerged by a river of enemies.

One man survived, a captain who had wrapped the colors around his body in an attempt to save them. Because he carried the colors, the Afghans assumed he was an important personage, and he was kept for ransom.

The terrible news came to the British garrison at Jellalabad on the thirteenth. The regimental surgeon, Dr. William Brydon, tottered into the town on a half-dead horse. He fulfilled the terrifying prophecy of one of the garrison officers, who had predicted that nobody would win through from Kabul, except one person "to tell us the rest are destroyed." Dr. Brydon had survived only by great good fortune and a fighting heart. He had three times fought his way past Afghans, the last time snapping his sword at the hilt.

The garrison of Jellalabad included the 13th Light Infantry, who had started the Afghan campaign so well these years before. Their commander, "Fighting Bob" Sale, had received orders to retreat to India, and called a council of war to decide whether to follow those orders or stand up to the inevitable attack. Influenced by the urging of two aggressive officers—including Henry Havelock, who would meet immortality and death at Lucknow—he elected to stand and fight. And in the event the 13th and some native infantryman hurled back repeated Afghan assaults on Jellalabad, and finally routed their besiegers with a sortie that captured the enemy guns, camp, and horses.

By this time help was on the way from India, and there would be retribution. By mid-September the British were back in Kabul and the prisoners were recovered, bought back from Akbar Khan for twenty thousand rupees. Then there was a good deal of killing and destruction in memory of those who had died on the long retreat, culminating in the burning of the Great Bazaar in Kabul.

Poor old Elphinstone died of dysentery—and perhaps bitterness—in April of 1842. Shelton's behavior during the debacle was examined by a court-martial after his release, but he was acquitted. He remained commanding officer of the 44th Foot, and continued to quarrel with everybody around him. Although he had covered himself with glory in the retreat from Kabul, the experience had done nothing to soften his nasty disposition. He left this life by falling from his horse in a Dublin barrack square in 1845, and legend has it that his regiment fell out and gave three cheers in honor of the occasion.

In time the British would leave Afghanistan, returning only

when the needs of imperial security required. In 1878 Afghanistan seemed again to be listening to Russian blandishments, and a small British force of some sixty-six hundred men crossed the Khyber to deal with the situation. This was another sort of army, however, a lean, tough fighting force, commanded by Sir Frederick Roberts—"Bobs" to his men and in the end Lord Roberts—and it routed an Afghan force three times its size on its way to a highly successful campaign. Perhaps in those murderous mountains Roberts' men heard red-coated shades in the uniform of the 44th murmur, "Well done."

A DAMN TOUGH BULLET TO CHEW

> To stand and be still to the Birken'ead
> drill is a damn' tough bullet to chew.
> Rudyard Kipling, *"Soldier and Sailor Too"*

In 1852 Victorian Britain was involved in another of her perpetual brushfire wars across the expanse of the empire, this time in South Africa. It was called the Cape War, or Kaffir War, and it was notable for very little, except that the troops learned how to forget their European training and fight in the bush, and for the use of the Brunswick Rifle, precursor of the rifles that were to make the American Civil War such a bloodbath in the next decade.

But the troopship *Birkenhead* provided one sad and memorable incident, another glowing chapter in the already considerable British military tradition. As was so often the case, the event mixed great courage and discipline with unnecessary tragedy, the soldiers paying for somebody else's stupid mistake, in this case several mistakes.

Birkenhead was an iron steamer, a paddle wheeler, on her way to South Africa with reinforcements, drafts for several regiments serving in the Kaffir War, including the 43d and 91st Foot, later the Argyll and Sutherland Highlanders. She also carried many women and children, families of British military personnel. And she was overloaded, the first in a series of tragic mistakes.

On the night of February 26, 1852, she was close to her destination, approaching the Cape. And then, at Danger Point, near Simonstown, she struck a rock. Her captain then committed his second error, and tried to back her clear. Had he kept her head against the rock, she might have survived a great deal longer than she did. But when he backed her away, he opened a monstrous hole to the sea, and *Birkenhead* was finished.

Save for those who died in the first rush of water below-decks, the troops aboard sinking *Birkenhead* kept their accustomed discipline. Parties were told off to help the women and children into the boats, and to help with the pumps. The others stood quietly in ranks, their officers out in front. It was soon clear to everybody that there were not enough boats, but there was no panic.

The dependents were gotten off without incident, and the overloaded boats pulled away. And still the troops stood in ranks, awaiting dismissal or other orders. The ship's captain then called out that it was "every man for himself." But still nobody moved.

Two officers now stepped in front of the troops and talked to them. Lieutenant Girardot of the 43d and Captain Wright of the 91st explained matter-of-factly that to swim away from the ship and try to board the lifeboats would only capsize the boats and endanger the women and children. They asked their troops to stand fast, and to a man the ranks stood unbroken until *Birkenhead* broke up and sank beneath them. Only then did those who could swim try to save themselves.

But the shore was several miles away, and the water teemed with sharks . . . and very few of the troops and their officers made it. Of the 638 passengers on board *Birkenhead*, 454 died, but every woman and child on the passenger list survived, thanks to the discipline and courage of men much of the British public regarded as the dregs of society.

King Frederick William of Prussia recognized the behavior

of the *Birkenhead* troops for what it was. Those who died could have no finer memorial than his order, to read an account of the incident to every regiment in the Prussian Army.

ANABASIS
DONIPHAN'S MARCH

The Missouri rolls placidly past the bluffs below Fort Leavenworth, where the great river bends to the south on its way to the Mississippi. In 1846 Leavenworth—like Liberty and Independence just to the east—was a jumping-off place for the vast empty spaces to the west, the plains, the great mountains, and the smiling land of California.

All of that intriguing, verdant westward land was Spanish, or at least the government of Mexico said it was. But America was about to try that claim, try it in the hottest furnace there is, the glowing retort of war. The immediate cause of hostility was the disputed Texas border with Mexico, a running sore of long standing.

But the causes of war ran far deeper. Stripped of rhetoric, it all boiled down to this: Was all this wonderful western country, made for cattle and farms and a young, virile people, to be governed by an effete, somnolent Mexico? Or would it be home to tough, brawny, pushy America, awakening to her great destiny, afraid of nothing, willing to dare any danger?

At least that was the way most Americans seemed to have seen it. It was a popular war, by and large, and ended in a series of astonishing American victories against enormous odds. It was a training ground for the men who would later command great armies in North America's most famous war: Among the young officers who dared Mexican bullets to learn their trade were names like Lee, Grant, Jackson,

Meade, Beauregard, and Johnston. It is a little surprising that the Mexican War is not better known. Perhaps that is because it is overshadowed by the terrible swift sword of the Civil War, to follow it in only thirteen years.

It was a war fought largely by volunteers, pugnacious, active men of courage and endurance, who learned to soldier as they went along. It could not be otherwise, for the entire American army numbered something like seven thousand men when war broke out, and a cheese-paring Congress was busily debating whether it should not abolish the Military Academy at West Point.

About a thousand of these volunteers were now gathered at Fort Leavenworth above the broad Missouri, arriving by horse and foot and steamboat to become an army. The architect of that army was Colonel Stephen Watts Kearny, the Regular Army commander of Fort Leavenworth. He had commanded the fort for some four years, and with three companies of dragoons he had policed thousands of square miles of Indian territory to the west. If that job had been tough, his current assignment looked monumental.

For Kearny was to command something rather pompously called the Army of the West. And he was to move out with it within three weeks, following the setting sun into the Mexican province of New Mexico. He was, of course, to whip any Mexican forces that got in his way, and incidentally put down any Indians who behaved in a hostile fashion. Once he had done all these things, he had left the small task of taking California as well.

Kearny was already sending wagons and herds of beef cattle out through the westward emptiness, all the way to Bent's Fort, 650 miles away through a lush, unpeopled land. At Bent's the supplies would await the army he would build. For beyond Bent's was the border claimed by Mexico, and once across it, he would be alone in a hostile land.

The size of his mission was staggering, and just now the entire Army of the West was Kearny's three companies. And the volunteers, of course, now camped every which way around Fort Leavenworth, busily engaged in electing officers, drilling (after a fashion), joking, quarreling, and gaping at Kearny's disciplined bluecoats. There was precious little time for training, twenty days at most, under the stern eye of regular officers and NCOs. At least the eager volunteers could learn something of saber drill, and how to charge home and rally afterwards.

So it would be a tiny army, and mostly very green. Still, Kearny reflected, orders were orders, and he would do what he could. The raw Missouri volunteers were hard and tough, at least, used to living out of doors, willing and eager, and mostly fine riflemen into the bargain. They were young—twenty on the average. They might just make an army after all.

They would.

They started by electing their own officers, sometimes wisely, sometimes not. On the whole they did not do badly, perhaps because each company had been raised within a single Missouri county. The men knew each other pretty well. They knew who was resourceful and intelligent and able to lead. They did an especially good job of choosing their colonel.

Big, amiable Alexander Doniphan was a transplanted Kentuckian, of a family that traced its roots to a Revolutionary War soldier from Virginia. Doniphan had practiced law in Liberty for fifteen years, served in the Missouri Legislature, and commanded a contingent during the bloodless campaign to expel the Mormons from Missouri in 1839. His integrity was a byword among Missourians. He had refused an order to execute the Mormon leader, Joseph Smith, and had successfully defended Smith in a criminal action after the campaign was over.

As a contemporary writer put it, in the flowery prose of the day:

> Never did Pericles gain a more complete
> ascendence over the minds of the Athenians,
> than Col. Doniphan . . . has attained
> over the people of Upper Missouri.

As soon as the call came for troops to march against Mexico, Doniphan had enlisted as a private. Within days he was elected colonel of the regiment. The Missourians knew a leader when they saw one. They would quickly discover just how well they had chosen.

Kearny got a contingent started toward Bent's on June 5, and by the twenty-sixth the Army of the West was moving,

moving out into the vast spaces between it and New Mexico. It was about sixteen hundred strong, a handful lost in an endless prairie, an ocean of grass as high as the back of a horse. There were three hundred regulars, almost nine hundred men of the First Missouri Volunteers, and some miscellaneous oddments, including fifty Indian scouts. Except for two companies of volunteer infantry, nearly everybody was mounted. There was also a monstrous logistical tail to the column, more than fifteen hundred wagons, over five thousand mules and horses, and nearly fifteen thousand oxen—rations on the hoof.

The column set off in high spirits, singing "Yankee Doodle" and other patriotic songs. They followed the national colors with its twenty-seven stars—Texas had just become the twenty-eighth state, but there had been no time to assemble a new flag. Another thousand or so volunteers, under Sterling Price, were to follow. Behind at Fort Leavenworth remained the dejected men of Weightman's battery, still waiting for the guns that would make them real artillery. They would follow, along with Kearny, who thoughtfully trailed the army to make certain everybody got where they were going.

Where they were going was Santa Fe, hub of Spanish New Mexico. After some seventy miles of the sea of grass, the column struck the well-marked Santa Fe Trail, coming in from Independence to the northeast. In broiling heat the column pushed on, covering a murderous twenty-seven miles on July 4, and ending the day with a whiskey-driven celebration of the nation's birthday. It was a fine beginning, and by the last day of July the whole force was together across the Arkansas from the thick adobe walls of Bent's Fort. The two infantry companies had marched six hundred miles in twenty-nine days.

Kearny did not stay long at Bent's. After a brief halt to rest the animals, he pushed on. By now he was in contact with Manuel Armijo, the Mexican governor, announcing that he came to take possession of New Mexico, but would guarantee the safety of its residents and their possessions. Armijo's reply talked about fighting battles, but the Mexican army was not in evidence.

It was bad enough without fighting. The column was struggling through largely waterless country, leaving a trail of worn-out animals behind it. It was on half rations as it

crossed seventy-five-hundred-foot Raton Pass, but still cheerful and anxious for a fight. It sang as it moved, to the tune of
"Hail, Columbia":

> *"We're marchin' west from Yankee land,*
> *A rough and ready fightin' band;*
> *Don't give a damn what comes along,*
> *The skeeter and the rattlesnake,*
> *The Injun and the bellyache ..."*

It was very tough going indeed, and even these hardened
frontiersmen suffered. Rations were flour-and-water fritters
fried with a little salt pork, and not a whole lot of that. The
horses could find no grass. As one man wrote to his wife, everybody was "sick and tired of the business ... Regulars
have spirit and volunteers would not make it without them."

And now there was every chance of a fight against great
odds, for rumor had it that Armijo and seven thousand men
awaited them up ahead. "Up ahead" was a narrow gut of a
canyon some fifteen miles from Santa Fe. It was called
Apache Pass, and it looked impregnable, especially when
held in such overwhelming strength. It could, as an American engineer later said, have been held by "one hundred res-
olute men." But Armijo lacked any resolution at all, and was
already fleeing his capital. Kearny got the good news from
the alcalde of a little settlement, who ambled in on his mule
to announce that "Armijo and his troops have gone to hell,
and the canyon is clear."

Armijo's abandonment of Santa Fe has never been explained. Neither has his refusal to fight at the superb defensive position in Apache Pass. Just possibly there was more
to his precipitate retreat than cowardice. One man might
have known, and that was James Magoffin, longtime trader
on the frontier and friend of Armijo in happier days. He
spoke excellent Spanish, and was an experienced man,
friend to powerful Missouri Senator Benton and well connected all the way to the White House.

Magoffin had joined Kearny's column at Bent's, carrying a
letter from President Polk, and Kearny had sent him on
ahead with a flag of truce and a tiny escort to summon
Armijo to surrender. Although apparently nothing came of
Kearny's offer, there had been no fighting either, only

Armijo's amazing disappearance. And after the war Magoffin lodged a fifty thousand dollar claim with the United States for what he called "goods lost." Typically, Congress reduced the claim to thirty thousand dollars before it was paid—and the suspicion still lingers that the sum had nothing to do with goods, but replaced some gleaming yellow gold with which Magoffin persuaded Armijo to decamp without a fight.

And so fell La Ciudad Real de la Santa Fe de Santiago, a Spanish town since the conquistadores first came upon an Indian village here in 1516. The Royal City of the Holy Faith of Saint James was the heart of this vast empty country. Kearny pushed hard for the city, marching twenty-nine miles on August 18. By sundown on that day, the stars and stripes flew over the town, to the thunder of a salute fired by Kearny's cannon.

Doniphan set to work drafting a constitution for the new territory, and an engineer lieutenant started construction of a little fort, designed to dominate the town. A hundred-foot flagstaff was erected, to proudly display the national colors. For their part, most of the inhabitants seemed content enough. Most of them were quick to take the oath of allegiance to the United States, for Armijo had been cordially detested. Kearny was quick to assure them that both their religion and their property would be respected.

The Santa Fe of those days was no metropolis. The volunteers called it "mud town," since most of it seemed to be made of that humble material. Nevertheless, the Americans found themselves welcomed, welcomed with fiestas and fandangos, with plentiful food and pretty girls. They ate and danced and reflected that this frontier war had some compensations after all. They would not have long to enjoy the fruits of victory.

Kearny, now a brigadier general, did not stay long in Santa Fe. There was much to do, and somewhere to the east reinforcements were on the way, Sterling Price's Missouri volunteers and a battalion of Mormons. Before they even arrived in Santa Fe, Kearny was on the move west. With just three hundred men of the Dragoons, he pushed off into the unknown on September 25. In time, with the help of the United States Navy, he would win California for the United States, but that is another story.

Doniphan's volunteers were also to leave Santa Fe. For

them, the road led south, toward the critical town of El Paso del Norte, and old Mexico. Somewhere, far to the south in Chihuahua, was a little American army under General Wool. Doniphan was to find and join him, pacifying along the way whatever part of this broad land he crossed.

But first there was the Navaho nation to deal with. The Navahos were tough and warlike, and they had amused and enriched themselves at the expense of the New Mexican settlements time out of mind. Now Kearny called on them to change their ancient ways. This broad land was part of America now, and the Great White Father would not put up with raiding and looting and slave taking. The Navahos were not impressed.

Kearny turned to Doniphan. Go forth and pacify, he ordered. Recover prisoners and stolen stock, and do whatever you have to do to persuade the Navaho to live in peace. Only then would the First Missouri set out to find General Wool. The First Missouri was not pleased.

Doniphan managed to calm them, standing on a wagon to talk to his men. "Boys, I don't like it any better than you do; but those are our orders, and we are going."

Go they did, for they would do what their big colonel told them to do. Their road led deep into the mountains, into a trackless land of cold wind and scant grass, until in time contact was made with the warriors of the Navaho. And the Navaho recognized other warriors when they saw them, so there was no fighting. To be sure, there was a little casual stock stealing to go with much fruitless riding up mountains and inconclusive palaver and sleeping in the snow. But at last, toward the end of a bitter November, the real leaders of the Navaho came to talk.

Doniphan did not mince words. The Americans were their friends, he said, but then he got to the point.

The United States first offers the olive branch, and if that is refused, powder, bullet, and steel.

That was plain enough for the Navahos, and a treaty was signed. The Indians explained that they could not return the stolen stock because, regrettably, "the animals had run off." Fair enough, said Doniphan, delighted to have this onerous task complete. Now he was free to do what he and his men had come to do. Now he could march to the aid of General Wool and conquer the vast State of Chihuahua, eight hundred miles away.

Doniphan took about eight hundred men with him, the fittest and strongest of his command. Colonel Sterling Price remained behind to support newly appointed Governor Charles Bent. Price's men were bitter, cursing the fate that kept them from the great Mexican adventure. They need not have worried. For in mid-January a rebellion struck New Mexico, Governor Bent was murdered and scalped, and other Americans killed in Santa Fe and elsewhere.

Before the end of the month, Price's men would fight two vicious pitched battles against heavy odds. In early February they broke the back of the uprising when they stormed Taos Pueblo, smashing in doors and scaling the walls on ladders. They ended by hanging fifteen of the leaders of the revolt, and they had had their war. They need envy Doniphan's men no longer.

Doniphan's Missourians took the road south in high spirits, whooping and eager to be off to the war. They considered themselves "gamecocks," ready to take on the whole Mexican army "on half rations, no salt, and no pay . . ." which was no exaggeration. In fact, they were very tough customers indeed, these survivors. They had been living on game and sleeping in the snow for months, clothing falling apart and filled with vermin. Mexico could be no worse, they thought, and cockily sang of their plight, to the tune of "Yankee Doodle:"

"My body is a field of strife from shoulders down to knees;
Where lice as big as chili beans are fighting with the fleas.
And as for high-grade cooking jobs, I'm hellish hard to beat.
I've made one thousand pans of bread the soldiers couldn't eat."

They were on the road south by December, and by the seventeenth had reached Valverde, with the worst of the trip yet to come. They filled every available vessel with water, even their saber scabbards, for there was none ahead. They were entering the moonscape called the Jornada del Muerto, the Journey of the Dead, three days of waterless desert. Even as they entered the Jornada, it clawed at them, a cruel, cutting wind that slashed their faces with sand.

By day the sun broiled them. By night they shivered in a chill wind. And always there was the knowledge that to fall behind meant death, death in a most horrible fashion, for this was Apache country. The animals suffered terribly, and men winced at their dreadful bellowing and neighing. They led their animals, sparing them at least an extra load, but keeping them going. The animal that lay down in that hideous place would never rise again.

On the morning of the third day, with dozens of beasts on their last legs, a solid image began to form amidst the ghosts of the mirage ahead of them. It was Dona Ana, only a tiny town, but a horn of plenty of water and fodder for the animals, and beef and mutton for the men. Here they rested a few days, after ninety miles of the worst country on earth. And when they started south again, Doniphan formed his men in three detachments, moving slowly and in close touch. Doniphan smelled trouble; this time, he was sure, it would be a human enemy. He was right.

The trouble came on Christmas day. It came on a little stream called the Brazito, an arm of the Rio Grande cutting through a prairie studded with chaparral. The leading elements of the army had halted early, and extra rations were being prepared in honor of the holidays. Perhaps half the men were in camp, the rest coming in gradually, rounding up stray horses as they came.

Doniphan was settling down with several others for a game of loo, the stake a beautiful stray stallion that had been found near the camp. The game had just begun when a sentry ran to warn him that a great cloud of dust was moving up the El Paso road, and that under that cloud were soldiers and cannon.

Doniphan gave the order to assemble the troops, and dropped his cards with regret. "Boys, I had you licked," he said, "but I'm damned if we don't have to play it out in steel!"

Confusion reigned in the American camp as the volunteers chased horses and tried to find their friends and units. Some were cooking, others carrying in bundles of firewood or buckets of water. Many simply grabbed their weapons and fell in with the nearest unit. A few were still running for camp when the first shots were fired.

The Mexican commander drew up his troops across the road from Doniphan's ragged men. There seemed to be about five hundred regular dragoons, plus hundreds more undisciplined peasants. From the Mexican ranks galloped an officer carrying a fanciful black flag bearing a death's head, and the slogan "Liberty or Death." He loudly demanded that Doniphan appear before the Mexican commander. The exchange that followed was vintage Doniphan.

"Tell him to come here if he wants to talk to me."

"If you do not come," said the Mexican, "we will take you by force."

Doniphan was unmoved. "Come and get me."

"Curses be upon you! Prepare for a charge!" the messenger cried.

Doniphan was even less impressed. "Charge and be damned!"

The Battle of Brazito was on. The Mexicans opened fire at about four hundred yards, firing five ineffective volleys, most of which went over the heads of the waiting Americans.

Now, as the Mexican army closed, the volunteers waited in silence. The Mexican dragoons came first, a roaring wave of frantic horses, green jackets, and gleaming helmets that threatened to swamp the little island of ragged frontiersmen. The Missourians held their fire until the mass of horsemen was within 150 yards, and then the whole Mexican front line dissolved in the roar of successive volleys, great billows of white smoke spattered with spiteful little jets of crimson fire.

The volunteers had been numbered off—alternately "one" and "two"—with orders that number twos were to hold their fire while ones let go their volley, then fire as the ones reloaded. The Mexican survivors simply could not stand that murderous rolling fire, and recoiled from the dreadful writhing mass of screaming horses and men strewn across the ground in front of the American lines.

Some of the survivors changed direction to charge the American wagon train, only to meet another terrible volley, poured into them from behind the wagons at thirty feet. And at that instant they were struck in flank by a tiny group of mounted Americans, fifteen sabers glinting in the sun, fifteen ragged horsemen screeching what the world would one day call the rebel yell.

It was too much for the dragoons, and the survivors fled for their lives, pursued by those fifteen mounted furies and their terrible war cry. The Mexican infantry, poorly trained and worse-led, fled before another of those dreadful blasts of rifle-fire, and Brazito was over, almost before it began. Thirty Howard County Missourians pushed forward on their own initiative to capture the Mexicans' four forlorn cannon, and silence fell across the field.

In thirty minutes the road to El Paso was open. There were seven or eight American casualties, none of them severely hurt. There were 71 Mexican dead, 150 wounded, and many prisoners, including the enemy commander. The field was strewn with flags, weapons, and horses, and best of all, liberal supplies of wine and fresh meat, thoughtfully provided by the Mexican army.

The Mexican troops had simply been no match for the deadly marksmanship of the volunteers. Many of Doniphan's men carried percussion rifles and Colt's revolvers. The rifles could deliver a deadly conical ball with some accuracy out as far as five hundred yards. The Missourians called their rifles "yagers," as close as they could come to the German *Jäger*, or hunter's rifle. They were a little slower to load but far more accurate than the flintlock musket, about which U.S. Grant commented, "At a distance of a few hundred yards a man might fire at you all day without your finding it out." And they were infinitely better than the Mexicans' ancient Tower muskets, wildly inaccurate beyond seventy-five or eighty yards.

To their astonishment, the Mexican wounded were treated and fed, their dead buried in a common grave. The battlefield policed and the army well fed, Doniphan's men moved inexorably south. Two days later they were met on the road by a mission from the citizens of El Paso, and the deputation carried a white flag. The road was open, and the town belonged to America. Two days after Brazito, Doniphan entered the city in triumph.

El Paso was paradise after the terrible march south. There was no end to the food and drink, races, fandangos, and other forms of what was chastely called "self-indulgence," including the unseemly spectacle of two drunken lieutenants settling a quarrel with knives. Nevertheless, with rest and food, the army grew stronger. And it added to its ordnance, for the town contained tons of ammunition, hundreds of small arms, and even four cannon, welcome replenishment for the American supply train.

Better still, on the first of February Weightman's long-disappointed artillery battery trotted into the town, six guns and more than a hundred men. And now that he had his cannon at last, big Alec Doniphan turned his eyes south.

On the eighth the volunteers were on the road again, headed for their long-awaited rendezvous with General Wool, and the assault on Chihuahua. But "Granny" Wool was not where he was supposed to be. Instead, his orders changed, he was far away in a town called Parras, almost a hundred miles west of Saltillo.

Trouble was, nobody had thought to tell Doniphan until now. Now the big Missourian sat down to consider. He had two options. First, he could return to Santa Fe, taking himself and his men out of the war. Second, he could push on into the unknown, to join Wool at Parras. In the typical, wonderful way of the frontier, he put the question to his men. The vote was nearly unanimous: Push on!

It was a daring gamble, and every man knew it. One soldier summed up the problem succinctly:

> Our situation is rather critical, leaving an enemy in our rear, marching into the heart of their country, expecting to meet a powerful one in front, depending upon them for subsistence, and our strength not exceeding one thousand.

And the enemy was not the only problem. Once more the army marched through a wasteland of dust and desolation, arid and waterless. Scrub fires threatened their wagons and beasts, even themselves. Each morning and evening the men shook boots and clothing to disperse the tarantulas, lizards, rattlesnakes, and copperheads that infested the country. To make matters worse, they were burdened with protecting dozens of traders' wagons in addition to their own. This Chihuahua road was almost as bad as the Jornada del Muerto, and the army expected to fight at every turn.

Doniphan was sure it would. Across his front he deployed three full companies of mounted men; he was not going to be surprised as he had been at the Brazito.

He was not. On February 28 he found his enemy in a very strong position at the crossing of the Sacramento River. Twenty-seven redoubts studded the Mexican line, and both of his enemy's wings were anchored on hills, bristling with cannon. As usual, the Missourians were outnumbered, their thousand or so opposed by anywhere from two thousand to five thousand Mexicans.

The Brazito forgotten, the Mexican army was confident in its elite cavalry and sixteen cannon, so confident that it had brought along plenty of ropes and handcuffs to secure the prisoners it was sure to take. For their part, the Americans were heartened by the sight of a large eagle, which spent much of the day soaring above them, sometimes dropping low over their colors. The mighty bird, emblem of their country, seemed the best of omens.

After an early advance by Mexican cavalry, driven off with some ease by Weightman's guns, the armies exchanged cannon fire for the better part of an hour. Then Doniphan ordered his whole line to advance, and the tattered volunteers moved in under a torrent of Mexican fire, most of which howled over their heads to kill and maim among the wagons and their teams. And then, as the Missourians closed to within a quarter-mile of the Mexican lines, Doniphan ordered Weightman to charge with his cannon.

Maybe it was good training, maybe long-frustrated pride, maybe both. Left behind at Leavenworth, absent at Brazitos, late at El Paso, Weightman's men had been waiting a long time to show they could soldier. Whatever drove them, Weightman's battery stormed at the gallop to within fifty yards of the Mexican line, unlimbered under heavy fire, and poured canister into the Mexican infantry at point-blank range.

Behind this astonishing charge, the rest of the volunteers closed in on foot, running through the smoke of their own deadly rifle-fire, and the Mexican line broke. Some Mexican units fought on for a while, and in places the fighting was hand to hand, with rifle butts, knives, Colts, and even rocks. One American knocked a Mexican lancer from the saddle with a well-aimed stone, then beat the man's brains out with his rifle butt. Another volunteer split his opponent's head to the shoulder with a single saber-stroke.

But by sunset, three hours after it had begun, the Battle of the Sacramento was over. More than three hundred Mexicans dead lay on the field, with at least that many more wounded. There were almost six hundred prisoners. The Mexican army had lost ten wagons and all its guns, and a great quantity of supplies. As much as one hundred thousand dollars worth of unreported portable loot, mostly money, had also stuck to the hands of the victorious volunteers.

Doniphan occupied Chihuahua on the first of March, and held it for a month and a half, a time of rest and refitting. There was a good deal of eating and drinking, and of other relaxations as well. In short order, much of the army was ill with venereal disease and unfit for duty. It was just as well that orders came from Zachary Taylor to join the main army at Saltillo.

Doniphan was quickly on the road, and made the six-hundred mile march in less than a month, fighting hostile Indians along the way. Again the army fought adversity, dust and heat and maggots, and a particularly voracious species of blue fly. At one point, dozens of animals were saved from death from thirst only by a rare and providential flash flood, which persuaded the local Mexicans that God must be in league with these gringos.

On the twenty-seventh of May the volunteers were reviewed at Monterrey by Taylor himself, then marched for Brazos, from which they moved by sea to New Orleans, and their first payday in a year of hard service. They were, as the *New Orleans Picayune* wrote, "the heroes of the town." And the paper added, perhaps tongue in cheek, "They excite unusual attention by their appearance."

Indeed they must have, for by this time they were attired in an amazing collection of their own rags of cloth and buckskin, liberated Mexican clothing, pieces of blanket, and whatever else they could find that would keep out the wind. It was time to go home. And when they went, they went in some comfort, up the great Mississippi to their own country.

And to a measure of immortality. They had marched more than thirty-five hundred terrible, sweat-soaked miles in hostile country, and covered a thousand more by water. The men knew they had done something extraspecial, and were appropriately proud. As one private put it, the march was "the most extraordinary and wonderful Expedition of the age."

Maybe the private waxed a little hyperbolic, but not much. It had indeed been an extraordinary achievement, by an extraordinary group of men. Lawyer Doniphan described them perfectly:

My men are rough, ragged and ready . . . After marching . . . miles over desert and mountain, they have not received one dollar of their pay, yet they stand it without murmuring. Half rations, hard marches, and no clothes! But they are game to the last, and curse and praise their country by turns, but fight for her all the time.

If Doniphan was no Xenophon, and the Mexican army no host of Persians, his anabasis was no less remarkable. It helped convince America—if it needed convincing—that Americans could do anything, and helped persuade a brawny young nation it ought to get on with its manifest destiny to conquer a continent.

THAT THE REGIMENT MIGHT LIVE
SAVING THE COLORS AT ISANDLWANA

On a bright January day in 1879, six companies of the Royal Warwickshire Regiment were dying before the great Rock of Isandlwana. They fought to the last cartridge, then struggled on with bayonets and the butts of their Martini-Henry rifles, until they were simply submerged by ten times their number of disciplined Zulu warriors.

Not a man ran; 581 enlisted men and 21 officers died together, and they took great numbers of their enemies with them. And at the end of it all, as the red infantry died grimly where they stood and irregulars and camp followers tried to save themselves, Lieutenant Colonel Pulleine called his adjutant to him.

Go, he said, ride hard out of this place and save the colors of the first battalion if you can. And then the colonel turned wearily back to his tent, sat down, and picked up his pen. Nobody knows what he was writing. It might have been a report to his superiors; it might have been a letter to his family; maybe it was both. Whatever it was, a Zulu burst into his tent before he was finished. Pulleine shot the warrior and was speared in return. He might have mounted his horse and survived, but that was not the way of a British officer.

And while Pulleine was calmly writing and dying, Lieutenant Teignmouth Melville took the colors over his saddle and rode hard for such safety as there was on that pitiless plain. If he could win through to the crossings of the Buffalo River, he might fight free, but the river was three and a half miles away, three and a half miles of rock and gulches and tangled undergrowth . . . and thousands of Zulu warriors.

Still, Melville did well, cutting his way to the river in spite of the cumbersome, clumsy flag case clutched to his saddlebow. Somewhere along the way he lost his saber, but he stayed in the saddle, clutching the precious flag, the symbol and soul of his regiment. Between the reins and the colors, the young officer had no hand to spare for his revolver; his only refuge was the speed of his horse. The riverbank was swarming with Zulus, and so was the opposite shore, but he urged his mount into the froth of the roaring current. He might well die in the river, or on the far side, but it was certain death to stay where he was.

The rush of the river ripped Melville from his saddle, and he was smashed against rock after rock until he was pulled onto a large boulder by another officer. Then both men were torn loose from their perilous refuge and swept downstream into a deep pool. Melville was exhausted and half-drowned, but he still clutched the colors.

Just behind Melville as he reached the steep banks of the Buffalo was Lieutenant Nevil Coghill. Coghill's knee was badly injured, a hurt so bad that he could not mount his horse without help. But he was well mounted, and as long as his horse lasted, he might well win clear. And win clear, he did, swimming his horse clear across the Buffalo, just a few hundred yards from open country—and life.

And then he saw Melville thrashing weakly in the river, recognized his unit's tattered colors, and instantly gave up all thought of escape. He kicked his horse back into the water, heading for Melville, and when he pushed into the river his horse crumpled as a bullet smacked into its forehead.

Coghill was thrown into the water, pulled down by his boots, shackled by his useless knee, but he struggled on to Melville and pulled him to land.

The colors were gone by now, slipped from Melville's hands in his desperate fight against the current of the Buffalo. Both men were done in, and Coghill could not walk on his bad knee. But Melville held his brother officer against him, and the two staggered up the bank a hundred agonizing yards. And then they sagged down against a big rock, exhausted but still defiant.

Time had run out for the two lieutenants. Zulus swarmed everywhere, and the two Englishmen had little to fight with. The cylinder of Melville's revolver was gone with his lost sword, although Coghill still had both saber and sidearm. They put their backs against the rock and waited . . . they would sell their lives as dearly as they could with what they had.

A third officer, scrounging for horses on the bank above them, rallied a few soldiers and ran back to help. He was too late. He could not see the end, but he heard the tumult and the shooting of the two lieutenants' last fight. And then a cloud of Zulus appeared on the trail, and he, too, had to run.

Early in February a British patrol found Melville and Coghill, or what was left of them. They were buried next to the rock against which they had put their backs to die. And against all hope, a quarter of a mile downstream an officer found the colors of the first battalion in a quiet pool. It was intact, a tattered silk flag, golden lion and crown atop the staff.

And when it was brought back to the British camp at Rorke's Drift, the soldiers stood to cheer it and the regimental commander shed unashamed tears. Battered as it was, the flag remained in service for another half century, leading the battalion across the Rhine in 1918. In 1933 it was finally retired to an honorable rest in Brecon Cathedral.

The Victoria Cross was as coveted and hard to win in 1879 as it is today, but there was no provision for awarding it posthumously. The best the army could do for Coghill and Melville was to announce that both officers "would have been recommended" for the VC had they lived. Cold comfort, that, until the regulations finally changed after the turn of the century; in 1907 Coghill and Melville became the first men ever to win the VC posthumously.

And the regiment lived on.

WHEN OLD ROCK BENNING HELD THE BRIDGE
AND THE 51ST PENNSYLVANIA GOT ITS WHISKEY

The seventeenth of September, 1862, was the bloodiest day in American history. More than twenty-two thousand Americans were hurt or killed on that awful day, maimed and gutted and mangled across the warm, fertile farmland near a little Maryland town called Sharpsburg. Just east of the village a clear, lazy, tree-lined little river meandered down to join the broad Potomac. It was called Antietam Creek, and it gave the battlefield its name.

Robert E. Lee commanded for the South, and pompous little George McClellan for the North. Bobby Lee was outnumbered two to one, and even that superb soldier should have been destroyed in the desperate fighting in front of Sharpsburg. Lee would have been badly whipped, too, even Lee, if only McClellan had attacked all along the line at once.

But he didn't. "Little Mac," efficient in training, bold in planning, timid in battle, put his fine infantry corps in to the attack piecemeal. The dusty blue lines struck Lee's troops a section at a time, starting generally at the northwest end of Lee's long, diagonal front, and working down to the southeast. Again and again the dogged Union infantry came within a hairsbreadth of victory. Again and again, in the nick of time, Lee moved troops to the threatened spot and threw them in to plug his leaking lines.

And so the ferocious fighting continued through the long, hot day, back and forth across pastureland and fields of standing crops and patches of dark green woodland. Under a dirty pall of powder-smoke the ceaseless hammer of the artillery, the roar of infantry rifle-fire, and the scream of hurt men went on and on.

Swarms of musket-balls hummed like huge bees, slashing down the standing corn, tearing flesh and splintering bone, leaving the fields spotted with writhing men in blue and gray and butternut. A sunken road filled up with corpses, stacked two and three deep. And the butchery went on and on through the morning, as unit after unit was wrecked in the appalling storm of rifle-balls and canister. As a soldier of the 9th New York wrote, "The whole landscape for an instant turned slightly red."

As the fighting dragged on into the heat of the afternoon, McClellan had failed everywhere. Lee had lost some ground, but his lines still held, and he knew that somewhere to the south, help was on the way. Coming up from Harper's Ferry, driving his men in a furious forced march, A. P. Hill was pushing his division hard for Sharpsburg. If he could get there before McClellan threw in the rest of his fresh, uncommitted infantry . . .

Over behind the Union lines, McClellan still hesitated. He was forever overestimating Lee's strength, and today was no exception. McClellan would not commit his reserve, Fitzjohn Porter's fine corps, nor would he hurry on an attack he had already directed. McClellan's sin on this dreadful day was not in failing to order a concentric attack on Lee's lines; that he did. Where he failed, and failed utterly, was by neglecting to insure that the attack went in all together, as it should have.

For down on the left of his line stood the Union IX Corps, under the leisurely direction of General Ambrose Burnside, a bluff, honest, courageous man without perceptible talent or energy. He cut a fine, imposing figure, tall and strong, his jaws bedecked with great thickets of whiskers to which he would lend his name. Everybody liked Burnside, including the troops. They knew he cared about them immensely; they did not know just how inert he would be this day.

And on this day, of all critical days, Burnside was miffed at receiving a rather silly reprimand from McClellan, that pompous ass the newspapers delighted in calling the "Young Napoleon." Burnside apparently was going to limit himself to strictly obeying orders this day, and the Young Napoleon would not make up for his subordinate's lassitude.

A bloody farce was about to be played out on the federal left, a stupidity that would never have happened had a Gustavus Adolphus or a Wellington or a Patton been in command. Sadly, there were no great captains leading the Union forces. At their best, McClellan and Burnside rose to heights of mediocrity, and neither was having a good day.

About nine o'clock, as the roar of violent, bloody fighting swelled up on the right of the Union line, McClellan sent word to Burnside to attack. McClellan's two right-hand corps were locked in desperate close combat, and Burnside's advance could help them by drawing off some of Lee's thin-stretched troops.

Now Burnside's men were east of Antietam Creek, and in front of them lay some open, flat ground and then the little river, winding along placidly between little copses of trees. West of the creek—toward the Confederate lines—the ground rose sharply to some steep little hills crowned with brush and trees. Antietam Creek is about fifty feet wide at this point, but its current is slow. Though the water near the bridge was between four and five feet deep, after the heat of summer the creek in many other places was as low as three feet.

And then there was the bridge, three graceful stone arches spanning the glittering, placid water. It was maybe 12 feet wide and 125 feet long, and it was known as the Rohrback Bridge back then—it has been called Burnside Bridge since the battle. It was about twenty years old in the fall of 1862, and it still stands today, placidly listening to the chuckle of the stream as it has for a hundred years and more. Beside it spreads a huge, graceful sycamore that was little more than a sapling in September of 1862.

Back then, nobody really needed the bridge to cross Antietam Creek, running low in the baking summer heat. Even so, unaccountably, the bridge attracted everybody's attention and held it. Because nobody on the Union side could think about anything but seizing the bridge, a lot of men got killed for nothing, and the Union Army of the Potomac drew a battle it should have won.

Although Federal troops had reached Antietam Creek the night before the battle, nobody had thought to do a proper reconnaissance of the little stream. Neither McClellan's head-quarters nor Burnside's had bothered to discover just how easy it would be to ford the creek. Apparently nobody had thought to wade out into it and find out. McClellan had further complicated matters by keeping at his headquarters all the cavalry, which should have been out on reconnaissance, prying into such things as handy fords and shallow crossing places.

There was some attempt to find a way across the creek downstream of the bridge—somebody had heard there was a crossing called Snavely's Ford. But even this search was a bit halfhearted. Nobody seems to have gone out and really looked; instead, officers rather vaguely cast about to find some local citizen who might know about the ford.

They found no citizen, at least nobody who would tell them anything. They did eventually discover a ford, but it turned out to be useless because it lay below a high, steep bluff, and the soldiers could not scramble down to it. When somebody finally did find Snavely's Ford, it turned out to be a long way downstream, and a whole Union division spent most of the day wandering around through the brush before it finally got across little Antietam Creek. Meanwhile the sun had long passed noon and opportunity was fleeing away.

All this milling about suited Bobby Lee entirely. He could spare very few troops for his far right. Nearly every man he had was locked in furious combat farther northwest, where soldiers were dying in thousands, and officers and orderlies were manhandling cannon into battery as their crews were cut down. There were no reserves at all, none whatever. Everybody in a Confederate uniform would have to stand or die where they were. There was no help to be sent to the handful of men assigned to defend the Antietam crossing.

Fortunately, the defenders were very hard men indeed. These ragged rebels were men of fire-eating Robert Toombs' brigade. Mostly they belonged to two understrength rifle regiments, the 2d and 20th Georgia Infantry. Downstream to their right, other troops were scattered along the creekbank, but around the bridge it all depended on these ragged Georgians. They held the high ground above the creek and they were getting a little artillery help, but they were alone.

The commander on the spot was Colonel Henry L. Benning, tall and dignified, deep-voiced, and very tough in-

deed. His men called him "Old Rock." Now, Benning was
hardly old—he was in his prime, an active man of forty-
eight—but a rock he certainly was. He would fight, this
husky Georgian, and if anybody could hold the Antietam, he
would. Before the war he had been a prominent Georgia lawyer. For some years Benning had been chief justice of the
Georgia Supreme Court. Now he was an experienced and
pugnacious leader of infantry, and he knew a fine defensive
position when he saw it.

He posted his two small regiments along the high ground
west of the creek. There was plenty of excellent cover there,
some rifle pits thoughtfully dug the day before and a fine
stone wall. Many of the Georgians found shelter in a rock
quarry. The rebels improved on their excellent defenses with
fallen trees and fence rails, and settled in. It would take a lot
of bleeding to make them move.

A few of them climbed up into some of the stout trees that
studded the hillside—here a man could find a branch for a
steady rest and a stout trunk to shield his body. And observation was matchless. Nothing could move in the open
ground across the creek without Benning's sharpshooters
seeing it. Covering the bridge itself, Benning posted about
four hundred men; he could spare no more.

A farm road coming west from Pleasant Valley struck
Antietam Creek about a quarter of a mile downstream of the
bridge, then ran parallel with the water up to the bridge.
Whether the Yankees used the road or moved across the
fields straight at the bridge, Rock Benning's Georgians
would make them pay. The range to the bridge was only
about a hundred yards, murderously close for good marks-
men.

And so, in the end, the Union effort was all concentrated
on the picturesque stone bridge. About ten o'clock the Feder-
als began to test the rebel defenses, pushing the 11th Connecticut down the farm road to the creek, and shaking it out
into a skirmish line along the water. The Connecticut men
achieved nothing but casualties from the steady fire of the
Georgians, who appeared to them mostly as puffs of smoke
up in the woods across the creek.

A courageous captain of the 11th led a party out into the
stream to wade across, but Georgia minié balls cut them
down in the water. Then the regimental commander was

down and dying, and the 11th Connecticut fell back, a third of its men out of the fight.

The valiant Connecticut effort was intended to cover an attack by Colonel George Crook's brigade of Ohio infantry. In the event, the Ohio boys marched down to find the crossing and missed the bridge entirely. Crook, who was a first-class soldier before and after Antietam, got his men down to the creek all right, but there they stuck. They began to take fire from the high ground across Antietam Creek, and so they found cover behind fences and trees and began to shoot back. And there they stayed.

The next Federal attempt to cross at the bridge was a disaster. About an hour and a half after the repulse of the Connecticut men, the 2d Maryland and the 6th New Hampshire came down the country road and charged upstream beside the water, turning their left flank to the flaming hillside across the creek, trying to reach the bridge. Everybody banged away to cover them, and Union artillery ripped the western hillside with shot and shell, but the assaulting column had no chance.

For the dug-in Georgians it was a turkey shoot, and they tore the two northern regiments into bloody fragments. The Union boys were good soldiers, but no troops in the world could stand the deadly musketry from the high ground across the creek. There was fire from Confederate artillery, too, and the Union advance collapsed. In just a few minutes, the Marylanders had taken 44 percent casualties.

It was noon by now, and absolutely nothing had been done to relieve the pressure on the Union army's hard-pressed right-hand corps. Couriers had begun arriving from McClellan trying to hurry Burnside on, but without result. Burnside was at his headquarters, a half mile from the point of decision, three hours behind time and still not showing much interest in pressing home any kind of effective assault.

At last McClellan's inspector general, Colonel Sackett, galloped up to relay the Young Napoleon's directive to attack again, and do so at any cost. Burnside was still on his high horse, even more upset at what he perceived as McClellan's interference: "McClellan appears to think I am not trying my best to carry this bridge."

No doubt McClellan thought exactly that, and for once "Little Mac" was entirely correct. But at least Burnside did give some more orders. They went off to General Sturgis's division again, the same unit that had launched the last abortive attack.

This time the job was up to Colonel Edward Ferrero, who commanded Sturgis' 2nd Brigade. Ferrero was a slugger, and a tough disciplinarian. Back in a little valley, perhaps two hundred yards from the bridge, Ferrero rode up to find the men he thought might give Burnside his precious bridge. Resting there, expectant, lay the 51st New York and the 51st Pennsylvania.

These dusty blue men were veterans, and characters to boot. The Pennsylvanians had a reputation as prodigious whiskey drinkers. They could find whiskey, people said, where nobody else could find water, and they loved their ration of firewater. But that ration depended on good behavior, and for some reason Ferrero, a tough commander, had recently cut off their whiskey. They were good soldiers, but the loss of their whiskey still rankled.

Now both the New Yorkers and Pennsylvanians watched their commander's familiar face somberly, guessing what was coming. Ferrero looked them over and raised his voice. "It is General Burnside's especial request that the two Fifty-firsts take that bridge. Will you do it?"

The answer came clearly from somewhere in the ranks of the Pennsylvanians. "Will you give us our whiskey, Colonel, if we take it?"

Ferrero was a disciplinarian, but he knew and loved his men. The little colonel laughed. "Yes, by God," he roared, "if I have to send to New York to get it!" And his men broke into cheers.

Ferrero had seen the horrible results of approaching the bridge up the creek-side road. This time, instead of exposing his soldiers' flank to that murderous musketry from the hillside, he elected to go straight for the bridge across the open ground just east of it. A couple of Union artillery batteries got into position just upstream, where they could sweep the rebel positions, and began to tear at that deadly hillside with swaths of canister.

Ferrero's two other regiments added their rifle-fire, and about half an hour past noon the Pennsylvanians and New Yorkers started their rush for that graceful, bloodstained bridge. They had about three hundred yards of open ground to cross, and the Georgia rifles ripped at them all the way. Men went down in scores as the northerners followed their colors across the killing ground, but the survivors made the foot of the bridge.

It was clear they could not muscle their way through that deadly Georgia rifle-fire to carry the bridge in a single rush. So the Pennsylvanians hunkered down behind a stone wall upstream from the bridge, and the New Yorkers found some cover downstream, behind a rail fence. From there, as a Union lieutenant wrote, with more enthusiasm than good spelling,

> we were then ordered to halt and commence firing, and the way we showered the lead across that creek was noboddys business.

Up on the high ground across the little stream, Rock Benning's whipcord Georgians were coming to the end of their tether. A ceaseless shower of canister and shell fragments and minié balls howled about their ears, slashing jagged chunks of wood from the trees and mowing down the grass and brush. They had been fighting hard for three solid hours, and they were horribly tired; worst of all, they were running out of ammunition.

And so, a few at a time, the Georgians began to pull back, back away from that dreadful fire from the blue men across the stream. Down along the creekbank Colonel Robert Potter waved his men onto the bridge, colors snapping out in front, and the New Yorkers hammered roaring across, jostling for elbowroom with the whiskey-loving 51st Pennsylvania, who came running from their stone wall, cheering.

Out in front of the Pennsylvanians was Captain Allebaugh, commanding C Company, and with him were the precious colors and his first sergeant, and behind trampled a river of yelling men and a thicket of flashing bayonets. Pennsylvania Colonel John Hartranft stood against the old stone of the bridge, waving his hat—forward, forward! He was gasping, his voice almost lost from urging his soldiers on: "Come on, boys . . . I can't halloo anymore!" The rest of the two 51sts went pounding on across that graceful, deadly bridge behind their regimental flags, and behind them the whole east bank erupted in cheering. However badly their leaders had failed, the Union infantry had done very well indeed—they were entitled to yell a little.

Rock Benning was a scrapper, but he was also a realist. His men could hold no longer, no men could. Down at the bridge a river of blue was swarming over the creek, and these Yankees obviously meant business. With the ammunition gone, Benning had little choice; he gave the order to fall back. Most of the remaining men of the 2d and 20th Georgia obeyed, leaving their pits and walls and trees to get back over the crest of the high ground, out of the storm of fire from across the river. A few surrendered; not many.

And one little band would not quit: Lieutenant Colonel William Holmes of the 2d Georgia, sword in hand, led a forlorn, quixotic little counterattack down the slope. It broke up under a storm of Union musketry, and Holmes went down, dying, to be sure, but certainly unconquered.

So the Young Napoleon had the bridge, and petulant Ambrose Burnside could say he had obeyed orders. The soldiers on both sides had suffered horribly. The commander of the 2d Georgia was dead, and more than half his men were casualties. Down below, in the wake of the last Union charge, lay more than two hundred Pennsylvanians and New Yorkers. Altogether, about 500 northern soldiers and perhaps 120 rebels had been hurt or killed in this vicious little fight.

Behind the 51st Pennsylvania and their brothers from New York, more soldiers from IX Corps streamed across the river. A little to the north, Crook's Ohioans finally got across—they waded—and at last the wandering division to the south got over at the elusive Snavely's Ford. More and more men reached the west bank, and artillery batteries, and great victory seemed to be only an arm's length away.

The Union men were on Bobby Lee's right flank now, with very little between them and the Potomac three miles away. They had perhaps twelve hundred yards to go, only twelve hundred yards to cut the Army of Virginia off from the Potomac fords and any hope of survival. Robert Toombs had pulled back to a stone wall about half a mile west of the bridge. It was the last place he could fight—a forlorn hope, certainly, but the fiery Georgian and Benning and their men would stick it out until the end.

Although the Union troopers seemed to have it all their way now, victory was still a little out of their grasp. For one thing, the leading Federal division had used almost all its cartridges, and, on this day of blunders, nobody had seen to resupply the ammunition. That division was replaced by another one and went back to replace its cartridges, and all this took time.

There was a traffic jam at the bridge, which became a monumental bottleneck. The troops got in one another's way, Burnside came down to direct traffic without noticeable effect, and still nobody thought about wading the quiet stream. And so a couple of hours passed, the sun galloped toward the west . . . and up the road from Harper's Ferry came Nemesis.

Nemesis was called A. P. Hill, and he was wearing his red "fighting shirt" this day. Up that dusty road, at the head of his panting, sweating men, Powell Hill came riding at his driving, fighting best. He pushed his ragged men mercilessly. for he knew what was at stake up ahead, and he left the baking road strewn with gasping stragglers. Those who could not keep up dropped by the wayside or hobbled along in the dust behind the column. But Hill drove on north with those who could keep up. Lee needed him, and Hill would not fail.

The Union advance finally got rolling west from Antietam Creek after a couple of hours of milling around and refilling cartridge boxes and getting reorganized. Much of the rest of the battlefield had quieted down, save for the spiteful popping of skirmishers' rifles and desultory cannon-fire. Both sides were tired and battered, pretty well fought out in the hideous bloodbath of the morning. McClellan had all his cavalry and a whole infantry corps still fresh and ready, but as usual, he dithered, his head filled with visions of hordes of imaginary rebels. He would not commit his fresh troops, which could have swept Lee's exhausted men from the field.

So if the Union were to win a victory, the push would have to come from Burnside's men. There were lots of them, too, two divisions abreast, each with an extra brigade attached. And now, at last, they were over in force, pushing inexorably west toward Lee's flank and rear.

There were fewer than twenty-eight hundred Confederate soldiers to stop them. The rebels had scraped together twenty-eight guns, however, and Lee, very much alive to the danger, was sending more artillery over to his right. The terrain was good defensive ground too, cut by ravines and gullies, crossed by stone walls and rail fences where riflemen could find a rest and reach out to pull down advancing men in blue.

Still, the advantage of numbers was all with Burnside, and his men made steady progress. On their right they were supported by a division from the neighboring corps, a very tough division that included two full regiments of experienced regulars. But here, too, McClellan failed—the regulars, on the verge of punching a hole in the thin line before them, were recalled. Although the Young Napoleon had promised to support Burnside, he failed to issue the necessary orders, and another chance went glimmering.

Still Burnside's men pushed on, "as thick," a Rebel wrote, "as Pharaoh's locusts." They cleared Confederate positions with the bayonet, running in yelling through a miasma of dust and powder-smoke. Around them friends were bowled over and dismembered by round shot bounding wildly through the orchards and the standing corn. Then, as they closed with the Confederate batteries, the rebels switched to grapeshot, swarms of iron balls that tore great gaps in the blue lines.

Eight men together were cut down in one Union regiment, but the survivors pressed on, and the deadly guns retreated before them. Now the blue lines roared, and stormed forward toward a line of grim gray men at a rail fence, and the two lines stood and murdered each other at fifty yards. Then the outnumbered rebels broke and ran, and the flag of the United States could be seen from Sharpsburg itself.

Lee himself was down in the streets of the town, rallying tired men, as Confederate ambulances pushed through the crowded ways, blood splashing from their beds. Union shells whistled into the town, bursting in the chaotic streets, knocking down pieces of masonry and glass on the tumult below.

Lee had nothing left to send to his right, and his ragged line was ready to dissolve. Time seemed frozen. As a great historian put it, the "sun seemed to stand still at the bidding of a Northern Joshua." Lee rode to a little knoll above the town, squinting toward the south and southeast, into the afternoon sun. He needed Hill desperately. He needed a miracle.

He got both. Looking past the debacle on his right, Lee

could see movement to the south. Powell Hill was close. Hill
and a few of his staff had galloped into Sharpsburg on spent
horses about two-thirty. But his troops were still panting up
the Harper's Ferry road, while the hammer of federal musketry came closer, closer, and there was nothing left to shore
up Lee's quaking, bending line. Holding tightly to hope, Lee
turned to a young officer who had a telescope.

"What troops are those?" asked Lee, and the young man
looked and said some of them were Union soldiers.

And the others? asked his general. What are they?

The youngster squinted into his glass again. As he answered, Robert E. Lee's heart must have leaped, although he
showed no emotion at all.

"They were flying the Virginia and Confederate flags."

They were. It was Hill's Light Division, famous through the
army for fighting and marching, and it had covered seventeen miles in seven hours, a prodigious march in the summer heat. It was strung out and lathered and panting, but its
blood was up and it was coming in on the flank of an enemy
that did not expect it.

Red-bearded Powell Hill was famous in both armies as a
furious fighter. Indeed, the northern soldiers believed Hill's
venom in combat stemmed from a competition with McClellan to wed lovely Ellen Marcy, who finally married Little Mac.
On one occasion, legend had it, as Hill's men attacked a
northern unit, a Union soldier grouched, "God's sake,
Nelly—why didn't you marry him?"

The tale was myth, probably, but Hill's ferocity in combat
was real enough. Now he threw his men into action as they
came up, panting and soaked with sweat, and they slammed
into the flank of the disorganized Union units moving west
on Sharpsburg. Screeching the rebel yell—"Whooo-eeee!"—
they came pounding in out of the smoke and dust, and the
Union left came unstuck under the ferocity of their charge.

Unit by unit, the northern advance ground to a halt,
bloodied by terrible volleys that tore into their flanks, and a
little at a time the whole Union line began to recoil. Men fell
in hundreds on both sides—both sides had a division commander killed here—but Hill had the initiative, and he would
keep it. By now, too, the rebels had more than forty guns collected east of Sharpsburg, enough metal to overpower the
Federal batteries.

In the end, Burnside's men were driven back almost to the bridge. They fell back fighting fiercely, but they lost most of the gains of the afternoon, almost everything but that damnable bridge.

And at this point McClellan's courage failed him utterly. Knowing the dimensions of Burnside's repulse, knowing that his left flank might be driven clear through the creek, he still dithered. Still he refused to commit any of the fifty-five hundred fresh troops quietly waiting for his orders, although, as a Union general dryly commented, "troops are put in reserve . . . to be used in a pinch." More than a third of McClellan's men had not popped a cap all day, while Lee had gotten the maximum effort out of every man.

And there, as Burnside's men stabilized their lines, and Powell Hill's tired men broke contact, it all ended. The worst day of carnage in American history was over. Before long night began to come down, and the dreadful business of collecting the wounded and the dead began. All across the ghastly fields around Sharpsburg danced little glimmering corpse-lights, the lanterns of medical personnel searching for wounded men.

Out on the battlefield burning haystacks glowed with fire in the gloaming, a soft, sweet evening hideous with the moans and screams and crying of horribly hurt men. They cried for water and they cried for their mothers, and in their delirium they still fought the battle and called on comrades silent and dead in the fields beside them. It was time to leave off killing for a little, and try to save those who could be saved. The surgeons would work desperately through the night, and with them worked a tough, tireless little woman named Clara Barton.

Lee spent the next day at Sharpsburg, brazenly staring McClellan down, then slipped away south in darkness, to rest and recruit. And come again. He had saved his army, an astonishing feat of arms. Fighting Powell Hill had come in the nick of time. McClellan and Burnside and others had fumbled away a great opportunity, but even then it had been a very close-run thing.

The extra minutes, the crucial minutes that cost the North its victory, those were the gift of Henry Benning and a handful of stringy, sunburnt Georgia foot soldiers. Benning, his superior reported, had fought his little force with "distinguished coolness, courage and skill . . . He deserves the special consideration of the Government." Indeed he did, for he had surely saved the Army of Northern Virginia.

A couple of good things did come out of the awful slaughter at Antietam. Although McClellan had failed to win, at least he had not lost, and the engagement looked more like a victory than anything the Army of the Potomac had done before. And so Lincoln made use of it as his chance to shake the South—and mold the future—with an astonishing announcement, the simple words called the Emancipation Proclamation.

And in November the President got rid of McClellan. Little Mac's replacement, unfortunately, was the plodding Burnside, the first of a series of short-lived command failures who would get a lot of good soldiers killed to no purpose. But at least a beginning was made, a beginning that in time would produce George Meade and Ulysses Simpson Grant . . . and victory.

And the thirsty, irrepressible 51st Pennsylvania? Well, Colonel Ferrero was promoted for his day's work, a promotion richly deserved. There was a ceremony, of course, and the 51st was there. And they still had something to say. It wasn't that they doubted Ferrero—he kept his promises—they just wanted to make sure. And so a little, anonymous voice piped up from the Pennsylvania ranks as Ferrero sat his horse among the music and the flags.

"How about that whiskey?"

Ferrero heard the little voice behind him, turned his head, and answered with a smile. "You'll get it," he said.

And they did, a whole keg of it, that very day. No doubt they drank to the health of the new brigadier.

Old Rock Benning fought out the rest of the war. He was shot, and badly, in the murderous, evil darkness of the Wilderness. But he returned to duty and walked the rest of a long, bleak road with the Army of Northern Virginia. He ended the war as a brigadier general, and he was still in harness on the very last day, that dreary, bitter April day when Bobby Lee's boys stacked arms for the last time, and a battle-hardened Federal commander brought his men to "carry arms," in a silent, final salute.

And then Henry Benning went back to Georgia, hung up his sword, and picked up his law books again. He was a fine

lawyer and a decent man, and respected on both grounds.
But nothing could ever top the warmth in the voices of old
Georgia soldiers when they spoke of the time they held the
Antietam bridge for Old Rock, trading blood for hours to
save an army.

The United States Army, which reveres scrappers, remem-
bers Henry Benning. For a long time, young officers from all
over America have gone to a big post in Georgia to learn to
lead, and men are trained there as paratroops and rangers
and Green Berets. The post is what it calls itself, The Home
of the Infantry, and it is named Fort Benning.

Old Rock would have liked that.

THE LITTLE DRUMMER BOYS

Army music was important to Civil War soldiers. Martial
melodies did wonders for fighting morale. Sentimental evening serenades reminded a soldier of home, and mother, and
the girl he left behind. When it came to work, however, to the
hard business of fighting, music was not just nice to have; it
was critical.

The telegraph might carry orders across the miles like
chain lightning. Flags and heliographs and galloping messen-
gers might transmit the commander's will to his subordinates on a hard-fought field. But a soldier down in the
battle-line needed something more. He was shrouded in
smoke, drenched in sweat, spattered with the blood and
brains of his friends. All around him comrades went down
writhing and screaming; his ears were full of the howl of
grapeshot and the endless din of hundreds of muskets.

Down in this butchery, soldiers could not see flags or heliographs; even if they could, they were unlikely to be able to

read their message. The infantry soldier on both sides, desperately loading and firing his Springfield or Enfield rifled musket, got his orders from the drums.

So the drummer was a critical cog in the Civil War infantry regiment, and he was usually a child. Most drummers were in their lower teens; a number of them were under ten. They were supposed to be treated as noncombatants, but at any distance a minié ball or humming grapeshot made no distinction as to size or years. The Civil War's mass armies did not bother much with such niceties as age. If a man was fit enough, he could serve. Medical examinations were cursory, when there were any at all; the first marches would sort out who would last and who would not.

The surprising thing is the immense courage these youngsters showed in action. One, a boy called Howe, won the Congressional Medal at Vicksburg. A drummer with the 55th Illinois Infantry, he was apparently used as a runner this bloody day. Badly shot up, the young soldier refused to leave the field until he accomplished his mission, reporting a shortage of ammunition to General Sherman. He was fourteen.

Some tiny drummers paid the ultimate price. As far as the records show, the youngest soldier to die on either side was a kid called Charley King, son of a tailor in Chester County, Pennsylvania. Charley was already an accomplished drummer before he was allowed to enlist. In fact, the commander of a newly formed company sought the lad's parents out and worked hard to recruit their accomplished son.

The captain was persuasive. He would watch over Charley himself. And anyway, he said, drummers stayed behind the battle-line and helped with the wounded; Charley would be safe. And no doubt the captain thought so. Nobody who hadn't been to war knew much about it in the late summer of 1861.

So, with misgivings, Charley's parents gave their consent, and boy and his drum marched south. Charley was indeed a fine drummer, and in short order became drum major of his unit, the 49th Pennsylvania. Now the youngster even drew pay, and he proudly sent it home to his parents, who banked it for him.

Charley should have survived Antietam, just as he had come through the peninsula fighting unhurt. His regiment missed the thick of the fighting, and there was little rebel activity in their section by the time they reached the battlefield. All the unit faced was a casual shell or two . . . but one of these burst near young Charley, and he went down with a shell fragment through his body. It would take him three days to die, not yet fourteen years old.

The most famous drummer of all, however, was Johnny Clem, who became a household word as the "Drummer Boy of Shiloh." Clem was eleven and looked like a cherub. But when those two raw armies clashed beside the Tennessee in April of 1862, he served stoutly through the battle, beating his calls resolutely even though a shell fragment had punched a hole in his drum. Later in the fight, Clem picked up a musket and fought shoulder to shoulder with the grown men of his regiment. Northern publications picked up the story of "Johnny Shiloh," and young Clem attained a measure of fame.

In the autumn of 1863, Clem, now all of twelve years old, drummed his regiment, the 22d Michigan, into the ferocious fighting at Chickamauga. Here, too, he fought as an infantryman, firing a rifle with a stock cut down to fit him. Legend has it that one of his minié balls knocked a Confederate colonel out of the saddle.

Captured by the Confederacy two months later, he again made news as southern papers trumpeted the capture of the North's most famous musician. Clem was soon released, presumably because of his age, and returned to duty, serving as a courier for General George Thomas, the "Rock of Chickamauga," in the Atlanta fighting.

Little Johnny Shiloh was mustered out in September 1864, but he had acquired a taste for soldiering. Commissioned after the war, he served until 1916, retiring as a major general. He had been forty-five years a soldier.

BAYONET!
The Twentieth Maine on Little Round Top

General Gouverneur Warren sat his horse in a little oasis of quiet. Except for a few signalmen, the little hill around him was empty, even peaceful. But down below, to the west and northwest and southwest, the lovely Pennsylvania countryside was a corner of hell itself. Down there was the terrible din of battle, the thunder of rifle-fire and cannon and the roaring of thousands of men. And out of the miasma of powder-smoke a line of men was coming, armed men in gray and butternut, bayonets winking in the sun, crimson battle flags out in front. And they were coming this way.

Warren spurred his horse back down the hillside. He had to find help, and he had to find it quickly. What looked like the whole Confederate army was headed for this little pimple, and there was nothing to stop it. This hill was called Little Round Top, and it was the left-hand anchor of the entire Union line.

Warren was chief engineer of the Army of the Potomac, and not in command of much of anything; he had no infantrymen to plug this gaping hole. But Warren had commanded in combat, and he knew big trouble when he saw it. If those pugnacious gray men got hold of Little Round Top, the rest of the northern position would be flanked; then Robert E. Lee would get some guns up here, his ragged infantry would lap around the Union rear, and the whole Federal line would come unstuck.

Up north of this hill the Army of the Potomac held a long, low elevation called Cemetery Ridge. It stretched on north almost to a quiet little town called Gettysburg, then curved back east and then south again, forming a long fishhook. It was a pretty fair defensive position, but it was nothing with Little Round Top gone. Just south of Little Round Top loomed a slightly larger hill called Round Top. It overlooked Little Round Top, but it was not a good position. It was so overgrown with thick brush that it afforded neither clear observation nor useful fields of fire. That left Little Round Top as the last piece of high ground at the southern end of the Union line. If it went, the rest of the Union line would go with it.

And so Warren sent officers galloping for help. One went hurtling cross-country to find Army Commander George Meade. Another, future Indian fighter Ranald McKenzie, found V Corps commander, crusty George Sykes.

Sykes took Warren's word for the danger, and sent a brigade pounding over to scramble panting up Little Round Top and form a breathless battle-line. Or maybe, as another and better story tells us, Sykes' messenger—searching for the division commander—ran into brigade commander Strong Vincent first.

"What are your orders?" asked Vincent.

And when the messenger told him, Vincent saw the danger and made a snap decision. "I will take the responsibility of taking my brigade there," he said, and began snapping out his orders. He gave them in the nick of time, starting his leading units for Little Round Top without delay. Vincent galloped toward the little hill himself; behind him his standard was carried into action, a little triangular pennant bearing a red Maltese cross.

Vincent's brigade was a good one. It was about a thousand strong, four regiments of infantry, and veteran Pennsylvania colonel Vincent was the best possible man to have around in a tight spot. Only twenty-six, Vincent was a lawyer by trade, a soldier by choice, and a ferocious fighter by instinct.

Vincent pushed his men hard up Little Round Top and got them into fighting positions across the southwest slope. From right to left, Vincent put in the 16th Michigan, the 44th New York, the 83d Pennsylvania, and the 20th Maine. They got to their posts with no time to spare.

For that brushy slope down below was alive with lean, rangy soldiers, John Bell Hood's formidable Texans coming through the smoke behind fixed bayonets. The air quavered with that unearthly keening rebel yell: "Whooo-eeee! Whooooo-eeee!" and popped and hissed with passing musket-balls. Vincent's men met Hood's men with a murderous close-range fire, and the two lines battered and smashed one another at ranges down to thirty yards.

The left of Vincent's tortured line—the left of the whole Army of the Potomac—was held by the 20th Regiment of Maine Volunteers, about 350 dusty blue soldiers who were promptly in the fight of their lives with a whole hillside full of southern hornets. Vincent knew how important this position was, and he was blunt with the commander of the 20th Maine: "This is the left of the Union line. You understand? Hold this ground at all costs!"

And hold it this commander would. The 20th Maine was led by an unlikely sort of soldier, a Bowdoin University professor-cum-clergyman from a scholarly family named Chamberlain. Chamberlain was a tall, slim, quiet-eyed man; with his long jaw and handlebar mustache he looked a little like a Victorian British officer. He had only been soldiering about a year.

Quiet Chamberlain was, but there was a lot to this quiet academic, a lot more than met the eye. Lots of men are not cut out to be soldiers; a few are born to lead men into battle, and Chamberlain was one of those few. Maybe his given name was some harbinger of the heart and talent of the man, for his parents had christened him Joshua.

Joshua he would be this day. He brought his men up Little Round Top on the double, panting in the heat, and shook them out facing Big Round Top. Acutely conscious that his left flank was naked, Chamberlain bent back his left-hand companies so that his line formed an acute angle, with its point toward the enemy. At the apex he planted the colors of the regiment and the United States.

Chamberlain must have wished that, like Joshua the Isra-elite, he could make the sun stand still. Not only was he the far left wing of the whole Union army—but down the hill just a little way were all the rebels in the world, coming on across a little valley that separated his position from Big Round Top. He pushed forward Captain Morrill and his B Company as skirmishers, out across the saddle between the two hills and up the slope of Big Round Top.

Almost immediately firing broke out to Morrill's right and rear, and the captain immediately pulled back behind a stone wall that crossed the saddle. Confederate shells came moaning in to burst among the brush and trees, and the sultry air was filled with death, pieces of iron shell case, fragments of stone, jagged splinters from shattered trees.

The first roar of heavy firing rose behind the Maine men, from the right of Vincent's line. Over there the 16th Michigan had reached out to its right, groping to link up with a Maine regiment down the hill to their north. An independent company called Brady's Sharpshooters helped extend the line, but the 16th and everybody else was getting dangerously thinned out.

And it was on this attenuated front that the first Confederate assault fell. Out of the scrub came the 4th and 5th Texas Infantry and parts of the 4th Alabama, tough veteran regiments trotting in from the southwest, across the lower slope of Big Round Top.

To Chamberlain's front, coming in higher across the same hill, were the 15th and 47th Alabama, two more experienced units. Both had marched a long way since the morning and attacked in the terrible heat of the day. Now they were out of water, but they were still full of fight. They halted, panting, around the crest of Big Round Top, rested a bit, then began to push on downhill. Some of the Alabama men had fallen out from thirst and heat exhaustion; a few had been hit; but the rest were coming on in that familiar lope, the eerie, banshee keen of the rebel yell already ringing through the din of the artillery fire. They were headed straight for the 20th Maine.

Now the real battle was beginning. Over on the Federal right the 4th and 5th Texas and the 4th Alabama had driven the blue skirmishers back uphill. Now the rebels dressed their ranks and began to push up the slope, past boulders and brush and scrub trees. And they quickly began to take an accurate fire from the top of Little Round Top. Their attack bogged down, and they fell back to regroup and try again.

This second rush was no more successful than the first one. The Union rifle-fire was murderous, and the ground was quickly littered with figures in gray and butternut. Again the three regiments fell back. In front of Chamberlain's men the 15th and 47th Alabama fared no better, met, as a Confederate officer wrote, by "the most destructive fire I ever saw." The gray lines staggered and stopped.

There was little respite. Again the firing rose to a roar, as the Alabamans came swinging in again against the 20th Maine. The southerners staggered in a ferocious fire from Chamberlain's grim men, but their colonel ran to the front to rally them, and they plodded on, closer and closer to the flaming Union rifles. A few more steps was all it would take, and then the South would have Little Round Top and a clear road to the Union rear, and just maybe America would be two nations instead of one.

The fighting was point-blank, bayonets and musket butts and pistols, and rifles fired close enough to burn a soldier as the bullet tore into his body. One Maine man was bayoneted as he seized an Alabama battle flag. A rebel soldier smashed in the face of a Maine man with a rock as a Union trooper broke an Alabaman's skull with a full swing of his clubbed rifle.

It was horrible, gasping, gut-tearing work, and the line of struggling men surged back and forth, panting, soaked with sweat, mouths cotton-dry in the July heat. Splashed with their own and their comrades' blood, the soldiers looked like devils incarnate, mouths open and gasping, ringed with smears of black from biting open their cartridges. It seemed to go on and on, the shouting, the screaming, the clanging of ramrods in hot barrels, the deafening roar of the big rifles.

Chamberlain was fighting along with his men, trying to keep some control over this pit-bull struggle in the dust and smoke. In the swirl of confused hand-to-hand fighting he had to depend mostly on his soldiers' native courage:

> At times I saw around me more of the enemy than of my own men; gaps opening, swallowing, closing again . . . all around a strange, mingled roar.

Chamberlain had everybody in the fight; even his musicians were in the firing line. Two accused mutineers from the 2d Maine, attached to the 20th as prisoners, grabbed muskets and pitched into the fight. Chamberlain saw them. If they live, he thought, I'll dismiss the charges. Thinking of his men in this hell, he knelt for just a moment in the midst of the carnage to promote a dying soldier to sergeant.

The Alabamans were also taking terrible losses. The regimental commander saw his brother fall, mortally wounded, along with at least half of his soldiers. A company commander cried out, "Oh God, that I could see my mother!" and then passed far from the terrible cares of command forever.

Chamberlain was hit twice. One bullet tore into his right foot; a second slammed his sword scabbard into his thigh, leaving a deep and painful bruise. And just yards away a Confederate sharpshooter spotted Chamberlain alone in the open, obviously an important officer, and drew a bead on him.

But the young rebel could not shoot; something held him back, although he aimed again at the redoubtable colonel in blue. Long after the war he wrote Chamberlain to say how glad he was something had kept him from pulling the trigger. His strange restraint may just have saved the Union.

On and on the fighting went. The Maine men had been fighting for their lives for more than an hour, and they were wearing out. Most of them had fired all sixty of the cartridges they had carried into the fight, and now they were rifling the cartridge boxes of their fallen friends to feed the hungry muskets. More and more men fell, and the Maine line grew pitifully thin. The left of the 20th Maine was bent almost double by now, twisted so far back on itself that rebel bullets were striking the rear of the rest of Vincent's regiments.

And then Chamberlain, half his men dead or wounded, the battle and maybe the war on the line, raised his sword and seized his moment. "Bayonet!" he roared into the hammer of firing. "Bayonet! Charge bayonet! Charge!"

And they went forward, those hardy Mainers, by instinct mostly, because nobody could hear much of anything over the thunder of musketry and the screams of the wounded and the wailing rebel yell. His men caught Chamberlain's urgency, and from the color company Lieutenant Melcher ran forward with his sword drawn, echoing his commander's urgency: "Come on, boys, come on!"

And then the flag bearers followed, and the call to charge "ran like fire along the line from man to man, and rose into a shout, with which they sprang forward upon the enemy, now not thirty yards away."

Chamberlain got his left started first, and then the rest of

his line, swinging in a wide right wheel a Pennsylvania officer
thought looked "like a great gate upon a post." By now all the
soldiers had caught the fire of the moment, and "with one
wild yell of anguish wrung from its tortured heart, the regiment charged."

Down the hill they went yelling, faces black with powder-
smoke and crimson with blood. Morrill swung his company
across the rebel right flank, poured in a terrible volley, and
joined the headlong charge. It was all too much for tired,
thirsty troops, even Hood's grim veterans, and the rebels, arguably the best infantry in the world, wavered and began to
shrink away. Astonished, they fell back faster and faster. And
then they broke.

They ran, as their commander wrote, "like a herd of wild
cattle," and the 20th Maine chased them. The northerners
charged on, cheering down the hillside and up the first
slopes of Big Round Top before Chamberlain could control
his jubilant men. They even took some prisoners in that wild
charge: Chamberlain personally captured a confused lieutenant colonel who offered his sword in surrender as he fired
his pistol with the other hand. In later years the Maine men
would boast of four hundred captives. It was a pardonable
overestimate: Their bag was probably more like half that
number.

The men of the 20th knew the quality of their enemies;
they knew they had gone in against the best. As a Maine corporal said, the 15th Alabama had "fought like demons" that
day. And in return, an Alabama prisoner gave the Maine men
their finest accolade. The 15th Alabama had never been
whipped before, he said, but they "never wanted to meet the
20th Maine again."

For a while, at least, Little Round Top would stay Union.

Chamberlain got his men back to their original position as
quickly as he could. He knew full well these rebs would take
a great deal of pounding. If they came again, he would need
every advantage: Of his original 386 men, only about half
were still on their feet. And a lot of them were wounded, including Chamberlain.

Meanwhile, sweating Union gunners were manhandling artillery up the steeps of Little Round Top. This was Hazlett's
D Battery, 5th U.S. Artillery, and just getting it up the hill
called for superhuman effort. Now its guns were dragged

into position by cannoneers and infantrymen and anybody else with his hands free; even General Warren dismounted to help heave the pieces into line. In a very few minutes Hazlett's men were hammering the Confederates down to the northwest, grapeshot humming through the gray lines, sounding like "partridges in flight" to one young rebel.

Warren, now bleeding from a shallow throat wound, galloped back downhill again, knowing that Vincent's thin brigade could not hold his hilltop alone for long. The first unit he found was the 140th New York Infantry, the leading regiment of a brigade commanded by Colonel Patrick O'Rourke.

"Paddy!" roared Warren. "Paddy, give me a regiment!" O'Rourke hesitated, knowing his own commander expected him elsewhere.

"Never mind," said Warren. "I will take responsibility!"

That was good enough for O'Rourke, and he promptly started the New Yorkers up Little Round Top. Some distance behind them, Sykes had ordered the rest of O'Rourke's brigade to Little Round Top, but it had a ways to go.

Vincent's men needed all the help they could get. The rebels were coming on again, this time with the 48th Alabama added to their left. The tired Union soldiers had lost a lot of comrades, and they were running out of ammunition. The right end of Vincent's line began to waver, somebody ordered the 16th Michigan's colors to the rear, and the line began to come unstuck.

At the last minute, Vincent ran in to rally his men in person, and some of the 44th New York wheeled to its right to fire into the flank of the attackers. For the moment the Michigan men held on, but Strong Vincent was down, down and mortally hurt with a bullet in the groin.

His brigade had slogged through Hanover, Pennsylvania, in the moonlight just two days before, fifes shrilling and drums banging, the colors uncased and spread to what breeze there was. As the tired, dusty troopers squared their shoulders a little and fell into step, Colonel Vincent halted his horse in the town square and watched his men pass. He took off his hat as the flags passed by, and the moment moved him, as it moved his soldiers. In the gloaming the tough Pennsylvania colonel turned to his adjutant, Lieutenant John Clark. "What death more glorious," the colonel mused, "can any man desire than to die on the soil of old Pennsylvania fighting for that flag?"

Or something like that. Or at least that was the way the lieutenant remembered it afterward. Maybe that really was what Colonel Vincent said, because men talked like that in those far-off days. In any case, Vincent was touched by the moment, and that was what he meant.

And now, in the awful din of shouting and screaming men and the hammer of hundreds of muskets, Colonel Vincent went in to rally his sagging line, waving his men on into the smoke and dust. And in that terrible moment Strong Vincent met face-to-face the death he found glorious: A southern rifle-ball found him, and he went down with his hands in the soil of Old Pennsylvania. Standing over his body, his men loaded and fired and died, and held their ground.

And then Paddy O'Rourke came pounding in out of the smoke, and behind him panted his 140th New York. Their muskets were not loaded and their bayonets were not fixed, but O'Rourke led them in anyhow. "Down this way, boys," the colonel shouted, and his men ran down to come in on the right of the battered Michigan men. Once in place, the New Yorkers began to frantically load and fire, and a murderous firefight developed at thirty or forty feet. The 140th held, all right, but in the course of this terrible point-blank exchange a rebel rifleman spotted O'Rourke and drilled a ball through the colonel's neck. Furious, his men almost blew the southerner apart; he fell with seventeen balls in his body, but the magnetic Paddy O'Rourke was down and dying.

Nevertheless, the 140th had turned the tide on the right of Vincent's line. The gray infantry recoiled; a few raised their hands in surrender. Then behind the 140th New York the rest of its parent brigade began to appear, and there was more help for the exhausted defenders of Little Round Top. It began to look as if the vital little hill might be held after all.

The defenders had to hold, now more than ever. For to their north and northwest the whole Federal line had come apart, dissolving into a maelstrom of shattered units and isolated artillery batteries, and everywhere gray battle lines were coming on through the smoke behind those brilliant crimson battle flags.

And if the Union soldiers had devastated those attacking Texans and Alabamans, they had paid dearly themselves.

Vincent and O'Rourke were down. Vincent's division commander would die there on the hilltop as well, and so would
young gunner Hazlett, shot through the head as he bent over
his stricken general. Around them were strewn hundreds of
Union soldiers, writhing in pain, quiet in death. Little Round
Top was a butcher's block, but it still belonged to the North.

And northern it would stay.

The last southern charge on Little Round Top petered out
over on the right, against the gutty survivors of the 44th New
York and the 16th Michigan. It died hard, in a wild storm of
bullets, bullets so thick, one soldier said, that "a man could
hold out a hat and catch it full." A company of the 5th Texas
got within about twenty yards of the flaming blue line, but
there it stuck. Hood's men had shot their bolt.

And so the bloody Second Day of Gettysburg was over for
Chamberlain and the 20th Maine. With the rest of the Union
defenders of Little Round Top, they began to care for the
wounded—the hurt men of both sides—and count their
losses. The little hilltop was at peace again, but it was only
a caricature of what it had been an hour before. The trees
were stripped of bark for six feet above the ground; some
saplings had simply been shot in two. Little rivulets of blood
trickled down into low spots in the ground and pooled there.

That night, Chamberlain's tired men occupied Big Round
Top, and returned later to bury their dead where they had
fallen, on tortured Little Round Top. It was a tradition in the
20th, a quiet sort of farewell to good comrades. They
marked the graves with crude headboards made from ammunition boxes, and carved the names of the dead into them
with jackknives. Later on, the remains of their friends were
moved to the growing national cemetery, but for now they
continued to occupy the bloody ground they had died to
hold. And that seemed only right to the men of the 20th
Maine.

It is tempting to say that the fledgling 20th Maine had
saved the Army of the Potomac. That would be something of
an exaggeration probably, because a lot of the other men had
fought and died and helped turn back Bobby Lee this terrible day. But the fact remains that the 20th held the line at
the very end of things. Had the rebels passed them, the way
to the Federal rear was open.

But they did not pass, and maybe the survival of the Union

army did depend, for a little while, on a couple of hundred
men from Maine. At least the commander of the gallant Alabamans broken by Chamberlain's charge thought so:

> There never were harder fighters than the 20th Maine men
> and their gallant colonel. His skill and persistency and the
> great bravery of his men saved Little Round Top and the Army
> of the Potomac.

It had indeed been quite a day for Joshua Chamberlain,
the Bowdoin academic. Whatever he may have been the night
before, as this day's sun went down, he was all soldier. "Bayonet!" he had roared, and lunged into the fire, and he had
done it at just the right time. He was plenty of officer and
plenty of man; soldiers know about these things, and his exhausted men would not have followed him otherwise. His
country agreed; this day's giving had won him the Congressional Medal (for which he was recommended on two other
occasions).

He had a long and ugly road ahead of him, too, much fighting and six wounds, and at the end a richly deserved promotion to major general. And in the twilight of it all, on a chilly
gray April morning two years later, Joshua Chamberlain
sat his horse next to a muddy road at a place called Appomattox.

Behind him his division stood silently in ranks, and in
those ranks were the remains of the 20th Maine. Down the
road trudged the tattered remnants of the Army of Northern
Virginia, on its way to lay down its arms, badly beaten but
never whipped. In its ranks were a few ragged survivors of
Hood's men, the old opponents of Little Round Top.

Chamberlain, the kindhearted warrior, responded entirely
in character. He took the southern surrender that quiet
dreary day; it was his duty to do so. But first he called his division to attention and to carry arms, a last salute and good-
bye to a gallant enemy. The silent lines of Confederate
soldiers returned the salute, and maybe the healing of the
nation's deep wounds was started there on that muddy country road. As a Confederate general commented, "They were
proud of their success, and we were not ashamed of our
defeat . . ." And that was the way to leave it.

On the twenty-third of May, 1865, there was a grand review

of the Army of the Potomac. The endless blue ranks swung down Pennsylvania Avenue past the White House and President Lincoln, bands playing, tattered battle flags snapping in the breeze—flags that had seen a hundred fights and skirmishes, and God only knew how much hurt and dying.

Out at the head of his division rode Chamberlain, and behind him fluttered his division flag, red Maltese cross on white pennon. He dismounted at the presidential reviewing stand opposite the White House, and joined the President and dozens of generals and other dignitaries to watch a mighty army pass from noonday sunlight into the mists of history.

Two nights later there was another sort of good-bye, a moving, spontaneous farewell by the soldiers themselves. There had been an issue of candles that day, and after nightfall men began to light them and stick them in bayonet sockets and musket barrels. And then they formed and marched to salute their generals, their column looking like "a line of living fire" in the night.

Chamberlain's men called on him to speak. He did so, responding with something his men cheered—what a pity we don't know what he said. Then the bands played and everybody sang patriotic songs and cheered their country and their officers and themselves . . . until at last the little candles began to wink out one by one, little sparks dying in the night. And with them passed the 20th Maine and the Army of the Potomac.

And then, all the misery and the celebration finally over, Chamberlain headed back north to a long and full career of teaching and leadership and honor. He would become governor of Maine in time, and in the end president of Bowdoin College.

Chamberlain had seen all the horror of war, and he hated the hurt and the dying. But he was wise enough to remember the good strong things that he had seen as well, and he said so:

In the privations and sufferings . . . as well as in . . . battle, some of the highest qualities of manhood are called forth—courage, self-command, sacrifice of self for the sake of something held higher . . . fortitude, patience, warmth of comradeship.

And when he wrote those words, he must have been thinking of the 20th Maine.

Chamberlain returned to Little Round Top nearly half a century later. He watched the sun go down from that quiet knoll he had held with the bayonet, and thought about that long-ago day of terror and transcendent courage. And he thought about his men and spoke of them, with that love that only good commanders know.

> They did not know it themselves, what were their lofty deeds of body, mind, heart and soul on that tremendous day.

Maybe they didn't. But Joshua Chamberlain knew. And Strong Vincent and Paddy O'Rourke would have understood entirely.

OLD JOHN BURNS FIGHTS FOR HIS COUNTRY

The storm hammered and rolled out along the gentle hills west and northwest of sleepy Gettysburg. Those were rifles firing out there, thousands of them, and cannon, too, and the thunder of firing was coming closer. Clouds of gray-white smoke drifted lazily against a burning sky, and long columns of dusty blue soldiers hurried through the streets under the brazen glare of noon.

Out west of town John Buford's union cavalry were firing and falling back, bloodying the gray infantry as it pushed in hard toward the town. The rebels at first thought they'd bumped into some Pennsylvania militia, local bumpkins who would disappear at the first volley. Now they knew better—especially since some of them had seen the distinctive black slouch hats of the fabled Iron Brigade, the first brigade of the first division of the first corps. This was the Army of the Potomac for sure, and the southerners knew they were in for a fight.

They were. More Union infantry was coming up to help their outnumbered comrades, but there were an awful lot of veteran Confederates coming down the pike, and the steady roar of firing drew ever nearer to Gettysburg.

White-haired John Burns could stand it no longer. There was one hell of a scrap building up out the Chambersburg Pike. Robert E. Lee's rebels were only a ridge away from the town, *his* town, and old John wasn't going to sit there and let them take it without a fight.

And so John Burns, civilian and almost seventy, went into his neat two-story white house and got his flintlock rifle and a little ammunition. He had served in the War of 1812, John had, and he knew what it was to stand up to a tough, determined enemy. So be it, he thought, and trudged off through the heat of the day, headed for the sound of the guns.

John Burns found his war quickly enough. Out near the McPherson Farm he attached himself to the 150th Pennsylvania. This regiment wasn't quite certain what to do with a superannuated civilian, but just then the Pennsylvanians needed every man they could find. Anybody who wanted to fight was welcome. And so old John rammed home a charge and pitched into the fight.

John Burns was hit three times that long, hot afternoon, but he stuck, and he did his level best for his country, and his country remembered. He became something of a celebrity—the "Old Patriot—" and had his picture taken repeatedly. At least one photograph still survives. From it a ferocious-looking old man scowls at the camera, hurt but undiscouraged. He is sitting in a chair and nursing a bandaged leg, trusty flintlock leaning against a wall by his side.

That November the President of the United States came to Gettysburg. He, too, remembered old John Burns, and the two men worshiped together at the Presbyterian Church. Abraham Lincoln could appreciate John Burns better than most; the president knew all about fierce, uncompromising devotion to the Union. Burns had risked his life for it; not many months later, Lincoln would give his own.

TRIPLE CANISTER
CUSHING'S BATTERY AT GETTYSBURG

It was hot, baking, gasping, sweat-sucking hot, and there was no shade worthy of the name. Only beneath a little copse of trees was there any appreciable amount of shadow. It was gratefully shared by infantrymen of John Gibbon's 2d Division, and a regular army artillery battery commanded by a slight, almost girlish lieutenant. All along the gentle rise of ground men called Cemetery Ridge, the long blue lines waited, squinting through the heat waves at the Confederate positions along the swell of Seminary Ridge in front of them.

Away to the west, a mile or more, lay the rebel artillery line, and there was dust and movement there. There was no firing, but more and more batteries were swinging into line, unlimbering, leading their horses to the rear, heaving at the handspikes to lay their pieces on this ridge line.

The veterans of the Army of the Potomac watched with professional calm. What was Lee doing? Was he coming or going, retreating or getting set to come after them again? General Henry Hunt, the Union chief of artillery, watched also, sitting his horse on the ridge, his field glasses registering each detail of the rebel movement. It could be preparation to cover a retreat. But Lee was a ferocious fighter, always ready to attack, and Hunt, uneasy, began to tell battery commanders to hold their fire if the enemy opened on them.

The veterans of the Army of the Potomac could read the omens too. It looked like the rebs were coming for sure. Bobby Lee was going to have another go. And they began to look to their weapons.

Both Hunt and the blue troopers were right. Over across

those silent fields the cannon of Longstreet's and A. P. Hill's corps were being concentrated. With some help from guns of Ewell's corps to the north, they would try to beat down the Federal artillery behind the stone wall around that little copse of trees. And behind their roundshot and explosive shell would come fifteen thousand of the finest infantry in the world, men of Pickett's division, and Pettigrew's, the raw-boned veterans of the Army of Northern Virginia, the army that had never been whipped.

The Federal infantry around the little grove were Winfield Scott Hancock's men, the II Corps, lean, lathy, tough veterans. They knew those raggedy, hard-nosed gray men across the fields—they had seen their crimson battle flags take the wind again and again and fought them in a dozen bloody stand-up fights.

They knew fear, these Yankees, for they had "seen the elephant," as the veterans put it. But they were also confident in their own strength and experience. They were well led, and they knew it. Gimlet-eyed John Gibbon, their West Point division commander, had won undying fame as commander of the immortal Iron Brigade. The imperturbable Hancock was also a regular army man, jumped from captain to brigadier general to fill the Union's desperate need for capable officers. Both commanders cared about their men and worried about their welfare. And the soldiers knew it. What the division and the corps were told to do this day, they would do. They could not dream, this sleepy morning, how terribly hard it would be.

Everybody was hungry. Most of the Union soldiers had not eaten this long morning, and some had missed their dinner the night before. Only now, as the heat of noon settled down like a shroud, was food reaching some of the units. Down in the grove, where the stone wall turned at a right angle, the battery had drawn its rations, and an infantryman of the 69th Pennsylvania walked over to the gunners and successfully bummed a hatful of hardtack.

His benefactors were the regulars of Battery A, 4th U.S. Artillery, and they had already seen action that day. A little after seven o'clock five of Hill's guns had opened on the grove of trees. One of their rounds had exploded three of A Battery's limbers with a deafening roar, killing several men, but the rebel guns had ceased abruptly under the lashing counterbattery fire of Federal pieces, and the morning had been silent since.

At about eleven a stillness had settled over the ridge, a stillness so profound that men spoke in whispers sometimes, as if afraid to break the spell. Men cooked when they had something to cook, and nursed their water, which was in short supply that broiling July day. Some made coffee, some even slept, finding shade under caissons or trees if they could.

General Gibbon's servant had scrounged several large chickens of uncertain vintage. He had also produced an enormous loaf of bread, salvaged after chasing down a large hog who had purloined the loaf and eaten part of it. So the general entertained both his army and his corps commander and some staff officers. There were butter and coffee and potatoes, too, and if the chickens were ancient of days and almighty tough, they were "large and in good running order," and there was plenty to go around.

After their repast the generals lit cigars and talked about what might come this afternoon. Meade gave orders to return the provost marshal's guards to their units, where they would be of more use than chasing stragglers. This was done, and before sundown more than half the provost's excellent men were casualties.

Down in A Battery its commander watched the rebel lines. First Lieutenant Alonzo Cushing was from Wisconsin, of a pioneer family that would give three sons to the Union cause. He was a West Pointer, slim, soft-spoken, quiet, "more like a schoolgirl than a warrior." For all his quietness he had already won two brevet promotions for gallantry, and was described by one of his NCOs as "the best fighting man I ever saw." His regulars were experienced soldiers, ready and watchful, but just now concentrating on filling their bellies, as thoughtful veterans do.

And so the day wore on, until, a little after one o'clock, a little puff of white smoke rose lazily from the southern end of the confederate gun line, and a shell screamed up over Cemetery Ridge and exploded. It came from number one gun of 3d Company, the Washington Artillery of New Orleans, a flamboyant veteran unit. A second shot banged out just behind the first, and then the whole rebel line roared, and 140 guns poured shell and roundshot into the Union lines.

It would go on like that for the next hour and a half, at a rate of anything from sixty to one hundred rounds a minute, and the worst of it would fall on the center of Hancock's line, around the little clump of trees.

Everywhere the Union infantry took cover behind boulders and trees, in depressions and behind walls and fences. Artillery ammunition chests blew up, horses screamed and thrashed in pain, men cried out as they were hit. One man tried to hide behind a small rock, bent over facedown, "like a pagan worshiper before his idol." Gibbon's aide, Frank Haskell, spoke to him. "Do not lie there like a toad. Why not go to your regiment and be a man?" But the soldier was too far gone in fear to respond, and remained in his ungainly posture even when a shell blew his rock to fragments literally under his very nose.

Another soldier, returning to his unit loaded with freshly filled canteens, had the pack ripped from his back by a howling roundshot. He stopped for a moment, then plodded on again into the storm of iron, unhurt, even his uniform coat untouched by the death that had come so near. Others were not so lucky, as men and horses were ripped and pulverized by the Confederate guns, roundshot thudding dully into the ground, Whitworth rifle bolts ricocheting across the fields with a sound "like hot iron plunged in water."

And now into this chaos rode Hancock, dignified and unruffled, his staff and color-bearer behind him, and the infantry cheered him as he passed. His shirtfront gleamed impeccably white, as it always did, and he had traded in a skittish horse for a more docile animal. The best officers led from the front, then as now, and Hancock was as good as they came.

In his quiet way, Gibbon was doing some leading of his own. On foot he and his aide strolled down through the little clump of trees and walked forward to where the 69th Pennsylvania lay behind the stone wall, chatting with the soldiers. Then he went still farther forward, to sit and watch the rebel round shot arch up toward the Union lines. On his way he passed Brigadier General Alexander Webb, whose brigade held the angle, calmly sitting on the ground smoking his pipe. Surely the bluecoats by the clump of trees did not lack for example.

Now some of the Federal batteries began to reply. Hancock

himself ordered some of them to fire, to cheer his battered infantry. Others fired slowly, conserving their ammunition according to Hunt's cautious order. Others did not fire at all, in particular Colonel Freeman McGilvery's thirty-six pieces to the south of the angle, sited to sweep the flank of any attack directed at the grove of trees.

The Union gunners were veterans, too, coolly choosing their targets, unmoved by the iron that struck and killed all around them. One officer noted a gunner stretched out on the trail of his piece,

> setting off his elevations by 1, 2 and 3 finger breadths, just as he measured his whiskey in happier times . . . Suddenly a round shot carried away the head of No. 1, and his body fell across the gun breech—blood and brains . . . splashing the gunner . . . Deliberately the gunner wiped the ugly mess from his face, cleared his eyes, lifted the corpse from the gun . . . and resumed his post . . . with scarcely the loss of a count.

Hard men, these blue-coated gunners. They did not excite easily, and they did not panic at all. In the midst of all the death, their shooting would remain deliberate, and murderously accurate.

Around them the infantry began to die in ones and twos and sixes and sevens as the shells rained in. One soldier of the 15th Massachusetts was killed when a solid shot struck just in front of his prone body and passed underneath him. "He has passed over," said an officer, and indeed he had. The round had thrown him high in the air, clear over the rank of men behind him. He was stone dead, without a mark on him.

Up and down the infantry line, others died. Seven men of the 126th New York were blown up by a single shell. Raking fire from the northeast battered the II Corps batteries, one round shot killing six horses standing side by side. Young Cushing lost one or two guns, and was wounded slightly by a missile that carried away one of his shoulder straps. One of his gunners went hopping to the rear on one leg, the other only dangling shreds of skin. Others moaned in bloody agony or lay twisted in the final ugly rictus of death.

But the veterans took it. Many of the more philosophical drifted off to sleep amid the roar of the cannonade. Only

once did a handful of men start edging to the rear. A lieutenant drew his sword and suggested they remain in line. He
did not have to repeat his order. A few hardy souls collected
canteens and trudged through the heat and the shells to
bring water to their units. Returning, one of them wryly commented, "The water is cold enough, boys, but it's devilish hot
around the spring."

It was indeed, for many of the rebel rounds were going
over the ridge line. The infantry called these long rounds
"quartermaster chasers," shells and roundshot that missed
the foot soldiers to kill and maim the support troops behind
them. They burst with terrible effect among the artillery reserves and other men on the reverse slope.

But now the Federal artillery began to fall silent, gun by
gun. This cease-fire was largely deliberate, canny Colonel
Hunt determined to conserve the remaining ammunition
against the infantry assault he knew was coming. But some
of the Federal batteries around the angle had taken a fearful
pounding.

Cushing's was a wreck, dead and wounded men and
horses strewn everywhere, caissons exploded, guns dismounted. The young lieutenant had no unwounded officers,
and only enough healthy gunners to man a couple of pieces,
but those stayed in action. The devastation all around him
was appalling, a howling wilderness of shell fragments,
roundshot, flying stones and splinters. Near him one desperately wounded gunner drew his pistol and ended his own
misery.

Across the way Longstreet's chief of artillery, Alexander,
noticed the slackening of the Union fire and sent a desperate
note to Pickett: "For God's sake, come quick, or we cannot
support you. Ammunition nearly out."

They would come. "Old Peter" Longstreet did not approve
of the assault. "I don't want to make this charge," he said. "I
don't think it can succeed." His heart was full of foreboding
for his soldiers, but an order was an order. He nodded to the
expectant Pickett, who handed his commander a letter to his
fiancée, quickly scribbling on the corner a last word: "If Old
Peter's nod means death, then good-bye and God bless you,
little one."

Pickett would escape the iron hail this day, but thousands
of his soldiers would not, and Longstreet knew it. Old Peter's

nod meant death for them, and as Pickett turned his horse away, he saw a tear glisten in his corps commander's luxuriant beard.

Those who would make the attack knew what the odds were, too. There was a good deal of prayer, led by the chaplains kneeling in front of the ranks. And the brigade commanders took counsel together. Dick Garnett looked out across the mile of bare ground at the battle flags of the Army of the Potomac.

"It is a desperate thing to attempt," he said.

"It is," said the devout Lewis Armistead, "but the issue is with the Almighty, and we must leave it in His hands."

A terrified rabbit sprang from cover and ran madly toward the rear—as he did so, one of the soldiers spoke for all the confederate veterans: "Run, ol' hare," he said. "If I was a ol' hare, I'd run too."

But the Army of Northern Virginia was dead game. Almost to a man, it would rather take its chances out in that coverless field than flinch or hold back. Armistead turned to the color-bearer of the 53d Virginia infantry. "Sergeant," he said, "are you going to put those colors on the enemy's works today?"

"I'll try, sir," said the NCO, "and if mortal man can do it, it shall be done." And he, too, spoke for the waiting infantry.

And so, after an hour and a half of this murderous quarrel of artillery, the decision was coming. Out of the woodline across that wide field from the battered II Corps the gray skirmishers came, flicker of sun on steel bayonet and tin cup, well spread, coming slowly, saving their strength. For a little while they stopped, and stood motionless and silent.

And behind them came Pickett's Virginians, the brigades of veterans James Kemper, Richard Garnett, and Lewis Armistead. To their left were parts of two of A. P. Hill's divisions. There were two solid brigades of North Carolinians, the men of Dorsey Pender, mortally wounded in the fire of the second day. Brigadier General J. J. Pettigrew would lead them this day, lead them well and survive, only to die in the last moments of the withdrawal across the Potomac. Just now he was waving his men up the long, gentle slope, calling to a regimental officer behind him, "Now, Colonel, for the honor of the good Old North State, forward!"

With Pender's veterans were the four brigades of wounded

Harry Heth, down with a head wound, saved from death by a wad of paper he had used to make his too-big uniform hat fit him. Today his men were commanded by ferocious old Isaac Trimble, men from Mississippi and Alabama, Virginia and Tennessee, and more men of the Old North State.

It was a sight nobody would ever forget, the regiments in beautiful alignment, coming deliberately behind a forest of blue and crimson battle flags, bayonets winking in the sun. It was about three o'clock, and something grand and awful was happening, a nation dying and another nation coming of age, and it would all center around that insignificant grove of trees.

Thousands of men had a rendezvous with destiny here, and some had come a very long way to meet it. For Armistead it had started all the way back in 1861, in the sleepy little village called Los Angeles, where he was part of the tiny regular army garrison. He was a friendly man, and was brother-close to his comrades of the Old Army.

After Fort Sumter fell, the officers at Los Angeles had to decide. North or South, state or Union, which was it to be? Those who chose the South, Armistead, Pickett, and Dick Garnett among them, attended a party at Hancock's home. Toward the close of the evening General Albert Sidney Johnston's wife sang "Mary of Argyle" and "Kathleen Mavourneen," two of Johnston's favorites, and the shadows of happy past and dreadful future filled the little house. Armistead, tears pouring down his face, put his hands on Hancock's shoulders and said good-bye. "You will never know what this has cost me," he said.

And then he gave Mrs. Hancock a little satchel, to be sent on to his family in case of his death. To her he gave a prayer book, which she kept ever after. On the flyleaf was written: "Lewis A. Armistead. Trust in God and fear nothing." And those few simple words pretty well summed up "Lo" Armistead, upright, tough, the soul of honor. Mrs. Hancock would never see him again. But Hancock would see him at the last, a sturdy gray figure tramping through the swirling smoke toward the stone wall, black slouch hat on the point of his raised saber.

Maybe Hancock remembered his old friend's words this blazing afternoon as he sat his horse on the ridgeline and watched the gray men and the crimson flags and the shining bayonets come grandly across the open ground in front. Pickett was there, too, following his brigades. And Dick Garnett, too sick to walk, but clinging to his big black horse . . . and Armistead, on his way to pay the last installment on the awful price his love of Virginia had cost him.

He turned to his brigade: "Rise, men!" His voice carried down the ranks. "Men, remember what you are fighting for—your homes, your firesides, and your sweethearts. Follow me!"

And follow him they would, as they had into the smoke so many fights before, grim, silent, deliberate. No better infantry had ever walked, and these dusty tattered men were going to prove it again. Out in front there was a popping of musketry, and lazy little puffs of white smoke as the skirmishers began to engage. Up on the Union line men began to cock their rifles, and shift cap and cartridge boxes around where they could easily reach them. It was beginning.

The Confederate infantry moved down into a little swale, a depression that hid them from the vengeful Union guns a little while. There they checked their alignment, and moved out into the open in perfect order. There was no going back now; it was make or break. Somebody was going to get whipped, and who won would depend on who could stand the pounding longest.

The massive gray line swept aside the Union skirmishers and began to close. As the range came down to four hundred yards or so, the Federal batteries switched to canister, flimsy tin cans that ruptured at the gun's mouth and spewed a storm of metal balls into the faces of the rebel infantry. Down to the left of the angle McGilvery's cannon were sweeping the gray ranks from end to end, and the Virginians began to drift toward their left, away from those awful guns.

But still they came, and now the blue infantry thumbed back their hammers and squeezed off a thunderous volley, sending a hail of minié balls scything through the men plodding up the hill. Gibbon was up front with his men, coolly moving along the infantry line and reminding his soldiers to hold low—they were firing a little downhill, where the tendency is to overshoot. The rebels had begun to return the fire, and pushed on into the hail of metal "as if," an admiring northern correspondent wrote, "they courted death."

Over in front of the Union right Pettigrew's decimated

ranks had begun to falter, and some had started to recoil. They had been struck by an appalling blast of artillery, a horrible storm of canister that tore the heart from them. One Union officer heard "a moan . . . distinctly to be heard amid the storm of battle" as the Federal fire blew weapons, equipment, and fragments of bodies into the air.

But still some of Pettigrew's men and Pickett's Virginians came on, and Cushing had his men push one gun down close to the wall, where the Pennsylvania infantry were firing as fast as they could load. Cushing had been hit again, this time a horrible wound in the thighs and testicles. The lieutenant clutched his groin as he gave orders, blood running down between his fingers. Stephen Vincent Benét caught the moment precisely:

> Cushing ran the last of his guns to the battle line. The rest had been smashed to scrap by Lee's artillery fire. He held his guts in his hands as the charge came to the wall. And his gun spoke out for him once before he fell to the ground.

Cushing leaned on his First Sergeant Fuger, an outstanding ten-year regular NCO, and he called for triple canister. Now his three-inch rifles leaped madly at every discharge, each shot spewing almost 150 murderous iron balls into the faces of Pickett's troopers. Down the line to his left Stannard's Vermont regiments had pushed out from the Union line, then wheeled to their right, and were pouring volleys into the right flank of Pickett's suffering men.

But the dogged gray soldiers were running now, and the shrill howl of the rebel yell rang over the ceaseless din of rifles and cannon. One southern captain stopped long enough to give a drink of water to his dying soldier son, and then ran on toward the blazing Union line.

Suddenly the remains of Pickett's division were across the wall, wraiths of men running in out of the swirling cloud of powder-smoke, and Webb's Pennsylvanians were falling back. Armistead was over the stone wall, still in front, hat still impaled on his saber-point. "Who will follow me?" he roared, and the remnants of his Virginians ran panting into the fire. Armistead was still miraculously unwounded, within reach of Cushing's guns, and only a few steps from the destiny he had chosen so long ago in sleepy Los Angeles.

Cushing's last gun was silent now, and the gallant young lieutenant had gone beyond the terrible ordeal of command at last, dead of a merciful rebel bullet that had entered his mouth and cut his spine. He had served to the last, his thumb burned to the bone from stopping the touchholes of his red-hot cannon while they were swabbed out between rounds.

First Sergeant Fuger was leading what was left of his gunners in a wild melee around the guns, a bloody brawl with bayonets, revolvers, handspikes, rammers, and bare hands. Hancock galloped to the point of crisis, shouting his orders to nearby regiments. "Go in there pretty Goddamned quick!" he roared, and the blue infantry ran down into that awful bloodbath in the little grove.

Webb's officers were bringing their men back, and from all sides Union soldiers were running in to help at the angle. The Union line sagged and bent, but it did not break. The file-closers of the 19th Massachusetts Infantry locked their hands together and strained against the pressure in front, strained with all their strength to hold their battered line in place.

Nobody was really in command anymore. Gibbon was down with a bullet in his shoulder, and another slug knocked Hancock from his horse, burying a saddle nail and other debris deep in the general's thigh. From all directions northern soldiers simply ran toward the heart of the fighting and pitched in, men from New York and Massachusetts, and more Pennsylvanians.

Gibbon's aide, Lieutenant Haskell, on his own initiative galloped to Gibbon's other brigade commanders. The line was breaking; could they help? They could, and without hesitation or question they sent their men pounding over toward the little clump of trees to get into the fight. Webb's three little regiments would have the help they needed.

Down the hill, Armistead still strode untouched through the fire, but Garnett and Kemper were both down, and with them virtually every regimental commander in Pickett's division. But the crimson battle flags came on, man after man falling, eager hands catching the precious colors and carrying them forward.

Hunt, the federal chief of artillery, could no longer control anything. His batteries were on their own, loading and firing with desperate haste, slamming double and triple loads of canister into the faces of the rebel infantry, or cutting their fuses to burst at the cannon's mouth. So Hunt was down there, in the smoke and dust, firing his revolver into the rebel infantry.

Officers and enlisted men simply fought it out with their enemies face-to-face. Armistead recognized his enemies. "It's the Philadelphia Brigade. Give them the cold steel, boys!" And then he, too, was down, gallant commander, and his men could stand no more. Back they went into the smoke and the dust, slowly and grudgingly, and then faster and faster, until at last the rebels began to edge away, and suddenly the gray tide lapped back over the wall and down the hill, and the southern dream was finished forever.

Now there was that awful mile to walk again, and the pitiful remnants of Pickett's and Pettigrew's men fell back across that open, coverless ground, still hammered by Union musketry and guns. Some pieces of units still hung together, some even halting to fire defiantly at the blue lines. But many, many went back in twos and threes and fours, helping their wounded friends, using rifles as crutches, staggering back across that endless mile.

Back by the trees and the angle rebels were surrendering. All around them was the horrible litter of war, the dead and the dying and the men shrieking in pain. Amid the heaps of gray and butternut was the crimson and blue of many battle flags, proud banners crumpled in the dust because there was nobody left to care for them. There were more than three thousand Confederate casualties strewn across that dreadful field, and another couple of thousand missing. Most of those were dead, too, or hurt, or just so dazed that they had simply wandered away from the war.

Lee rode out into that terrible field to see his men home. He moved among them, rallying and encouraging, gentle and fatherly. And as a brigade commander reported his awful losses, tears in his eyes, Robert E. Lee shook his commander's hand, and took the blame for the repulse where he knew it belonged, on his own great heart.

"Never mind, General Wilcox," said Marse Robert. "All this has been my fault. It is I that have lost this fight, and you must help me out of it the best way you can."

Back at the angle, Armistead was dying. He had gotten as

far as one of Cushing's guns, and had his hand upon it, when he was struck by several bullets. Even as he fell, a Union colonel was urging his horse through the melee, trying to reach this courageous rebel, knock him down, and save him.

But it was over for Armistead, all of it, the charge, the war, the gallant life. Union soldiers began to carry him to the rear for medical help, but there would be no saving him. As his day faded swiftly into night, Lieutenant Mitchell, Hancock's aide, dismounted to ask the Confederate officer if he could do anything for him.

Yes, said Armistead, as his life ebbed away. Yes. And he gave his watch and spurs to Mitchell, asking that they be taken to his old friend Hancock, to be kept for Armistead's relatives. He asked also to be taken to Hancock's tent, but was told the General was wounded himself.

Mitchell delivered these small mementos to Hancock as the general lay nursing his own serious wound, and then Hancock let himself be carried from the field. His job was done. He had held his line, made his report to Meade, and urged immediate pursuit of the rebels. His troops were no longer in danger, and he could rest.

There is a story that Armistead sent a message to his old friend, a message that included these words, or something like them:

Tell Hancock I have done him and my country a great injustice which I shall never cease to regret.

Maybe so, maybe Armistead did say something like that. But it is far more probable that the aide did not hear the dying officer clearly, or maybe the aide elaborated on what he thought he heard, or maybe the newspapers invented it all, because it was surely good copy. On balance, the probabilities are very much that the words attributed to Armistead are apocryphal. As one writer neatly put it, "Armisteads don't die that way."

Down at the angle, Cushing's battery was only wreckage. None of its guns was serviceable, and none could be moved. Of the battery's ninety horses, eighty-three were dead. Casualties among the men exceeded 50 percent. The redoubtable

Fuger remained in command, cleaned up the field as best he could, and cared tenderly for his commander's body. Fuger would be commissioned for this day's dreadful work, and would finish his military career long years thence as a colonel.

Pickett's Charge cost the Confederacy terrible losses. In addition to the veteran infantry, the loss in officers was dreadful. In Pickett's division alone, two of three brigade commanders were dead, the third badly wounded. Twelve of the fifteen regimental commanders had been killed, two more wounded.

A British Guards officer, watching the fight, admiringly gave the rebel infantry their finest eulogy . . . and their obituary. He praised the Confederate troops warmly, "but," he added, "they will never do it again. Don't you see your system feeds upon itself? You cannot fill the places of these men . . . Your men do wonders, but every time at a cost you cannot afford." And the Englishman was right, of course. These dead and mangled men were the best the South had left. There were no more Armisteads and Garnetts and Kempers. They could not be replaced.

And so the last day of Gettysburg petered out in exhaustion, and a final spiteful spatter of musketry. Both sides were fought out, too hurt to start up the carnage again. And it began to rain, torrents of water accompanied by a spectacular thunderstorm. At first the rain brought some relief for the parched survivors and the wounded, but later relief changed to misery as the soil turned to mud, and the deluge soaked the southern wounded as they jounced horribly in springless wagons back to the Potomac and safety. Seventeen miles their wagon train stretched, seventeen miles of dying and indescribable suffering.

Their day of martyrdom was the Fourth of July, the birthday of America, and far away Vicksburg was surrendering, and the South was forever cut in two. It was all over, although no one could clearly see it then. There was still a lot of dying to be done before the guns fell silent for keeps.

In years long after, Pennsylvanians and Virginians would meet again at the little stone wall. There would be hand shaking and picture taking and a lot of story telling. And one hot day there was a keg of cold beer at the angle, and the rebel veterans joked that had there been beer in the little grove that faraway afternoon, nobody could have driven them away. The old wounds were starting to heal.

HAIL AND FAREWELL

It was a dreary, sickly morning, this twelfth of April, 1865. It was a day of dying, of mourning, for it was the last day in the life of the Army of Northern Virginia. The surrender was signed. U. S. Grant, the sword arm of the North, had already left Appomattox. He would not stay to gloat, or seem to. In spite of Grant's very generous surrender terms, he knew how terrible this day would be for the ragged, proud men in Confederate gray. For on this pale, chilly day the army would lay down its arms forever. And it would do so under the eyes of its old enemy, the Army of the Potomac, its foe and companion through so many days of agony and pride and hurt and gallantry. And it would make its last march with its head up, in spite of its tattered clothing.

The Army of Northern Virginia began to stir early in its camps on the rain-soaked ground. And then it formed, regiment after decimated regiment, and began to march in silence down to the place where it would stack arms for the last time. It still carried its battle flags proudly, except those few already hidden by the men of the regiments, or torn into small pieces as precious keepsakes of better days.

On the rebels came in silence, no drum, no bugle, only the sound of tired feet in the mud of the road, and the rattle of tin cup and bayonet frog and saber scabbard. In front rode John Gordon at the head of II Corps, behind him a mass of crimson where the flags flew close together over the remains of great regiments. A Union officer was struck by the sight:

The regimental battle flags crowded so thick by thinning out of men that the whole column seemed crowned with red.

The Union soldiers watched in silence. They did not cheer, or laugh, or speak, or call out. Like Grant, they would not gloat. No bands played. And at last, ahead of them, on both sides of the road, the southerners saw a mass of blue, the precise ranks of the 1st Division of V Corps, United States Army, its own battle flag and the national colors at the right of the line. By the colors was a little cluster of northern officers, including Brigadier General Joshua Chamberlain, who watched Gordon's weary men approach.

And then, as the silent gray column drew near, a magical, wonderful thing happened, a heart-tugging thing nobody there would ever forget. Chamberlain gave an order, and a bugle call split the dreary day like lightning through midnight gloom. Regiment after regiment, the Union division came to "carry arms," the marching salute, a last honor to a respected enemy.

Gordon's sword snapped down in acknowledgment, and he turned in his saddle to order his men to return the salute. Good-bye, good-bye, we fought you as hard as we knew how, but oh, how we admired you.

General Chamberlain put it pretty well:

On our part not a sound of trumpet more, nor roll of drum; not a cheer nor word nor whisper of vain-glorying . . . but an awed silence rather, and breath-holding, as if it were the passing of the dead.

After this came the stacking of arms, and it was all over. But at least it had ended in respect, whatever might come later.

TWELVE TO ONE
The Fight at Beecher's Island

It was hot and silent, and the world was empty. The grassy buffalo country of northeastern Colorado stretched away to the horizon in all directions as far as the eye could see. Through this flat, lush land meandered the Arikaree Fork of the Republican River, now almost dry in the baking heat of mid-September.

Major Forsyth was not enjoying the tranquility around him, for he was following Indian sign, a broad, unmistakable trail well chewed up by many horses and many travois. There were a great many Indians somewhere ahead of him, the best light cavalry in the world. And they were hostile, and the trail was fresh.

Forsyth constantly checked his little command. He had forty-eight men with him, mostly civilians, some of them experienced frontier hands, some not, about half of them veterans of either the Union or the Confederate armies. Many of these had held commissions during the war. They were an unknown quantity in a fight, but at least they were hard-nosed, willing, hardy, and well armed. In the event, it was as well that they were.

General Sheridan was now commander of the Department of the Missouri, an enormous area of vast empty spaces roamed at will by horse Indians, many of them actively hostile. They had abandoned their reservations during the agony of the Civil War, and they did not want to return, determined to resist the march of the foreign civilization remorselessly eating up their lands. The railroad, symbol of settlement, was headed for Denver, and was already at Fort Wallace, Kansas. The Sioux and Cheyenne were both out, and in a single month had killed or captured more than eighty men, many with families. They struck at isolated homesteads, and at railroad gangs, and were gone before pursuit could begin.

To make matters worse, Sheridan was very short of troops. And so he had called on Forsyth, whose ability he knew, to raise a civilian force of fifty men to scout against the plains Indians, and to command that force. "Sandy" Forsyth had little trouble enlisting his fifty around the army posts of Fort Hays and Fort Harker, a little way east of Hays on the line of the Kansas-Pacific Railroad. For want of other specific authority, Forsyth signed them up as employees of the Quartermaster Department, to draw one dollar a day, plus thirty cents a day for the use of their horses. He also promised that the United States would pay for any horse used up during the campaign. In the event, the government was going to buy a lot of horses.

Forsyth himself was new to Indian fighting, but he was a good officer, onetime Civil War aide to little Phil Sheridan, and had ridden with the little general on that famous ride at Winchester. He had enlisted in 1861 as a private soldier in an Illinois dragoon company, and finished the conflict as a brevet brigadier. And he had brought along an experienced second-in-command, First Lieutenant Frederick H. Beecher of the 3d Infantry, a Civil War veteran who had shown conspicuous gallantry at Gettysburg.

Forsyth's first sergeant, W. H. H. McCall, had been a brigadier general of Pennsylvania volunteers, and he, too, had a record of great courage under fire. The column was guided by a veteran scout, Abner (Sharp) Grover, and an experienced physician, Dr. John H. Mooers, rode along as surgeon to the expedition.

Forsyth was confident of the equipment of his untested little force. His men carried the dependable Colt Army revolver and the Spencer carbine, a lever-action repeater holding seven rounds of .52 caliber ammunition, fed from a tube in the butt of the weapon. It was state-of-the-art firepower for 1868. And Forsyth, though traveling light in other respects, had required each of his men to carry 170 rounds, and had 4,000 more in reserve on his pack animals. He would need them.

Otherwise, the scouts carried no extras. Besides their weapons, ammunition, and horse furniture, each carried a blanket, a tin cup, a knife, and a haversack. There were rations for a week and a few medical supplies, but no tents or other luxuries. The major would not be weighed down with extras.

Forsyth's scout company had left Fort Hays, Kansas, on August 29, looking for sign of hostiles. His initial scout had at first been fruitless. Eight days out of Hays, he had paused at Fort Wallace, far up the Smoky Hill River, almost to the Colorado line. There he loaded seven days' rations, and received word that a band of Cheyenne had struck a wagon train near Sheridan City, a short distance east. Moving quickly to the site of the attack, he picked up the hostiles' trail and began to follow it to the north.

It did not last long. By next morning the trail was cold, the war party having split up, as usual, to confuse pursuit. But Forsyth didn't quit. He pushed on to the north, aiming always for the headwaters of the Republican, excellent buffalo country, and therefore much frequented by the Indians. And his guess had been correct—the only trouble was, he was following something much bigger and more dangerous than a hit-and-run war party. Moreover, his rations were almost gone, and some of his men had already suggested that it was time to turn back.

The little column guessed the Indians knew they were being followed, for they came upon fresh meat, cooking utensils, and similar camp items dropped along the trail and left there, things that the Indians normally would have stopped to collect.

And so the hot afternoon of the sixteenth of September dragged on, until the little column came upon a small valley, covered with grass and about two miles in each direction. Down its center ran what was left of the Arikaree Fork of the Republican, and at the point where Forsyth stopped to make camp there was a little island in the middle of the stream. It was well covered with brush and grass, and a decent place to make a fight if trouble came.

Forsyth took great care. He posted the guards himself, and saw to it that the animals were picketed close in for the night. Meanwhile, Sharp Grover and young Simpson E. (Jack) Stilwell walked over and took a look at the little island. It was certainly the best place around to make a stand, about in the middle of the almost dry Arikaree, some 140 yards from bank to bank.

Forsyth reckoned he would make contact the next day, striking the Indians somewhere upstream of his bivouac. But here he miscalculated. There were indeed two large villages nearby, but they were *down*stream of his position, not the other way. They were Sioux, Pawnee Killer's Oglalas, and the Cheyenne dog soldiers of Tall Bull, White Horse, and Bull Bear, and there were six or seven hundred of them. And among the dog soldiers was the fabled warrior Roman Nose, no chief, but a powerful leader in war, with medicine that made him invincible. To make matters worse, their scouts had seen Forsyth's little column and had been stalking him all day.

The Indians had also miscalculated. Forsyth was actually moving away from their villages, and the Sioux and Cheyenne assumed he must be moving downstream toward them instead. And so they looked without result throughout the sixteenth, and on into the night. Finally they had camped, puzzled, all but eight young braves, who pushed on up the Arikaree. And these men saw Forsyth's fires very early on the seventeenth, just at the break of dawn, and kicked their horses toward the camp, intent on surprising the white men in their bedding.

But Forsyth, good soldier that he was, was up and alert, and caught the movement of the eight braves just as they struck the camp. He and a guard opened fire, rousing the rest of the scouts, as the Indians dashed through the bivouac, cutting out two horses and two mules. Forsyth gave the order to saddle up. Whatever was to happen next, it was better not to wait for it on foot.

The little group of scouts never made it. For the main body of Indians was not far behind the daring young braves, and had already spotted Forsyth's camp. The Oglalas and Cheyenne did not hesitate. They kicked their ponies to a gallop, spread into a long line, and rode flat out for the little grassy valley.

Grover and others saw them on their way in, and Forsyth made an instant—and correct—decision. Their only chance of survival was the island, and he immediately ordered his command to make for that dubious refuge, pulling their frantic horses with them. Forsyth was one of the last to reach shelter, personally making certain the reserve ammunition was brought along.

On the island, the scouts tied their horses in a rough circle and began to pour fire from their Spencers into the tidal wave of Indians bearing down on them. The blast of fire was a surprise to the onrushing braves, and their mass charge—a rare thing in Indian warfare—split on both sides of the island, passing it by and taking casualties from the heavy Spencer bullets.

They quickly took up positions on both banks of the river and began to pour gunfire and showers of arrows into the little island. The pitiful horses died quickly, and Forsyth's men began to cry out and slump as slugs and arrows found them. Somebody yelled that they must leave, and not stay behind to be shot down like dogs. Forsyth instantly hefted his Colt and snarled that he would personally kill any man who tried to leave. There was no more talk of running.

Under the hail of Indian missiles, the scouts dug frantically with knives and tin cups and tin plates and bare hands, pausing from time to time to return the Indians' fire. Little by little they deepened their rifle pits, tossing the dirt up around them to form a parapet, for the fire was coming from all directions. Throughout this critical early stage of the fight Forsyth remained erect, walking calmly around his tiny perimeter, indifferent to the cloud of bullets and arrows all around him.

And then, suddenly, Forsyth was down, a bullet in his right thigh. Almost instantly he was hit again, his left leg shattered by a bullet. Dr. Mooers dragged him into a rifle pit, but it was not long until the gallant major's skull was fractured by still a third bullet. But Sandy Forsyth was made of iron and whipcord, and he was not about to quit. Conscious and in terrible pain, he nevertheless remained in command, urging on his men as they hammered back still another mass charge down the Arikaree.

The afternoon dragged on, and one by one the little band of scouts were hit. And another charge was making up, and this time Roman Nose would lead it. The great war leader had held back from the fight up to now, for he believed that the magic of his war bonnet, the extraordinary medicine that had kept him bulletproof until now, had been broken. But he had been taunted by another warrior, and now, convinced he would die in the attack, he let shame push him into joining the charge.

Watching the charge forming up, Forsyth shouted orders to cease fire, reload, and wait for his order. The island was quiet as Roman Nose and the hundreds behind him broke into a trot and then a gallop, and poured like a flash flood down the bed of the Arikaree. Then, at a range of about fifty yards, Forsyth shouted the command to fire, and the scouts poured carbine fire into the Indian front as fast as they could work the Spencers. The charge broke on that deadly little island, and as the dust of his third assault drifted away, Roman Nose was dead in the sand of the dry riverbed.

Now the evening began to close down, and a drizzle of rain began to fall. It was balm to the embattled men on the little island, those who could still feel it. For Dr. Mooers was dying, shot through the forehead, and Lieutenant Beecher was dying as well. After Roman Nose's charge had broken, Beecher crawled over to Forsyth to tell him matter-of-factly he was mortally hurt.

"No, Beecher," said Forsyth. "It cannot be as bad as that."

"Yes," said the lieutenant simply. "Good night." He would die by sundown.

Two other scouts were dead, and two more were mortally wounded. Seventeen more were wounded, several of them badly, including Major Forsyth. A scout named Farley lay with a bullet in his shoulder. Near him his father, dying, had still fought all through the day. He died with the evening. Scout Harrington had been struck in the forehead by an arrow early in the fighting. He had jerked loose the shaft, but the arrowhead remained embedded in his flesh. A little later on an Indian bullet knocked the arrowhead from its wound without injuring the scout badly. He simply tied a piece of cloth around the wound and reloaded his Spencer. He would survive the action.

The iron major was still in command, rising above his pain, and there was still plenty of ammunition. Under the kind shelter of darkness, the scouts dug a well and hacked off enough horsemeat to make a meal. The wounded were moved to a new pit dug in the island's center, and Forsyth called for volunteers for a terribly hazardous mission.

For the major knew they would all die in this place unless help came. The nearest assistance was at Fort Wallace, about

125 miles away to the south, and somebody would have to get to the fort and tell of their plight. Two men answered the major's call. One was young Jack Stillwell, nineteen years old and afraid of nothing. The other was hunter Pierre Trudeau, an old man, but wise in the ways of the frontier. As soon as it was full dark, the two men disappeared into the darkness, and the remaining scouts waited for the dawn. In the distance they could hear chanting as the Indians mourned their dead.

Daylight brought more Indian fire, but the pressure was a little less. The Oglalas and Cheyennes had learned the terrible power of the Spencers and Colts, and the few charges that they began were not pressed home. The third day was much the same, a desultory exchange of rifle-fire and arrows, but without massed attacks. That night another pair of volunteers—John Donovan and Allison Pliney—slipped out into the darkness, carrying a written dispatch addressed to the commanding officer at Fort Wallace.

As the fourth morning of the siege dawned, the defenders were in desperate straits. Conditions on the island were ghastly, as the wounded—some of them delirious—suffered horrors from maggot-infested wounds, and Dr. Mooers died early in the day. Forsyth, still in command, decided he had suffered enough from the ache and throb of the bullet in his right leg. And so, bending forward to reach the wound, he opened his straight razor and carved and probed until he found and removed the bullet. He could do little about the maggots.

To make matters worse, the specter of hunger joined the horrors of infected wounds. The horsemeat had turned rotten in the September sun, and there were no rations. As the fourth day passed, and the fifth, and the sixth, the cramp of starving bellies added to their misery. There was a little cactus, some wild plums, and a coyote who walked into the island, but those meager rations would not keep the little band alive.

They had seen no large groups of Indians after day six, but nobody could be sure the dog soldiers and the Oglala were actually gone. And even if they were, they could return at any time. In any case, without horses the wounded could not be moved any distance. It was better to abide the maggots and the pain and the empty bellies and wait.

And so at last on the morning of the twenty-fifth of September, the ninth morning of the siege, one of the scouts picked up movement on the far-off hills. Squinting into the haze, he hoped against hope that the distant horsemen were not the Indian enemy, returning for a fresh attack. And then he whooped in joy, for the riders wore Federal blue, and there was an ambulance in the faraway column. Help had come at last.

The help was a company of buffalo soldiers of the all-black 10th Cavalry, led by Captain Louis H. Carpenter. Trudeau and Stilwell, moving under cover of night, had reached Fort Wallace in five days—twenty-five miles a day in hostile country.

It had been a hard time for Trudeau and Stilwell. Carrying their boots, they had gotten clear of the island in the darkness, crawling almost two miles before dawn, then lying up during the day. The next two nights they made good progress, passing groups of Indians unseen.

But the next morning came the worst time of all. Hidden in a shallow buffalo wallow, the only shelter available, the two men lay almost without breathing as a large war party halted within a hundred feet of them. And then into the wallow crawled a rattlesnake. Unable to move, or to hit or shoot the snake, young Stilwell nailed the unwelcome reptile with repeated gouts of tobacco juice across its head. The rattler, disgusted, crawled away without rattling or striking, and the two men waited out the war party, which rode on within a half hour.

And so they came to Fort Wallace, dirty, hungry, and exhausted, and made their report. The commander at Wallace, Lieutenant Colonel Henry C. Bankhead, had immediately sent a galloper after Captain Carpenter, then scouting west from Cheyenne Wells. Bankhead then immediately set about assembling a relief column of his own, with tough young Stilwell as his guide.

Carpenter was an old friend of Sandy Forsyth, and the two had served together on Sheridan's staff. He turned north immediately, alternately trotting and walking his horses, and when the command snatched a few hours' sleep that night, it had covered an astonishing forty-five miles. Next day he and his troopers pushed hard north, striking the Dry Fork of the Republican after a twenty-mile march.

Carpenter, unsure of his location, followed this branch for a while, to be certain he would not miss Forsyth, then turned north again, riding up on the Arikaree and striking a broad, fresh Indian trail. He then bivouacked for the night, and the next morning overtook Donovan. Donovan had also slipped through the Sioux and Cheyenne, reached Fort Wallace in the meantime, left the exhausted Pliney there, and was now loyally pushing on with five men recruited at Fort Wallace, back to his embattled unit.

Now guided by Donovan, and sure of his location, Carpenter took thirty men and an ambulance and pushed hard upstream, galloping into the island to the wild delight of Forsyth's exhausted men. Their thirty-one-year-old eagle of a commander was sitting up reading *Oliver Twist* as the maggots crawled in his gaping leg wound.

Forsyth's people were moved about a half mile from the island, away from the horrific stench of bloating animal corpses, and the surgeon went to work. The doctor wanted to amputate the major's shattered, infected leg, but Forsyth would have none of it. Another scout was not so fortunate, and lost his leg to the doctor's field surgery in the valley by the Arikaree.

Lieutenant Colonel Bankhead's column, complete with a surgeon and two howitzers, rode into Beecher's Island the next day, and the whole column then moved slowly back to Fort Wallace. Lieutenant Beecher was buried where he had fallen after the custom of the day, Dr. Mooers and the others beside him. Six scouts had died on the island, and fifteen more had been wounded. Indian losses, as usual, were very hard to establish with any accuracy. Forsyth estimated they had suffered thirty-two dead and perhaps a hundred wounded; the Indians would not admit to more than nine dead, including Roman Nose. Another estimate puts the Indian losses as high as seventy-five dead and two hundred seriously wounded. Considering the violence of the close-range fighting, and the firepower provided veteran fighting men by the Spencers, Forsyth's estimate seems conservative.

Only the name now remains of Beecher's Island, long since washed away by the waters of the Arikaree. Sandy Forsyth faced two years of agony from his wounds, but in the end would emerge more or less whole, a brevet brigadier general. In later years, still on active service, he chased Geronimo and other Apache leaders through the Southwest, still the careful but daring commander. Whatever he may have experienced in those later years, we may be reasonably certain nothing eclipsed those dreadful days of pain in the heat and squalor of Beecher's Island, when young Major Forsyth refused to think of quitting.

LAST POST

February 1891. William Tecumseh Sherman was dead. Outside the general's New York home there was an ocean of black crepe, muffled drums, soldiers with arms reversed, all the panoply of a military funeral. And it had rained that chill winter day, drearily, steadily, as if the heavens joined in the nation's gloom.

Perhaps even more than U. S. Grant, Sherman had been the Union's hero, symbol of a nation's determination to have its victory, and damn the price. No soldier could have been harder, grimmer, more determined. No soldier better understood the horror of war. No soldier did more to end it.

Sherman had fought through it all, from bloody Shiloh to the end. He had left a swath of destruction ninety miles wide from Atlanta to the sea. He had made himself deeply hated in the South. For Sherman was a very modern soldier. He knew that wars are meant to be finished, finished any way you have to do it, and damn the blood and destruction.

But this grim soldier knew something else as well. He understood clearly that the men of the South fought from deep conviction, just as he did. He knew that this bloody victory would be wasted, all the lives and treasure, unless the two ends of the country got on with the business of becoming one, again and forever. And so, once the powder-smoke had blown away, he had buried any animus he may have had, and done what he could to help the healing.

And that is why, among the honorary pallbearers standing in the damp and cold, there stood the erect, soldierly figure of General Joseph E. Johnston, late Army of the Confederate States: old opponent, old friend, Confederate soldier par excellence. Bareheaded he stood in the cold, as Sherman's casket, covered with his country's flag, was carried to the waiting caisson.

Johnston was an old man, eighty-four that very month, veteran of the war against Mexico and every weary mile of the Civil War's long road. No doubt he should have been seated comfortably by a cozy fireside that bitter day. He had earned his rest many times over. But there he stood, bareheaded, for Sherman and for America.

A concerned bystander leaned forward. "General, please put on your hat; you might get sick."

But Johnston would not. His warrior's heart would not let him deny his old friend a soldier's last honor.

"If I were in his place," Johnston said, "and he were standing here in mine, he would not put on his hat."

Ten days later, Joe Johnston was dead. He had crossed over that same placid river for which Stonewall Jackson had called out in his own last moments. And he had died of pneumonia, pneumonia contracted that bitter day on which he stood bareheaded to honor his friend.

It is pleasant to think that as he went to make his final report, he met William Tecumseh Sherman, hat in hand.

THE BIGGEST FIGHT OF ALL
KIT CARSON AT ADOBE WALLS

The spring and summer of 1864 were a bad time along the Santa Fe Trail and the lonely uplands of Colorado and New Mexico. From the time the new grass would support Indian ponies, the clear skies were smudged with the smoke of burning homesteads and settlers' wagons. Lonely graves multiplied along the vast, unforgiving reaches of those unsettled lands.

For the Cheyenne, the Comanche, and the Kiowa were out, and no life was safe along the Santa Fe trail. "No train crossed the plains without being attacked," wrote an officer of volunteers. Even those ranches and wagon trains on which no lives were lost were stripped bare of livestock.

Far to the east blue and gray armies hammered at one another in the last bloody summer of the Civil War. There were no regular soldiers to spare for the western lands, and precious few volunteers, and the horse Indians knew it. And so, as the fair weather came to the empty spaces and the snow melted, they painted for war.

To be sure, the Comanche and Kiowa had a grievance. They owned, they said, all the land from Texas to the Platte. They had agreed to the white man's use of the Santa Fe Trail, but now the whites were spreading all over the country, *their* country. Since the white man was an oath-breaker, there would be war.

In the autumn of 1862 the Comanches had destroyed the Wichita Agency. The next summer they harried the settlements along the Texas border. Now they carried fire and death along the Santa Fe Trail, vital artery of supply, not only for New Mexico and points west, but for the California and

New Mexico volunteers in Union blue. Something had to be done, and quickly.

General James Carleton was just the man to do it, and he had the right weapon at hand. Carleton commanded the United States Department of New Mexico. He had few soldiers to spare, and those local volunteers, but he had the very best of leaders, a man whose very name symbolized success against odds. He called for Kit Carson.

Carson's name was legend across the sprawling lands of Colorado and New Mexico. He had been mountain man, trader, soldier, and Indian fighter extraordinary, victor against odds in dozens of skirmishes with hostile Indians. It was he who had finally driven into the canyon lair of the elusive and ferocious Navajos, and vanquished that defiant people. Just now Carson was colonel of New Mexico Volunteers, and he answered Carleton's call.

Carson, barrel-chested and stocky, was graying now. He still had the square jaw and keen blue eyes of his youth, but the years had told on him. He had less than three years to live as he rode in to take command of General Carleton's expedition. He already carried in his chest the aneurism that would kill him. But for now he was still the active, decisive, careful commander. It was as well he was—he was soon to ride into what was probably the biggest Indian fight in western history. He would need all his skills.

Carleton's orders were simple; Carson's discretion was complete. His superior's orders left decision to him:

> I . . . desire that you give those Indians, especially the Kiowas, a severe dubbing . . . I do not wish to embarrass you with minute instructions. You know where to find the Indians; you know what atrocities they have committed; you know how to punish them; . . . now all the rest is left with you.

As the leaves fell and the first snow flurries swirled in out of the north, Colonel Carson began to gather forces at Fort Bascom, down on the Canadian River near the Texas line. General Carleton's intelligence reported that the Comanches and Kiowas—together with some Arapaho and Kiowa Apaches—were going into winter quarters along Palo Duro Creek, near the Canadian. As the cavalry horse walked, they would be some two hundred miles down the Canadian from Fort Bascom.

There would be several large villages, perhaps four to five thousand adults altogether. If they could be found, and their camps destroyed, next summer's menace might be blunted before it began. Other horse Indians had been and would be similarly conquered in winter campaigns, their people scattered, their horses captured or killed, their lodges and food and buffalo robes burned.

Carson scraped up men from all across the New Mexico Territory, nearly all of them either California or New Mexico volunteers, 14 officers and 321 enlisted personnel. Carson was able to form five companies of cavalry and two of infantry. One of his units was Company K, 1st California Volunteer Infantry, commanded by a hard-nosed young lieutenant named George Pettis. Pettis' undermanned unit served two lilliputian cannon, small mountain howitzers that threw a twelve-pound shell.

These little guns were smoothbores, handling all the same munitions as their bigger sisters, the famous twelve-pound Napoleons. They were much smaller, however. The bronze tube was less than three feet long and weighed only 220 pounds. The carriage weighed in at 157 pounds; a pair of wheels was lighter still. The weapon's range at five degrees elevation was only nine hundred yards, as compared to over sixteen hundred for the Napoleon.

The howitzer would break down into a two-horse load. Or, as Carson's men probably did it, the small trail of the piece could be attached to a single horse by two poles. It was then towed, without a limber. In any case, the ammunition was packed eight rounds to a box. One box, weighing 112 pounds, was strapped to each side of a horse's or mule's packsaddle.

Carson also found a regular army officer to handle his supplies, a surgeon to care for his sick and wounded, twenty-seven supply wagons, and an ambulance. Finally, he recruited seventy-two Indians to scout and screen his movements. A few were Jicarilla Apache, but most were Utes, including their chief, Ka-ni-ache, a longtime friend of Carson. Both tribes were eager to strike at their hereditary enemies, the Kiowa and Comanche, and thirsting for loot. Carson ar-

ranged to equip them, provide them with much-prized coffee
and sugar, and feed their families while they were away.

And so, on the sixth of November, Carson and his little
army splashed across the Canadian and plodded east along
the north bank of the river. They followed the old Mexican
wagon road from New Mexico, a road unused for years. Carson did not hurry, and moved warily. He knew his enemy,
and knew that the slightest lack of caution could destroy his
little command. The soldiers and their Indian scouts found
nothing at first, however, and for the next two weeks they
found more of the same.

On the fifteenth, still having seen no hostiles, the column
camped at Canada de los Ruedes—"wheel gulch." Here the
Mexican trains had stopped in the old days, repairing their
wheels from the stand of large cottonwoods that still grew
there. Here the old Mexican road veered due north. Carson
determined to press on east, following a long-disused Indian
trail along the river.

For the soldiers, the days were notably chiefly for the cold.
Snowstorms held up the march for two days. The nights
were worse. As the troops tried to sleep, the Utes and
Apaches made the night hideous with interminable dancing
and singing in preparation, as the soldiers thought, for war.
Lieutenant Pettis wrote afterward that the war dance

> . . . became almost intolerable, it being kept up on each night
> until nearly daybreak, and until we became accustomed to
> their groans and howlings incident to the dance, it was impos-
> sible to sleep.

At last, late on the twenty-fourth, the command halted
near Arroya de la Mula (Mule Spring) in the Texas Panhan-
dle, about thirty miles west of a desolate place called Adobe
Walls, a place Carson's command would come to know well
before another day was out. Carson's Indian scouts fanned
out into the empty spaces east of his camp, and some of
them soon cut a broad trail some fifteen miles out. They reported back: There were many, many Indians ahead, many
Indians and much livestock. The Volunteers looked to their
weapons: This was what they had ridden so many dreary
miles for.

Carson immediately issued his orders. All the cavalry, and

the guns, would move out at once. The infantry would cover the supply train and follow at first light. His horsemen were in the saddle by sundown, and by midnight had found the broad fresh Indian trail down the valley of the Canadian. Carson could not tell how near the hostiles' camp might be. So, to keep from stumbling into the camp in the darkness, he dismounted his men and waited out the night.

Carson's decision was the only correct one, but it was a miserable wait, each man standing stock-still by the head of his horse, counting the dragging seconds of the long darkness. There was no fire, no smoking, no talking, no news— only cold and anxiety, 13 officers and 246 men standing through the bitter night. At last, with the first wan daylight, Carson sent his cavalry along the Indian trail. His scouts led, wrapped closely in buffalo robes against the biting cold, followed by most of the volunteer cavalry, the cannon, and a mounted rear guard.

Almost immediately the Ute scouts spooked an outpost of three Indians just across the Canadian, dumped their robes and other clothing, and galloped whooping after their fleeing quarry. Carson reacted immediately, sending most of the cavalry charging after his scouts into the cottonwood thickets and high grass along the river bottom ahead. Time was critical now. He had to strike the Indian camp before the Kiowa and Comanche had time to prepare for battle.

Carson himself followed with a single company of cavalry and the little howitzers. Although the guns were on wheeled mounts—called "prairie carriages"—the mounts were too small for the gunners to ride on. They were, moreover, narrow-tracked and prone to tip over, and could not—unlike regular horse artillery—be moved at cavalry speed.

Carson pushed on as fast as he could, moving alternatively at "walk" and "trot" to help the panting cannoneers keep up on foot. It was tough going, keeping the little guns upright and pushing through grass sometimes taller than a mounted man.

Up ahead, the scouts and cavalry hit the village—it was Kiowa and it was big, 170 lodges—and achieved some surprise. There was a short, hard fight around the buffalo-skin lodges, but the Kiowa soon scattered, moving downriver to rally about four miles away at a place called Adobe Walls.

The Ute and Jicarilla scouts were jubilant: Their enemies

were routed, and each of them had acquired a small herd of
Kiowa horses. They were already changing to fresh horses,
leaving the old horses with their stolen remuda to mark it as
their personal booty. They were exhilarated with success,
ready to continue the fight. Before they saw the last of Adobe
Walls, they would have all the fighting any healthy warrior
could ever want.

Adobe Walls had once been an outpost of the great
Bent–St. Vrain trading empire. The stout building had been
erected in 1845–46, just on the north side of the Canadian,
in what is now Hutchinson County, Texas. But for once as-
tute William Bent had miscalculated, for the Indians stayed
aloof and hostile, and trade was paltry. Bent had cut his
losses and abandoned the place, and abandoned it stayed,
except for the occasional daring traveler or hide hunter. But
Bent had built well, and his thick adobe-brick walls would
save Carson's little command this day.

When Carson reached Adobe Walls, he found his cavalry
fighting on foot, their horses penned within the ruins. They
were up against some two hundred mounted braves, galloping back and forth in front of the Volunteers' skirmish-line,
hurling taunts at the white men. Bodies hidden behind the
bodies of their horses, they fired from beneath the animals'
necks.

Behind them another thousand or so fighting Indians were
approaching. Most of them seem to have been Kiowa, under
Sierrito, Stumbling Bear, and Satanta. And behind them a
mile or so was still another village, this time a monstrous
one of five hundred lodges or so. Everywhere more bands of
Indians were headed for the fight around Adobe Walls. Carson's men had kicked open a hornet's nest.

In fact, Carson and his volunteers were up against a huge
gathering of fighting Indians. There were somewhere between
one thousand and three thousand braves descending on his
little command, perhaps as many armed and mounted warriors as would confront Custer's ill-fated cavalry less than a
decade later. And they were better armed. There were already several Volunteer wounded being cared for in the shelter of the walls.

One body of more than a thousand warriors was being
whipped up to attack by their chiefs—they looked like they
were about to charge. Carson immediately played his trump

cards: the tiny howitzers, which were wheeling into position near him on a little knoll.

"Pettis!" he shouted, pointing at the mass of Indian reinforcements. "Pettis! Throw a few shell into that crowd over thar!"

"Battery, halt!" roared Pettis. "Action right—load with shell—*load!*"

"Number one, fire! Number two, fire!"

At the crash of the first round, the hostiles began to fall back. By the fourth shot, they were galloping madly out of range. But they were far from defeated, as the soldiers were about to discover.

Carson gave his men the order to water and feed the horses, which were then picketed along a clear stream amid lush grass. The men he ordered to eat and rest while they could. Impressed by the Indians' pell-mell retreat, he was not sure they would return to the fight. He began to consider moving farther downriver to destroy the big village in the distance. But then, as the troops gnawed their raw bacon and hardtack, he turned his field glasses on the Indians: They were plainly not finished. This retreat was only temporary, a reorganization and reinforcement. They would come again, and that soon.

They did come, in enormous numbers, and they came again and again through the long afternoon. By staying well scattered, the braves were able to diminish the horrific effect of the mountain guns, but still the little explosive shells caused casualties. One round went completely through a Comanche horse at full gallop. The pony disintegrated, hurling his rider twenty feet through the air into a senseless heap. Two braves instantly dashed through the soldiers' fire, leaned down from their horses, and lifted their fallen comrade to safety.

Some of the braves crawled forward to keep up a steady and accurate fire on Carson's men. Most of the rest galloped back and forth across the soldiers' front, "yelling like demons, and firing from under the necks of their horses at intervals."

Somewhere in the Indian ranks rode a brave who not only carried a bugle, but understood the army's calls. Throughout the battle at Adobe Walls, he responded to the calls of Carson's bugler, blowing "retreat" when the soldier blew "charge," and "advance" when Carson's man blew "retreat." Whoever the bugler may have been, he did not manage to confuse the soldiers, who laughed, even under fire, at his parody of the American calls.

The Indians said the bugler was one Set-t'ainte, who owned a "French brass horn which he was accustomed to blow as signal for meals and other assemblies." Carson thought he was a white man, but nobody else saw any evidence that the mocking calls came from anybody but one of the braves.

(In one of history's great coincidences, an Indian bugler was also present at Adobe Walls in 1874, when an outnumbered band of hide hunters fought off Quanah Parker's Comanches. His calls were recognized by ex-servicemen among the defenders of the old building. This time the musical hostile was thought to be an American deserter, perhaps from the 10th Cavalry. Whoever he was, a heavy-caliber buffalo gun reached out to pull him down and silence that bugle forever. Could the buglers at both fights—ten years apart—have been the same man?)

And so the afternoon wore on. All through the dragging hours more Kiowa, Comanche, Apache, and Arapaho joined their opponents, until the little party of soldiers faced—by one estimate—as many as three thousand braves. They were well supplied with guns, the product of steady raiding and continual trading with both Comanchero and "respectable" traders. In fact, Carson reported that he had found tracks of traders' wagons headed downriver, toward the Indian camp.

But all the Indians' superb horsemanship, all their courage and numbers, could not overcome the steady fire from Carson's troopers. Even so, casualties steadily mounted among Carson's men. Although four or five Indians went down for every soldier, the Indians continued to press in, and upriver Carson could see them entering their village to empty it of anything useful.

Carson considered. His orders were to chastise the marauders who had terrorized the Santa Fe trail and all the country around it. His fighting blood was up, and he longed to attack and destroy that huge village so tantalizingly close. But he was also coldly realistic. There were just too many Indians out there. They were still being reinforced, and already bands of them were moving past him to the west.

Behind him someplace was his slow-moving supply train and its tiny escort, cold meat for the number of braves Carson's command was facing. Moreover, Carson's horses were worn-out; many of them were wounded. He had wounded men to protect. Perhaps worst of all, ammunition was running low.

In spite of odds and casualties, most of Carson's officers and troopers were still full of fight, eager to press on to attack the huge village up ahead. But they had not seen the miles and the blood that their commander had seen. Carson was supported by the leaders of the Ute and Jicarilla scouts: They knew bad odds when they saw them, and besides, they were losing their booty, principal source of fame and glory on their return.

And so, about three-thirty, Carson did the only thing he could: He ordered a retreat. He moved slowly, one man in each four leading four horses, the others fighting on foot as skirmishers. The little mountain guns brought up the rear, banging away with shell at the swirl of pursuing warriors. Carson reported afterward:

> The Indians charged so repeatedly and with such desperation that for some time I had serious doubts for the safety of my rear . . . but the steady and constant fire poured into them caused them to retire on every occasion with great slaughter.

Step by desperate step Carson's men fought their way back upriver, through a storm of bullets and arrows, through a raging grass fire set by their pursuers. The fire threatened to engulf Carson's rear guard, who double-timed out of its way. Carson avoided the blaze by setting a back-fire, and forted up temporarily on a rise where the grass was short. Clouds of braves charged him out of the smoke and flame, but steady musketry and the little howitzers beat them off yet again.

At times the smoke was so thick that the braves charged to almost point-blank range, looming suddenly out of the smoke to fire and dash away. Here the only scalp of the fight was taken, ripped from a fallen brave by a Mexican boy fighting with the soldiers.

Colonel Carson and his embattled men reached the Kiowa village just before sundown, to find it full of Indians trying to save their supplies and possessions. Carson did not hesitate. He and his men shot their way in, launching a hell-for-leather cavalry charge through the lodges.

They were again covered by the steady fire of the guns. Pettis found a twenty-foot sandhill near the village, and loaded his pieces in its shelter. Then it was "by hand to the front!" and each piece was manhandled to the top of the rise, where one gunner jerked the lanyard and sent the shell on its way.

The recoil did the rest, returning the howitzer abruptly to the bottom of the sandhill, sometimes rolling smoothly backward, sometimes toppling end over end. While this piece was reloaded, the second was muscled to the top, to fire and return on its own.

Some of the fighting was point-blank: Iron Shirt, the Apache chief, died in the doorway of the lodge he would not abandon. Two old squaws, traveling with Carson's scouts, proudly displayed the remains of four blind or crippled Kiowas they had hacked to death with axes.

Among the lodges the soldiers found pitiful evidence of the border war, white women's and children's clothing, photographs, and a cavalry sergeant's hat. There were even a buggy, a wagon, and several sets of harness, supposed to belong to Sierrito, a major chief of the Kiowas. Tragically, as Pettis later learned, seven captive white women and several children had been hidden nearby during the fight. They were never discovered.

Then, while half the soldiers fought off the clouds of warriors galloping around the village, the rest set fire to the lodges, 126 of them, lodges filled with critical winter supplies, buffalo robes, and ammunition. They saved enough robes to equip each volunteer against the cold. The rest was ashes, including Sierrito's prized vehicles and harness. The little mountain guns again helped the troops disengage, sending a last shell into the midst of a group of braves.

Then the retreat continued, plodding on across a prairie now dark and bitter cold, the wounded loaded on the gun carriages and ammunition carts. The wounded were suffering terribly; the rest of the command was stumbling-tired. But within three hours, Carson's column saw bivouac fires in the distance, and soon were challenged "in good, clear, ringing Saxon, 'Who comes there?' "

They had found the supply train, intact, alert and ready to fight. Now, after thirty hours of combat, the exhausted volunteers could breathe a little easier. They settled in, posted sentries, and waited out the night. Carson's troopers rolled into their blankets. Although they had eaten little or nothing since the hasty meal at Adobe Walls, many fell asleep without eating. Even the Indian scouts were too tired for the customary dance. For the next twenty-one nights they would dance the scalp dance with a solitary scalp, the trophy bought from the Mexican boy. But this night would be silent, the silence of utter exhaustion.

Next day Carson called his weary troopers to stand-to at dawn, but there was no attack. After a monstrous breakfast of wild turkey and venison, the command rested. Carson's men were ready to fight again, but they were terribly tired. So were his horses, and he had twenty-five wounded. If he had to fight again, it might as well be here. But there would be no fight, even though many of Carson's men wanted to return to attack the large village off to the east. There would be no attack on Carson's command, either; although they could see bands of warriors all through the day, the expected attack never came.

And next day, the twenty-seventh, the Indians were gone. Carson put his command on the road home, and took stock. Thanks largely to Carson's careful handling of his men, his losses were remarkably light: two soldiers and an Indian dead and twenty-odd total wounded, two or three of whom later died of wounds. Carson estimated Indian casualties at sixty, about half-and-half dead and wounded.

However, three years later Pettis would meet two Mexicans who had been trading with the Kiowa and Comanche when Carson's column marched down the Canadian. These men said they were in the big Comanche village just downstream from Adobe Walls during the fight, and estimated Indian losses at almost a hundred dead and between a hundred and a hundred fifty wounded.

Thus the fight at Adobe Walls. Carson had not achieved what he and General Carleton had hoped for, the complete punishment of the hostile horse Indians. Then and later, some observers were moved to call the battle a defeat for Carson. George Bent, half-breed son of trader William Bent, would later write that:

Kit Carson told me in 1868, three weeks before he died, that the Indians whipped him in this fight. What saved him was Adobe Fort ... I bought a race horse from Kit Carson in 1868, the horse he rode during the fight ... [It] had white spots on each side of his back. Carson told me he had the saddle on ... four days during this fight, and when he took the saddle off the skin came with it.

Another officer commented that Carson had honestly said, "had it not been for his howitzers, few would have been left to tell the tale."

As to that, Carson was probably right. The explosive shell from his well-served little guns had a dramatic effect on the clouds of braves who attacked him. The Indians were certainly impressed by Carson's artillery. As Pettis learned years after the fight, the Indians said that had it not been for the "guns that shot twice," no white man would have escaped.

Carson knew he had been in the Valley of Death. In his report on the action he declared himself pleased with the results. But he cautioned that further campaigning against the Kiowa and Comanche would require at least a thousand men and four guns.

But the fact is, Carson had the foresight to bring artillery, and he used it well. Whatever he or anybody else may have thought or said of the fight in the valley of the Canadian, it is hard to call Adobe Walls a defeat. It was the sort of coup that impressed the Indian enemy: Carson had cut deeply into their territory, inflicted considerable damage, and suffered little loss himself. Adobe Walls was a major factor in bringing the Comanche and Kiowa to the treaty talks in 1865.

Carson had succeeded in destroying one substantial village; he had preserved his command and brought it out whole and battle-worthy against tremendous odds. The excellent discipline and steady shooting of his volunteers had inflicted many more casualties than Carson's command had suffered.

Probably most important, he had convinced the hostiles that the army's arm was long and strong. It is fact that raiding along the Santa Fe Trail was reduced after Adobe Walls, and the Comanche and Kiowa moved their winter camps far to the east, on the Cimarron in Indian Territory (later Oklahoma).

General Carleton considered the Carson expedition a success, and was generous in his praise of its commander. It was a "brilliant victory," he wrote, "another green leaf to the laurel wreath which you have so nobly won in the service of your country." Washington agreed. In March 1865, Carson was brevetted brigadier general of volunteers.

And history proved the general and the War Department were right. At the end of 1865 the Kiowa, Comanche, and Apache signed a treaty under which they agreed "to cease all acts of violence or injury to the frontier settlements, and to travelers on the Santa Fe road."

Carson had a hand in arranging the 1865 peace conferences. The Indians had confidence in his honesty, and as an American general wrote about his dealings with the Utes, Carson "returned their confidence by being their most steadfast and unswerving friend." William Tecumseh Sherman— who later educated one of Carson's sons—would write of him,

> These Red Skins think Kit twice as big a man as me. Why, his integrity is simply perfect. They know it and they would believe him any day before me.

Indeed, Carson understood and respected the Indians far more than most other white men, and believed in dealing with them fairly. He made no secret, for example, of his loathing of the murder of a peaceable Cheyenne band at Sand Creek in the fall of 1864.

And so, whatever the critics said, Carson's expedition down the Canadian got results. Thereafter Army escorts still protected wagon trains on the Santa Fe Trail. Thanks to Carson, they had little to do.

COPAINS

In the French Foreign Legion, a man's most important relationship was always with his *copain*. The word is not precisely translatable, but means at its best some combination of buddy, friend, and brother. Your *copain* shared the last drop of water in his *bidon*, his last cigarette, even his ration of *pinard*, the red wine that has fueled the Legion for a century and a half. Your *copain* ran through a hail of fire to get you as you lay in the open with a bullet in your guts. And you would do these things for him without question.

Stories of devotion between *copains* abound in the history of La Legion. Often they were odd couples, unlikely pairs who nevertheless kept faith with one another to the death, no matter how immoral they might otherwise be, no matter how they might steal and cheat others. But of all the tales, none is more strange and touching than the story of the American and the Englishman who really shouldn't have been in the Legion at all, but whose friendship became a rich part of its legend.

The story comes out of the First World War, in which the Legion left the sands of North Africa to cover itself with glory in France—and almost bleed to death. For the Legion had always been contemptuous of death, and that very willingness to take casualties had enabled its units to take objectives other units could not reach. When the last shot had been fired, some thirty-one thousand of the forty-four thousand Legionnaires who had fought in France were either dead or missing, including virtually all of the eight thousand old Africa hands who had begun the war. The Legion was the most decorated of all French units, and the most fabulous.

John Ford Elkington had joined the Legion in the fall of 1914. Traditionally, nobody asked a Legionnaire where he came from or why he was in the Legion, or even what his real name was. But in Elkington's case, his comrades were certain of a few things at least. Elkington was plainly British and a gentleman. And it very soon became apparent that he was also an experienced soldier, and a very good one. Beyond that, nobody asked, and nobody cared. Legionnaire 2d Class Elkington was a good man to have next to you in a fight, and that, in the Legion, is the best of recommendations.

And then there was David Wheeler. Wheeler was an American, and also a man of breeding, and, like Elkington, not a young man. The two men got acquainted in a restaurant in Lyons, where both had gone for a decent meal. Each liked what he saw, and the two became *copains*. A little at a time, they learned about one another, a truth that was far stranger than all the fiction the Foreign Legion novels could create.

For Wheeler was a surgeon, and a good one. He had left the quiet of Buffalo to treat wounded men in France, and his wife had come along as a nurse. But as he saw more and more ripped abdomens and shattered limbs, Wheeler became convinced that he was not doing enough to help end that filthy war. Even though he had been working in a forward-area hospital, he was determined to take a direct hand against the Germans. Ignoring all pleas to stay on in the hospital, he enlisted in the Legion.

And if Wheeler's case was strange, Elkington's was stranger still. For Elkington had been a professional soldier in the British Army, and had gone to France with the "Old Contemptibles," the little long-service expeditionary force that helped blunt and hold the first German push. A lieutenant colonel, he had commanded the 1st Battalion of the Royal Warwickshire Regiment. The Warwicks fought well in the desperate retreat from Mons and Le Cateau, taking heavy casualties but ripping terrible holes in the German infantry with their murderous rifle-fire. At last, late on August 26, the battalion stumbled, exhausted, into Saint-Quentin.

Elkington had to rest and feed his men, but the mayor of Saint-Quentin refused both food and rest unless Elkington agreed in writing to surrender if the Germans attacked the city. Instead of simply taking what he needed at gunpoint,

Elkington acceded to the mayor's desire to save his town from destruction, and signed the requested pledge to surrender. In the event the battalion went back into the fighting, but somehow Elkington's superiors found out about the agreement.

A court-martial followed, and Elkington, characteristically, took responsibility for what he had done. He was cashiered from the service, but he would not sit out the war. He said good-bye to his family in England and set out for the anonymity of La Legion.

Even Elkington's hard-bitten comrades admired his cool courage. Indeed, neither he nor Wheeler appeared to be afraid of anything at all. And through the worst of the fighting, the two men fought on with Legionnaires falling all around them, miraculously untouched themselves.

Their luck ran out in the Champagne, in a slogging attack through deep mud on a strong point called the Navarin Farm. They worked their way through a torrent of machine-gun bullets and shell-fire, crossing two belts of barbed wire unscathed. Elkington, as usual, was out ahead of his section, clearing trenches with grenades. And then, as the surviving Legionnaires neared the farm, Elkington fell, his right leg shattered by several machine-gun bullets. Wheeler ran to him, and was hit as he dropped into the trench near his *copain*.

Elkington's leg was a bloody wreck, and Wheeler neglected his own hurt to dress Elkington's wounds and give him morphine. The American doctor managed to bandage his own leg, then passed out on top of Elkington. And there they lay for hours in the mud, rain falling on them until the blessed darkness came and the litter-bearers could reach them.

For Elkington, life in the infantry was over. He would lie in a Paris hospital for almost a year, and the surgeons would save his leg. But only just, and he would walk with a limp for the rest of his days. In the summer of 1916 he was awarded both the Military Medal and the Croix de Guerre for his extraordinary gallantry before the Navarin Farm. Typically, Elkington would not wear his decorations—"I don't wear medals" was all he would say. But the citations for his awards had been published in the French official journal, and it is here that his story becomes stranger still.

For King George V read the French journal, and the king

was familiar with Elkington's sad trial and dismissal. And so it was that the *London Gazette*, a few weeks later, carried still another notice naming John Ford Elkington. It went like this:

> The King has been graciously pleased to approve the reinstatement of John Ford Elkington in the rank of Lieutenant-Colonel of the Royal Warwickshire Regiment with his previous seniority, in consequence of his gallant conduct while serving in the ranks of the Foreign Legion of the French Army.

The same *Gazette* issue announced the award of the British Distinguished Service Order to Elkington. There would be no more question of the colonel's courage. His tunic still hangs in the regimental museum.

He returned to England in the autumn of 1916, a vindicated man. Always modest, he still wore none of his hard-won decorations, saying only that he had done "nothing of particular note. I was with the others in the trenches."

It is not known whether he ever again saw his *copain*, David Wheeler. It is certain that he never forgot him, for Elkington always maintained that the doctor had ignored his own painful wounds to save Elkington's life. Like Elkington, Wheeler remained true to his own ideals. He left the Legion in 1917, but not the war in which he so passionately believed. He went on serving, this time with an American unit, and was killed in action with it. The war had only four more months to run.

THE HAND OF CAPTAIN DANJOU
THE FOREIGN LEGION AT CAMERONE

Near Marseilles, at a place called Aubagne, stands the new home of the Foreign Legion. Its spotless grounds include a massive stone pile, the Monument aux Morts, which commemorates the Legion dead of a century and a half. When the legion left its spiritual home, Sidi-bel-Abbès in Algeria, the Monument was dismantled stone by stone for the return to France. At the same time, the treasured mementos of the Legion were tenderly brought back to new places of honor in the Legion crypt and museum.

These few mementos represented an immense military tradition, a tradition of absolute loyalty, unswerving courage, and contempt for death. There were medals and swords and pictures, and the flags of the Legion, dripping with more decorations than any other unit in the French army can boast. And most curious of all, there was a little wood and glass casket . . . containing a simple wooden hand.

The hand belonged to Captain Jean Danjou, a quiet, thin officer whose left hand had been lost in the service of France. He was *un brave,* a veteran of desperate fighting in Algeria, the Crimea, and the slaughterhouse of Magenta. Danjou still had his saber hand, and had equipped himself with a wooden hand sufficient to manage his horse's reins. He was a Legionnaire, after all, and the Legion has always done more with less.

And this is the wooden hand that lies in state in its little casket at Aubagne. It is not an imposing sort of trophy, but it is the most sacred talisman the Legion knows, and it is shown with reverence to new recruits, who in time will come to understand what it means.

For to understand the meaning of Danjou's hand is to understand the mystique of the Legion, of its incredible courage and sublime contempt for danger. To understand Danjou's hand is to understand why defeat is not part of the Legion vocabulary. Men may die, and units may be destroyed, but the Legion is never whipped. The key to that unique philosophy is that little wooden hand, and the fight it commemorates, Camerone.

In the Invalides in Paris there is a Latin inscription about Camerone. It goes something like this:

> The men who lie here, fewer than sixty of them, fought a whole army before they were buried by weight of numbers. Life left these French soldiers before honor did. April 30, 1863.

The inscription is entirely accurate, except that the soldiers were not exactly French. They fought for France, it is true, but they were Foreign Legionnaires, which for one thing means that most of them were not born in France. It also means that their primary allegiance was not patriotic, but that profound, mysterious, undefinable loyalty to the unit in which they served, La Legion. Inscriptions and banners are all very well, but to the Legionnaire, even today, Danjou's hand is infinitely more important.

Camerone is a dreary, shabby village, or was so in the spring of 1863. It lay on the fever-haunted road that connected Vera Cruz and the French fleet with Puebla, on the Mexican plateau. At Puebla the French army lay, trying to win an empire for Napoleon III and his Hapsburg puppet, Maximillian, younger brother of Emperor Franz Joseph. And the French army, hammering at the Mexican defenders of Mexico City, needed regular supplies from its beachhead at Vera Cruz—not only ammunition and food, but money, gold francs, and lots of them. And the critical road, along which the gold and supplies came from the sea, was guarded by the Legion.

It was terrible duty, the isolated little Legion companies stewing in the heat, fighting Mexican raiders and dysentery and malaria, and a terrifying disease called the black vomit. And *le cafard*. *Cafard* was—and is—that terrible craziness that makes men go berserk, named for the black beetle that

crawls in a man's brain after too much drink or sun or isolation. It made a man assault his officer or his *copain*—his
buddy—run screaming and drooling like a rabid animal, or
fall on his bayonet for relief. It was born in the little Beau
Geste forts of Africa, and now it thrived in Mexico, too,
brought on mostly by too much pulque and mescal, the
white lightning that turned a man's head to crawling maggots.

And then one night at the end of April an Indian spy
brought word to Legion Colonel Jeanningros that the next
convoy would be attacked by powerful Mexican forces, including regular troops. The convoy was big—60 carts and
150 mules—and it was critical, carrying not only food and
ammunition, but four million francs in gold. The column
would need help along the road, and that help could only be
the Legion.

Jeanningros had few troops to send. He could spare only
a single company, the 3d Company of the Legion's 2d Battalion, already down to half strength. But the colonel could
send the experienced Danjou as its commander. The captain
was thirty-five, a graduate of the French military academy at
Saint-Cyr, and he had a world of experience. Danjou would
have two other officers, both second lieutenants: one, Napoleon Vilain, was a boyish ex-enlisted man; the other, Clement
Maudet, was an old sweat, who rose through the ranks to
sergeant-major before winning his commission.

Danjou had sixty-two NCOs and enlisted men, men from
all over the world. There were Belgians, Swiss, Germans,
Frenchmen, men from Poland, Holland, Denmark, and who
knows where. In short, it was a typical Legion company,
fiercely loyal to the Legion, its officers, and each other, and
to little else. Shortly after midnight on April 30, Danjou set
off down the fever road to cover the convoy, passing through
a series of thoroughly forgettable hamlets, still meeting no
enemy. The company passed in peace through miserable
Camerone, and marched a little farther on.

But now, shortly after daylight, at a halt to refill the *bidons*
with water and make a little coffee, they saw their first Mexican cavalry. Danjou reacted instantly, falling back toward
the village of Camerone and the all-important road. He was
fired on from a dilapidated hacienda in the village, and a
man was wounded. And then he saw them, hundreds of Mex-

ican cavalrymen. The company formed a hollow square, and its disciplined volley-firing twice broke Mexican charges, littering the ground with fallen horsemen. But Danjou knew he must find cover; the enemy was far too strong to take on in the open.

The Legion took shelter in the run-down hacienda. The main building was already occupied in strength by Mexican troops, but Danjou posted his men at windows and walls and broke every attempt to rush the little company. His Legionnaires used rock and rubble to plug doorways and breaches in the walls, and settled down to a siege. The day was already getting very hot.

Danjou's men began to take casualties early from the heavy Mexican fire. They returned it, but they fired carefully, choosing their targets. Not only was fine fire discipline a Legion tradition, but their pack mules had bolted at the first Mexican charge, taking with them the reserve ammunition.

And the water. As if eight hundred–odd Mexicans were not bad enough, the company must bear the horrors of thirst in the ovenlike enclosure from which they fought. It was especially horrible for the wounded. Before the day was over, they would be reduced to licking the blood from their own wounds for moisture. Nevertheless, about 9:30 A.M. the Mexican commander sent a flag of truce, and the Legionnaires were offered the chance to surrender. Danjou scornfully refused.

The murderous fire continued, and the Legionaries continued to drop. Their disciplined fire inflicted heavy losses on the Mexicans, but there seemed to be no end to the attackers. Danjou, the old professional, could read the omens. And so he called to his German batman to bring the captain's daily liter of wine, carefully carried all the night and morning. To each man Danjou gave a sip of the raw *pinard,* and required of each soldier an oath to die rather than surrender. Each man swore, and before the end of this broiling, hellish day, each man would keep faith with this strange communion.

And a little while before noon Danjou kept his own rendezvous with destiny. He was running from one building to check a detachment behind a barricade when the bullet hit him. He was struck in the chest, and lived only moments.

Young Lieutenant Vilain got to him; Danjou tried to speak and could not, and then he was still forever.

Vilain took command of the forty remaining men and fought on. For a little while, at noon, there was a flash of hope. There were drums in the distance, and bugle calls. The company for a moment caught at the fantasy of relief. But the music was Mexican; another thousand infantry surrounded them now, and hope was finally extinct.

Lieutenant Vilain was killed as he, too, crossed the open area to check his men. Maudet, the ex–sergeant-major, took command of the pitiful little band that remained. Nearly everyone was wounded by now, and the barrels of the long Le Gras rifles were far too hot to touch. The heat was nearly unbearable; the wounded were in agony, and one by one the survivors went down into the dust. Those still able to shoot emptied the cartridge pouches of the wounded and the dead. And still that deadly, deliberate rifle-fire held the attackers at bay, and dropped them in scores.

Until at last nearly all the blue-coated soldiers were still in the dirt. Only five still stood, the hard-eyed Lieutenant Maudet, husky Corporal Maine, and three privates. They were down to a cartridge apiece now, and Maudet looked around at the remnants of his little command. He gave his last orders, and his men nodded. They would fire a last volley together, and then they would follow him with the bayonet into the mob of Mexicans drawing ever closer.

They fired and charged out into the blazing sun, and a blast of Mexican fire stopped them in their tracks. Maudet was down, and one of the privates, and now the ammunition was entirely gone. And still their baraka, their luck, held. For the mass of Mexicans was halted by their officer, Colonel Combas, who miraculously was of French extraction and called on them in French to surrender.

Maine was the ranking man now, and all Legion still. "Yes," he said. "Yes. But only if we keep our arms and you care for our officer."

And so ended the stand at Camerone. Thirty-nine Legionnaires were dead in the hacienda. The terrible heat and their wounds would kill most of the rest, including Maudet, over the next few days, in spite of Mexican attempts to save them. The few survivors passed into captivity. The ground was littered with Mexican casualties, at least three hundred of them, and the convoy would go through untouched.

After the war was over, the French army gone and Maximillian well and truly shot by the Mexicans, Maine and another Legionnaire returned to the army, and both became officers. The other man was later killed in a duel, but Maine would serve on through the Franco-Prussian War.

The relief column, arriving much too late, buried the dead Legionnaires in a common grave, and retrieved by the way the wooden hand of Captain Jean Danjou. And that symbol of disaster would come to mean everything that makes the Legion both different and great.

For April 30 is still the high holy day of the Legion, Camerone Day, when Legionnaires are forgiven virtually any transgression short of murder, and the great deeds of the past are celebrated with great ceremony wherever the Legion may be. At the Monument aux Morts the Legion parades, and some highly decorated former Legionnaire has the honor of bearing the hand of Captain Danjou in solemn procession. And there the 1st Regiment of the Legion stands in ranks while an NCO reads the story of Camerone.

Camerone has been celebrated in many strange and dangerous places, not least of these the witches' kettle of Dien Bien Phu, where the only wine was the dreadful Vinogel concentrate, and the day's special treat was two American cigarettes per man.

Much of even that Vinogel came from an air-dropped container that had fallen well out into no-man's-land, beyond the battered French bunker line. A small force of volunteers from the 1st Battalion of the 13th Legion Demi-Brigade had crawled out in the darkness, to destroy several Vietminh bunkers and kill perhaps a dozen of the Communist enemy. Their sortie was duly reported as a successful raid—for they took no casualties—but all the Legion knew the object of the exercise was not the enemy but the Vinogel. At least now each Legionnaire would have a little sip for Camerone Day.

So the holy ritual was strictly observed, and in the shadow of death the Legionnaires sang "Le Boudin," the slow, solemn marching song about the blood sausage, the anthem of the Legion.

And the lesson of Camerone is never lost. While the Legion keeps faith and dies well, there is never defeat. Men may die, but the Legion lives on, nurtured by the hearts of thousands of troopers long gone to dust, led by the men of Camerone.

THE BLOOD SAUSAGE

The Foreign Legion is at once the pride and the despair of the French army. Its history of victory against odds, its sang-froid and contempt for death, have won it an indelible place in the military history of France.

But on the practical side, the Legion can be a pain. It is not always easy to control, except by its own officers and NCOs. From time to time it has been inclined to consume too much *pinard;* when it does it sometimes wrecks bars and raises lumps on the police, both civil and military. And on parade it is impossible.

It must always march at the end of any column, for its boots hit the pavement at an old-fashioned 80 paces per minute, instead of the modern 120 steps per minute. Some romantics have speculated that the slow, ponderous cadence dates from the Legion's thousands of miles of marching in the shifting sands of North Africa. In fact, the pace appears to be only a relic of the eighteenth century, when all units marched at that rate. In any case, the Legion declines to change—it has always marched to a different drummer any-way, and does so, literally, to this day.

It sings on the march and it sings in garrison. It has also been known to sing in action. It chooses to sing its own marching songs, some of which are French, and some Ger-man, such as "Annamarie." Many of these songs are moving, some sad, some exultant, some joking. But the anthem of the Legion is a nonsensical sort of ditty, about a sausage of all things, and it is sung seriously, with a meaning only Legionnaires understand.

It is called "Le Boudin," "The Blood Sausage." Its music dates from just after the Crimean War, the melody almost hymnlike. It was played by the Legion bands, but it had no words until 1870, until somebody wrote some rather silly lyrics. And it caught on. It mentions Camerone and the memorable stand at Tuyen Quang in Tonkin. It nods to the Legion's constant companion, death, "which never forgets us." And its refrain goes something like this:

"Here's the blood sausage, the blood sausage, the blood sausage;
For the Alsatians, the Swiss, and the Lorrainers;
There's none for the Belgians,
Because they're shirkers."

"Le Boudin" is sung in the barracks, in the bars, and on the march. It is also sung in the officers' messes, often after a toast to the dead of the Legion. Even there, it is sung to the very slow cadence of the Legion on the march.

As long as the Legion exists, "Le Boudin" will be sung. No matter that its lyrics sound a little silly to the world at large; what, a song about a sausage? The Legion knows what "Le Boudin" means, and that is enough.

PLEVNA

"I drink and drink," said Skobeleff, "I drink and drink, but I still see that breastwork of dead bodies . . . I can't sleep . . . and the screams still ring in my ears." As hard as the flamboyant Russian general drank and feasted and whored in festive Bucharest, he could not forget the piles of torn, contorted corpses stacked in the mud and drifting rain. Skobeleff, good soldier, could not erase from memory the heaped corpses of his own devoted infantry, lying stiff and silent before the battered little Bulgarian town of Plevna.

Ancient enemies, Russian and Turk were on the march once more in the spring of 1877. The czars had always coveted Constantinople, dreamed of control of the critical Bosphorus, schemed for access to warm water. Cross and crescent had clawed at each other's throats again and again over Russia's unchanging avarice, over this as much as over the undying religious enmity that lay perpetually between them.

Now they were at it again. The festering Balkans were the immediate cause, as they had been over and over. In the provinces of Bosnia, Herzegovina, Montenegro, Serbia, and Bulgaria, revolt and repression grappled for control. In the previous spring, Europe had been sickened by news of widespread Turkish massacres in Bulgaria: rapes, executions, burnings alive. Villages had been razed and burned, children violated. In depopulated villages, rotting Christian corpses were heaped three feet deep. The American consul himself estimated that the Turks had butchered at least fifteen thousand people.

The czar, instantly and publicly indignant in his role as protector of Balkan Christianity, seized at the justification for invasion, and the Russian army was on the march. Some of its units, heading for trains to the west, might have passed through the streets of the middle Volga town of Simbirsk. They might have slogged past a boy of that town called Vladimir Ulyanov, a boy who one day would call himself Lenin.

The czar's commanders, always rich in willing manpower, launched two enormous armies at the traditional enemy. That enemy was just now personified by Sultan Abdul Hamid, ugly, intelligent, suspicious, and, like others of his family, more than a little crazy.

History would know Abdul Hamid as Abdul the Damned. A better name would have been Abdul the Paranoid. He had begun his unhappy reign by building—mostly on two large Christian cemeteries—a sort of shabby palace at a place called Yilditz, an unappealing spot north of the city of Istanbul. Catering to Abdul Hamid's paranoia, this sinister, rambling maze was honeycombed with secret passages and doors, and everywhere the sultan stashed loaded revolvers, a thousand of them altogether. Abdul spent much time in isolation at Yilditz, closely surrounded by guards, his food tasted by cooks and palace favorites. No one dared touch his pockets in the sultan's presence, and Abdul once shot and killed a gardener because the man sprang suddenly to attention as Abdul passed by.

Such government as there was, he managed from his lunatic palace, and from Yilditz he received reports from his army of spies. He was terrified of assassins, especially poisoners, and his fears pervaded his entire life. Haggard, sleepless, his face heavily rouged, the sultan was hardly the wartime leader beleaguered Turkey needed.

And war it was to be. Quickly the czar's armies pushed south into Turkish Balkan territory, moving swiftly through Rumania with the blessings of its government, pushing easily across the Danube into Turkish Bulgaria. They were confident, these 180,000 Russians, elated at their cheap captures of the strategic Danube town of Nikopol and the critical Shipka Pass.

In their massive columns rumbled eight hundred guns, and there seemed to be no good reason why they should not rumble all the way to Sofia . . . and, maybe, Constantinople, the dream of blood-soaked centuries. The Russians did not hurry. Their progress was described as a "promenade."

After all, the only obstacle anywhere close by was an insignificant provincial town about twenty miles south of the Danube, a somnolent place called Plevna. Sixteen or seventeen thousand people lived there in 1877, about evenly divided between Turks and Bulgarians.

It was a pretty spot from a distance, all red-tile roofs and minarets. Up close, it was just another dreary, shoddy Balkan town, a maze of trash heaps and stinking narrow streets. On one side loomed a marsh; on the other lay a foul stream called the River Vid. An Englishman serving as a Turkish lieutenant found it a fairly typical Turkish town, full of "palsied hovels . . . and heaps of offal, the thousand-and-one stenches characteristic of urban Turkey . . . The [creek] served as the main drain." Another Englishman, a correspondent, agreed, calling it "labyrinthine . . . its streets paved on the principle of one huge boulder to three great holes."

Plevna was surely an insignificant place, even by Balkan standards. Undefended, it could not delay the Russians even a day.

But trouble was on the way. Marching hard toward Plevna was a husky, tough Turkish general called Osman Pasha. Osman was a disciplinarian, a professional, far more of a soldier than his effete commander-in-chief deserved. Mushir Osman Nuri Pasha was then forty-five, a veteran of fighting in Syria, Crete, Yemen, Serbia, and the Crimea.

Behind him were fifty thousand men, ten miles of hardy Turkish soldiers. They were obedient, and they were remarkably tough. They pushed on hard east down the Danube, the road behind them littered with sick and exhausted men. They marched deep into each night and started again before dawn, swiftly covering 120 miles on hardtack so rocklike, it had to be beaten into pieces and soaked in water before a man could eat it. And they beat the Russians to Plevna by a few hours.

Well led, these men were doughty fighters, especially in defense. And they would be very well led indeed. Osman Pasha was not in the slightest intimidated by Grand Duke Nicholas, the Russian commander and younger brother of Czar Alexander II. The experienced Turk quickly saw the value of sleepy Plevna and the high ground around it.

For Nicholas would have to stop and fight at Plevna if Osman held it. He could not bypass the little town, for a Turkish force there could easily cut his supply lines if he marched past toward the south. And so Osman's hardy peasants dug madly, working in shifts around the clock to entrench the ridges that surrounded the town. At the same time Osman built a series of monstrous redoubts to bolster his line. Each of them was equipped with dugouts and underground magazines. Some would hold a thousand men.

By the end of July, Osman's fortifications were nearing completion. He stocked them heavily with food and water, and paid special attention to ammunition, food for the voracious barrels of the Turkish ace in the hole.

For carefully laid out before the Turkish infantry were not one, but two rifles, precision killing tools made in America. First, for long-range work, the Turkish troopers would use the Rhode Island–made .45 caliber Peabody-Martini, a remarkably accurate single-shot, falling-block rifle, designed to pull down a man as far away as a thousand yards.

Then, if the determined Russians still pressed on, closed in to two hundred yards or less, Osman's men would reach for their ultimate weapon, the old, reliable lever-action Winchester, chambered in .44 caliber Turkish. Thirty thousand of these saddle guns had been bought for the Turkish cavalry. But since horsemen were of no use inside the trenches of Plevna, Osman issued these American man-killers to his frontline infantry. The result would be astonishing.

By the first days of August, the stage was set. The Russian lines were pushed close to the little town, close enough that the czarist infantry could hear muezzins calling the faithful to prayer. The Russian peasant soldier was eager to close with the infidel, who had murdered and horribly mutilated a number of Russian prisoners. The Russian infantryman detested the enemy, and he was just as tough a customer as his Turkish foe.

He was uniformed in dark olive green, with high boots and a gray greatcoat or a sheepskin jacket. He carried a heavy pack, rifle, and bayonet, and sometimes a heavy short sword as well. He wrapped his feet in cloth strips in lieu of socks and thrived on a diet of cabbage, onions, and a sort of buckwheat gruel, plus meat when he could get it. He was brave and devoted, and he could stand a great deal of pounding. He was about to show just how much.

Both Russians and Turks struggled with the sea of viscous mud and a steady, depressing deluge of rain. These horrible conditions were especially hard for Nicholas' supply lines, on which teams struggled, foundered, and died, and supplies rotted in the wagons on the march. More than twenty thousand horses perished miserably in the slimy morass, and purifying carcasses lay everywhere.

Both sides banged away with their artillery, the Russians with their swarm of obsolescent bronze cannon, the Turks with excellent Krupp steel breechloaders. There were casualties on both sides, but this struggle would not be decided by the big guns. It would be won by men's flesh and by rifles . . . especially by rifles.

Osman's men waited, protected by yards of earth, each soldier well supplied with rations and ammunition. Food was in good supply, and even the town was at peace. Osman had thoughtfully hung several soldiers for crimes against the Christian Bulgarian residents, and the townspeople had opened their stores and behaved themselves.

Outside the town, Grand Duke Nicholas' massive army had deployed and spread its camps. Heavy in artillery, the Russians still did not understand the tactical dominance of the rifle. Confident in numbers and the valor of the Russian soldiers, the Russian command pushed on with preparations for a grand assault. Their infantrymen, tough and hardy as the Turks, were not nearly as well armed. The elegant Russian officers and their rough peasant soldiers both worshiped the bayonet.

Some of the Russian troops carried the .42 caliber Berdan, developed by, and named for, American Civil War commander Hiram S. Berdan. It was a reasonably reliable rifle, but did not have either the deadly accuracy of the Peabody or the murderous firepower of the Winchester. Other Russian units were equipped with something called the Krnka, a .63 caliber breechloader developed by a Bohemian gunsmith. It could be as dangerous to the firer as to the target, since its design left it dangerously weak behind the breech. Even if it did not blow back into the firer's face, it had a nasty habit of failing to extract spent cartridges once it got a little dirty. The harried infantryman then had to knock the fired case out of the breech with his ramrod, a distinctly unhappy experience under fire.

Nonetheless, the Russians were supremely confident, as men are who do not understand the dangers they face. By contrast, Osman seems to have missed nothing of the dreadful lessons of the American Civil War. He perfectly understood the deadly partnership between earthworks and rifles, and he made the most of it. Because of what he knew, and their own officers did not, the sturdy Russian soldiers would pay the butcher's bill.

It fell due on the thirtieth of July, 1877. At eleven o'clock that morning, under the eye of the czar himself, thirty-five thousand Russian troops rose from their trenches and charged cheering toward the Turkish lines. A cloud of smoke rose above Plevna's fortifications as Osman's men opened at long range, and the Russians began to go down in windrows.

Horrified by the carnage amongst the Russian infantry,

some Russian officers later claimed the Peabodys began to kill out beyond two thousand yards. However they may have stretched the lethal range of the American breechloader, it is certain that the Russians suffered staggering casualties even before they began to close with the Turkish trenches.

They had come too close to the deadly Turkish fire while still bunched in close order. The doctrine of shock—the attack with the bayonet—was holy writ in the Russian army. But, as an American eye-witness commented, "the shock of heavy columns is powerless before the rain of bullets poured out by breech-loading muskets."

Still the Russian infantry slogged on into the pitiless fire, until it looked for a moment as if raw courage and sheer numbers might make up for command ignorance. And then, with success just a few yards away, the Turks laid down their Peabodys and opened fire with the lever-action Winchester. The effect was appalling. Each of Osman's men, as a Russian general later wrote,

> carried 100 cartridges, and had a box containing 500 placed beside him. A few expert marksmen were employed to pick off the officers . . . The Turks did not even attempt to sight, but, hidden behind the trenches, loaded and fired as rapidly as they could.

The Russians went down in struggling, screaming heaps and piles, and still more of their comrades pushed on into that hideous fire. Divisions lost 50 percent of their rifle strength in minutes. Even the stolid Russian infantry wavered and sought cover.

Furious at the repulse, the Russian command threw in ten thousand more infantry, and at last these new masses began to push into the forward trenches of the Turks. The survivors of the Turkish riflemen began to waver and fall back, and some of the Russians began to smell success. "We shall sup tonight in Plevna!" shouted one Russian officer, and just for a moment it seemed that all the blood and suffering might not have been in vain. And then a bugle shrilled in the Turkish lines, and Osman's own reserves crashed into the exhausted Russians.

They came in close order: "Feel each other's elbows!" their officers shouted, and they poured in rifle-fire and then closed with the knife and bayonet. It was too much for tired men, too much blood and too many hours, and the Russians were driven out of everything they had captured.

And so, as the sun went down, the Russians were back where they had started, bloody, tired, and dispirited. More than 7,000 Russian soldiers and almost 170 officers were down, many of them still lying between the lines. Through the hideous night, the howling of wolves played counterpoint to the moans and screams of countless wounded. Out in the gloom between the lines there were human wolves as well, Turkish irregulars called Bashi-Bazouks, who murdered prisoners as a matter of course, and spent this night looting, and cutting the throats of helpless wounded men.

The Russian command was appalled at the bloody repulse. Some officers advised retreating. Stragglers crowded the roads back into Rumania. Grand Duke Nicholas cabled in panic for help: "The Turks are annihilating us. The Christian cause is lost!"

It was not lost at all, of course, and Osman knew it. In fact, very little had really changed. The Russians were still outside Plevna, and he was still inside, as badly outnumbered as ever. As the Russians regained confidence, he knew, they would come again, and this time there would be more of them.

Osman put his men to work, steadily improving his lines with more and deeper fortifications, terrible redoubts with walls twenty feet thick, surrounded by ditches ten feet deep. His blue-clad soldiers were accomplished diggers: "The Turk," said an American officer present at Plevna, "stopping for a day, installs himself as if for a month." The garrisons were issued six hundred rounds per man, with another thousand in reserve. With abundant rations, each redoubt could hold out alone.

The American Civil War might have been fought on Saturn, for all the Russian command and staff had learned from it. Or from the first assault, for that matter, that horrible bloody failure. To the Russian leadership, that debacle had been regrettable, of course, but there was a remedy: Send more men. They brought up reserves, and began to prepare.

And so, out of a thick white fog, Russian shells howled into the Turkish lines on the morning of Tuesday, September 11. The Russian command had chosen this day for reasons of somewhat dubious military validity: It was the czar's name day. The Little Father would watch the assault from a specially built timber platform—with railings and a cover, of course, appropriate wines, a monstrous samovar of tea, and suitable dishes of caviar and wild game. Perhaps his presence would inspire the troops.

They would need inspiration. The Russian bombardment lavished shells on Osman's lines, and managed to kill some five hundred Turks. But it actually made little impression on the mass of that stolid infantry, and still less on the massive entrenchments. Nevertheless, about three in the afternoon, the Russian infantry arose and began to slog up through the glutinous mud toward the waiting Turkish rifles.

There were three attacks, and all three were quickly in trouble. Those terrible Peabodys and Winchesters began to reach out through the rain and pull the plodding Russians down in the mud and muck. Only one assault kept going at all, an attack against the southern sector of the Turkish lines by a mixture of Russians and Rumanians. It was led by the prodigious Michael Skobeleff.

Skobeleff was six feet tall, a barrel-chested fearless fighting machine, son of another Skobeleff who commanded a cossack division for the czar. Skobeleff the Younger was a magnetic leader, given to wearing white in battle, riding a great white stallion, and flaunting a large white flag bearing the letters *MS*.

Worshiped by his soldiers, he carefully cultivated his flamboyant appearance, "so that my men can see that I am always with them." He was that rare leader who could mix and joke with his men without abandoning his position as an officer. He was fond of telling young soldiers that they, too, could become generals. "My old grandfather was a peasant like you, yet I am a general, and so may you be, if you are brave."

Skobeleff cared deeply about his men, spending thousands of rubles of his own money to care for peasant soldiers with trouble at home, chartering a ship to carry wounded men back to Russia. His soldiers replied by idolizing him, following his white banner into the worst fire without hesitation.

Skobeleff was part Scots and all fighting gentleman. The English correspondents paid him their highest compliment. He might, they said, be taken for an Englishman. The Turks also knew him well. To them he was the White Pasha, or the White Devil.

The general was not only a talented leader but an engaging companion, an accomplished merrymaker who spoke six languages and was fond of singing "Auld Lang Syne" in English toward the end of a hard-drinking evening. He was also something of a mystic in his obvious contempt for danger. "We must all be prepared for death, and go to meet it as we are when going to take Holy Communion."

Now, with four thousand of his men dead on the slopes behind him, Skobeleff at last, in ferocious hand-to-hand combat, carried one of three major redoubts barring the way into Plevna. Inside the redoubt walls bodies were piled up five and six deep, and the ground outside was covered with more corpses.

But the other redoubts still stood, and their fire swept the captured ground. Attacking uphill with bands playing, charging through a field of corn, Skobeleff was driven back from another redoubt with hideous casualties. He threw in more men, and still the Turkish stronghold stood defiantly, spewing fire. And then Skobeleff dashed into the fire himself, waving his men on. "Follow me!" he cried. "I'll show you how to thrash the Turks!"

And in went Skobeleff at the head of his survivors, never hesitating when a round cut his sword in two and most of his staff were killed around him. The famous white horse went down, but the general was thrown clear and ran on at the head of his roaring infantry. And up he led them, up, up across the ditch and over the parapet, and in a flurry of bloody bayonet fighting, another redoubt fell. Three thousand Russian dead littered the ground below and inside the walls, but the double eagle flew exultantly above the redoubt at last.

Osman reacted at once, pulling men from the northern redoubts. He must counterattack at once, with everything he had, or Plevna was finished. And from all directions, as night came on, Turkish troops poured south for Osman's counterstroke.

Skobeleff's men were weary, caked with mud, soaked with rain, and battered by steady Turkish fire from every direction. They dug in desperately with bayonets and mess tins, knowing the enemy would be back. Skobeleff could read the omens as well as Osman could, and desperately appealed for reinforcements. He must have men, his urgent messages said, men and ammunition, and both at once.

He got neither. In stark contrast to Osman's energy, the Russian command managed only to reply that there were no troops to be sent, apparently never thinking of stripping other sectors for fresh soldiers. A little ammunition was forthcoming, but it fit only the Krnka rifle; there was nothing for the Berdans, which took a different cartridge. Skobeleff managed to get a little Berdan ammunition at last, cartridges carried in horses' nose bags by galloping Cossacks. It was not nearly enough.

About dawn, Osman's counterattack came in out of a clear, brilliant morning. He was repulsed at first, leaving five hundred dead men littered in front of the redoubt. But he pressed on, until as many as twelve thousand Turks pushed grimly into what remained of the ridgeline entrenchments. And as the day wore on and the Turkish bayonets came closer, Skobeleff's men reached the end of their tether. They had fought for thirty-six hours. They could do no more.

And so the White Pasha saved what he could of his gallant men and fell back. Skillfully he withdrew the bloody, exhausted remnants of his command, all except a tiny group who would not budge, and died to the last man in the redoubt. Their young commander, Major Gortalov, had promised Skobeleff he would hold the redoubt or die. As he covered the retreat of the rest of Skobeleff's men, he shouted to an officer, "Tell the general I have kept my word . . . Tell him I am here, dead." Now, with his handful of men dying around him, Gortalov kept his promise, lifted squirming into the air, impaled on Turkish bayonets.

By the end of the day the whole bloody episode was over. Skobeleff had lost more than eight thousand soldiers, well over a third of his force. The czar's long-suffering men had gained nothing. The three failed assaults together had cost fifteen thousand in just two days of bitter fighting. Even the lion Skobeleff was staggered. He left for a leave in Bucharest, to try to forget the horror of the bloody struggle for the ridge above the town. Later he would write:

> Until the third battle of Plevna, I was young . . . It is a nightmare . . . I will tell you honestly, I sought death there. If I did not find it, it was no fault of mine.

The magnitude of Russian losses shocked the czar. There would be no more of these frontal assaults, he ordered. Instead, the Russian army would settle down to a siege. Perhaps hunger could do what men could not.

Indeed it could, and nobody knew that better than Osman Pasha. He had soundly whipped the Russians twice. The sultan had awarded him a ceremonial sword and the title *Ghazi*—Victorious. Enough was enough. It was time to save his army and go. His men were the best the sultan had, and could do no good penned up and starving in Plevna, which after all had no real intrinsic value.

No, Osman decided, he would get out while he could, get out to the south to join other Turkish forces. He would have to go quickly, too, before the Russians closed their siege ring around the town and trapped him forever. His decision was eminently sensible, of course, but his master was not, and Osman made the mistake of telegraphing his plan to Abdul Hamid in his curious lair by the Bosphorus.

No, came the reply. Absolutely not. Plevna was a symbol. It must be held to the last man. After all, all of Europe was watching, and much of it had come to admire the talent and courage of Osman Pasha. And admiration there certainly was, especially in Great Britain, a land not given to admiring the barbarian Turk but partial to spunky underdogs. In Britain, as historian Rupert Furneaux wrote, there was widespread

> glorification of the courage . . . of the bulldog Turk, and Osman . . . became the man of the hour. Innumerable dogs, not a few cats, the son of an English peer and a new type of lavatory-pan were christened Osman.

Politically this admiration was all very well, but the sultan's order was cold comfort to Osman and his hard-bitten soldiers. But orders were orders, and at least the sultan's message also said that a relief army was being formed to break through to embattled little Plevna. Osman would obey, and wait. He made good use of the several weeks it took the Russians to completely close the ring around his fortress, running in reinforcements, hundreds of wagons of provisions, and whole herds of cattle.

The Russian command now brought in experienced General Franz Todleben, engineer extraordinary and veteran of the Crimea. Todleben would ably advise his royal masters, and insure that the net was drawn tight around Plevna. Osman's last major resupply came early in October, and after that, supplies dried up to a trickle.

By the middle of the month heavy snow was falling, and the iron shackle around the town closed entirely by the end of the month. It did not take long before the ghastly specter of starvation became as big a threat as the Russian guns. As the bitter cold deepened, so did the suffering of Osman's men.

Worse still, Abdul Hamid's armies were everywhere retreating in defeat, and all the sultan's grandiose talk of relief was just so much hot air. As Plevna ran out of fuel in the bitter weather, as the temperature fell to ten below, as rations declined to bare subsistence, as the wounded died in the cold and bandages were taken from corpses for reuse, Osman got news that a wretched caricature of a relief army had run away without a fight.

Osman decided. Orders or no orders, he would not keep his suffering men in this pesthole any longer. In profound secrecy, he began to organize a breakout, scheduled for December 10. Ammunition and the miserable remnants of food were redistributed, gun carriage wheels were muffled, and the civilian Turks were assembled. They would have to come out, too, for if they stayed behind, they would be murdered by the Bulgarians in the cordial tradition of Balkan conflict. Osman extracted an oath from the elders of the Bulgarian church to respect the Turkish wounded he could not move, gathered his men, and peopled his redoubts with a garrison of dummies.

Osman almost made the breakout work. The Russians knew of the planned escape as early as the seventh, although they were not certain of the time. Early on the tenth, however, a spy reported to Skobeleff that Osman was coming out. Even so, Osman's attack smashed through the inner lines of the circle around Plevna and might even have punched through into open country . . . except for the chance Russian bullet that found Osman and knocked him from his horse.

In moments, all the army knew, and the heart went out of Osman's emaciated men. They broke and were surrounded, and by nightfall the shooting died away to a spiteful popping, and then to silence. The siege was over, and Osman's army passed into captivity.

Osman had a leg wound, and would survive. He was lionized by the Russians, who generously acknowledged his genius and drive. Skobeleff called him "the greatest commander of the age, for he has saved the honor of his country." And Osman answered in kind, shaking Skobeleff's hand to tell him, "One day you will be commander-in-chief of the Russian army." The czar returned Osman's surrendered sword, and the doughty Turk was shipped off to honorable captivity in Kharkov.

There, unfortunately, Russian gallantry ended. The Bulgarians lost no time in breaking their oath and butchering Osman's helpless wounded. The rest of his men were left in miserable conditions for weeks, with little food and no medical attention, then marched off through the snow to Russian prison camps. Forty-two thousand soldiers started that death march, most of them weak, many of them without shoes. Their dreadful track was marked with thousands of snow-buried corpses and clouds of watchful ravens. No more than fifteen thousand Turks reached Russia.

The war ground on into the heart of winter, as the Russian juggernaut smashed southeast in horrible weather, down roads packed with frozen and dying refugees, both Turk and Bulgar. Christian and Moslem murdered one another along the road, and pursuing Russian cavalry killed and killed. One story held that the course of the River Maritsa had been changed by a dam of two thousand children's corpses, thrown into the water by the cossacks.

The czar's men, smelling final victory, pushed on past ancient Adrianople and closed in on the Bosphorus. Skobeleff was in the lead, marching an amazing 275 miles in twenty days. The old specter of a triumphant Russian empire holding the Bosphorus was too much for Great Britain. The British flexed their military muscle, and Englishmen sang the favorite music hall tune:

> *"We don't want to fight;*
> *But by jingo if we do,*
> *We've got the men, we've got the ships,*
> *We've got the money too."*

In the end, although Turkey was finished as a European power, Constantinople remained unoccupied. A Royal Navy flotilla cruised ominously in the approaches to the Bosphorus, and Austria began to quietly mobilize troops. And so the shame of occupation, at least, was spared the crumbling Turkish empire, perhaps because the Russians did not want to try conclusions with those terrible ironclads flying the white ensign. An armistice was signed on January 31, 1878, and a peace treaty in March.

A great many good men had died miserably at Plevna, many more than needed to. On the Russian side the leadership, except for the bold Skobeleff, had been dreadful. Russian military doctrine had paid no attention to America's Civil War, which had proved forever that raw courage was no match for the minié ball, let alone the breech-loading rifle.

Skobeleff was promoted to full general, and commanded again in Central Asia. But he would not rise to lead the Russian army, where he might have done much good. He died of a heart attack in Moscow in the summer of 1882. He was only thirty-nine. One of his veterans spoke for every Russian soldier: "God is angry with Russia."

Osman had commanded well, but he served a worthless ruler. Abdul Hamid, gaunt, ill, terrified, far gone in insanity, was at last deposed by his own people in 1909. Osman returned from captivity to command the sultan's guard, but he, too, would never rise to the highest levels of command. He died in 1900.

The real heroes had been the infantrymen on both sides, good soldiers who deserved much better than they got. The ugly futility of their struggle was pretty well expressed in a British newspaper story about fertilizer-making, written some time after the guns fell silent at last:

Thirty tons of human bones, comprising thirty thousand skeletons, have just been landed at Bristol from Plevna.

It wasn't much of an epitaph.

FATE AND GLORY
BATTERY L AT NERY

The early morning of September 1, 1914, was blessedly quiet. A cool mist hung over the blooming French countryside near the village of Nery, as L Battery, Royal Horse Artillery, stretched its aching muscles, cooked breakfast, and watered its horses. Some of the men were washing up, stripped to their shirts. The guns and limbers were not yet harnessed to their teams, the horses still tethered to the wheels or the guns and limbers.

For a little while, at least, both men and animals could rest a little from the nonstop desperate fighting of the retreat from Mons. Battery L had been in action again and again during the retreat, always successfully. On one occasion the battery had fought off four German batteries for almost three hours, finally disengaging neatly with all its guns intact and most of its ammunition gone.

But this morning it was still only five-thirty, and the veteran gunners thought there might be a quiet hour or so to eat a decent meal and have a smoke before the unit trotted back onto the dusty roads of France. There were friendly patrols out to the west, and there was French cavalry on the ridge above the battery. But there would be no rest, for the French cavalry was gone. In the mist, no one had seen them leave, and their commander had not thought to tell Battery L.

Nobody in Battery L knew that about three o'clock that morning, a Frenchman had reported seeing a great many *uhlans*—German lancers—and forty guns. They were supposed to be heading in the general direction of Nery. The report had been made to II Corps headquarters, but it had not yet been passed down to the neighborhood of the resting battery.

A few British gunners saw movement on the little ridge and watched it, veteran soldiers concerned about high ground they did not occupy.

"Some of our scouts out there, aren't they?" said a farrier. "Or is it French cursers (*cuirassiers*)?"

"Looks more like Germans to me," said another man, "arf a mo," and he turned the battery telescope toward the little ridge.

"Yes, it is," he said, "Germans, I can see their spiky helmets! . . . I'm off to report to the captain." And he ran to find his officer.

Too late the quiet was broken by a patrol of the British 11th Hussars galloping into the encampment, shouting a warning that large German units were close and closing on Nery. The patrols reached Battery L's bivouac about the time an alarmed gunner ran up to tell Captain Edward Bradbury what he had seen through the telescope. "Beg pardon, sir," he panted, and at that moment the first German shell howled in out of the mist to burst among tired men and tired horses. Without warning, the uhlans were there, elements of a whole cavalry division, six regiments and two six-gun batteries.

Instantly the battery's peaceful bivouac was a shambles of screaming horses and bleeding men, as shell after shell smashed guns and limbers, tore men and animals to bloody shreds. Passing transport elements dashed for cover as Battery L's gunners dropped razors and pots and cups of tea, and sprinted for their guns.

Above the battery, near the little village of Nery, twelve German guns poured rapid fire into their defenseless target. The range was no more than six hundred yards, almost pointblank for the cannoneers of von der Marwitz's 4th Cavalry Division. To the terrible destruction of their guns, the German troops added the fire of massed carbines and machine-guns.

"Action rear!" roared Bradbury, and the surviving gunners sprinted for their pieces, manhandling the guns into firing position, dodging through dirty clouds of black and crimson to carry shells from their limbers. Major Sclater-Booth, the battery commander, ran desperately back from Brigade headquarters, where he had gone for the morning orders. He never made it, knocked down and out by a shell-burst, unconscious and temporarily blind.

Nearby, cavalrymen of a squadron of the 2d Dragoon Guards (the Queen's Bays) ran for cover, many of their horses stampeding in terror through the bivouac area. Caught in the open like Battery L, the men of the Bays kept their heads and their rifles, and began to gather in a sunken road near the battered battery. They got a machine-gun into action as well, and gradually their aimed fire began to knock down men in pickelhaube helmets up on that flaming hill. The murderous "fifteen-rounds-a-minute" musketry for which the British were famous began to tell on the German gunners and dismounted cavalrymen.

Captain Bradbury, second-in-command of Battery L, ran to his guns through a scene out of hell. All around him the air erupted with whining shrapnel. Wild-eyed horses bolted through the bivouac, screaming with pain, falling, thrashing in the agony of death. Ammunition and caissons exploded around him, but he could see his gunners react with the stolid calm and efficiency expected of the Royal Artillery.

These were the men whom Kaiser Wilhelm had called "that contemptible little army." These same old sweats ever after called themselves the "Old Contemptibles," and now they reacted to disaster with traditional Regular Army calm and precision. They went into their gun drills as if they had been on the range in England, and their shells began to fall among the Germans on the high ground.

The British guns were the reliable thirteen-pounders—so named for the weight of the shot they fired. The piece was the 1904 offspring of a three-inch gun designed by Vickers, the great armament maker, and a carriage made at Woolwich Arsenal. The gun was lighter than its eighteen-pound cousin of the field artillery, light enough, with its six-horse team, to keep pace with fast-moving cavalry.

It was a handy weapon, designed primarily to fire shrapnel, 263 small pellets around a bursting charge that hurled the pellets forward when it exploded, showering death over troops and animals in the open. It weighed about a ton, and threw its 12.5 pound round out to almost six thousand yards.

But the battery was terribly outnumbered, and the Germans scored hit after hit. Three of Battery L's six guns never got into action at all, knocked into junk by German shells before their crews could get them laid and loaded. Two of the other three thirteen-pounders opened on the German artillery and dismounted cavalry above them, but could not sustain their fire.

Gunner after gunner dropped under the howling hail of German shrapnel, but the survivors carried on. Lieutenant Gifford was wounded four times as he ran to bring ammunition to one piece. In spite of his hurts, the officer still dragged himself back and forth with ammunition until the last round was gone from the limber.

But one by one the thirteen-pounders fell silent, the ground around the guns littered with bloodied men in khaki. Man after man went down, until at last only a single piece remained in action.

This was number two gun, and on it the Germans concentrated their fire. More and more gunners fell around it, until it was down to a most unusual five-man crew. Captain Bradbury scrambled between gun and limber, carrying ammunition, while the gun was laid by Gunner Derbyshire, Driver Osborne, Sergeant Nelson, and Battery Sergeant-Major Dorrell.

And the God of Battles smiled on this solitary gun and its scratch crew. In spite of a storm of German gunfire, all of it concentrated on this single piece, number two kept up a steady fire on the German position. A lieutenant and a corporal fell, helping carry ammunition for the gun.

Young Lieutenant Munday moved out from behind the gun shield to stand in the open to observe the gun's fire and call corrections.

"Five minutes left," he called. "Add twenty-five."

And then, as one German gun went silent, "Ten minutes more right; drop twenty-five."

Munday calmly stood erect in that maelstrom of fire until three of the German pieces had ceased fire. And then his luck passed from him, and he went down, mortally wounded.

At first Gunner Derbyshire laid the piece, staying in the aimer's position for twenty minutes, until blood poured from his ears and nose from the concussion of the rapid fire. His replacement, a lieutenant, was blown completely off the piece when a round exploded beneath the shield. Bradbury took his place for a while, then handed over to others and ran back to organize the ammunition supply.

Almost immediately Captain Bradbury himself was down with a hideous wound, both legs shattered just below the waist, but he continued to call to his men, encouraging their disciplined fire. Derbyshire commented admiringly:

> Though the captain knew that death was very near, he thought of his men to the last, and when the pain became too much to bear he begged to be carried away, so that they should not be upset by seeing him, or hear the cries which he could not restrain.

The gun crew stayed grimly at their places. While Sergeant Nelson laid the gun, Sergeant-Major Dorell loaded, reaching back for the shells handed him by Osborne and Derbyshire, who scrambled through the hail of fragments between gun and limber.

A German shell burst directly above the gun, the same round that mortally wounded Captain Bradbury, and fragments tore into Dorell, Osborne, Nelson, and Derbyshire. But the fire of the piece never slackened until Osborne and Derbyshire fainted from loss of blood, lying in the open between gun and limber.

But still Dorell and Nelson kept up the fire, scrambling back to bring up their own ammunition. And the fire was beginning to tell. Several of the German pieces had gone silent, and from the sunken road came a cheer for the solitary gun and its tiny, bleeding crew. The fire from the sunken road was also hurting the Germans up on the high ground. The general commanding the British brigade was down there with the Bays now, and so was his staff, everybody firing on the German units above them.

By now the unequal fight had gone on for some two hours, and at last the thirteen-pounder fell silent. Dorell and Nelson were weak from loss of blood, and their ammunition was gone. But now help was close, and the exhausted gun crew and the embattled Bays could hear the howl of shells from the horse gunners of Battery I, and watch their shells bursting among the Germans above. "There was never," said a gunner of Battery L, "grander music."

Now the Bays could hear the hammer of rifle-fire off to

their left, and the Germans began to disappear in haste. The infantry of 1st Battalion, the Middlesex Regiment, had worked around the right flank of the Germans, and their fire was driving the German cavalry and guns rapidly from the high ground, leaving even some of their wounded behind.

The German retreat quickly turned into a rout under the disciplined fire of the Middlesex and the Bays. The British infantry swarmed over the rise above Nery to find eight German guns still in place, two of them loaded but unfired. They were beautifully built and finished pieces, bearing the imperial crown and the legend "ultima ratio regis," the "last argument of kings." Dead and wounded gunners lay around them, and prisoners threw up their hands as the infantry carried the high ground. British cavalry galloped after their late tormentors, and almost eighty more German prisoners were taken during the chase.

But gallant Battery L was a shambles. All its officers and 80 percent of its gunners were casualties, and there were terrible losses among its horses. Nevertheless, the battered guns were given new wheels and other repairs, and some horses borrowed from Battery I. And slowly what was left of Battery L was gotten on the road to the west. Battery L would return to England to get new guns and new personnel, and would fight again in France.

Total British casualties in the fighting on both sides of Nery were fewer than five hundred. Their German attackers had lost some seven hundred, plus eight of their twelve guns. And next morning, near Ermenonville, British cavalry came upon an area strewn with German equipment and lame horses, every sign of a panic retreat. They had found the track of the cavalry division that had attacked Battery L. And among the loot the British troops took and carried away were the other four of those deadly German guns.

Captain Bradbury, Sergeant-Major Dorrell, and Sergeant Nelson would all win the Victoria Cross, that simple, almost drab decoration inscribed simply "For Valor." Both NCOs would also be commissioned. Gunner Derbyshire and Driver Osborne were both awarded France's coveted Medaille Militaire. The individual gallantry of these men had been outstanding, but it had also represented well the steady, undramatic courage of all Royal Artillery gunners, the men whose motto was "Where Fate and Glory Lead."

THOMAS ATKINS

Oh, it's Tommy this an' Tommy that,
and 'chuck 'im out, the brute';
But it's 'special train for Atkins'
when the guns begin to shoot.
                    Rudyard Kipling, *"Tommy Atkins"*

Time out of mind, "Tommy Atkins" has been the archetypical British soldier. "Tommies," the world called Her Britannic Majesty's troops, long before Kipling's day. The great poet extolled Private Atkins for what he was, the guts and backbone of the empire, and at the same time a simple, intensely human person. Tommy was not above the occasional taking of loot or the more frequent drunken spree. In Kipling's words, he "took his fun where he found it," and could gripe and shirk with soldiers of any era.

He was also an exceedingly tough customer in the clinches, famous for dogged bravery and a disinclination to leave wherever he was before he was ready. Properly led—and he usually was—he won some startling victories against odds, and whipped a variety of excellent fighting men in places Tommy never heard of, places like Inkerman and Suakin and Swat.

Tommy has had a very long life, though he is still alive and well. He was born sometime during or just after the Napoleonic Wars. Whether he was a real soldier or not, nobody knows, but he became the best-known private of all time. His father and mother were both General Sir Harry Calvert, who in 1815 was Adjutant-General in residence at the War Office in London. As part of his duties, Sir Harry created a sample of the new army pay book, and made it out in the name of Private Thomas Atkins. Tommy, born in Odiham, Hampshire, belonged to number six Company, 1st Battalion, 23d Regiment of Foot.

Now, Sir Harry had served in the 23d Foot—later the Royal Welch Fusiliers—during the war. It may be, therefore, that Tommy was a soldier Sir Harry knew, perhaps even his batman, but there is no certain proof of this. What is sure is that samples of the new book were sent to all units in the British army of the day, and Tommy gained a life of his own. It has been a long and honorable one, and although the book is long gone, Tommy is still with the colors. He is less profane and lawless these days, but just as tough as ever.

SAINT GEORGE'S DAY
THE BLOCKING OF ZEEBRUGGE

The spring of 1918. World War I was well into its fourth year, and still the armies bled in bottomless mud across the wastes of Flanders. Imperial Germany, freed of the need to engage Russia, moved troops west and desperately threw assault after assault against the exhausted French and British, driving the allies back across the moonscape of France. Thus far the lines had bent, but they had not broken. And the Americans were coming, hundreds of thousands of fresh, eager troops, new blood to finally end the appalling stalemate on the western front.

But there was another danger. The German U-boat menace, growing steadily more dangerous as the war went on, might starve Britain before the Americans arrived, might decimate the convoys carrying fresh troops and munitions for the hungry guns in France. The U-boats were slipping through to infest the North Atlantic and the waters west of

Great Britain and Ireland. Whatever it might take, they had to be stopped.

A major part of the stopping had to be done by the Dover Patrol, a collection of destroyers, trawlers, drifters, monitors, and motorboats whose function it was to stop the infiltration of German submarines through the English Channel. They were assisted by minefields and submerged nets in certain areas, but the job was not getting done.

Documents lifted from a German boat sunk off Ireland told the story. The German U-boat skippers had strict orders to pass the Channel in darkness on the surface, diving at any chance of discovery. For all their hard work and dedication, the little craft of the Dover Patrol seldom sighted the almost invisible German boats before being spotted themselves. Those boats that traveled the much longer route around Scotland were ordered to let themselves be seen, so that the British would assume the Germans were sending most of their boats to sea that way.

And not all of the *Unterseebooten* were coming from Germany. Many were based right across the Channel in occupied Belgium, particularly at the ancient inland city of Bruges. From Bruges they—and squadrons of torpedo boats—would wend their way eight miles to sea through a canal system that emptied into the sea at a tiny place called Zeebrugge.

Bruges would hold some thirty submarines and even more torpedo boats, which could also go to sea through the more difficult canal to the port of Ostend. The boats based in Belgium had a radius of action much greater than that of the boats sailing from Germany, and their crews remained far fresher while in their operational areas.

But all that was about to change. Three days past Christmas in 1917, a new and dynamic force took charge of the Dover Patrol. This was Sir Roger Keyes, a slim, tough rear admiral who had served his country at sea since he was a boy. He had served in the Boxer Rebellion, winning early promotion, and had been at the Dardanelles. He was a very tough sea dog indeed in spite of his soft-spoken manner, and he began to make changes at once.

The nets were largely removed, and the minefields were extended to new areas and depths. The night surface patrols were stepped up, and much greater use made of searchlights and a white flare of blinding brilliance, developed by Wing

Commander Frank A. Brock, scion of a fireworks manufacturer. Within a month five U-boats had been destroyed by the patrol. One was sunk by depth charges, but the others had been forced to dive into the minefields by searchlights of Brock's flares. They had died there.

But Keyes was not satisfied. Bruges and its ports, Zeebrugge and Ostend, were still a running sore in the side of the British war effort. He began to lay plans to deal with them. Such plans had been considered before, but they had usually involved shelling with heavy artillery. The Dover monitors had unsuccessfully hurled fifteen-inch shells at Zeebrugge's lock gates, an exercise very much like throwing a golf ball at a hole you cannot see a hundred yards away. There had also been a surrealistic scheme to force a major landing on the coast, then set up an eighteen-inch gun *inside* the Palace Hotel in Westende village to bombard Zeebrugge.

But Keyes' daring plan was more practical. While the Zeebrugge lock gates were half a mile up the canal—too far to ram—the channel leading to them might be blocked permanently by a well-organized raid. And even if the blockships could not entirely bar the channel, sufficient drifting silt would pile up against them to clog the channel forever.

The difficulties were legion. Zeebrugge is sixty-five miles from the English coast at its nearest point, a very long way to sail undetected. In addition to the Zeebrugge guns, the coast on both sides of the harbor mounted almost 230 more cannon. Some were as large as fifteen-inch, firing a projectile that stood six feet high and weighed almost a ton.

The Belgian coast itself is a maze of sandbanks and twisting channels, constantly changed by a powerful tidal flow running fifteen feet between high and low tides. The Germans had long since removed all channel buoys, so nobody knew precisely where and how extensive the shallows now were.

The harbor itself was a hornets' nest of guns and obstacles. And to make any blocking expedition more difficult, the ship channel leading to Bruges from Zeebrugge harbor was only 116 yards wide. Its mouth was extended from the coastline by a pair of arms—piers, called *estacades*—270 yards long and 200 yards apart at their mouth. The whole channel required constant dredging, because of the accumulation of silt brought in by the tidal current. Any ship drawing more than twelve feet could only enter the channel by staying precisely in the center of it.

But the guns, and the difficulty in getting far enough up the channel to block it, were not the only problems. For the canal mouth was enclosed by a monstrous mole or breakwater, which made an artificial harbor surrounding the canal entry. It started half a mile west of the canal, and curved northeast for a mile and a half.

First, next to the shore there was a three-hundred-yard causeway, followed by a viaduct or open pier made of steel girders, also three hundred yards long. This served as a sort of sluice, so that the western tidal current could wash the inside of the mole clear of silt built up by the drift from the east. Both of these sections carried a road.

Next came the breakwater itself, about eighty yards wide and more than a mile long. The road continued down it, and on the seaward side was a tall parapet, towering thirty feet above the sea even at high tide. The last section of the mole was a narrow three-hundred-foot pier, ending in a lighthouse. This also had a parapet.

This last section mounted at least six artillery pieces, which could tear apart at point-blank range any block ship sailing by them to get at the canal. Moreover, a barge boom obstructed the channel off the tip of this pier. This obstruction was made of four Rhine River barges cabled together and filled with stone. There was also another boom made of heavy nets supported by buoys, waiting to foul the screws of any ship coming too close to them.

Back on the main part of the mole was a battery of heavy 5.9 inch guns, which could also cover the entrance to the channel. Worse still, the mole was infested with concrete positions for machine guns and antiaircraft guns, infantry trenches, and a wilderness of barbed wire. The garrison numbered more than a thousand. German destroyers were normally moored on the inside of the mole, and their guns could also sweep the channel entrance.

But Keyes thought it could be done. The trick was to attack the mole first, putting ashore Royal Marines and naval landing parties to attack the guns. Even if the guns could not be knocked out, the landing parties might raise so much hell that the garrison would not notice the blockships until it was too late, and they were into the canal entrance itself.

First Keyes requisitioned six obsolete light cruisers, headed for the breaker's yards, but now reprieved to end in grander style. *Thetis, Iphigenia,* and *Intrepid* would be the Zeebrugge blockships. For proud old *Vindictive* there would be another role to play, for she would carry the marines and bluejackets who would storm the mole.

Fitting out of *Vindictive* had to begin immediately. Because of the enormous height of the mole above the water on its seaward side, extensive modifications had to be made to get the landing parties up onto the top of the mole.

Vindictive received eighteen narrow ramps, which could be dropped on top of the mole and mounted by the landing parties. There were grapnels for securing these gangways, which were hinged to a false deck built the whole length of *Vindictive*'s port side.

The false deck got the landing parties closer to the top of the parapet on the mole, but they would still be five to eight feet below it when they started up the bucking, swaying gangways. The marines and bluejackets would also carry scaling ladders to get *down* the sixteen-foot drop from the parapet to the road behind it.

Vindictive kept her weaponry, and got some more. Two 7.5-inch howitzers and an 11-inch howitzer were mounted on her decks, permitting high-angle fire over the mole. In her fighting-top, which towered above the mole, were placed six Lewis light machine guns and three quick-firers. Ten more Lewis guns were placed on the false deck, and Stokes mortars were scattered everywhere. Sandbagged huts were built fore and aft, each one enclosing a flamethrower. Lastly, all her exposed positions were covered with sandbags and mattresses, and her foremast was cut away and lashed across her stern to prevent her port propeller from banging against the mole.

Because *Vindictive* had a very deep draft, there was always the chance she would strike a mine in the uncharted shallows off Zeebrugge. To provide some shallow-draft support, Keyes acquired two most unlikely warships, the Liverpool ferry boats called *Iris* and *Daffodil.*

For all their squatty, benign appearance, they were tough; both had double hulls. And they would hold lots of people once their inside fittings had been torn out and some armor bolted on. They, too, were sandbagged and mattressed, and fitted with smoke-making equipment, grapnels, and scaling ladders for climbing the mole.

And then there were the submarines. HMS C-1 and C-3 were in fact floating bombs. Each carried a crew of six and some five tons of amatol, and their mission was to work westward around the curve of the mole to the open pier, wedge themselves beneath it, and light the fuses. If all went well, the steel girders of the pier would disappear in a flash of white light, leaving the Germans on the mole without rein-forcements.

Altogether 162 vessels were to participate. Besides the blockships, *Vindictive*, the submarines, and the Mersey-side ferryboats, there were two heavy-gun monitors for shore bombardment, a covey of destroyers to cover the operation, and a whole cloud of small, quick motorboats for rescue work. Fast coastal motorboats would close the shore to make smoke, and enter the harbor to torpedo anything hos-tile moored there. Moreover, a number of Handley-Page heavy bombers were to raid Zeebrugge during the attack, creating even more confusion and distraction for the garri-son.

The blockships also carried extra crews to man the ship on her way across the channel, giving some rest to the crew that would actually take her into the harbor. *Vindictive, Iris,* and *Daffodil* also had two complete crews. One would re-main on board to take the ship home in the event most or all of the first crew became casualties or did not make it back from the mole.

Alterations to the blockships consisted mostly in providing an artful cargo of concrete. Concrete, of course, made them very hard to move once sunk in place. More important, if placed correctly in the hull, it made almost impossible the salvage expedient of cutting up the hull and removing the pieces. They also retained their armament, for they would go in shooting.

The operation would have to go in as close to high tide as possible, to give the landing parties their best chance to climb the mole, and the blockships the maximum water be-neath them as they drove in toward the narrow channel. The attack would have to be on a moonless night in reasonable weather. It must be late enough for most of the approach to be under cover of darkness, but early enough to permit most of the retirement to be completed before dawn. During the dark of the moon, there were only four or five nights that fit all these criteria.

To provide further cover, Keyes again called on Wing Commander Brock, and that pyrotechnic genius responded by developing a particularly dense smoke, which could be generated by the covering ships. The smoke was critical, but it required an onshore breeze to keep the cloud in the Germans' faces.

Progress to the target would be controlled by a strict timetable and by buoys, prelaid in the Channel by the small boats. Further position marking would be done by floating calcium flares, also developed by Brock.

The men were easiest to find. Even though Britain was terribly tired, and her manpower reservoir was drying up, there were still far more hearts of oak than Keyes could take along. Even though his officers could not tell the fleet anything about the nature of the mission, both officers and ratings responded in droves. One of Keyes' most painful duties was turning away the dozens of officers who pleaded with him to go along in any capacity.

One of the lucky officers was a member of *Vindictive*'s old crew, still temporarily on board. He knew something was up, and reported to Carpenter. He was terse and convincing: "I don't know, sir, what the old ship is going to do, but it looks like dirty work, and I should like to be there." He was, and in Carpenter's words, "covered himself with glory."

In the event, there would be a number of enlisted stowaways, and every man of the blockships' "extra" crews had volunteered to remain on board all the way into Zeebrugge.

At one point, a part of a Navy crew, discovering that it was not to go all the way to the objective, came perilously close to mutiny. Their spokesman put it plainly: "Well, sir, me and my mates understands as how some of the crew have got to leave the ship on the way across to Zeebruggy. The jaunty [master-at-arms] says it's us lot, and we ain't a-goin' to leave."

The officer hearing their complaint, a wise and understanding man, decided on the spot to take along the extra gun crew, and told the men to draw lots for places on it. In the event, the whole crew went on to Zeebrugge when their pickup boat broke down, and all returned safely.

There were also volunteers from among the cooks and

other support personnel, and even from the civilian employees of the company that provided the men's canteen. Some of these volunteers were taken along to help with the wounded, and performed exceedingly well.

Nobody wanted to be left out. One officer received another irate deputation from the engine room. Their spokesman addressed him: "Me and my mates, sir, understand that we ain't allowed to leave the stokehold and have a go at the Hun." And after the officer confirmed that this was so, the stoker continued: "Well, sir, we wants to know if we may guard the prisoners in the stokehold." The request was denied, as Carpenter later wrote, because "it spelt too much discomfort for the prisoners."

A battalion of Royal Marines—the fourth—was formed at Dover, and began to rehearse the operation on King's Down, outside the town. Many of the residents were bemused at the sight of hundreds of marines going through strange evolutions on and around strips of canvas laid out on the hillside, strips that represented the fortifications on the mole. The marines rehearsed over and over, by night and by day, thinking they were getting ready for an attack somewhere behind enemy lines in France.

In addition there was a Royal Navy landing force of two hundred bluejackets, plus fifty more trained in demolitions work. The whole force was commanded by Navy Captain Stuart- Halahan, who would sail in *Vindictive*. Commanding *Vindictive* and directing *Daffodil* was Commander Alfred F. B. Carpenter—Keyes promoted him acting captain on the spot before the raid, and his confidence would be fully justified.

By the end of March the preparations were complete. All that remained now was the right combination of moon and weather. The men were trained to their peak, and waiting, jammed into the ships, was agony. Twice the signal to go was given and the motley fleet set sail—twice conditions worsened before the strike and ships turned for home without firing a shot . . . but also without being discovered by the Germans.

But at last the day came. It was the twenty-second of April, appropriately the eve of the feast day of Saint George, patron saint of England. That afternoon the various contingents of the force began to sail, and by seven-thirty that evening the flotilla was assembled and turning for the Belgian coast. Before night fell, Keyes—in destroyer *Warwick*—semaphored to the fleet the ancient battle cry: "Saint George for England." It was an apt farewell. By eleven, conditions were still right, and Keyes transmitted a single code word by radio: The operation was on.

A little after midnight the ships reached D buoy. At this point the blockships were to drop the crews that had brought them from England, going on under the crews that would take them into the mouth of the canal. The small boat assigned to remove the spare crew from *Intrepid* had broken down, and so her spare crew, to their intense delight, went on into the objective. Some of the men on *Thetis* and *Iphigenia* hid well enough that they, too, "missed" the launch that lifted off the extra crews.

Now it began to drizzle. It helped hide the little armada, now cruising into a thick screen of Brock's smoke, but it prevented the diversionary strike by British bombers. Still the ships sailed on in silence; still the Belgian coast was dark. Then came the first rounds from the German shore batteries. The defenders knew something was up, but obviously not what it was. Their shells wailed eerily overhead in the smoke, bursting far behind the invasion fleet.

And then it happened, with *Vindictive* only a quarter mile from the mole. At four minutes to midnight the north wind shifted, and the friendly cloud was jerked away from the ships just when they needed it most. Instantly the sea around them churned with bursts from German shells, and Carpenter grimly called for full speed and put his helm over, steering the shortest course for the stone mass looming before him.

German shells tore into the ungainly old cruiser, destroying the forward howitzer, killing men among both crew and landing party, tearing her upperworks to scrap. But the old ship bored in, flames shooting from holes in her funnels, her deck and superstructure ablaze with German shell hits and the muzzle-flashes of her own guns.

Carpenter swung her hard against the mole, where at least her hull was protected from the torrent of fire out of Zeebrugge. But she was a quarter-mile west of her intended landing area, and one anchor was jammed in place. He dropped the other and ran astern as far as he could, but *Vindictive* was still too far from the mole.

Out of the night loomed the chubby Mersey ferryboats, *Iris* and *Daffodil,* already taking hits from German guns, but chugging steadily in toward the mole. *Daffodil*'s captain, Lieutenant H. G. Campbell, wounded and half-blind, saw Carpenter's predicament and neatly swung his little ship bow-first into *Vindictive*'s starboard side, pushing the old cruiser against the mole.

The marines and bluejackets stormed up those gangways that still were undamaged, running across the wildly bouncing planks to reach the parapet of the mole. They ran into a storm of fire, and began taking casualties immediately. Officers struggled in the flash and roar of explosions to attach *Vindictive*'s grapnels to the parapet, covered by the steady fire from the cruiser's foretop. The marine gunners there raked the infantry positions on the mole and turned to scrap the upperworks and gun positions of two German destroyers moored on the inside of the mole itself.

Out in the harbor British Coastal Motor Boats raced through the hail of steel. One torpedoed a German armed vessel trying to leave port; another got a torpedo into an Imperial Navy destroyer moored inside the mole. Others pushed into the harbor to fire mortars at targets around the inside curve of the mole.

Captain Halahan was killed in the opening moments, as German shells slammed into *Vindictive.* Near him fell the Royal Marine colonel commanding the landing parties and his second-in-command. Carpenter, miraculously untouched, calmly went about keeping his battered ship against the mole as missiles of all sizes crashed around him. Both flamethrowers were out of action, one from a break in the fuel line leading to it, the other with a smashed ignition device. Nearly every man in and around the conning tower was down, dead or wounded.

But through all the chaos the leaders maintained that wonderful calm long bred in the Royal Navy. Carpenter found lieutenant Hilton-Young chomping on a huge cigar as he supervised the firing of *Vindictive*'s forward guns. Young nodded to his bandaged arm and cheerfully remarked that he had "got one in the arm." He had. It would be amputated as a result of the wound, but the smiling officer would survive.

Up at the head of one of the ladders lay young Lieutenant H. T. C. Walker, his arm torn off during the assault on the mole. Seeing Carpenter, he waved his remaining hand and called good luck to his commander. Walker, too, would survive.

Meanwhile, down on the mole, Lieutenant Commander Harrison led a storming party in spite of a broken jaw, suffered when a shell fragment had knocked him cold on *Vindictive*. Running into the teeth of German machine-guns, Harrison would die on the mole, in spite of the efforts of his men to pull him to safety. His courage and example would win him a posthumous Victoria Cross.

Through the fire and smoke strode a Church of England chaplain named Peshall, once, like Harrison, an international rugby star for England. His comfort was the last kindness many fatally injured men would know. Throughout the night he went calmly back and forth across the rickety, shell-swept bridges between *Vindictive* and the mole, carrying one wounded man after another away from the German fire. On *Vindictive* a petty officer jumped into the flames of burning boxes of mortar rounds, ordering others to take cover while he stamped out the fire.

Just to the west of *Vindictive*, little *Iris* rode against the wall of the mole, trying to land her parties. Two officers in a row were killed in the hail of fire along the parapet as they tried to anchor the pitching ladders and get the men ashore. Meanwhile, men from *Daffodil* laboriously worked their way across her bows onto *Vindictive* to try to reach the mole.

At this moment two lucky German shells struck *Vindictive*'s foretop, killing or wounding every man there. Only one marine, Sergeant Norman Finch, could move enough to drag himself to an undamaged Lewis gun and open fire again on the Germans. He fired pan after pan of ammunition, raking the mole defenses, until another shell struck the top, wounding him again. Even then, Finch found the strength to drag another badly wounded man from the foretop to safety before Finch himself passed out.

Finch's heroism would earn him the Victoria Cross this night, but now there was no suppressive fire on the German defenses, and the landing parties were taking terrible casualties as they grenaded their way down the mole. Their losses were ghastly, including Brock, who could not stay out of the attack he had done so much to make successful. Wounded men went on and on, still pushing toward the mole batteries until they were killed.

But the selfless work of the landing parties was accomplishing what it was meant to do. The Germans had no eyes for anything but these persistent, pestilential Englishmen on the mole. And so they missed the approach of submarine C-3 entirely as she slid in from the west. Save for a couple of errant shells, there was no opposition until she was close enough to see the outline of the steel girders ahead.

Then she was suddenly framed in the beams of three searchlights, and her skipper, young Lieutenant Sandford, sent her straight for the pier. She struck the latticework of girders flat out, wedging herself between them up to the conning tower, and raising her bow two feet out of the water. Twelve feet overhead was the roadway to the mole.

Sandford lit his fuses and jumped down onto his hull and into a little motor-skiff brought along for the purpose. He was not pleased to find that the propeller would not operate, but he and his men began to row, paddling desperately against a current that threatened to push them back against the monstrous bomb that was C-3.

To make matters worse, the little boat began to take a hail of German automatic-weapons fire from almost point-blank range. Sandford was badly wounded, and two of his men were hit. Still they paddled, hoping the automatic pump could keep up with the cold channel water rushing into the skiff through bullet holes. As they began to make a little headway, the German fire increased, and things began to look hopeless for the little crew of C-3.

And then C-3 blew up. A brilliant flash and the colossal roar of five tons of amatol shattered the night, and the iron girders disappeared. Disappearing with them were the leading elements of a German bicycle unit, peddling madly out to reinforce the garrison on the mole. As the trailing ranks of the bicycle unit skidded and braked and fell into the gaping hole in the pier, a seaman on blockship *Iphigenia* watched a German soldier, complete with bicycle, fly through the air over the mole.

Now the blockships were coming through at last, led by *Thetis*. They had been passed a bearing and distance by a waiting motor-launch, and emerged from the remains of the smoke headed straight in toward the channel. Thanks to the sacrifice of the landing parties and C-3's amatol, the block-ships were well on their way to their objective before the Germans reacted.

But when the German fire came, it was devastating, particularly the point-blank fire from the mole battery. As *Thetis* crashed into the gap between the barge-boom and the net, she was struck again and again, until her hull was filled with smoke and steam, and water was pouring into her. Pushed by the tide, she smashed into the net barrier, dragging it with her until she grounded well short of the channel.

Even then, *Thetis* served well. Her own guns firing non-stop, she drew the mass of the German fire on herself. Meanwhile, *Iphigenia* and *Intrepid* charged into the harbor. Guiding on the green light on *Thetis'* starboard quarter, they forged past her into the entrance to the canal, *Intrepid* leading.

Her captain, Bonham Carter, got well into the canal entrance, and began to back and fill until he got his old cruiser across the channel. Satisfied with a perfect position, he got his men into the boats, started his smoke generators, and prepared to blow *Intrepid*'s bottom out. Before he could, however, his ship was struck by *Iphigenia,* driving down the canal in the cloud of *Intrepid*'s smoke, after ridding herself of a barge she had rammed in passing. *Intrepid* was knocked a little out of position by the collision, but there was no fixing the problem, and Bonham Carter blew his charges, settling the old cruiser across the channel.

Iphigenia's commander, a twenty-two-year-old lieutenant named Bilyard-Leake, fought his ship immaculately attired in a leather coat and steel helmet, looking like a uniform advertisement. Commanding unperturbed in a blizzard of gunfire, he forced the bow of his ship into the silt-bank in a gap between the bank and *Intrepid,* and got his stern into the bank on the other side. Satisfied, he blew his charges also and got his men off. When Keyes saw him after the raid, he was still immaculate and still unperturbed.

Meanwhile, old *Thetis* had managed to get one engine working again, and had pushed her way still farther toward the canal entrance, finally getting crosswise in the channel and scuttling herself. All in all, it had been a remarkable achievement for all three ships.

Getting out again would be pure hell.

On the western side of the mole, C-3's gallant crew had been picked up by a motor-launch commanded by Lieutenant Commander Francis Sandford, brother of the submarine's commander. Under a curtain of fire that turned the water to froth, the fragile little boat headed for the darkness of the channel and safety.

Back in the channel, desperate evacuation efforts were under way, the blockship crews jammed into the remaining undamaged small boats. *Intrepid* had to get off her two complete crews, but there were miracles happening out there in the shell-ripped darkness. One of her two overloaded cutters was found by destroyer *Whirlwind*, and the other by an unarmed motor-launch that had already picked the crew of *Thetis*.

Iphigenia's crowded cutter, battered and almost sinking, was lashed to another motor-launch and nursed out of the rain of fire around the canal mouth. And only then did one of the rescue crew realize Bonham Carter had been left behind in the water—so the little boat turned again to pick him up, finally starting her run for the open sea. Her captain, a young lieutenant named Dean, took the launch in so close to the mole that the big German pieces could not depress to fire on him, and the little boat tore past them to vanish into the night.

Among the mortally wounded was *Iphigenia*'s lieutenant, a youngster named Lloyd, who still carried, wrapped around his body, *Iphigenia*'s white ensign. He was gutshot, and knew he was dying, but he lived long enough to see Keyes after the raid. The admiral did what little he could for the dying boy: He made the young officer a gift of that blood-soaked ensign, the flag he had died for.

On *Vindictive*, Commander Carpenter knew it was time to go. Now that the blockships had charged home, his mission was complete. His ship was jammed with dead and wounded, the surgeons below operating steadily in a blood-spattered imitation of hell. It was the same on all the attack ships: On *Iris* an army doctor, attached to the marines, operated for thirteen and a half hours on end in the blood-spattered purgatory of the sick bay.

The remains of the marine and bluejackets landing parties were still fighting on the mole, but the only result of keeping them there longer would be increased casualties. The withdrawal signal was a blast on *Vindictive*'s siren, which had been long since shot away. But little *Daffodil* still had hers, and its scream finally cut through the roar of battle. At once the troops began to fall back down the mole, fighting little rearguard actions as they came, carrying their wounded and some of their dead.

Lewis guns on the parapet covered the retirement, while the wounded were hauled up the sixteen-foot climb to the roadway, then up to the swaying gangways and across to *Vindictive*. Unwounded men in the comparative safety of the ship ran across the gangways, back onto the hell of the mole, to assist in carrying the wounded to safety. By now, shells were hitting *Vindictive* from batteries down the coast, against which the mole gave no cover.

Carpenter was hit about this time, along with his first officer and quartermaster, but all three men stayed at their posts. Then, as word was passed that the landing parties were back on board, Carpenter walked up a gangway onto the mole, standing calmly in the hail of German fire to make certain no one had been left behind.

Now *Vindictive* and the two motherly Mersey ferries turned for home, belching covering smoke as they pulled away from the mole. Before they could hide themselves entirely in the smoke, *Iris* took a hit on the bridge, which mortally wounded her captain and knocked out both her navigating officer and quartermaster. Drifting off course momentarily, she took shell after shell from the German batteries, until the two wounded men on her bridge put her helm over and headed for the open sea. As she turned, a fragile little motor-launch cut between her and the blazing shore, shrouding her in more of Brock's impenetrable smoke.

Iris was not out of the woods yet. A fire raged forward of the bridge, and ammunition lay everywhere in its path. Able Seaman Lake and Lieutenant Henderson, the only survivors of the damage-control party, fought the fire alone and gradually beat it back. Lake dealt with the threat of the hot ammunition by grabbing it with his bare hands and throwing it overboard. Then, as the wounded steersman finally collapsed, Lake took the wheel in his blistered hands and nursed *Iris* home to Dover in midafternoon.

Behind Lake, sitting up against the bulkhead, was Signalman Tom Bryant, his legs shattered during the fight at the mole. Carried below, he realized he was only the signalman on board, and insisted on being brought back to the bridge. And there he remained until he finally passed out.

Of all the small craft involved in the attack, only two motor-launches had been lost to German fire. In both cases, most of the crew got off in small boats and were picked up by other Royal Navy units. Destroyer *North Star* was crippled by shellfire only four hundred yards off the end of the mole. In spite of valiant attempts to tow her clear by sister destroyer *Phoebe*, *North Star* was finally abandoned, her crew saved by *Phoebe*.

It was over now, all but getting home. *Vindictive* made Dover at eight o'clock next morning. *Daffodil* was towed in five hours later by destroyer *Trident*, and *Iris* chugged in at 3:00 P.M., down by the head but moving on her own engines.

There is still controversy about the effect of the raid. Aside from the casualties inflicted on the German defenders, there is evidence that the blockships substantially closed the channel for a reasonable period of time. German figures indicate it made little difference in their ability to get their boats to sea. However, postwar salvage crews worked long to clear Zeebrugge, and it was not until January 1921 that the channel could be freely used.

The Ostend raid failed, and so did a subsequent attempt. There was no landing operation there, just the old cruisers and their attendant small craft. There was the usual gallant work by the boats that fought the shore defenses and got off the blockships' crews. And at Ostend proud old *Vindictive* went to her death at last, this time as a blockship.

British casualties at Zeebrugge were about 170 killed, 400 wounded, and 45 missing, mostly dead. And the spirit of the survivors was incredible. As they selflessly cared for one another during the long voyage home, their pride shone about them, and overcame much of their pain. One man, who had lost both legs, was asked if he was sorry he had gone. He answered for the whole force: "No, sir, because I got on the mole."

Whatever the long-term effect of the raid, Zeebrugge was a gallant flash of the old sea-dog spirit, and a badly needed stimulant to British morale. Eleven Victoria Crosses were awarded between Zeebrugge and Ostend, a remarkable number of that very rare decoration.

The British nation was cheered by the knowledge that the navy and the marines were as full of spirit and courage as they had ever been, the same gallantry that won Trafalgar. Nelson—who had lost an arm in a similar attack on Tenerife in 1797—would have been proud of the men of Zeebrugge.

GOD'S FAITHFUL SERVANT

Desmond Doss was an ordinary soldier, a PFC from Lynchburg, Virginia. He trained as a medic, and was assigned to the United States Army's 307th Infantry Regiment. As a medic, he was expected to take chances to help his fellow soldiers; self-denial was simply part of the job. In fact, an unwritten rule in the army made the Silver Star the top award a medic could get.

Until Okinawa.

At the end of April 1945 the 307th was locked in vicious, close-quarters fighting for a four-hundred-foot-high ridgeline called the Maeda Escarpment. It was so sheer that the American infantry scaled it with ladders and navy cargo nets. They met a brutal fire as they crawled to the top, a hail of metal that struck down some seventy-five Americans, and stopped the attack cold.

Desmond Doss went into action. Moving steadily across the fire-swept escarpment, he methodically carried a man at a time to the edge of the ridge. He got the worst-hurt down the cliff on a litter rigged to ropes, then went back for more.

During the next week the 307th lost the ridgeline to a Japanese night attack, then took it back again the next morning. Doss was in the thick of it again, tending to the wounded and dragging a shot-up soldier two hundred yards through the open to the shelter of friendly lines. Four times he crawled within twenty-five feet of a fire-spitting Japanese cave, each time dragging a wounded American back to safety.

Doss wasn't through. On the twenty-first of May he crawled through the darkness in the midst of a wild night battle, treating American wounded in his usual nerveless style. Even when a Japanese grenade filled his legs with iron shards, Doss carried on, dealing with his own wounds rather than call for another medic and expose a buddy to danger.

Five hours of pain later, litter-bearers found Doss and began to work their way to the rear with their uncomplaining load. They did not get far. Caught in a Japanese tank attack, the litter party hit the dirt, and Doss went back to work. Spotting a badly wounded American nearby, Doss dragged himself from the litter and ordered the litter-bearers to take the other man to safety.

While they were gone, Doss was hit again, this time a nasty wound that shattered his arm. Still unwilling to endanger others by calling for help, he somehow managed to splint his own terrible compound fracture with a rifle stock and crawl three hundred yards over rough ground to safety.

Remarkably, Doss, this quiet, selfless, astonishing man, was not of the stuff of which traditional heroes are made. He would not touch a weapon, not even to save his own life. For Doss was a Seventh-Day Adventist, a conscientious objector, whose faith forbade him to kill.

One of the abiding strengths of the United States Army has been its willingness, in a proper case, to turn a blind eye on rules, unwritten or otherwise. The army did it again for Desmond Doss. It understood high courage, and it knew how to reward.

Desmond Doss got his Congressional Medal of Honor.

WHEN THE BUTTERFLY WHIPPED THE EAGLE
Over the Western Front

Lieutenant Albert Woodbridge hunched over his bucking Lewis gun, pouring a stream of tracers into the bloodred Albatros fighter rushing at him. Behind him pilot Captain D. C. Cunnell kept their antique F.E. 2d bow-on to the German fighter, as Woodbridge drilled burst after burst in between the muzzle-flashes of the Albatros's twin Spandaus.

Around Woodbridge lead from the German's guns ripped through the flimsy wood and canvas of the ungainly British fighter, reaching for the flesh of its crew. "Thank God," said Woodbridge later, "my Lewis didn't jam . . . I could see my tracers splashing along the barrels of his Spandaus, and I knew the pilot was sitting right behind them."

And then, as the two aircraft closed at 250 miles per hour, the Albatros was suddenly gone, diving beneath the lumbering F.E., no more than twenty yards away. Cunnell rolled the F.E. on her side, and he and Woodbridge saw below them the Albatros falling like a dead leaf, her engine full on, plainly out of control.

But there was no time to celebrate, or even to watch the crippled German all the way into the ground. The air was still full of German fighters, and the British aviators had their hands full just staying alive, Cunnell throwing the creaking old plane around the sky, while Woodbridge slammed quick bursts into anything with Teutonic crosses on its side.

When at last their ammunition was gone, they broke for home, dodging "archie"—German antiaircraft—on the way to their grass field at Marie-Chapelle. They had survived one of the longest air fights on record, forty minutes of fear, sudden death, and wild aerobatics. Woodbridge's hands were burned and blistered from the red-hot barrels of his guns, but he and his pilot had reason to celebrate back in the mess that night.

For the archaic British planes of 20 Squadron, Royal Flying Corps, had knocked down seven German fighters for a loss of only three of their own. And even one of these had managed to crash-land on the British side of the trenches. No fewer than four Albatros fighters were credited to Cunnell and Woodbridge. They had not even claimed the all-red fighter, which nobody had seen go down. They could not know that they had just shot down the German ace of aces, Manfred Freiherr von Richthofen, the Prussian "Red Baron."

The sixth of July, 1917, was quite a day for the F.E.s, so obsolete they should not have been flying at all. They were, as Woodbridge put it later, "butterflies sent out to insult eagles." For the Farman Experimental was a grotesque pusher biplane that looked like a two-seater bathtub with a small oil derrick sticking out behind it. At the end of the derrick was a tail assembly, and the whole thing was held together with a forest of guy-wires . . . and the luck of the Royal Flying Corps.

The pilot handled the plane from the rear seat in the tub. Behind him was a big, 160-horse Beardmore engine, perfectly placed to come crashing through the pilot's spine if he crashed; that is, if the exploding petrol tank did not get him first. The F.E. was nimble enough, but it would not fly above ninety miles per hour without a tail wind.

Nevertheless, the "Fee" was a tough old bird, and carried a considerable punch. The pilot had a forward-firing Lewis gun fixed to the side of the cockpit, which he aimed by pointing the whole plane. The observer, sitting up in the front of the bathtub, fired a pivot-mounted Lewis with a wide field of fire; this was the gun with which Woodbridge knocked down the baron.

There was a third machine-gun, another Lewis mounted on a sort of pedestal behind the observer's cockpit. With this weapon, the observer could fire back over the upper wing at an enemy closing in from the rear. To use the gun, however, he had to stand up, turn around, and put both feet on the edges of his cockpit. Springing from gun to gun while the pilot hurled the Fee through the maelstrom of a dogfight was a considerable feat. Only very brave men flew as observers in F.E.s.

This fight had started over the German lines on a beautiful summer morning. The British were following their usual tac-

tic of aggressive patrolling, six F.E. 2ds out looking for a
fight. They found it quickly, in the form of several fighter
squadrons under Richthofen's overall command. And this
day the baron himself was leading. In no time the half dozen
obsolete British aircraft found themselves tangling with
some forty fast, agile fighters.

The Englishmen stood and fought, turning in a defensive
circle, snapping and biting at the German fighters roaring in
against them. In the midst of the melee four Sopwith tri-
planes of 10th (naval) Squadron pitched in to help the Fees,
and knocked out four Germans without losing a plane. Still
the odds were too long, and the F.E.s edged toward the British lines, turning to slash at their tormentors again and
again. At least there was an east wind to help their clumsy
kites home, instead of the steady westerlies that regularly
forced crippled RFC planes to earth inside the German lines.

"My word," said Woodbridge afterward, "I never saw so
many Huns in the air at one time in my life before." He
sprang madly from gun to gun, firing on some German aircraft from no more than thirty yards. Some of the Germans
burned, horrible splashes of crimson and black, turning to
torches as the dry wood and doped fabric flashed into flame.
"Nasty sight to see," said Woodbridge, with typical British
understatement, "some poor devil who might just as well
have been I. I'll never forget that chap's face . . . I must have
got the petrol tank, as there was a terrific flame and cloud of
black smoke. He saw everything was up, and simply threw
his hands up and clasped his head . . ." And died horribly.

Maybe the young officer's comment seems casual for a
man who was only nineteen when he sent other men to flaming death over the moonscape of devastated France. But an
airman grew up swiftly in those terrible days, or he did not
grow up at all. The life expectancy of young pilots on the
western front was measured in days or weeks, sometimes
only hours. As German ace Kurt Wolf put it, "It was either
him or me—I would rather it was him." One day it would be
Wolf, in a burning aircraft riddled with slugs from a British
Sopwith Camel. Only the strong and the lucky survived.

For Captain Cunnell, veteran pilot and flight commander,
luck ran out only a week after the fight with the baron. But
young "Pip" Woodbridge would survive. Like so many English youngsters of the day, he dutifully wrote regular letters

to his mother—"the mater," as he called her—sparing little detail of the war he fought each day for king and country. "I also got another chap," he wrote of the fight on July 6, "but didn't claim him because, as far as I could see, he was only 'out of control.' " And he added, "Well, W.S.G.S." As he shyly admitted after the war, that meant "watch still going strong," a reference to his mother's treasured gold watch, which she had given him to take to war when he smashed his own in a training crash.

Von Richthofen himself would not make it through the war. In the end, in dreary 1918, he would fall as so many of his victims had fallen, dead of a bullet from the guns of a British Sopwith Camel—or perhaps a slug from the Vickers of an Australian infantry outfit. Nobody will ever know for sure.

But this day he would survive. The British slug ripped through the leather helmet he wore, and tore at the head beneath. The blow was glancing, but it splintered the bone of von Richthofen's skull and drove a fragment against a vital nerve. In an instant the most feared killer of the air war was helpless, his arms and legs temporarily paralyzed, his vision gone. His own simple account underscores the stark terror of the moment.

> I feel my machine tumbling down—falling. At the moment, the idea struck me, "This is how it feels when one is shot down to his death." Any moment, I wait for my wings to break off . . . I forced my eyes open—tore off my goggles—but even then I could not see the sun. I was completely blind.

Richthofen groped for his switches and cut the motor, but still his aircraft tumbled, out of control. The baron knew he must have fallen two or three thousand feet; he must be within a thousand feet of the earth by now; he was running out of time. And then, a little at a time, he began to perceive small flashes of light, little black and white spots, and he realized he was staring straight at the sun, seeing it as if his eyes were covered with thick, dark lenses.

But at least he could see something, at least he could right the sturdy Albatros and try to find someplace to land. He glanced below him at the desolation of shell holes. He could see no safe place to put down, but at least he was within the German lines—there was a wood he recognized. He was in no condition to fight and turned east for home, skimming the torn, shapeless landscape at fifty feet.

He would not reach his home field. Almost immediately von Richthofen realized that his strength was fading, ebbing away with the blood streaming down his neck over his leather flying jacket. The world was turning black before him. It was time to set the bloodred fighter down, and his Prussian luck was in. There it was, a little piece of ground not ripped by shellfire, and he slammed the Albatros down in a space free of shell holes, bouncing across the ground trailing a festoon of telephone poles and wire.

The baron had been saved by his own iron constitution . . . and by his sturdy airplane. The Albatros DV was the cream of the fighters of 1917, a rugged biplane driven by a big Mercedes power plant producing 175–180 horsepower. Its top speed of 116 miles per hour and two synchronized 7.92 mm Spandau machine guns made it an efficient killer, for months outperforming anything the British or French could put in the air against it. More than fifteen hundred of them would fight on the western front alone.

And now the tough Albatros had got von Richthofen safely on the ground, and from everywhere soldiers in field gray were running to help. They knew who flew that blood-red fighter; they knew the hero of Germany was down, and they hurried to get to the Albatros. If it burned, von Richthofen had no chance. Above them two of von Richthofen's young pilots circled anxiously, like falcons above a fallen chick.

Among those who ran to help were Lieutenant Schröder and a corporal from the *Flugmeldedienst*, the efficient German early warning system that telephoned reports of enemy aircraft direct to a fighter control center. Gasping for breath, they reached the Albatros, to find the baron collapsed in a patch of thorns next to his fighter. He had managed the strength to pull himself up and out of the cockpit, but he could go no farther.

Sending the corporal running to telephone for an ambulance, Schröder tenderly removed von Richthofen's helmet and covered the wound as best he could with a field dressing. It was a horror, a rip through the skin of the head four inches long. A patch of white skull as big as a dollar shone through the blood, and the baron was deathly pale. His breathing was so shallow that Schröder was not sure the baron was alive.

But at last von Richthofen began to stir and look around him, and awareness began to return. When a soldier offered him a drink of cognac, the baron had presence of mind enough to ask for water instead, knowing that he should not have stimulants as long as he was bleeding so badly. He had been fortunate, too, in landing near a road, and a field ambulance arrived quickly.

Richthofen, suffering badly from headache and alternate spasms of heat and cold, was taken to the hospital at Menin, but refused to be treated there. For some reason, he had more confidence in the staff at Field Hospital 76, set up in Saint Nicholas Hospital at Courtrai. He had his way. At *Feldlazarett* 76 a surgical team, already alerted and standing by, quickly had him on the table, suturing the long, ugly wound.

He would do, the surgeons said, but a fraction of an inch to the left and there would have been no saving him. Now he must rest, rest absolutely. His nurse, pretty Kätie Otersdorf, would make sure he did. However much the baron might yearn to return to the air, he would recuperate under Kätie's watchful eye until the surgeons were ready to release him. And that was that.

For days von Richthofen fought terrible headaches, headaches drugs could not conquer. But within a week he was able to sit up, to begin to relish the telegrams and letters that poured in from other pilots and from his family. But not from the German public, who had not been told he was down. It would not do to tell all Germany that its idol had fallen, the invincible baron, holder of the Pour le Merite—the Blue Max. Germany could not learn of the defeat of the leading *Kanone*—ace—of the whole air war. The war was going badly enough without that sort of news, even though he had survived.

As he rested, von Richthofen also found time to order five more of the little silver loving cups he kept to commemorate his victories. With these latest additions, his collection of little trophy cups numbered fifty-seven. He had killed sixty-one men in the air. And now he began to think about killing more. He even reflected on his rivalry with his fighter-pilot brother Lothar, also down from an English bullet. As the baron wrote home,

> As I write, I wonder whether my brother or myself will be able to board his plane first. My brother fears that it will be I, and I fear that it will be my brother.

Among the letters that Kätie read to him were a number from two very special correspondents. There was a series from a young girl in a convent in the lovely hills above Oberammergau. There is an air of mystery and purity about these letters, which so moved the baron that he answered several of them, always explaining that he could not think of his own desires as long as the war lasted.

The girl wrote that only a crucifix and von Richthofen's picture hung on the bare walls of her convent room. And when her mother superior had ordered her to take down this picture of a man of the world, the girl had painted out his helmet and uniform, and painted over it a nun's wimple. And when the baron died in that bloody April of 1918, the girl sent the camouflaged picture to Richthofen's mother, took her vows, and passed from the world.

The other treasured letters were from a woman who remains nameless to this day, apparently the only real love of the young baron's life. Other love letters there were, in plenty, and many of these he read aloud to the laughter of the mess. But not these. They came regularly, but they were never shared. Often von Richthofen's orderly would meet him as he returned from a mission, to hand his officer one of the precious letters.

Neither von Richthofen's comrades nor the inquisitive Berlin newspapers ever learned this woman's identity. The baron's mother knew, and so did Kätie Otersdorf. And indeed, there is a story that a tall, beautiful woman visited von Richthofen each day at *Feldlazarett* 76. But as far as is known, neither Frau von Richthofen nor Fräulein Otersdorf ever revealed the name of the baron's one love. And to this day, nobody knows who she was.

Along the way the baron took time to help Lieutenant Schröder, the *Flugmeldedienst* officer who had run to the fallen Albatros to help. Threatened now with court-martial for leaving his post to help von Richthofen, the lieutenant appealed to the baron, and von Richthofen said the right words in the right places. The lieutenant would not be punished.

Now the Red Baron had to try to help himself. After nineteen days in the hospital, he returned to his airfield at Marcke, eager to fly and command again. But he was not the same man. Although he would fly again, and would kill another twenty men and aircraft before a British bullet caught him, something was lost inside him.

To begin with, his wound did not heal well, and for months he fought headaches, dizziness, and a buzzing in his ears. He was thinner and quieter, and twice he returned to Field Hospital 76 to have bone splinters pulled from the gaping hole in his head. But the wound was not the only torment the *Rittmeister* was suffering.

It was certainly not a loss of courage. The baron never lacked for guts. But some of his confidence seemed to have ebbed away along with the blood from his torn scalp. His mother noticed the change when her son took six weeks' leave at their Silesian home in Schweidnitz:

> Manfred was changed after he received his wounds. I noticed numerous differences in him. His fears for Lothar's safety increased, and he was no longer certain that victory would come . . . He said that people in Germany did not realize the power of the Allies.

They did not. For when von Richthofen returned to his unit toward the end of October, there were many empty places around the mess table. Two of Germany's finest squadron leaders were absent, absent forever. Kurt Wolf was gone, and so was the brilliant Werner Voss. Richthofen must have seen the implacable future in the empty chairs and turned-down glasses. Germany was losing the war.

The baron would fight on. He was a soldier, son of a family of soldiers. He had another six months to live, and he would spend it grimly stalking his country's enemies. But it was getting harder and harder. There were more and more of the aggressive British Camels and SE5As. As 1918 began, German losses steadily mounted. On the twenty-fourth of March alone, Germany lost sixty-seven aircraft to only ten RFC planes. The baron could see the handwriting on the wall. In a letter to his mother in February, he wrote a prophetic line:

I am sorry . . . that I could not come . . . to say good-bye. It would have been so pleasant, and I was looking forward to it. Now I think I will not come back to Germany for a long, long time.

He would not come back at all, at least not until his remains were returned to Berlin's Mercy Cemetery in 1925. In spite of the protests of left-wing organizations, his funeral was attended by countless mourners, led by Marshal von Hindenburg, now president of Germany. His people had not forgotten him.

And among them, fittingly, were men of the old Royal Flying Corps, men who had fought against him. They had not forgotten him either, and had come, as friends, to say good-bye.

A MATTER OF HONOR

As the bloodied remnants of Japan's eastern armies fell back before the British in Burma, hard-nosed Field Marshal William Slim gave a little thought to the last act. He knew the Japanese well. He knew that to understand and accept their total defeat, they could be left no way to rationalize their loss.

And so Bill Slim ordered that all senior Japanese officers would surrender their swords to British officers of the same or higher rank. Even more important, they would do so in front of formations of their own troops.

Slim gave this order knowing that it contradicted MacArthur's directive that the "archaic" ceremony would be dispensed with. He also ignored the advice of allied "experts" on Japan, who objected to the surrender of swords on three grounds.

First, they said, the samurai sword was so important to a Japanese officer's honor that he would fight on, rather than surrender. Second, even if he did hand over his treasured blade, he would lose all face with his men, and with it all power to command. Third, opined the experts, a Japanese officer who surrendered his sword would be so shamed that he would be obliged to commit suicide.

Slim was unmoved. He had been at war in Burma for a long time, and he had seen too much. He was a humane man himself, but he remembered too much brutality by his enemy, especially their mistreatment of prisoners. He had no pity, and replied to the experts directly.

"(i) If the Japanese liked to go on fighting, I was ready for them.

(ii) If the officers lost their soldiers' respect, I could not care less, as I intended to separate them from their men in any case.

(iii) If the officers committed suicide, I had already prepared for this by broadcasting that any Japanese officer wishing to commit suicide would be given every facility."

And so, with Lord Mountbatten, he presided at the overall Japanese surrender, in Singapore on September 12, 1945. Outside the place of surrender the Union Jack snapped in the breeze. In a touch typically British, it was the selfsame flag hauled down in surrender three years before.

Mountbatten formally received the sword of Field Marshal Terauchi. To Slim went General Kimura's blade, which in later years reposed on Slim's mantel. "Where," wrote Slim, "I always intended that one day it should be."

GOODBYE, MY SON
The Siege of the Alcazar

The ancient fortress-palace of the Alcazar sits on high ground overlooking the river Tagus and the storied city of Toledo, city of El Greco and matchless swords. The Alcazar has been much rebuilt since 1936, but in that year it was a massive place, old but strong, and built of stone, a complex of buildings that included the fortlike military governor's quarters. It was approachable only on one side, across the Plaza de Zocodover.

Once a Moorish stronghold, it had long lain quietly under the Spanish sun, musing mutely on its past days of blood and heroism and glory. And now, in the broiling July of 1936, it would have another time of high courage, as bitter civil war swept ancient Spain.

The Fascist rising had begun in many places across the country, in the Canary Islands, and in Spanish Morocco, from which would come many of the hard-core troops of Franco's armies. But in these early days forces loyal to the republic, supported in some places by vast mobs of civilians, had in many places defeated soldiers and Falangists trying to topple the government.

All across the land there was murder and torture and rape by both sides, but in these early days the rebels suffered most. Many of them were driven to make a desperate stand in whatever strong place they could find. And they took their women and children with them when they could, for there was no safety in age or gender.

One of these refuges was the Alcazar. For in Toledo the rebels had been driven quickly from the city after an initial success. Vast crowds of militiamen and *Asaltos*—assault police—had descended on Toledo from Madrid and the north to join the local Loyalist militia, and the Fascist forces were terribly outnumbered.

The rebel commander, Colonel José Moscardo y Ituarte, would have made a fine conquistador. He was one of those fearless, unbending types who raged through Peru and Mexico to build the Spanish Empire in centuries long gone. He was, in short, the perfect man to keep a rebel foothold above Toledo until help could fight through to him, for "surrender" was not in his vocabulary.

On July 18 Moscardo had been in Madrid, preparing to travel to Berlin for the Olympic Games. He was at that time director of the military School of Gymnastics, just outside Toledo on the Madrid road. Getting news that the revolt had begun with risings in Africa, he quickly returned to Toledo to lead the rebellion there. Fighting had already begun in the streets of the city, and that evening the Communist rabble-rouser La Passionaria broadcast an appeal to the masses to rise against the revolt.

Moscardo knew well that help might never come, for there was no strong rebel force anywhere close to him. The rising had failed in both Madrid and Guadalajara, northeast of the capital. He knew he would long be a tiny island in a hostile sea, a sea that might well rise to drown him. He was not at all bothered by the thought, and proceeded to organize a defense.

At first he was able to hold strongpoints in the city itself, but as ammunition and water ran low, he pulled back his scattered outposts to the citadel itself. By the afternoon of the eighteenth, under Loyalist air and artillery attack, he had concentrated his force inside the Alcazar. He took inventory of his resources, and found that he had little to work with.

There was a reasonable supply of water inside the fortress, and enough food to subsist on short rations for months. There was wheat to make bread, but the very limited capacity of the garrison's tiny mill kept the bread ration down to around 180 grams per day. There was some carefully rationed meat, mostly horse and mule.

Colonel Moscardo's young cadets, about two hundred in number, were ardent nationalists, and were determined to hold the Alcazar to the last cartridge. In addition, he commanded some eight hundred men of the *Guardia Civil*, the paramilitary police. The *Guardia* troopers were trucked into Toledo from all the surrounding countryside, and they brought their families with them. It meant that many more mouths to feed, but if they were left outside, it meant death . . . or worse. There were also some one hundred unattached officers and about two hundred civilian rebels belonging to right-wing nationalist organizations. Finally, there were some two hundred noncombatants, fifty of whom were children.

Ammunition there was, in plenty, thanks to an incredible oversight by the loyalist Ministry of War in Madrid. On the evening of July 18 a ministry functionary telephoned Moscardo, ordering him to take delivery of a million rifle-caliber rounds stored at the Toledo Arms Factory. Moscardo, short of ammunition, moved swiftly to gather in this treasure, of which he had had no notion prior to the call.

Less than an hour afterward the ministry called again. This time it was loyalist General Riquelme, ordering Moscardo to surrender. Moscardo replied that he and the other defenders "preferred to die than to see the Alcazar transformed into a dung heap . . . by surrendering it to the enemies of our country." So the colonel had made his decision, and sent a force for the ammunition. He would fight it out.

He would persist in that view, in spite of further appeals not to expose the Alcazar, "this precious jewel," to the ravages of war. He would not, he said, surrender ever, but would resist the Marxist government to the end.

There was an ample supply of weapons. In addition to the rifles, Moscardo had thirteen 7 mm Hotchkiss machine guns and thirteen quick-firing guns of the same caliber. There were several cases of hand grenades, and an assortment of bombs and other explosive devices. The only artillery were two little mountain guns, with only fifty rounds of ammunition. Since all power to the Alcazar was cut by the enemy, there was no communication with the outside world except a jury-rigged receiver run on automobile batteries.

In late July, during the first week of the siege, Moscardo received a terrifying telephone call from Toledo, through the Loyalist-controlled switchboard there. The caller was a Loyalist officer named Cabello, commander of the Toledo militia, who demanded that Moscardo surrender within ten minutes. If he would not, the caller said, Moscardo's sixteen-year-old son, Luis—captured elsewhere—would be executed. Luis was put on the telephone, and father and son spoke briefly.

"Papa, what are your orders?"

"What is happening, my son?"

"Nothing. They say they will shoot me if you do not surrender the Alcazar."

"Well then, I order you in the name of God to cry out, 'Viva España' and 'Long live Christ the King' and die like a patriot. Good-bye, my son."

"I give you a hearty embrace, Father."

And that was that. Moscardo told the loyalist officer to forget the ten-minute grace period. There would be no surrender.

There is no doubt that this terrible conversation took place, and it is also certain that young Luis Moscardo was shot, although not until another month or so had passed. It was all, as one correspondent wrote, "in the best—and worst—Spanish tradition."

The garrison dug in, using priceless books from the ancient library as sandbags, and prepared for the worst. It was not long in coming, for the Loyalist besiegers were determined to take the ancient citadel. It was becoming a symbol for both sides, and the question soon became which side could stand pounding the best.

Loyalist artillery steadily shelled the Alcazar, and the garrison could not respond, having no guns of their own. The granite walls chipped and cracked here and there, but thousands of artillery rounds produced no breach through which infantry could go. Inside the fortress, as the garrison suffered casualties, the bodies were simply inserted into the massive walls. They could not be burned, somebody said, because the garrison were Catholics.

As the siege dragged on, besieged and besiegers sang patriotic songs at each other across the bullet-torn Plaza de Zocodover. And they hurled insults back and forth, singing their cheerful slanders in spontaneous *coplas*.

On the loyalist side, there was a good deal of oratory about not destroying a "priceless work of art," and killing or injuring the women and children inside. How much of this talk was sincere, and how much an excuse for not going in hand to hand to eliminate this hornets' nest, is unclear to this day.

At any rate, as September began, the loyalists took the decision to capture the Alcazar whatever the price. First they again tried negotiation. On the ninth a former instructor at the Cadet School went in under a white flag to try to persuade Moscardo to at least evacuate the women. The doughty colonel refused, but did ask for a priest.

The besiegers responded by moving all women and children out of Toledo, and stepping up the bombardment, using artillery as large as 155-mm against the stubborn granite. During the siege some fourteen thousand shells struck the old fortress, more than three hundred of them 155-mm. Loyalist aircraft bombed the Alcazar almost daily with bombs, containers of gasoline, and teargas canisters. The gas caused the garrison the worst problems, for they had no masks, but it could not drive them from their posts overlooking the Plaza.

After the first day of heavy bombardment, the attackers made another effort to negotiate, and this time did honor the garrison's request for spiritual help. The government troops sent in one Father Camarasa, a highly respected priest who was admired even by much of the anticlerical left. He was carefully observed as he approached and entered the Alcazar, checked by officers who knew him, to be certain he was not a disguised government officer sent to assess the strength of the garrison.

Father Camarasa celebrated Mass, giving a short sermon in which he spoke to the garrison of the glory they would find in the world to come; he was plainly certain they would go there soon, that their defense of the Alcazar was hopeless. Because he had no time to hear individual confessions, he gave a general absolution to the garrison. Finally, he gave Communion to all who wished it, moving from the chapel to minister to the seriously wounded in the infirmary. He even found time to baptize two babies born in the Alcazar's cellars during the siege.

He spoke with Moscardo in an effort to end the fighting and save lives, but the colonel was determined to hold out. Moscardo retrieved from the priest notes he had made identifying families of the garrison. Father Camarasa would no doubt have sincerely visited these people to reassure them of their men's welfare. But Moscardo feared the government would make hostages of them to further pressure the garri-

son to surrender. And then the priest returned to the Loyalist lines and the guns began again.

Moscardo had other worries as well. Twice in July the
government had announced the fall of the Alcazar, even pub-
lishing faked pictures of the garrison surrendering.
Moscardo was concerned, fearing that the Nationalist command might believe the reports, and redirect its relief columns to other objectives. And so he asked for a volunteer to
win through to the nationalist lines and reassure their commanders that the Alcazar was alive and well.

The volunteer was a Captain Alva Navas, a professor at the
School of Gymnastics. Dressed as a laborer and carrying a
Communist party card taken from a hostage, he worked his
way through the battered city to the Tagus, then swam the
broad river in the dark. Working down the left bank of the
river out of the town, he then recrossed the Tagus and made
for open country.

About forty kilometers from Toledo he ran an astonishing
bluff. Calling on a local Red Committee, he demanded a car
to take him farther on his "secret mission" for the government. Persuaded, the committee found an automobile for
him, but as he stepped into it a bystander—once a student at
the School of Gymnastics—recognized him. It was a fatal
greeting, and the gallant captain was immediately shot on the
Toledo road. Tragically, the captain's heroism was wasted,
for the Nationalist command was not deceived. The drive toward Toledo continued, and the defenders could not hold it.
The government forces were getting anxious. In the North
and along the great River Tagus, the loyalist cause was coming unstuck. Strong rebel forces were advancing everywhere,
and a victory was desperately needed.

Meanwhile, inside the Alcazar, nobody knew whether the
captain had won through to friendly lines, nor what the rebels' next move might be. Would they raise the siege, or starve
out the garrison? Did any friendly forces even know they
were still fighting on?

It did not take long to find out. A strong Nationalist column under General Yague, deliberately passing up a chance
to wrest Madrid from the government, turned its head toward Toledo. Relief of Moscardo's embattled people would
be an incredible moral victory in this very Spanish war of
morality and mystique, and the besiegers knew they must

crush Moscardo before nationalist help could fight its way through to Toledo.

They decided on a maximum effort, whatever the cost, and even invited correspondents to Toledo to watch the fall of this nationalist bastion. The besiegers were reinforced with more *Asaltos,* and tunnels were begun that would undercut both the towers on the landward side of the Alcazar.

These were to be monstrous mines, laid at the end of the tunnels driven by Asturian miners. There were two separate charges, totaling some seven tons of dynamite. It was not a surprise to the defenders—for days they could hear drilling beneath them, and it needed little imagination to know what was coming. But since there was no engineering equipment but a few spades inside the Alcazar, the garrison could only wait, and hope to move out of harm's way in time.

Preparations for the government attack began early on September 18, with a heavy barrage of artillery fire against the east face of the Alcazar. Among the torrent of projectiles were at least ninety 155 rounds. After half an hour or so of bombardment, the mines were finally sprung, and the attack was on. With a shattering roar that broke every remaining window in Toledo, one of the mines went up, and the Alcazar's southwest tower collapsed. Great fragments of the wall showered over the precipice into the broad Tagus, and into the dust and smoke came the loyalist infantry. They charged from two directions, against both the north and south wings of the building, and the defenders met them head-on.

But only one mine had gone up; the second had not exploded, and the drilling had warned the garrison, who had moved from the threatened area. And now, as the Loyalists fought their way into the courtyard in a shower of grenades, they found themselves face-to-face with the *Guardia,* and the professional officers, and the cadets of Toledo. The fight lasted for several hours at very close range, but the attackers could gain no foothold. Casualties piled up, and the defenders counterattacked again and again. At one point the north tower was held by just four officers, armed only with pistols. But it held.

The attackers fell back, licking their wounds. Obviously something else was required. The garrison knew it was not over, but they had no idea what to expect. They did not have long to wonder, for the next day five fire engines full of gasoline began to drive into the back of the Holy Cross Hospital, across the Zocodover. And then, to the defenders' horror, government militiamen began to advance under heavy covering fire, spraying the walls of the Alcazar with fire hoses gushing gasoline.

Suddenly a young cadet ran from the Alcazar, seized the nozzle of one of the hoses, and turned it back on the militia. He was shot down quickly, however, and the soaking of the Alcazar's walls went on. Then hand grenades exploded along the wall of the building, and the facade was engulfed in flames, which burned on with a vile smell all through the afternoon.

Now dynamite specialists blew charges along the Alcazar's old walls, tearing gaps in the defense, but the ceaseless fire from the garrison drove back every attempt to enter. As night came down, both sides lay exhausted, and rain began to fall across the corpse-littered square and the blackened, torn front of the old fortress.

But the fighting went on. The militia pushed in again with grenades and more dynamite, and poured gasoline into the interior of the building. But through the smoke and flame the garrison's steady firing barred the attackers' way. As the fighting went on through the twenty-fourth, the cadets and *Guardia* still held, and now there was new hope to feed their courage. For there were rebel aircraft circling the Alcazar, dropping messages for the garrison: Hang on, hang on; the relief column was coming hard, only ten miles away.

At last, on the twenty-seventh, the attackers tried their last hope. They blew their last and biggest mine and came on again. But this time the mine—three thousand kilos of powder—had been driven too hastily. It had been pushed in through a sewer toward the northeast tower . . . but the diggers had miscalculated, and stopped short of the foundations. The tower came down, all right, but the rubble behind it was still full of well-served rifles and machine guns.

The explosion left a crater about one hundred feet across and twelve or thirteen feet deep, but the building stood. Again the defenders were waiting with cocked rifles when the Loyalist infantry came in. The attack stalled, and this time it would not be renewed. Outside the city units of the Nationalist Army of Africa lined the hills, tough, experienced Moorish infantry, and the loyalist forces could not hold them. The militia broke and streamed away, and the assault police, and last, a handful of the tough volunteers of the International Brigade.

In the town the Nationalist troops took no prisoners. They had found the bodies of two Nationalist aircrew outside the city, mutilated by the Loyalists, and they took their revenge. Some wounded militiamen were murdered, and forty anarchists, forted up in a building, drank themselves into a stupor and then burned themselves up, building and all.

It was over except for one last gesture. As General Varela led relief forces into the Alcazar on the evening of September 27, Moscardo stepped forward to meet him, snapped to attention, and saluted. *"Sin novedad,"* he said. "Nothing new, General"!

"Sin novedad"! It was a truly Spanish ending, a last flare of the same sort of half-arrogant, half-heroic determination that had held the citadel these sixty-nine long days.

Although the siege of the Alcazar won most of the headlines during the civil war—due no doubt to the accessibility of Toledo to correspondents—it was only one of several fights against odds by garrisons in strong places.

One of these was in Asturias, the battle for the Simancas Barracks in Gijón. The barracks there were held by only 180 men, short of everything, especially water. Each night they had to undergo the torment of listening to the arrogant Queipo de Llano smacking his lips over a glass of wine on radio Seville. But by mid-August 1936 the garrison was still holding on, helped from time to time by shells from the Nationalist cruiser *Almirante Cervera*, anchored off the town.

In Gijón, as at Toledo, the government besiegers tried to force surrender by threatening to shoot hostages, this time the two sons of the commander, Colonel Pinilla. Pinilla, like Moscardo, refused, and his two boys were promptly executed. Still the garrison hung on, fighting off charges by miners armed with dynamite bombs. Until, on August 16, overrun by enemies, Pinilla radioed the Nationalist men o' war off the town: "Defense impossible. Barracks burning and the enemy starting to enter. Fire on us!"

And so the ships shelled Simancas, and the last of the garrison went down fighting in the burning building, taking with them the attackers killed by the ships' guns. It was the stuff of which legends are made; the garrison would not be forgotten.

And then there was Santa Maria de la Cabeza, a church flanked by two mountaintops up in the Sierra Morena, between Castile and Andalusia. Here had gathered some 250 *Guardias* with their families, perhaps one hundred Falangists, and a thousand or so middle-class civilians. They collected food and dug in, and for a while they were left alone.

And then, in a gesture purely Spanish, they decided to take a stand in this bitter and emotional war. They sent a declaration of war to the Popular Front Committee of Andujar, and the siege was on. Santiago Cortés, a *Guardia* captain, took command of the defenders, in spite of the fact that his family were already political prisoners of the government. He faced a besieging force of at least ten thousand militiamen, but for the moment there was no serious assault.

The garrison communicated regularly with friendly territory by carrier pigeon, and the defenders were regularly resupplied by air. Some 150,000 kilos of food were dropped to the defenders during the siege. More fragile supplies were attached to turkeys, whose strong wings generally wafted them—and their cargo—safely to earth within the lines.

But in April 1937 the government had had enough of this running sore inside its own territory. This time real shock troops would lead an attack on the little Nationalist position, the XIII International Brigade, led by General "Gomez"—in fact, the German Communist Zeisser. One hilltop was lost, but the garrison fought on. Franco sent permission to surrender, but Cortés and his officers knew better than to trust the government besiegers. Hammered by artillery and air strikes, they resolved to fight on to the end.

And on the first of May—the great day of international Communism—the International Brigade and republican militia broke into the burning church, and the terrible passions of civil war ran loose in a welter of blood. Not until a great many people had been murdered—including many noncombatants—did the orgy of killing subside. At last most of the women and children were trucked away, and the surviving defenders made prisoners. Cortés, wounded on the thirtieth of April, died later of his wounds. He was as tough a nut as Moscardo . . . but not quite as lucky. He, too, would find a permanent place in the legends of the new Spain.

FOREBODING

When I knew him, Herr Becker was an instructor at the Army Language School in Monterey. He was a superb teacher and a charming man, full of wisdom, much given to laughter and high spirits.

In his time, however, Becker had been a first-class soldier. He had rolled into Poland in September of 1939 as a regular army *Fähnrich*, an officer-candidate. He finished the war as a major, fighting to the very end, and along the way he fought virtually all of Germany's foes at one time or another.

In September of 1944 Becker had just emerged from the hospital with his fourth wound. "By the British," said Becker. "It was always the British who shot me. I liked the Englishmen I met; I still do. But I was never popular with them."

Experienced officers were in short supply by that point in the war, and so, instead of fully recuperating, Becker was sent to command a scratch company of boys and invalids near a place called Arnhem. As part of Operation Market Garden, the British 1st Airborne Division had landed there to capture the vital crossing of the Lower Rhine. It was critical to eliminate the British airhead before Allied help could reach the paratroopers. And so the Germans threw in everything available, including Becker's feeble company.

Becker drew a quiet part of the ring around the British, because of the youth and inexperience of his men. During the night, however, he was awakened by one of his few experienced NCOs.

"Herr Major," said the sergeant. "I have two of our young soldiers outside. I think you had better talk to them."

Becker faced the two youngsters. To his astonishment, they were crying.

"There, there," said Becker, in his best fatherly voice. "You are unhurt. It cannot be that bad. Tell me what has happened."

Between sniffles the young men answered. "Our machine gun, Herr Major; they stole our machine gun!"

Ah, thought Becker, who knew replacements for automatic weapons were scarce. Some neighboring unit has up-gunned itself at our expense.

"Describe them, men," said Becker. "Tell us what they looked like, and perhaps we can recover the weapon."

"I remember this, Herr Major," said one youngster brightly. "They wore red berets."

Becker and his veteran NCO looked at one another in silence, and then Becker gently dismissed his young soldiers.

"They were a British patrol, of course," said Becker later. "They looked at these two young soldiers of mine, these two boys, took the machine gun, and went on their way without harming my youngsters. I never fought tougher men than the British paras. But they would not kill children who had no idea of what soldiering was about.

"If I had not been convinced of it before, I knew now the war was over."

THE NAVY'S HERE
THE BOARDING OF *ALTMARK*

Captain Dau could breathe easier. His big tanker, *Altmark*, was in neutral waters, in a Norwegian fiord, safe from her enemies in the deep water outside. He was almost home. It was only a short run to Wilhelmshaven, and he could wait.

The British could not keep ships outside his haven forever; when they left he would sail south, hugging the Norwegian coast, until, covered by the Luftwaffe from German bases, he could run across the narrow neck of the Baltic for home. He would bring his ship and crew back intact, and with them he would bring almost three hundred British prisoners, merchant navy officers and crew taken off ships sunk by pocket battleship *Graf Spee* in the opening weeks of the war.

It was February of 1940, dark and frigid, as *Altmark* lay in her fiord. She had left Germany in the summer that now seemed so very long ago, and many thousands of miles had passed beneath her keel since. Her warship, *Graf Spee,* had had success after success against British merchant ships in the far-flung shipping lanes of the South Atlantic, and had even crossed into the Indian Ocean to sink another merchantman. But in December her luck had run out. She had reprovisioned from *Altmark* and headed west for the mouth of the mighty River Plate, the shipping artery that fed both Montevideo in Paraguay, and Buenos Aires, Argentina. She hoped to find a small merchant convoy, but she had never returned.

Spee had been at sea before war began. She and her sister ship, *Deutschland,* had both left Wilhelmshaven for the open sea, and their intended career as commerce raiders. The Polish invasion was prepared and ready to go, and the *Reichsmarine* wanted its surface raiders far at sea before the first shot was fired, lost deep in their waiting areas near British shipping lanes.

Graf Spee left port on August 21, 1939, and *Deutschland* was three days behind her. Both ships, using darkness as best they could, sailed through the trackless seas north of the Faeroes without being seen. Their support vessels, *Westerwald* for *Deutschland* and *Altmark* for *Graf Spee*, were already at sea. *Altmark* had sailed on August 6, traveling openly down the English Channel in the last sunny days of peace, bound for Port Arthur, Texas. There she filled her tanks with fuel, then turned south for the empty wastes of the South Atlantic, and her rendezvous with *Graf Spee.*

Captain Heinrich Dau of *Altmark* was not a pleasant man, nor one beloved by his crew. He was short, graying, and wrinkled, sporting an old-style Imperial Navy beard and mustache. He seems to have been something of a petty tyrant, fond of exercising his authority, and given to constantly reminding his officers of his long experience. "A lifetime at sea . . ." he would say, effectively discouraging suggestions from his subordinates.

He and his officers were at dinner on Sunday, September 3, when the steward murmured softly to him, and the captain abruptly jumped up from the mess table and quickly left the room. He was back within minutes, waving a decoded radio message, and immediately gave orders to fall in the entire ship's company, pulling the men from their Sunday meal rather than wait even a few minutes. It was only then that *Altmark*'s crew learned of their mission. They would not be sailing to Rotterdam as they had thought; instead, they were going to war. "England and France have declared war," he announced with great drama. "The task which the führer has selected for us is to act as the indispensable, floating supply base for a German battleship."

The response was silence. The crew was not anxious for war, especially not after the series of bloodless triumphs Hitler had achieved in the Rhineland, Austria, the Sudeten, and finally the rest of Czechoslovakia. But Dau, already in his mid-sixties, was apparently enthusiastic, and sure that the führer was right again. He still vividly remembered the great days of the First World War, when he had commanded a frigate of the Imperial Navy.

Dau immediately put the crew to work. *Altmark* was to be painted a light yellow, better suited to the harsh sunlight of the South. And she became the Norwegian *Sogne,* home port Oslo, just as fast as her hands could paint in the new identity. Dau pushed south for a rendezvous point in the great blankness about midway between Trinidad and Dakar.

In the end, the meeting was easy. In fact, *Graf Spee* came up so suddenly, northwest of the Azores, that Dau at first thought she was a British man-of-war, and turned to run at *Altmark*'s best twenty-two-knot speed. But quickly the fighting top of the pocket battleship loomed above the horizon, and her signal "Gustav—Sophie" reassured *Almark*'s commander. In short order small boats were towing the six-inch pipeline between the two ships, and the storekeepers were preparing to transship supplies.

By day's end *Graf Spee* pulled away to the south. *Altmark* would follow closely, keeping radio silence. But first, every evidence of the resupply operation was fished from the water; not even a wooden box slat would be left behind, although nothing could be done about the dark oil slick, visible to a searching aircraft miles away.

By September 13 the two ships reached the great emptiness in the center of the South Atlantic, about midway between South America and Africa, and there waited for orders. They had been fortunate; they were in position to strike at three different major shipping lanes, and the Royal Navy still had no idea they were there.

They had had one close call. On the eleventh *Spee*'s Arado seaplane, out on a routine reconnaissance flight, had spotted trouble. On a day of wonderful visibility, she had sighted HMS *Cumberland*, an eight-inch gun cruiser, on her way from Freetown, Sierra Leone, to Rio de Janeiro. The Arado had turned away before the British lookouts saw that tiny dot in the sky, and had warned *Spee* and *Altmark*. They had been able to turn out of *Cumberland*'s way in plenty of time. *Spee* was much the more powerful ship, but *Cumberland* was faster, capable of hurting the pocket battleship badly, and sure to warn other British warships no matter what the outcome of any engagement between her and *Graf Spee*.

At last, on September 26, *Graf Spee* was released by orders from Berlin, to begin savaging British shipping up and down the South Atlantic. *Spee*'s first victim, on the thirtieth, was the little tramp freighter *Clement*. She was the first of nine merchantmen *Spee* would send to the bottom.

But little *Clement* had ignored *Spee*'s order not to use her radio, and sent a clear message, pinpointing the raider's position before she died. The little freighter had begun the process that would doom her killer. Brought on board *Graf Spee*, *Clement*'s skipper, F. C. D. Harris, faced *Kapitän-zur-See* Hans Langsdorff defiantly. Langsdorff, aware that his orders had not been obeyed, eyed the English captain:

"You have defied my orders?"

"Indeed I have."

Langsdorff shrugged. "I strongly disapprove; but then, I should have done the same thing."

Langsdorff, a gallant gentleman, understood the Englishman's courage and strong sense of duty. They were brothers under the skin. The German could not know that *Clement*'s message had sealed the fate of his ship, and would in time insure salvation for Harris and his men. Harris and the others were sent below, prisoners.

Meanwhile, *Altmark* would have a scare on October 9, when she was seen southwest of the Cape Verde Islands by aircraft from HMS *Ark Royal.* But Captain Dau and his crew were fine actors, and persuaded the inquisitive pilots that *Altmark* was the American SS *Delmar.* The carrier and her aircraft could not know that *Delmar* was even then in New Orleans. *Spee*'s supply ship would live awhile longer.

On October 14 *Altmark* and *Spee* met again. Dau overflowed with fulsome accolades for Langsdorff, eloquently celebrating the sinking of *Clement* and three more British merchant ships. But Langsdorff, the old-line officer, had no time for flattery and Nazi slogans. He brushed aside the compliments and went directly to the point. He now had 150 captives aboard *Spee;* he could not keep them. They would be transferred to *Altmark.*

Dau was appalled. The prisoners numbered as many as his own crew. Why could not some other arrangement be made? Langsdorff was unmoved. *Spee* would transfer a small armed guard to help. But the prisoners *would* be held in *Altmark,* and that was that.

Dau held his peace; his orders were clear. But to the British merchant navy officers he was brusque, arrogant, rude. His hatred of everything British showed clearly. His crew, at least most of them, behaved to the captives with decency, even kindness, when their captain was not around anyhow, as had Langsdorff and the crew of *Spee.*

By evening the prisoners were settled in steel storerooms ranged vertically in *Altmark*'s bow and stern, pillowed on heaps of carpet off-loaded from *Spee*'s last victim, the freighter *Huntsman.* They knocked together their own latrines from old ammunition boxes and empty oil drums. That same scrap lumber would soon become tables and other crude furniture under the skilled hands of the ships' carpenters.

It was as well they made themselves as comfortable as possible, and organized themselves with typical British discipline. They would remain in their cramped, airless steel prison for months to come.

Cold, pompous Dau, with his silly little beard, was promptly named "Knitty Whiskers" by the prisoners. He would be called little else—aside from a choice selection of obscenities—for the rest of that eventful voyage. Dau grew no more lovable with time. When on October 28 he received more prisoners—this time from freighter *Trevanion*—the little tyrant harangued them. Red-faced, his absurd beard twitching, he spluttered saliva as he yelled at them.

"I do not like you; I do not like the English! Britain will be crushed!"

It is not recorded whether he remembered that vainglorious little speech early in the new year, far to the north in icy Norwegian waters.

Spee next left the South Atlantic to run around the Cape into the Indian Ocean, a move designed to convince the Royal Navy's searching ships that she had moved her area of operations. She sank only a single merchantman there, however, and the whole point of the move was lost shortly after her return to the shipping lanes off the coast of West Africa.

For she fell in with the refrigerator ship *Doric Star*. This time *Spee* opened fire from long range, ordering her prey to keep radio silence as usual. But *Doric Star*'s courageous skipper and radio operator were not deterred. They sent their "raider" signal nevertheless, and the Admiralty would soon know *Spee* was back in the South Atlantic.

But on *Altmark* life was uneventful, even dreary. Gradually the rations grew smaller as Dau economized. More serious for many of the captive seamen, the tobacco supply dwindled away. There would be no more. But the British seamen stuck together, and their discipline remained intact. One sailor, angered by the arrogance of a guard, hit him, and drew solitary confinement punishment in a tiny tank set aside for the purpose, bread and water his only rations. Others were confined for other offenses, such as smoking in unauthorized places. But their spirits remained high. The worst enemy was boredom, followed closely by the dead stale air of the prison flats, and the lack of any real news.

And the crowding. As more and more prisoners were taken by *Spee*, the congestion became almost unbearable, until 299 merchant seamen were jammed into the prison flats. All of the captive crews were there, with the exception of a few ship's officers, who were retained on *Spee*. The stench, the foulness of the air, and the terrible closeness grew worse and worse by the day.

On December 6 the two German ships met again—for the last time, although neither commander could guess it. Langsdorff insisted on moving his last lot of prisoners into *Altmark*, much to Dau's dismay. And the battleship's commander commented that *Spee* needed an overhaul; he could contact naval high command for orders, recommending they return to Germany.

Dau was horrified. "It's up to the führer!"

"Nonsense!" said Langsdorff. "It's up to the grand admiral. Raeder knows these things. Only a sailor understands."

The exchange typified the two men: Langsdorff, the model of the professional German naval officer, no political fanatic, but a sailor; Dau, the passionate Nazi. That night Dau would describe Langsdorff in his diary as "defeatist."

In the end, *Spee* steamed off westward, heading for the fateful estuary of the Plate, and the vital shipping lanes to and from Argentina and Paraguay. *"Auf weidersehen,"* she signaled, *"auf wiedersehen."* *Altmark*'s crew watched the sleek warship go hull-down over the horizon. They would never see her again.

Langsdorff had learned that a small British merchant convoy of four ships was to sail from Montevideo on December 10, a rich prize indeed. But Langdorff's luck had run out. This time he would find, not a handful of defenseless merchant ships, but the Royal Navy, pugnacious and ready.

Admiral Graf Spee was a pocket battleship, built to be able to run from almost any battleship with a punch greater than her eleven-inch guns. Her own ordnance and armor were much heavier than that of any cruiser fast enough to catch her. She had a cruising range of some ten thousand miles, infinitely extended by resupply from *Altmark*. She had been designed as a commerce raider, but now she would have to fight for her life on this brilliantly clear early morning of December 13, 1939.

For *Kapitän-zur-See* Langsdorff was about to meet a sea-dog in the finest British tradition. Commodore Henry Harwood led three cruisers, searching for his raider quarry, and his orders were to disable or destroy her at any cost. The blood of Britain ran through her arteries at sea, and no price was too high to pay to keep those vital lines open.

Harwood knew he would fight at long odds. His two small cruisers, *Ajax* and *Achilles*, carried only six-inch guns; they were really only big destroyers. His only real cruiser, *Exeter*, was armed with an eight-inch main battery. But neither she nor her smaller consorts could hope to stand up to hits from *Spee*'s eleven-inch guns. Their armor would not bear it. Nor were their guns liable to hurt *Spee* very badly: The combined broadside weight of all three British ships was little more than half that of *Spee*. Harwood's only assets were speed and four centuries of tradition.

Nevertheless, Harwood cleared for action and closed.

The little ships, *Ajax* and *Achilles*, fought as one unit, and *Exeter* as another. This tactic forced Langsdorff to shift his fire, and allowed the two units to observe the fall of each other's projectiles, a considerable help to their relatively inefficient ranging equipment. *Exeter* bore the brunt of *Graf Spee*'s main battery fire, and she suffered heavily, until she was firing with only a single turret, and her wounded captain was steering with a portable small-boat compass.

But she had hit *Spee*, and in the end it was Langsdorff who turned away, pursued by the two little cruisers. Their six-inch shells bounced off the main armor of *Spee*, although their repeated hits caused casualties and damage to her superstructure and secondary armament. And although he had avoided two salvos of torpedoes from *Exeter*, Langsdorff knew *Ajax* and *Achilles* also carried torpedoes. And so he ran for the estuary of the Plate, followed by *Ajax* and *Achilles*.

Battered *Exeter* turned south for Port Stanley in the Falklands, and from Stanley eight-inch cruiser *Cumberland* steamed hard north to replace her off the Plate. Still shadowed by the little cruisers, *Spee* sailed up the broad river. She was safe, and in neutral Paraguay she could seek the repairs she needed.

But outside in the swells of the Atlantic, Harwood would be waiting. *Cumberland* would be there, fresh, undamaged, with her full load of ammunition. And other heavy units were on the way. If they could not reach the mouth of the Plate in time to meet *Spee* on her way out, they might at least make certain she would not get far if she escaped the waiting cruisers.

But *Spee* would not come out. She could make such repairs as were possible within her own resources, but Montevideo's shipyard would not help her. Neither could

Langsdorff leave immediately, even had he wished to. For international law required that no belligerent ship could leave a neutral port within twenty-four hours of a merchant ship flying her adversary's colors. The British minister in Montevideo was prepared to send out British merchantmen then in port, one at a time, twenty-four hours apart, to keep *Spee* in port. But the Uruguayan government solved the problem by ordering *Spee* to leave port not later than the evening of the seventeenth.

Langsdorff asked Berlin for instruction. All he got was an answer that dumped the problem back on him. The only clear instruction was to avoid internment at all costs. At last poor Langsdorff, alone and without orders, made his terrible decision. Vast crowds lined the river as *Spee* steamed slowly toward the sea, apparently headed for a renewal of the battle. At sea, the Royal Navy cleared for action. But Langsdorff, in what agony of heart, took off his crew and blew up *Graf Spee* in the middle of the river.

Three days later, the gallant Langsdorff wrapped himself in the ensign of the German navy and shot himself. There is a certain irony in the fact that in that same month, in 1914, Admiral Graf von Spee, for whom Langsdorff's ship was named, went down with his small fleet before the guns of the Royal Navy off the Falklands to the south. One wonders whether Captain Langsdorff thought of that long-ago fight in the last hours of his life.

And now Dau, alone, had to decide his course of action. He ignored Langsdorff's order to land the British prisoners in some neutral port. Although he had 299 aboard, and they had to be constantly guarded by his own men and the armed party from *Spee*, Dau knew that landing his prisoners anywhere would certainly mean that the British would quickly learn his ship's general location. He could not take that chance. His only hope now lay in remaining invisible, far from the vigilant eyes of the Royal Navy.

So Dau turned south, sailing into the trackless vastness of the South Atlantic, far from any shipping lanes, and thus presumably far from the weathered gray ships of his enemy. He stayed in his oceanic wilderness for five weeks.

Dau's hatred and contempt for the British grew deeper and more obvious. His latest reason for sneering at them was that the British sailors shared their quarters with eight

African seamen from *Spee*'s last victim. His temper was not helped when inevitable rumor filtered down into the prison flats to tell the prisoners that the Royal Navy had caught *Spee.*

Dau kept his crew busy, overhauling *Altmark*'s engines as best they could, but belowdecks the boredom and frustration grew. Small arguments between prisoners grew easily into shouting matches and fights. A British captain, brought to Dau to complain about the miserable conditions in which his men had to live, was given five days solitary confinement simply for complaining, and had to be restrained from attacking the pompous captain.

But at last both crew and prisoners could feel something in the air, a sense of expectation. At last the engines were reassembled, and *Altmark* test-fired her machine guns and light cannon. The signs were unmistakable: *Altmark* was going to run for home. British spirits rose; they knew the Royal Navy would be waiting.

The voyage back would be fraught with danger for *Altmark,* even though the British were hard-pressed at sea all over the world. Dau knew where the points of greatest danger were. So did the captive officers. In fact, they were marked down in the prison decks on a lifeboat chart, kept hidden from German eyes by the pinup girl drawn on the other side of the page.

On January 22, 1940, Dau turned north, staying far from the shipping routes, and crossing the equator on the thirty-first, still unseen. Now, pushing hard, Dau headed for home. He could not steam up the English Channel. It was a British lake. The road home had to be the long, hard way, north through the Atlantic far west of the British Isles, then east into the North Sea, and finally south to one of Germany's Baltic ports. The shortest route east was between the Orkneys and the Shetlands, or between the Shetlands and the storm-haunted Faeroes. But those routes were too dangerous, covered as they were by British air and naval patrols. So Dau wisely opted for that wilderness of terrible storm and almost perpetual stygian gloom between the Faeroes and far-off Iceland, deep in the long Arctic night.

Dau was lucky, and a fine sailor to boot. Using the foul weather and the long nights, he made his turn safely between the Faeroes and Iceland, far to the north of Great Britain, still unseen, and coming closer to home with each storm-tossed day. Rough seas, cold weather: *Altmark,* empty of fuel, rolled badly in the big seas of the North Atlantic. But at last she was in sight of Norway. Her luck had held, and the hopes of the British prisoners steadily declined. Only one obstacle lay ahead of her now: the run south down the Norwegian coast. If deliverance for the prisoners was to come, it would have to come quickly.

But at that moment, at the Royal Navy's desolate base near Rosyth in the Firth of Forth, a party from cruiser *Aurora* were boarding the sleek destroyer, flotilla leader *Cossack,* short-handed from a flu epidemic. *Cossack* and her flotilla were making ready for sea, and would fill their complements to strength from other ships. And the men from *Aurora* knew there might be something different about this trip, for they carried steel helmets, rifles, bayonets, and web equipment.

They got their orders from *Cossack*'s first officer, Lieutenant Commander Bradwell Talbot Turner, a tall, quiet officer who looked more like an Oxford don than a typical seaman. But his words were crisp and plain. He instructed them precisely on two alternate plans to board, one from small boats, the other directly from the deck of *Cossack.* They learned their assigned places and duties and were sent below.

And so *Cossack* put to sea, leading her flotilla of *Sikh, Nubian, Ivanhoe,* and *Intrepid.* In company was the swift cruiser *Arethusa.* The official mission was "ice patrol" in the Skagerrak, but that was only a cover story. They were going to look for *Altmark,* and on the bridge of *Cossack* Captain Philip Vian, tough, lean, and aggressive, knew it.

For the Admiralty guessed that *Altmark* was making for home. The few British prisoners freed from *Graf Spee* in Montevideo had revealed that *Altmark* had many British seamen on board. Provisions would not last forever, either. So *Altmark* would have to try to run the picket line of scarred gray men-of-war, somewhere in the North Atlantic. The Navy would be watching for her.

Time was short. *Altmark* had made the Norwegian coast, and turned southeast along it. She was in neutral waters at last. On February 14 Dau was awakened from a restless cat-nap to be told that a Norwegian torpedo boat had signaled *Altmark* to stop. It was little *Trygg,* and she put an officer aboard. But his inspection was a gesture only, and he courteously accepted Dau's lies that *Altmark* carried neither prisoners nor weapons. He even put a Norwegian sailor on board, to act as pilot until a regular pilot could be obtained, farther down the coast at Alesund.

Dau indeed found pilots at Alesund, but aboard with them came another Norwegian naval officer, asking the same questions again. This time the British prisoners spotted him coming aboard, and the captive seamen began to beat on the doors, bulkheads, and latrine drums with chunks of wood, shoes, and even fists. A party of the younger men ripped a steel girder from the bulkhead and began to smash it against the heavy wooden hatch cover overhead. Hungry and worn-out as they were, they kept it up until the hatch began to splinter, and a small hole started to appear in it. When a German guard sat on the cover to help keep it in place, one Englishman seized a jagged tin can and stabbed the German in the behind, sending him springing off the hatch cover. The girder party carried on bashing.

The uproar was tremendous, but the Norwegian, in Dau's cabin, did not react. The German crew ran every winch on the ship in an attempt to drown out the tumult, and finally the prisoners were driven down into the prison decks with fire hoses and rifle butts. The Norwegian returned to his ship, and Dau spitefully put the prisoners on bread and water.

Altmark was stopped twice more by Norwegian vessels, mainly concerned that Dau did not pass their Bergen naval base in darkness. Both times the same questions were asked and answered as before, but no search was made. However, Dau was forced to turn farther to sea, away from Bergen, although he still retained Norwegian pilots. The prisoners ate their biscuits and water in angry silence. The German guards were afraid to go belowdecks; they could feel the hatred all around them.

But *Altmark*'s phenomenal luck had begun to change. She had been seen near Bergen, by a Norwegian sympathetic to Britain. In less than an hour the news was passed to the British vice-consul, who relayed it to the embassy in Oslo, and a coded message was sent on to the Admiralty in London. *Altmark* was found. Just after noon on February 16, a Coastal Command Hudson bomber saw her running close to the coast, and immediately radioed her position. And his call was happily monitored in *Cossack*. Vian turned hard for the Norwegian coast.

Altmark steamed on to the south, well inside neutral waters. She was safe for the moment, but she could not lose her shadows. The original Hudson had gone home, her fuel running out. But there were three more RAF aircraft in her place, circling above *Altmark*. And in midafternoon *Altmark*'s lookouts called down that they could see the masts of warships, closing fast. Soon they were visible to everyone on *Altmark*'s decks: *Arethusa*, sleek and deadly, and her covey of destroyers. Dau turned and ran farther into Norwegian waters, headed for the cover of neutral territory. The Norwegian pilots smiled.

Dau still had reason for optimism. He was nearly home, thanks to the weather, his own seamanship, and the democracies' stupid adherence to the letter of neutrality law, while Europe caught fire around them. Soon he would be within the Luftwaffe's range, and the rest would be comparatively simple.

But down on the Mall in London, just a very brief walk from Trafalgar Square, an extraordinary man thought otherwise. The First Lord of the Admiralty, Winston Spencer Churchill, was cast from the same mold that had produced the sickly little admiral who had won the seas for Britain almost a century and a half before.

In Trafalgar Square Nelson stood thoughtfully on his tall pillar, high above the brooding lions. One-armed, one-eyed, he would never have let a matter of paper neutrality stop him doing what he thought best for his beloved England. It was he, after all, who at the battle of Copenhagen put his blind eye to his telescope during the hottest of the fighting, and then blandly announced that he could not see the fainthearted signal to withdraw raised by his superior. He had gone on to win. So would the square-jawed bulldog at the Admiralty this day.

The time for decision had come. Two British destroyers had gone into the coastal waters after *Altmark*, but as the gray ships closed in, the Norwegian torpedo boats *Kjell* and *Skarv* steamed close alongside *Altmark*, and the destroyers could not stop or board her. Dau turned his ship in to Jossing Fiord, one of the tremendous deep-water gorges that push back into the Norwegian mainland.

Altmark was still free, but she was in a trap. She crunched through the drifting ice of Jossing Fiord, her captain only too aware that the Royal Navy had plugged the only exit behind him. For the moment, *Altmark* was safe. The two Norwegian gunboats lay near him in the fiord. But Dau, who had several times criticized Langsdorff for allowing *Spee* to be trapped in the Plate, was now well stoppered himself. One of the gunboats approached him and again asked whether he carried British prisoners. As before, Dau lied, and the little Norwegian returned to her anchorage. Darkness settled over the deep cold of Jossing Fiord.

After dark, captain Vian took *Cossack* in close to the coast. He advised the senior Norwegian officer present of the British belief that *Altmark* carried British prisoners. However, that officer replied that he had orders to resist any British attempt to capture *Altmark*, and Vian signaled the Admiralty for instructions. Churchill's response came within three hours, and could not have been more plain:

> Unless Norwegian torpedo boat undertakes to convoy *Altmark* to Bergen with a joint Anglo–Norwegian guard on board and a joint escort, you should board *Altmark*, liberate the prisoners and take possession of ship . . . Suggest to Norwegian captain that honour is served by submitting to superior force.

The orders were precisely what Captain Vian wanted. It would take about twenty minutes to run into the fiord and alongside *Altmark*. "Right," said Vian quietly, "we're going in."

Quiet, scholarly Turner called his men together, silent and armed to the teeth, to give the age-old order: "Stand by to board." There was nothing more to be said, and the party checked their weapons and found their places on *Cossack*'s deck. Her weapons trained and her railings down, the destroyer pushed in under the lowering gloom of the Norwegian coast, the black waters lit by a full moon.

Cossack was one of the powerful Tribal-class destroyers, commissioned, like her fifteen sisters, in 1937. Her turbines generated some forty-four thousand shaft-horsepower, enough to drive her sleek nineteen hundred tons at thirty-six knots. She carried eight 4.7-inch guns, sundry lighter weapons, and four torpedo tubes. But her heavy weaponry would not fire a shot this night: She would do what she had to do as it had been done in Nelson's time, in the days of wooden ships and iron men.

Dau ran wearily to the bridge, his eyes still sticky with sleep. At first he thought the slim black shape was another Norwegian, especially when she stopped to hail and talk to one of the little gunboats. He turned his searchlight on her and hailed her, but received no reply. But now she came on, moving slowly but very surely toward him through the drifting ice. It was a little after eleven o'clock, and there was no longer any doubt. *"Ein Engländer,"* Dau said, and gave orders to go astern and ram the destroyer.

But Vian had thought ahead of the German, and pivoted *Cossack* neatly, avoiding the much larger tanker, slipping most of the force of the blow while keeping the ships close together. Turner, standing by with his party to board over *Cossack's* starboard side, quickly moved his men to port, next to *Altmark.*

Now he turned to them and shouted, "Come on, then, what the hell are you waiting for!" and hurled himself onto *Altmark's* deck, revolver in hand. A few of the party were able to jump behind him before the gap between the ships widened, and Vian quickly maneuvered *Cossack* tightly against the German's side, so the rest of the boarders could follow.

There was firing now as some of *Spee's* guard raised their rifles, and the British boarders shot them down. Other boarders pushed on deeper into the tanker, using their rifle butts to scatter the crew. One sailor smashed a German to the deck with his revolver, splintering the butt into a dozen pieces. Another looked up at the bridge wing in time to see a German aiming his rifle. The Englishman lunged hard upward with his bayonet, and his enemy screamed and fell.

Altmark, still running in reverse after her unsuccessful attempt to ram, grounded on the rocks, and on her bridge Dau, the pugnacious Nazi, surrendered without a fight. Elsewhere on *Altmark,* the fighting died away. It was over.

But not quite. Below, the prisoners waited in an agony of apprehension. They had felt the shock as the two ships ground together, and heard the shooting and the sound of running feet and shouting voices. They could only guess at the outcome of the battle above their dark steel pen. At last they could hear the hatch being opened, and see the dark outline of heads against the gloom of the night above them. In the cold Norwegian night, Turner leaned over the edge of the hatch, peering down into the blackness of the hold. He shouted into the darkness: "Any British down there?"

The answer was a roar from 299 throats: "Yes! We're all British!"

"Come up, then," said Turner. "The Navy's here!"

The prisoners left *Altmark* quickly, crossing to *Cossack* on a gangway Vian had thoughtfully rigged. There was need for haste: One German had falsely told the boarding party that *Altmark* was rigged with scuttling charges, set to explode at midnight. For all that, the merchant seamen left in joy, dancing and laughing. One man took a moment to knock out a particularly obnoxious German guard; another plaintively asked a *Cossack* officer for his revolver, in order to shoot Dau. But most were simply too happy to care, happy just to be back on a British deck, out of the stench and darkness and stale air of their prison.

Last, Vian recalled his boarding party, and just before midnight *Cossack* moved slowly out of Jossing Fiord. Belowdecks, with its traditional practicality, the Navy was already beginning to feed the ex-prisoners their first good meal in many months. Their ordeal was over.

"The Navy's here!" Those words were quoted in the British papers, and in that bleak winter provided a delicious ration of good cheer at home. *Altmark*'s prisoners came ashore at Leith on the seventeenth, to a tumultuous welcome.

Norway protested at length to the British government, but her sensibilities were soothed to some extent by the discovery that *Altmark*, contrary to Dau's protestations, *had* had prisoners aboard, and weapons, a fact she had also lied about. In any case there was little time for Norway to mull over the violation of her neutrality by *Cossack:* On the ninth of April Hitler not only violated her neutrality, but seized without warning her whole country and people.

Altmark finally returned to Germany, reaching Kiel on March 28. She had lost seven dead, six wounded badly and five less so. Goebbels did what he could to minimize Germa-

ny's embarrassment, raving at length about British "piracy."
Dau was retired immediately, and poor *Altmark,* which, like
her captain, had done a pretty fair job, was renamed
Uckermark, as if to expunge the memory of Jossing Fiord.
She deserved better, as did her captain.

The tanker would sail again as a supply ship until, on November 30, 1942, she blew up in Yokohama Bay, taking with
her the raider *Thor* and another storeship. Fifty-three of her
crew died with her, many of them part of the original crew.
About fifty more were badly hurt by the blast. The official explanation of the explosion attributed it to gasoline vapor, but
the odor of sabotage has clung to the incident ever since.

Poor Dau committed suicide in May 1945, apparently unwilling to survive the defeat of Germany. Most of his British
prisoners returned to sea. Some survived the war; many,
sadly, did not. At least two became German prisoners again,
meeting once more in a prison camp in Germany.

Cossack would go on to greater glory. She fought brilliantly in the British sorties into Narvik, where ten big German destroyers were sunk or wrecked beyond repair.
Cossack was badly damaged in that fight, but would sail
again. She played a leading part in the successful hunt for,
and final sinking of, the German superbattleship *Bismarck.*
Still leading the 4th Destroyer Flotilla, commanded by the
redoubtable Captain Vian, she was in at the kill, sending at
least one torpedo into mighty *Bismarck.* She died finally as
she had lived, torpedoed and sunk in the Atlantic in 1941.

Captain Vian, the quintessential sea dog, went on to command larger forces in the Mediterranean. On the afternoon
of March 22, 1942, his small force of light cruisers and destroyers, covering a critical convoy to Malta, fought a brilliant action against a force of Italian heavy cruisers and a
battleship covered by dozens of aircraft. All Vian had to
counter the fifteen-inch, eight-inch, and six-inch guns of the
Italian navy were the 5.25s of his little cruisers and the 4.7s
of his destroyers. Nevertheless, he stayed between the attackers and the convoy, his little ships darting in and out of their
own smoke screen. Their daring and aggressiveness saved
the convoy.

In later days, Vian commanded even larger formations, finishing the war in command of a carrier group in the Pacific.

He retired at last in 1952 as Admiral of the Fleet Sir Philip Vian, rich in well-deserved rewards.

Commander Turner won a DSO for his leadership of *Cossack*'s boarding party. And in time, when the war was only a memory, he became, appropriately, the naval attaché at the British embassy in Oslo.

The boarding of *Altmark* was a brilliant flash of the flame of the old tradition, a proof, if one was needed, that if equipment had changed dramatically since Nelson's day, men had not changed at all. If the ships were no longer wooden, the men were still iron. Churchill, as he generally did, put it pretty well in an address to *Exeter*'s crew:

> In this sombre dark winter . . . a flash of light and colour on the scene . . . an action in the old style . . . which will long be told in song and story . . . carrying us back to the days of Drake and Raleigh . . . [You] can say to them, "We, your descendants . . . have not forgotten the lessons you taught."

More than forty years after, in their old campaigning ground in the Falklands, the Royal Navy would again sail and fight in the spirit of Drake and Raleigh. From seventeen-year-old gunners to a Prince of the Blood, the Navy was still there.

ALL ALONE

The great waves were huge and black, the tentacles of the North Sea clawing and snatching at the battered ships struggling in the icy dark. The night was wild as a witches' Sabbath, cold as death. Through it units of the Royal Navy and Germany's *Kriegsmarine* groped blindly for one another off the coast of Norway.

Both nations knew the value of the little Scandinavian nation. Just two months before, HMS *Cossack* had startled and infuriated Hitler when she bore into Norwegian waters to board German supply ship *Altmark,* and release hundreds of British prisoners.

Hitler fumed publicly about British violation of Norwegian neutrality, conveniently forgetting that *Altmark* had been carrying weapons and prisoners, both violations of that same neutrality. But der führer had done more than rant; he had also decided to act.

Now it was the eighth of April, 1940. The day before, Hitler had launched *Weserübung,* the surprise invasion of neutral Norway. The British had reacted hesitantly, unwilling to land troops on Norwegian soil until there was clear evidence the Germans were set on occupation. Most Major British units remained well offshore, determined to prevent any German breakout into the Atlantic—the precious convoys were still the Admiralty's chief concern.

Closer in, small Royal Navy units drove north to mount mine-laying operations off Norwegian ports. The tiny destroyers took a terrible pounding in the mountainous seas, and during the night one of them lost a man overboard.

Little destroyer *Glow-worm* turned back into the night to look for the lost sailor. *Glow-worm* was a tiny ship, four little four-inch popguns and some torpedo tubes, a prewar ship with a lot of miles behind her. She knew that German units were at sea, and she was alert, but she was hardly prepared for what she was to find.

For in the faint, dreary corpse-light of dawn, *Glow-worm* ran head-on into Germany heavy cruiser *Hipper* and her escort of big fleet destroyers. *Glow-worm* wasn't strong enough to fight even one of the big destroyers, let alone *Hipper* with her eight-inch guns. But tiny *Glow-worm* was Royal Navy, a ship and crew in the tradition of Nelson and Rodney, Drake and Jellicoe, and she turned to fight.

She used everything she had, her little guns and her torpedoes, but she was swamped by a torrent of German shells. As explosions rocked her again and again, *Glow-worm*'s radio room got out the vital news: heavy German units, close inshore off Trondheim. She got her message through, and far south in London the Admiralty drew the right conclusion: The invasion of Norway was on.

Glow-worm had finished her vital work, and now it was time to die as well as possible. Sinking, burning, *Glow-worm* altered course painfully toward big *Hipper*. *Glow-worm*'s skipper, Lieutenant Commander Gerard Roope, was a man of Nelson's breed. His little ship dying beneath his feet, Roope turned calmly to his helmsman on the battered bridge: "Ram her."

And with every knot she had left, the tiny destroyer charged her huge adversary and slammed her sharp prow into *Hipper*'s steel flank. The destroyer's prow slashed a monstrous 120-foot gash in *Hipper*'s side. The big cruiser survived, but she was listing, and more than five hundred tons of icy North Sea water weighed down her massive hull.

Little *Glow-worm* exploded and disappeared in those wild seas, and her gallant captain died with her. Most of her crew went down with her as well, although the Germans did what they could to save a few men from the greedy, greasy swells. Roope's icy courage earned him a Victoria Cross, and a warm place in the history of the sea.

And so passed *Glow-worm*, who sent her vital message and did what damage she could and died well. But the Royal Navy does not forget signal courage and dedication, and teaches her new sailors about such things. Every new generation of recruits will learn about *Glow-worm* and what she did, and a little of her spirit will live on in them.

And that is not a bad legacy.

IN THE WITCH'S KETTLE
Papi Wenck at Stalingrad

Colonel Walther Wenck commanded nothing. He belonged to nothing. He was alone in a seething caldron of broken units, leaderless fugitives, and burning equipment. Behind him lay Rostov, gate to the Caucasus. Before him lay a frozen waste and masses of Russian armor and infantry, all surging south from Serafimovich and Kletskaya, all heading for critical Rostov.

Wenck had no troops to stop them. Only a few days before, on the twenty-first of November, 1942, Wenck had been flown from his unit in the Caucasus to become chief of staff to the Rumanian 3d Army. Wenck's first move was to fly to the front, and what he saw appalled him. As his little Fieseler Storch circled over the frozen desolation west of the Don, he realized that there was no defensive position, no line of resistance.

For on November 19, over ground made rock-hard by frost, Marshal Rokossovsky's tanks had smashed into the Allied formations north of Stalingrad, and in two days were across the Don at Kalach. The blow had fallen first on the Rumanian 3d Army, holding about ninety miles of front. In spite of warnings of their relative weakness, Hitler had brusquely refused requests to shorten their front, obsessed with holding on to every inch of ground. Their antitank weapons were obsolete as well, and nothing had been done to remedy that failing either.

And so, when the hammer fell, Rumanian 3d Army collapsed, and their left-hand neighbors, Italian 8th Army and Hungarian 2d Army, came unstuck with them. And there were no reinforcements.

In an attempt to shore up the Rumanians, German XLVIII Panzer Corps had received orders in mid-November to move to the area of Serafimovich. But the corps was a weak formation, one German panzer division, 22d Panzer, and one Rumanian armored division equipped with obsolete equipment. Even 22d Panzer had not received its full complement of Mark IIIs and IVs, and was still using many Czech T-38s, no match for the Russians. Moreover, it had lost its *Panzergrenadier* regiment, and its engineer battalion was bleeding to death in Stalingrad.

There was worse to come. For XLVIII Panzer Corps had been long static, dug in in straw-filled pits, deprived of fuel to at least start up its vehicles. And when the move began, it was discovered that mice, living happily in the straw, had gnawed through hundreds of electrical leads, cutting off engines, turret power, sights, and guns. Only 39 of 104 tanks would even start, and by the time the Russian tidal wave hit, the division could muster only 42 armored vehicles. The Rumanian division was in no better shape: Of its 108 tanks, 98 were old Czech T-38s. The corps was not nearly strong enough to stem the enormous flood of Russian armor.

Then, on the twentieth of November, Yeremenko's offensive punched into the Rumanian 4th Army south of the city, and now there was nothing but air on both sides of German 6th Army, isolated in and around Stalingrad. And on the twenty-third of November, the Russian encirclement closed. It was crystal-clear to every competent soldier that 6th Army could still withdraw, and easily, if it moved quickly, attacking to the west and scattering the top of the Russian spearheads behind it. But Hitler, ever inflexible when it came to giving ground, refused. And so, at about 4:00 P.M. on the twenty-third, the trap snapped shut on some three hundred thousand Axis troops.

Now, as Wenck's Storch circled above the desolation west of the Don, the full magnitude of the disaster was plain to him. Rumanian battle group Lascar was still fighting, somewhere in the vast emptiness west of Kletskaya on the Don. Elsewhere in the white wilderness other little groups of men sold their lives as dearly as they could. But the front was gone. There was only a terrible emptiness of dreadful cold, studded with towers of black smoke from burning equipment, populated only by scattered fugitives . . . and by the dead and the dying.

Wenck took charge. Professional that he was, he set his fears aside and began to organize a skeletal front. If Rostov and Army Group A were to survive, he must hold the line of the curve formed by the Chir and Don rivers. For if the Russians took Rostov, Army Group A, a million men, would be cut off forever in the Caucasus to the south.

Wenck needed troops and equipment, and they were precious few. He took command of German ad hoc battle groups under Colonels Stahel and Adam, Lieutenant Colonel Spang, and Captain Sauerbruch, scratch units of a few assault guns and tanks, a little artillery, oddments of infantry. They were few, but at least they were German, experienced and willing. There were some Luftwaffe field units as well, and a few Rumanians still fought on, either as the remains of units or as individual volunteers with German outfits.

Wenck also found a few veteran German NCOs, and in the immemorial tradition of experienced noncoms, they began to get their commander what he needed. One found a fuel dump "belonging to no one," and put up signs directing passing vehicles to it. And as fuel-starved crews topped up, they became part of Wenck's Army, willing or not. Communication equipment, motorcycles, and other gear were "found," to use Wenck's own euphemism, until Wenck had begun to build a little headquarters and an organized fighting force.

As his NCOs swept the rear areas for stragglers and lost soldiers, Wenck himself ordered a Wehrmacht propaganda company to show films at road junctions around Morozovskaya. Men who stopped for a little to watch the films were organized and rearmed, and led off into the maelstrom to the northeast to meet the Russians. his NCOs intercepted men returning from leave, walking wounded, anybody who could hold a weapon.

Wenck's patchwork force was stiffened a little by the arrival of what remained of 22d Panzer Division. Wenck used this veteran unit like a rapier, lancing into the exposed flanks of the Russian advance in counterattack after counterattack. Within a few days 22d Panzer was down to a half dozen tanks, an 88 dual-purpose gun, and a few armored personnel carriers, but still it fought on.

Replacement material came from maintenance shops and motor pools. Disabled vehicles were repaired and sent into battle. Tank transporters entering Wenck's area were stopped and relieved of their tanks, no matter whom the vehicles belonged to. Wenck was desperately short of armor, and did not care where he filled his need.

And the patchwork defense began to hold. Beyond all hope, the motley units fought extremely well, ably commanded by veteran officers and NCOs. For they knew everything depended on them. They could give some ground, but they could not break. As they held grimly on, they were cheered by the news that at last a new commander had taken charge of the whole area, the genius of France and the Crimea, Manstein.

Field Marshal Erich von Manstein took command on the twenty-seventh of November, his mission to stop the burgeoning disaster west of Stalingrad, save Army Group A, and somehow organize this confusion of desperate units newly dubbed Army Group Don. Help was on the way, he knew, 6th and 17th Panzer Divisions from France, other units moving from within Russia. But for a few days, at least, all depended on Wenck's handful.

Manstein knew it. "Wenck," he said, "you'll answer to me with your head that the Russians won't break through to Rostov. The Don-Chir front must hold. Otherwise not only the Sixth Army in Stalingrad, but the whole of Army Group A in the Caucasus will be lost."

And Walther Wenck held on. He was using anybody who could hold a weapon, cossack volunteers, Todt Organization labor units, even groups of Reich Railway employees. His scratch units counterattacked over and over in the snow, striking repeatedly at the Russian spearheads in temperatures well below zero.

Manstein knew the caliber of his energetic commander, and backed him. One evening at a situation briefing, Wenck's G-3 made the mistake of referring to "our panzer battalion."

"What panzer battalion?" asked Manstein. "Our records do not show that you have one."

So the fat was in the fire, and Wenck told his commander the truth. He admitted he had been purloining other people's armor, and offered to face a court-martial for what amounted to misappropriation. But the field marshal smiled a little, and only forbade further liberation of other units' tools. And Wenck, unrepentant, thereafter employed his armor "in no more than company strength, so that they should not attract attention from higher commands."

At last, by the end of November, organized help began to arrive for Wenck's battered little units. The first force to arrive was XVII Army Corps, commanded by General of Infantry Hollidt, and Wenck, professional and unselfish, proposed Hollidt take command of every unit in the Don-Chir sector. Manstein agreed, and with the formation of *Armeeabteilung* Hollidt, Wenck's odd little army passed into history. Wenck would win the Knight's Cross to his Iron Cross for his incredible stand. More important to him were the unspoken thanks of the million men of Army Group A.

WHEN MAD MIKE CALVERT TOOK UMBRAGE
THE CAPTURE OF MOGAUNG

When you go home
Tell them of us, and say
For your tomorrow
We gave our today.

Monument to British dead. Kohima, Burma

"Ayo Gurkhali!" The thin line of exhausted Gurkhas broke into a shambling run. Spraying submachine-gun bursts, hurling grenades, the little men in dirty, tattered green rushed a rickety bridge, swamp on both sides, the rattle of Japanese automatic weapons ahead. As the rush faltered twenty yards in front of the Japanese positions, Captain Michael Allmand threw more grenades and charged into the teeth of the Japanese fire.

As Allmand closed on the Japanese positions, the light flashed from the wicked knife in his right hand, the half-moon blade of the Gurkha kukri. Then he was in among the Japanese, and as his kukri rose and fell, red and slick with Japanese blood, Allmand's men roared and ran to join him. *"Ayo Gurkhali!"* "Here are the Gurkhas!" And with kukri and bayonet the ferocious little men of Nepal charged home. The Japanese broke.

It was June 1944, and up ahead of these battered remnants of British 77 Brigade lay the town of Mogaung, and the vital railroad line from Rangoon to Myitkyina. Up at Myitkyina, "Vinegar Joe" Stilwell's American and Chinese troops were still stalled, still unable to take that vital town, though Stilwell had already announced its fall back in May. Upwards of thirty thousand Chinese had been stopped cold by about one tenth their number of Japanese, and would remain stopped until August.

The Japanese could only reinforce Myitkyina through Mogaung, if Myitkyina was to be held at all. A Japanese intelligence officer had slipped through the encirclement at Myitkyina and returned; it could be done, at least by small groups. The British block called White City that had closed the way to Myitkyina was now gone. Now, if troops could be gotten past Mogaung, perhaps Myitkyina might be held, at least for a while.

Brigadier Mike Calvert had other ideas. He and his men had marched many miles to take this place, and take it, Calvert would. He chose to approach the city from the southeast, avoiding the major rivers that protected the town to north and west. It would mean crossing marshy ground and a ridgeline to the southeast of the town, but he had been promised help from a Chinese unit, although the Chinese had yet to appear.

As 77 Brigade closed on the town, it constructed a light-aircraft strip to speed evacuation of its wounded. In the swirling rain of the monsoon, the RAF liaison officers had coconut matting air-dropped. Laying this over a foundation of cut brush, they created a strip usable virtually constantly, in spite of the foul weather.

After one little aircraft failed to lift off the short strip in time, the RAF added its finishing touch: a bump at the end of the strip, which tossed into the air any aircraft having difficulty taking off. The builders kindly refrained from telling the pilots that the bump was built of dud mortar shells—presumably on the theory that there was no use adding more stress to an already difficult job.

Resupply, as usual with the Chindits, was by air. Calvert had only the highest praise for the British and American pilots who flew runs in the worst of weather. These weary pilots were flying an average of three hundred hours a month during this period. They never failed to respond.

Mogaung had long been prepared for defense by the Japanese. It was infested with well-concealed bunkers with overhead cover and tiny firing ports. Each one would have to be taken out individually. It also contained extensive ammo dumps and two large hospitals, many of whose wounded fought from their beds. Some, less badly hurt, tried to escape by swimming the flooded defiles and fleeing into the bush. Many of these died of exposure and starvation in the jungle. Others met groups of Kachin tribesmen—many of them British-led. The Kachins loathed the Japanese in any case, but if they had any reluctance in exterminating these invaders, Calvert had thoughtfully offered one rupee for each Japanese right ear.

His 77 Brigade was on its last legs, torn to pieces by scrub typhus, cholera, cerebral malaria, typhoid, encephalitis, trench foot, jungle rot, and a dozen other hideous diseases. Huge mosquitoes and other voracious insects swarmed in millions. One officer in another unit, swimming a river to scout the enemy, returned so covered with leeches that a transfusion was needed to save his life.

For there was no worse place on earth in which to fight than Burma. For the Chindit units like 77 Brigade, evacuation of the wounded ranged from difficult to impossible, and men soldiered on as scarecrows, ravaged by dysentery, shuddering with malaria. Unspeakably difficult jungle terrain made five or six miles a good day's march—a fact apparently not understood by Stilwell and his staff, called the Stuffed Baboons by American and Briton alike. These worthies were obsessed with things made of paper, march tables and squiggly little lines on maps.

Their standard practice was to measure the distance to the objective on the map, divide this by the book-speed of a marching infantryman—two and a half miles per hour—and then fail to understand why it was impossible to carry the objective in the time the formula produced.

Vinegar Joe and much of his staff hounded field commanders for not fully carrying out their missions, and seemed to make no allowance for the hideous conditions under which their men operated. Stilwell's own tough, dedicated American infantry—the fabulous Merrill's Marauders—hated the callous, ruthless indifference of their boss, who had left them in the jungle until the unit quite literally fell apart. He was "bloodless and coldhearted, without a drop of human kindness," said one American officer. And an enlisted Marauder put it more bluntly: "I had him in my rifle sights. I coulda squeezed one off and no one woulda known it wasn't a Jap that got the son of a bitch."

Conditions had become so bad for the Marauders that

some of the men were so racked with dysentery, they cut the
seats out of their trousers. Some soldiers threw up their rations; others fell asleep during battle. Still they were not relieved.

While Stilwell was using up his own men, he never ceased
believing that the British were not pulling their weight. As
one British commander later wrote, "It was Stilwell's misfor-
tune that he had only to think of the hated Limeys for his
wits to fly out of his head." Even casualty figures did not convince him. They should have, for during a period of time in
which the Marauders suffered about five hundred battle casualties, 77 Brigade took almost sixteen hundred, and another British brigade about seven hundred. And that did not
count the terrible losses to sickness.

Stilwell's staff was, if anything, hated more than their
boss. It was widely believed that the Stuffed Baboons deliberately catered to Stilwell's deep dislike of the British, and
otherwise told Stilwell only what they thought he would like
to hear. One staff officer was regularly sent to imply to the
Chindits that they were gutless for not doing whatever-it-was
that week.

There is a story that Calvert stood with this man in areas
on which he knew the Japanese had zeroed in machine
guns. And Calvert admitted later that he hopefully escorted a
particularly obnoxious American liaison officer into an area
swept by Japanese fire. "He looked so much more imposing
than I," wrote Calvert. "But unfortunately the Japanese are
bad shots."

This is probably the same officer whom, later on back in
India, another British officer set out with a pistol to kill. The
Marauders hated this staff officer equally: "I had not realized
that his qualities had transcended national boundaries to
such an extent," wrote one Marauder officer.

Otherwise, Stilwell's staff seldom bothered to visit the
Chindits in the field. On one occasion a written complaint
was handed to the British command, at a time when
Stilwell's headquarters was a ten-minute walk away and a
staff officer could have easily walked over to discuss the situation.

No account was taken of the fact that Chindit units had no
artillery bigger than a mortar, and so lacked the fire-power
of conventional organizations. Nor was any interest taken in

the terrible terrain over which the Burma war was fought. At one point, a Gurkha unit was ordered to use a route flooded deeper than the average height of a Gurkha soldier.

But in spite of scorn from Stilwell's headquarters, in spite of the ravages of endemic sickness and high battle casualties, 77 Brigade would give Mogaung a try. They were a veteran outfit, made of famous regiments. And they were Chindits, part of the long-range penetration force raised by the fabulous Orde Wingate, and named for the *Chinthe*, the legendary Burmese pagoda guardian, half bird, half lion.

There was indeed a Chinese unit on the road to Mogaung, a unit with artillery. But the Chinese saw no reason to hurry to attack, and were very late in arriving. They had, after all, been fighting for a very long time, and knew there would be still more fighting against Mao's Communists.

And so the work on the ground would be done by the British and Gurkha infantry. There were only a couple of thousand of them left when they began the last push to Mogaung, and many of these were walking hospital cases. Calvert's battalions included the 3/6th Gurkhas, and the first battalions of the King's Regiment, the South Staffords, and the Lancashire Fusiliers. Along with them were detachments of the Burma Rifles—tribesmen led by British officers—and an assortment of engineers, RAF liaison personnel, and medical personnel.

Their leader was a soldier's soldier, tough, profane, and relentless, cut out for bad places and bad times. Brigadier Mike Calvert, born in 1913, was a sapper, part pirate, part crusader, all born leader. Capable of ferocious rages, he nevertheless kept his sense of humor. He cared deeply about his men, and literally never asked a soldier to do what he did not regularly do himself. Calvert has been called both rowdy and flamboyant, with good reason. But he was also entirely professional, thoughtful, intelligent, and articulate.

Calvert was the youngest of four brothers, all soldiers. He first saw fighting as the Sino-Japanese War swirled around the British garrison in Shanghai in 1937. After fighting the Germans in Norway, he helped make England's southwestern coast a maze of mines and booby traps for the expected German invasion. He then taught commando technique in Australia and New Zealand.

In the early stages of the Burma war, Calvert, then a major, commanded something called the Bush Warfare School, in an obscure place called Maymyo. While there, he had come to know the messianic Orde Wingate, before that Lawrence-like officer had been called to form and command the famous Chindits.

When the war came close, Calvert, thirsting for action, wanted to go and kill Japanese, not train people to go and do it. And so he chose a solution typically Calvertian: He equipped himself with a bottle of whiskey and some matches, sang off-key to himself as he burned heaps of directives and correspondence he deemed nonessential, and set about organizing his own unit.

Calvert took with him the small staff of the school, including a handful of Australians—some of them ex-jailbirds—there for training. His leaders included several of the hard-nosed captains who staffed the school, including a Black Watch demolition expert, a Rhodesian who was said to have been a hangman in civil life, and a captain who loved cigarettes, but only to eat. Calvert included about twenty school duty personnel—all of whom had substantial disciplinary records.

He found a couple of allies, a Royal Marine major with a few men and a launch, and the captain of a civilian river paddleboat, an elderly Royal Navy veteran with only one kidney. With this motley crew Calvert sailed up and down the Irrawaddy blowing up anything of possible use to the Japanese invader. He first struck a place called Henzada, and in a wild gun battle killed more than a hundred Japanese for the loss of only four of his own.

Calvert went on to recruit still more men for his private commando, dragooning walking wounded, underemployed rear-area types, restless military policemen, mess attendants, and various minor offenders from the military jails. As Peter Fleming later wrote, it was a unit of "odds and sods, including several lunatics and deserters." He did not lack for brash young British officers, eager to fight and tired of whatever they were doing.

Oddly enough, many of Calvert's odds and sods turned out to be surprisingly good material. One was a private from the Yorkshire Light Infantry, who had evaded the Japanese by swimming a river, wounded and pushing a raft with five nonswimmers clinging to it. He then found a bottle of beer, opened it with his teeth, and walked twenty-five miles bare-foot to a friendly town. He was Calvert's kind of soldier.

Calvert continued to haunt the Japanese, accompanied still by the fierce Royal Marine major, but without his paddleboat, whose captain had been forbidden to risk his venerable craft in unlikely warlike excursions. Calvert, adored by his men, took them perpetually in harm's way. One raid, led by the marine major, pitted a small detachment of Calvert's men against four times their number of Japanese who surrounded them at night in a village called Padaung.

In a wild melee in the darkness, Calvert's men fought hand to hand, bloodying their enemy badly. One NCO shot three Japanese and took out another two with his gunbutt. Another sergeant split a Japanese skull with the rim of his helmet, disabled another enemy with a knee to the groin, and finished by killing a Japanese officer with his own sword.

Even when time came for the dreadful retreat from Burma, Calvert's ruffians walked out as a unit, dirty, bearded, and bedraggled, but still soldiers ready to fight. Calvert led them, as dirty and disheveled as they were, very much in command, unwashed certainly, but also undaunted. He would be back.

Calvert was a natural leader for the Chindits, when that long-range strike force was formed under Orde Wingate's almost mystical leadership. He was initially second-in-command of 77 Brigade, Wingate's original unit, then its commander. He had come a long way with them since his veteran brigade, through the years and the miles of bloody, merciless jungle war against the Japanese.

For this Burma war was unsurpassed in viciousness and hardship. It had begun with Japanese victories and British humiliation, compounded by widespread Japanese murder and mistreatment of prisoners, soldier and civilian alike. And then, as the British grew stronger under able Field Marshal Bill Slim, as they retrained, reequipped, and returned, the fighting was man to man, inch by inch, marked by anger and hatred unsurpassed anyplace else.

Much of the fighting was at very close range, some of it with bayonet, knife, shovel, and sword. During one close-quarters fight to clear a vital pass, a Gurkha shot a sword-waving Japanese officer in the belly with his PIAT antitank

weapon. As Calvert put it tersely: "The officer and the counterattack rapidly disintegrated."

In another head-on engagement fought by Calvert's men a
South Staffords lieutenant had his arm cut off by a Japanese
officer's sword. Ignoring the blood and pain, the young subaltern shot the Japanese, then picked up the sword and
hewed at every enemy within reach until he collapsed.
Calvert ran to the young officer and knelt beside him.

"Have we won, sir?" the lieutenant asked his commander.
"Was it all right? Did we do our stuff? Don't worry about me."
And then the youngster simply died, another good man gone
in the spiteful, no-quarter jungle war.

Such heroism and tragedy was commonplace in the pitiless jungle. In Lieutenant Colonel John Masters' brigade,
number 111, a captain would win the Victoria Cross leading
a wild Gurkha charge that drove the Japanese from an impregnable position, against all hope. But the captain paid for
the victory, as an inordinate number of British officers did,
dying with several of his devoted men. And when it was over,
nobody had the strength to bury the captain and the
Gurhkas who had fallen with him. Only three months later
would a detail find and bury them, bamboos growing six feet
tall through their remains.

It took a different breed of man to command here, to command and survive not only the privation and the illness and
the enemy's bullets, but the terrible burden of command. In
The Road Past Mandalay, perhaps the best book about war
ever written, Masters told of a hideous command decision,
as he and his brigade fell back after heavy fighting. On the
muddy trail before him lay nineteen stretcher-loads of desperately wounded men.

> The first man was quite naked and a shell had removed the
> entire contents of his stomach. Between his chest and pelvis
> there was a bloody hollow, behind it his spine. Another had
> no legs and no hips . . . A third had no left arm, shoulder or
> breast, all torn away in one piece. A fourth had no face . . .

Only a few of these human wrecks seemed even semi-
conscious. Masters' doctor shook his head, standing beside
his boss in the pouring rain. These men could not be saved,
but maybe another thirty up ahead would live, if they could

be carried. As bullets whined around him, Masters made his decision.

"Very well. I don't want them to see any Japanese."

He could not spare any more morphine, the doctor said. All right, said Masters, just give it to those whose eyes are open. And move on. You have five minutes.

As he walked up the trail, Masters could hear single carbine shots behind him, the last kindness for these hideous wrecks that had been his men. He put his hands over his ears, but could not shut out those final shots. "I'm sorry," he muttered, "forgive me." And then he went back to the terrible business of command, the atrocity of war in the jungle.

That was the kind of man it took to command successfully in this green hell. Masters was that kind of man, and so was Mike Calvert. And now, as Calvert looked across the river at the town of Mogaung, he could see his most important objective clearly. And he could see, if not the end of the Burma war, at least the beginning of the end.

And so started the final push on Mogaung. Starting the day after Allmand's gallant charge at the bridge, the Gurkhas fought two days to take a crucial village. Allmand was again in the front of the action, leading a charge into machine-gun fire that overran the gunners and carried a critical piece of high ground. He went on to lead the assault on a strongpoint called the Red House, a position crammed with automatic weapons.

Using flamethrowers, grenades, and PIATs—the spring-loaded antitank grenade projector—Allmand's Gurkhas cleared the position. But Captain Allmand's luck had run out. He was down and dying by the time the position fell, shot down as he slogged through thick mud to attack, his feet too ravaged by rot for him to run. His grenades had killed the Japanese machine gun he was hunting, and he would receive the Victoria Cross.

Another Victoria Cross went to Gurkha rifleman Tulbahadur Pun, who charged along across thirty yards of open ground. Firing his Bren gun from the hip, he captured two Japanese machine-guns, killed or routed their crews, then covered the advance of the rest of his platoon.

The going was tough. There were at least thirty-five hundred Japanese in Mogaung, more men than Calvert had. And there was no way to go but straight ahead. The Japanese had fortified every village, cutting deep bunkers beneath the houses. Each one was methodically taken: fighter-bombers first—American Mustangs—then mortars, then grenades and flamethrowers and bayonets and kukris. Consolidate, then do it again.

One Lancashire Fusiliers officer was killed because he advanced standing up; he was simply too exhausted to crawl. There was little rest for anybody, and then only for a few hours. "Heaven was a letter from home, dry feet, and a tin of British steak-and-kidney pie."

The British were cheered a little by the knowledge that their enemy was weakening too. The Fusiliers, cooking rations in positions taken from the Japanese the same day, watched in amazement as a weary Japanese patrol walked in to the British position and began to shed their weapons and equipment. The Fusiliers finished the patrol quickly, then returned to the important business of food.

The British patrolled incessantly at night, tossing grenades into Japanese bunkers, penetrating all the way into Mogaung town to ambush stray Japanese soldiers and booby-trap equipment and food. One favorite occupation was to cut Japanese telephone lines, booby-trapping the cut ends with grenades.

The trees were full of Japanese snipers, the patches of scrub concealed hidden riflemen and machine gunners. The British losses mounted, until Calvert's battalions were down to company strength. The casualties in officers were particularly high. In the South Staffords, only one lieutenant remained of those who had marched to Mogaung. Major Archie Wavell, son of the Viceroy of India, walked calmly to the rear, holding his almost severed hand, still in command, still giving orders. After treatment, his hand amputated, Wavell refused to be evacuated until every soldier more seriously hurt than he had been flown out.

Evacuation of the wounded was more difficult now, as the weather grew worse and worse. The Brigade surgical team labored desperately to save lives in mud and rain, only to have critically wounded patients lie for weeks awaiting evacuation. Calvert had lost control of any of the light aircraft, and was entirely dependent on planes controlled by Stilwell's headquarters.

Many days he was told no aircraft were available. But even

during the worst weather, a single American NCO pilot flew mission after mission to Mogaung, often against orders, one day flying fourteen sorties to bring out critically wounded Britons and Gurkhas. Wrote Calvert simply in later years, "I salute him."

Calvert's men were moving like automatons, shot with a dozen diseases, soldiering on with unhealed wounds. When Calvert urged one South Staffords soldier to keep up with his section, the man showed him a freshly reopened wound covered by a bloody bandage: "The bullet's still in, sir, but I wanted to join in this last attack."

Lieutenant Wilcox of the same unit was shot through the neck just below the chin. He was quickly back with his unit, fighting on with a roll of gauze stuffed clear through the wound. In breaks in the fighting, he would pull the gauze through the wound to clean it. Later he was shot in the head, had the scalp sewn up, and returned to his platoon to serve until Calvert personally ordered him evacuated. Wilcox would win both the DSO and the American Silver Star. To Calvert he was "a worthy representative of all the other sub-alterns who did not last so long."

To the end, British discipline remained tight, unit spirit and morale amazingly high. After the war, a senior Japanese commander in Burma commented:

> The British forces maintained their traditionally high standard of discipline throughout a most difficult campaign. The high standard of morale and discipline of the colonial forces surprised the Japanese troops.

Tropical diseases and wounds were not the only dangers in the quagmire of Mogaung. Concerned by the great number of soldiers hobbling from trench foot, Calvert asked for gum boots to protect the feet of soldiers perpetually in deep mud. A distant pompous headquarters irrelevantly responded: "It is the medical opinion that . . . wearing gum boots injures the feet . . . The best insurance against trench feet is to keep the feet dry."

But bunker by bunker, village by village, 77 Brigade closed on Mogaung in spite of vicious Japanese resistance and foolish messages from higher headquarters. Calvert held an officers' call in a bomb crater, pervaded by the sick-sweet stench of Japanese killed and wounded by flamethrowers; some were still screaming as Calvert gave his orders. The final push was coming. The brigade was down to some 550 effectives, 550 out of the 2,355 who had come to Mogaung.

On June 14 Calvert ordered a British captain commanding a Burma Rifles patrol to go and find the Chinese, and not to return without at least a regiment. Four days later the captain simply reported to Calvert that he had indeed found and brought a Chinese regiment, now waiting just across the Mogaung River. Now there would be some help in keeping the town absolutely isolated, and some help from the Chinese 75 mm artillery. Calvert was moved to comment on the officer who had produced this miracle:

> We had all come to take these wonderful Burma Rifles officers for granted. You would say, "Bring me six elephants," or "a river," . . . or a "Chinese regiment," . . . and they would look at you from behind their moustaches, salute, disappear followed by a worshipful company of Kachins, Chins, or Karens, and then appear with whatever you wanted.

The final major obstacle was the railway embankment, running roughly north and south, carrying the vital Myitkyina railway. The British went in before dawn, South Staffords first, clearing the Japanese strongpoints along the embankment with grenades and flamethrowers. Then through them passed the Fusiliers and a Gurkha company to hold the gains. American Mustangs flew mission after mission in close support, often six sorties per plane per day. Their accurate bombing saved dozens of lives among Calvert's tired soldiers.

And then, on the twenty-fifth of June, suddenly, anticlimactically, it was over. The remnants of the Japanese defenders were gone. Calvert's Gurkhas were in Mogaung unopposed, to be followed immediately by a swarm of Chinese, looting and destroying. It had been, as Calvert described it, "a pleasant place with wide tree-lined streets," substantial buildings, and a thriving commerce. Now it was a wreck, ravaged by bombs and artillery. Its only occupants now were abandoned dogs and cats.

The Japanese had fled on improvised rafts, gone on down-river to join the remainder of the imperial forces. Only a couple of dozen Japanese officers and men remained, hiding on the riverbank, probably men who could not swim. A Gurkha patrol dealt with them.

It had taken sixteen days, sixteen days of concentrated fighting, and a hideous casualty list. 77 Brigade and its commander had every reason to be deeply proud. Only one irritant remained. "It was," as one historian pungently commented, "a victory marred by those necessary lice on the military body, the public relations staff." For the announcement from Stilwell's headquarters was that the *Chinese* had taken Mogaung.

Calvert was furious. There were too many graves behind 77 Brigade, too many good men gone back to India without arms or legs, too many soldiers whose health had been broken forever. But Calvert's revenge was, especially for him, remarkably restrained; it was certainly subtle. His signal to Stilwell's headquarters is a military classic:

The Chinese having taken Mogaung, 77 Brigade is proceeding to take Umbrage.

And at Stilwell's headquarters the staff—the Stuffed Baboons—searched diligently through their maps all one long night, looking for this mysterious place called "Oombrah-gay." One story has it that the baboons even returned Calvert's signal, asking him to repeat the invented map references of this tantalizing place they could not find.

Then, as if the untrue and insulting award of Mogaung to the Chinese were not enough, Calvert received orders to bring whoever could still walk to, of all places, Myitkyina. Calvert could see no sense in bringing a few hundred sick, exhausted Chindits to help attack a place already infested by thirty thousand Chinese and divers Americans.

His response was vintage Calvert. He closed down his radio link with higher headquarters and marched his survivors fourteen days out to Kamaing, in hopes of saving what was left of 77 Brigade by evacuation to India. Although in later years he would write that his decision was a mistake, it is impossible to blame him. He knew his men had taken Mogaung on sheer courage and not much else. They were used up, and he would not see the rest of them sacrificed. In fact, the brigade was now down to three hundred effectives. Even those still on their feet were in such bad shape that two Lancashire Fusiliers died of simple exhaustion on the march to Kamaing.

Calvert was fully confident his disobedience would earn him a monumental chewing-out at best, perhaps even relief and a court-martial. He could not have predicted what actually happened, a summons to report to Stilwell's headquarters. Calvert's boss, Brigadier W. A. Lentaigne, went with him to meet Stilwell. They found the general supported by Brigadier General Boatner and Stilwell's son, a lieutenant colonel on his staff. (His son-in-law also served on the same staff.)

It must have been a daunting moment even for Calvert, who was never noticeably afraid of anything. Stilwell spoke. "Well, Calvert, I have been wanting to meet you for some time."

"I have been wanting to meet you, too, sir."

"You sent some very strong signals."

"You should have seen the ones my brigade major wouldn't let me send."

Stilwell laughed, and commented he had the same trouble with his own staff officers.

Calvert then told Stilwell bluntly what his brigade had done, and the terrible casualties it had suffered. Stilwell interrupted only to say to Boatner, "Why wasn't I told?" He was reverting, one author says, to a tendency to blame his staff for not keeping him informed, just as he had done when confronted with the Marauders' terrible losses.

Calvert, however, believed that Stilwell really had not fully known what 77 Brigade had endured, and that his staff had carefully edited and slanted reports of the Mogaung fighting. In the end, at least, Stillwell commented, "You and your boys have done a great job," and directed that 77 Brigade receive five Silver Stars. One of them went to Calvert.

It was over for the Chindits—Masters's 111 Brigade had left only a composite company of more or less fit men, including the brigade commander. The remaining Chindits were withdrawn to India, marching into their camps in step, with all the spit and polish these scarecrows could muster. One out of two of them was medically unfit for further service; some of them would never entirely recover. They were to be retrained, but in the end, in February 1945, the word came down that Special Force, their parent organization, had been disbanded.

Calvert did not stay to see the disbanding of the Chindits. He moved his men back, "shaved and polished" as befitted proud soldiers. He visited his wounded in the hospitals, including a brother officer and close friend who had soldiered through Burma with a terminal case of tuberculosis. And then, in Calvert's words, he "went out and got drunk, and joined in quite a nice fight in a Chinese restaurant." His friend died a week later.

Many of the Chindits would fight again, brought back to some sort of health and reassigned to other units. Masters, himself a Gurkha officer, would have the privilege of seeing the end of it, the final brilliant advance past Mandalay to Rangoon. It was, he wrote afterward,

> the old Indian Army going down to the attack, for the last time in history, exactly two hundred and fifty years after the Honorable East India Company had enlisted its first ten sepoys on the Coromandel Coast.

It was nearly over by then, for in that month of July 1945, British 14th Army killed and captured 11,500 Japanese, for a loss of 96 dead. It had been a long and tragic road, but it was ending now, and some of the worst of it had led through the ruined town called Mogaung.

Mike Calvert finished the war with two awards of the Distinguished Service Order in addition to his Silver Star, and a rich assortment of foreign decorations. After leaving Burma he commanded an SAS brigade during the last days of the war in Europe, one Belgian and two French parachute battalions. With British SAS elements, he led the Allied return to Norway, taking the surrender of thousands of sullen German troops.

After the war Calvert served in Trieste and Hong Kong, then went to Malaya to train and command the Malayan Scouts, an antiguerrilla force designed to find and kill the Communist rebels in the bush.

A bout of malaria cut short his Malayan assignment, and he was reassigned in Germany, a lieutenant colonel again, and again a Royal Engineer. He is the author of two excellent books on the Burma war, and editor of a number of works on military history.

THANKS, MAJOR

Shelford Bidwell's fine book, *The Chindit War,* contains this fine little story about the closeness men of different races can attain in the agony and dedication of battle.

During the terrible Burma campaign against the Japanese in World War II, the British forces included West African troops, tough, cheerful Nigerians who communicated with their leaders in the "Coast Pidgin" English of their native land.

A British major, down from headquarters to check on the efficacy of air support for the Nigerians, chatted with some of the soldiers. They had enjoyed the RAF's help.

"Dey planes done come," said one. "Dey go boom-boom-boom. De Japans, dey die plenty."

And then the Nigerians asked the major whether he was the man responsible for the fine air support "dey planes" had provided. "Sah, you-self, you done send planes?"

The major said that was, indeed, his department.

There followed some discussion and rummaging about amongst the Nigerians, who gathered and formally presented to the major a collection of K ration cigarettes.

"For sen' na planes, sah."

Once in a while something nice happens in war, even to staff officers.

FOR VALOR
The Fight for Toktong Pass

Fox Company had to hold or die. It was just that simple. For just below the windswept hill on which these tired Marines dug in lay Toktong Pass, and just now Toktong was the most important single spot in all of Korea, north or south.

Up ahead about seven miles lay the North Korean town of Yudam-ni, the Fifth and Seventh Marine Regiments, a howling wilderness of snow and bitter wind, and what looked like the whole Chinese army. Behind Toktong about the same distance was Hagaru-ri, more Marines, and a critical airfield, still under construction. If the two hard-pressed Marine regiments were to survive, if even one man was to escape death or imprisonment, Toktong Pass had to be held.

Captain William Barber commanded Fox, and he got his orders on the morning of November 27, 1950. Barber was an experienced officer, a "mustang" up from the ranks, who had won a Silver Star on Iwo Jima as an enlisted paratrooper.

Barber knew immediately how critical a task he'd been assigned, and quickly did a recon of the pass with his platoon leaders and battalion commander. He selected a prime piece of high ground above the pass, a shoulder of the monstrous mountain called Toktong-san. The spot was rugged and steep, studded with fir and scrub pine and a couple of abandoned huts. In spite of the bitter cold and drifted snow, a little spring still flowed at the lower end of the position.

From this vantage point, nothing would move through Toktong Pass unless Fox Company let it, as long, at least, as Fox Company survived. Barber knew there was big trouble coming, coming down out of the north behind a hideous north wind, a Chinese wind.

Up until a few days before, the UN advance had seemed to be going well in spite of zero weather and a Siberian wind. The UN troops were four corps abreast. From left to right the line was held by the U.S. I and IX Corps, and the Korean II. On the far right was X Corps, a combination of Korean and American troops, including the 1st Marine Division. All in all, the attack went so smoothly that many thought this would be the final offensive, maybe the last step to peace.

The Chinese had smashed that illusion utterly, striking south the day after Thanksgiving. They had received the Korean II Corps advance in the *hachi shiki* formation, a vee with the open end pointed south, a sort of gaping mouth poised to swallow its enemy. Then, with the Korean corps well into the mouth, the jaws snapped shut, and a tremendous counterattack came flowing south through the arctic night. They came in under a bright moon, in unspeakable cold, making the night horrible with shrilling bugles and clashing cymbals.

The Koreans, still shaky from a Chinese mauling the month before, came unstuck quickly. Then they began to dissolve entirely, and suddenly the whole UN force had a monstrous hole in it, no line, no cohesive units, only great masses of the enemy rushing south against negligible opposition. The Chinese attack spread and spread, and in no time all of allied 8th Army was pulling back.

General Walker, the 8th Army commander, fed in Turkish and British brigades and America's 1st Cavalry Division in a desperate attempt to plug the hole. These units fought well and killed a great many Chinese, but they could not halt the enemy. There were too many Chinese and not enough friendlies, and so the retreat went on.

The two American corps to the west had troubles of their own, but their fighting withdrawal went better than the Koreans' debacle. On the east, most of X Corps fought its way back toward the port of Hungnam, keeping its cohesion and bloodying the attackers at every step. However, the other major corps unit, the 1st Marine Division, was far north, seventy-eight miserable miles northwest of Hungnam, in the incredible cold of the Chosin Reservoir and the Chinese border.

If Korean winters were generally miserable, the weather up near the reservoir was unbelievable. Daytime temperatures rarely got above zero, and at night the thermometer plummeted to twenty or thirty below. Everything froze in that shocking cold, flesh, weapons, lubricating oil, blood plasma, everything. Ice fragments clogged transfusion tubes; wounded men froze as doctors cut away clothing to reach shattered flesh and bones.

When the bottom fell out of Korean II Corps, the Marines had been ordered to advance west to help stem the torrent of Chinese rolling south. It was not a practical notion, based as it was on a gross underestimation of the magnitude of Chinese involvement. It also failed to consider the incredible difficulty of the mountainous, arctic terrain into which the Marines were being told to go: The weather was appalling, and there were virtually no east-west roads.

As far as anybody knew, there were now eighty miles of frozen nothing between the Marines and the first friendly forces to the west. Fortunately for the Marines, Major General Oliver Smith smelled a monstrous rat.

White-haired, soft-spoken Smith was fifty-seven, highly intelligent, experienced, deliberate. He neither drank nor swore, and seldom raised his voice. But he had seen combat in the Pacific in World War II, and he was born to lead. He was not going to hurl his twenty-thousand-man division west into a void without a lot of thought. In fact, he was not going to hurl it at all. His advance was slow and careful, the more so because his men had fought Chinese units repeatedly on the way to the reservoir. They had taken prisoners who openly boasted of the great offensive that would destroy the Marines once they had pushed out into the trackless wilderness west of the reservoir. Smith's intelligence officers had already identified elements of six Chinese divisions.

In spite of the ominous information they had gathered, Smith's staff could not convince higher headquarters of the enormous force poised to strike south. MacArthur was still adamant that China would not intervene; if it did, he said, he would "slaughter" it from the air. He had ignored the reservations held by General Walton Walker, 8th Army commander, about starting this offensive at all. He had also rejected a British plan to stop and leave a sort of neutral zone between the two antagonists.

MacArthur's assessment was shared by his X Corps commander, an otherwise able officer profoundly loyal to MacArthur. On a visit to a scratch Army task force east of the reservoir, Lieutenant General Ned Almond told its concerned and capable commander, "The enemy who is delaying you for the moment is nothing more than remnants of Chinese divisions fleeing north. Don't let a bunch of Chinese laundrymen stop you."

Well aware that his boss was not seeing the situation clearly, Smith made his own decisions. He would save his men.

Smith's division was already strung out much more than he wanted, stretched for thirty-five miles along that precious ribbon of highway from Yudam-ni, west of the reservoir, all the way down to Chinhŭng-ni, northwest of the port of Hungnam. Smith's instincts told him that his two leading regiments at Yudam-ni were in the presence of an enormous enemy force.

Smith's instincts were entirely correct; there was a trap waiting for his Marines. Hidden in the snow, covered by the blizzards and clouds of the north, were ten Chinese divisions, over one hundred thousand men under General Sung Shinlun. And Sung was waiting eagerly for the main body of the Marines to push west. Once it was well extended into the icy hills, his trap would snap shut, and the two leading Marine regiments would die. The rest of the division he would kill as he pushed south to Hungnam, and the sea.

Sung's Chinese were tough soldiers, mostly peasants inured to hard living from birth. His divisions each contained three infantry regiments, plus a few support personnel; the terrible terrain of North Korea had forced him to leave behind his artillery.

The Chinese soldier wore a reversible quilted cotton uniform, a sort of yellow-brown on one side, white on the other. He had a thick cap with earflaps, a blanket, a small pack, and his weapon. Usually he was issued with leather or half-leather footgear, although some Chinese went into action wearing rubber-soled canvas shoes.

For all his toughness and his numbers, the Chinese soldier was handicapped by a primitive supply system, which meant he often ran short of food and ammunition; he carried only four days' food and eighty rounds of ammunition. His radio net extended only to regimental level; below that, he had to depend on runners, light signals, and bugles. This lack of communication, together with his doctrinal rigidity, made him inflexible and slow to adapt to new or changing situations.

All Sung's careful planning was to be wasted. It soon became clear that this canny Marine commander was not going to walk into the jaws of the dragon; Sung would have to take the initiative. And so, on the twenty-seventh of November, the Chinese counteroffensive came rolling out of the north to strike the 1st Marine Division in the hills around Yudam-ni. They came in darkness, with bugles shrilling, screaming, "Son of a bitch, Marines, we kill . . . Son of a bitch, Marines, you die!"

But instead of units on the march, the Chinese hammer struck dug-in, ready Marines, and the Communist attack broke down in savage night-fighting. Everywhere there were extraordinary feats of raw courage among the Marines, as the fighting got down to knife and bayonet and rifle butt in the frigid gloom.

Staff Sergeant Robert Kennemore of the Seventh Marines took over when his platoon leader went down, and led his men in fierce hand-to-hand resistance to the charging Chinese. As ammunition and grenades failed, Kennemore collected a new supply from the wounded and the dead. Under a shower of Chinese grenades, Kennemore scooped up the deadly missiles and threw them back at the enemy . . . until two grenades landed in the midst of an American machine-gun crew. This time he could not throw them back.

Kennemore did not hesitate. He simply stamped one grenade into the snow and kept his foot on it, then calmly knelt on the other. The explosion tore his body terribly, but he would miraculously survive to receive the Congressional Medal of Honor.

Smith could not stay in Yudam-ni. East of the reservoir, far to his right, another huge Chinese force had submerged Task Force Faith, an Army unit, killing its gallant commander and scattering its shattered remnants. It had badly hurt the Chinese 80th Division and held up the Chinese advance for most of five days. But now Task Force Faith had taken casualties approaching 50 percent, and there was nothing east of the reservoir to stop the Chinese flood.

Now Smith had Chinese pouring down both his flanks, striking at the road behind him. If the Chinese could permanently sever that vital umbilical of road behind him, his regiments would die in the snow. It was time to go, and quickly. Radio Peking was already ranting about the imminent "annihilation" of the American Marines.

Smith, for all his paternal manner and appearance, was a warrior to his bootheels. "We are not retreating," he told a correspondent. "We are merely attacking in another direction." He meant every word of it, and in fact he exaggerated very little. In spite of the killing, heart-stopping cold and the ocean of Chinese all around them Smith's Marines would go back deliberately, taking out their wounded and most of their dead as well.

Back to the south help waited, hard-nosed, flamboyant Chesty Puller's First Marine Regiment, reinforced by an Army infantry battalion. But even Puller was stretched thin. He had a battalion posted at Hagaru, one at Koto-ri, and the third at a forsaken place called Chinhŭng. His battalions were some ten miles apart, and their men could not cover all of the precious road at once.

Engineers were hacking an airfield from the frozen ground at Hagaru as well. They would complete it in just twelve days, and transport aircraft would brave the terrible weather to haul in food, ammunition, and a few replacements. Best of all, the faithful C-47s could evacuate Smith's wounded on the return trip. Before the long retreat ended, the planes would lift out some forty-three hundred wounded, helpless burdens Smith's men would not have to carry and guard.

There would be other help from the air as well. C-47s and Flying Boxcars dropped tons of desperately needed food and ammunition, and from carriers off the east coast, from Yongpo airfield in Hamhung, Marine, Navy, and Australian pilots would rain high explosives and napalm, cannon and rocket-fire, on the Chinese.

There would be times when the weather would ground them. But when, as an Aussie pilot put it, the overcast and snow improved to "no worse than bloody awful," the faithful fighter-bombers were in the air looking for targets. In contrast to the cumbersome Army system for requesting air support, Marine units would call down fire from the sky quickly and efficiently. Excellent close air support was a Marine trademark. It would save countless lives along the frozen road to Hungnam and the sea.

Even so, even with the Marine spirit and firepower, even with the air cover, it all came down to Toktong Pass. The Chinese 59th Division had already cut the vital road between Yudam and Hagaru. And on the night of November 29–30 the Chinese came in out of the night against Fox Company at Toktong Pass.

Barber's men were on 100 percent alert and ready, and they knocked the little soldiers in their quilted suits back down the sides of the hill above the pass. Fox had a good deal of welcome help: 105-mm howitzer rounds howling in from the tubes of How Battery, Eleventh Marine Artillery Regiment, firing from the edge of the Hagaru perimeter.

Down at Hagaru the Marine perimeter held firmly. Chinese dead, fifteen hundred of them, piled up outside the Marine positions. The attackers' total casualties exceeded six thousand, and one regiment was virtually destroyed. But there were more Chinese, many more, and heavy casualties would not stop them.

The Marine regiments at Yudam-ni had also held firmly, but it was high time to go, attacking south, in General Smith's words. The commanders of the Fifth and Seventh Marines, Colonels Murray and Litzenberg, made thorough preparations. Sadly, the Marine dead could not be taken out; all rolling stock was reserved for the wounded. And so a sad little service was held on the first of December, and eighty-five Marines were laid to rest in the frigid ground.

Every man not part of a rifle platoon, gunners, drivers, headquarters clerks, was assigned to one of twenty-six provisional platoons. The Marines would need every rifle, for the whole road south was one vast roadblock, frozen solid and stuffed with Chinese.

The basic movement plan was simple: The Marine infantry would clear and hold the high ground along the vital road; the mechanized column, supplies guns and wounded, would follow the road. The solitary Marine tank at Yudam would lead the march down that terrible road. A special task was reserved for Lieutenant Colonel Ray Davis' 1st Battalion of the Seventh Marines. As the main force broke out, he would lead his men on a night march east of the road, pushing through the terrible terrain to link up with Fox Company at Toktong. The main column would push through to him.

And so, about eight o'clock on the morning of December 1, the "advance south" began. First, units of Fifth Marines disengaged from Chinese troops besieging their hilltop positions north of Yudam-ni. It was a dicey operation, since the Chinese were at some points within grenade range, but the Marines managed it well, covered by artillery and Marine close air support.

Next, as three Marine battalions held a temporary stop line against the pursuing Chinese, other Marine units carried high ground overlooking the highway, and lone tank D-23 pushed off south, surrounded by infantry and combat engineers. The fighting for the high ground was close up and brutal, with Marine units repeatedly attacking uphill through the snow against much larger Chinese units.

In one such vicious, face-to-face exchange Marine Sergeant James Johnson covered the withdrawal of his battered platoon, making sure each man pulled back, then standing his ground to hurl grenades into the attacking Chinese. He was never seen again, and the writers of his Congressional Medal citation could not even be sure of the date of his death.

A second Medal of Honor went to Staff Sergeant William Windrich, who led a squad to support elements of his unit in desperate trouble. In hand-to-hand fighting, Windrich held off the Chinese, in spite of a bad head wound from a Communist grenade. He organized a group of volunteers to evacuate wounded Marines, and was hit again seriously, this time in the legs. He turned down evacuation and medical assistance—"There isn't time. They're only small holes, anyway." Even after he could no longer stand, he fought on for another hour. And then, his stout heart literally broken, Windrich went down in the cold and died from loss of blood and exhaustion.

Down on the road the vehicle convoy pushed doggedly on. Sniper fire killed driver after driver, but new men climbed into the seats. Occasionally a Chinese thrust carried to the road, but those that did were quickly driven back. Up on the high ground to either side, Marine units cleared hill after hill, fighting yard by yard to cover the vital road.

All through the second of December, the column pushed slowly on, under an umbrella of close air support. A blown bridge covered by Chinese fire held up the advance for a time, until Marine Corsairs dumped their deadly loads on the Chinese covering force, and combat engineers cleared a bypass around the bottleneck at the ruined bridge. At last, past midnight on December 3, the leading Marine unit, 3d Battalion, Fifth Marines, could do no more. Their commander pulled his men into a defensive perimeter for the night; they were about a mile from the crest of Toktong Pass.

Up above the pass, Fox Company was still hanging on. After five days and nights the Chinese 59th Division still could not budge this stubborn bunch of Marines from their little piece of high ground, now called "Fox Hill" all along the road. The 59th's mission was to strangle American traffic along the fourteen miles between Yudam and Hagaru, and this little company of Americans would not let them do it.

Barber had chosen his position perfectly. Fox Hill stood a little by itself, just north of the vital road and near its highest point. From any direction, the Chinese had to come uphill to get at his Marines. And he had firepower aplenty, for Fox was reinforced by the machine-gun and mortar sections of the battalion weapons company.

Barber had deployed his unit in a rough U shape, the open end toward the pass, the closed end on the highest part of his hill. The tops of the U, and his command post and mortars, were down the slope closer to the road. A steep roadcut below the CP protected Fox against attack from the road itself.

The first major Chinese attack came in on the early morning of the twenty-eighth, in that ghastly time of day when human energy is at its lowest ebb. It is the hour when men react and think most slowly; it is the hour when men die. The attack struck the closed end of the U in absolute silence, and two Marine squads were instantly overrun. In wild, hand-to-hand fighting, fifteen Marines died and part of the base of the U was lost.

Through the rest of the night, the Chinese came in again and again, but the Marines gave no more ground. At the west curve of the Marines' horseshoe position, under a shower of grenades, a handful of Marines heaped up Chinese dead in front of their positions. One man, Private First Class Hector Cafferata, was the only man between the Communist infantry and in the rear of the Fox perimeter. He stood his ground in the flaming dark, killing at least fifteen Chinese all by himself, and wounding many more.

Cafferata, the biggest man in the platoon, had been rubbing his cold feet when the Chinese struck. Without time to get his pacs back on, Cafferata fought in his bare feet, emptying rifle after rifle as a wounded Marine reloaded for him.

Standing alone, wounded Marines down all around him, Cafferata mowed down charging Chinese with rifle-fire and grenades. As a Chinese grenade landed in a hollow filled with wounded Marines, Cafferata stooped, snatched it up, and threw it back. It went off just as it left his hand, tearing off one finger and chewing up his hand and arm. Unfazed, Cafferata fought on.

Near Cafferata a Marine machine gun jammed; the gunner coolly drew his .45 pistol and cut down six onrushing Chinese. Other Marines killed the rest, and the fragile line still held. Marines swung clubbed rifles and lunged with bayonets in ferocious hand-to-hand fighting, struggling like troglodytes in a gloom lit only by a little moonlight and the flash of grenades.

Other Marines swung entrenching tools at squatty figures in padded uniforms, then used the little shovels like bats to drive back Chinese grenades. Men died in silence, died screaming defiance or crying in agony, and still the line held. It held all night.

And when daybreak at last brought a little respite to Barber's beleaguered men, Fox Hill still belonged to them. The amazing Cafferata could at last stand down and have his wounds treated. A Chinese sniper had hit him again about daybreak, hit him badly. Happily, he would live to receive his Congressional Medal. And he could get some help for his feet. For the big man had fought for five hours barefoot in the snow.

It had been a tough night, though, in spite of victory, for Fox had taken twenty dead and fifty-four wounded. The hill was a hideous place for a wounded man; some of the worst-wounded had died during the night because the blood plasma that might have saved them was frozen solid.

And there were three Marines missing, three men who would never be seen again. Out in front of the Fox position, the Marines could count at least 450 Chinese dead, not counting the dead and wounded their enemy had been able to remove.

During the day, Australian Mustangs hammered the Chinese on the high ground north of Fox Hill and along the valley south of the road. Chinese fire died away, and the Marines had a little relative peace. Barber received permission to withdraw that day, but wisely decided against it. He was surrounded, with no nearby help, and he had fifty-four wounded men to carry. Any attempt to pull out would surely fail; all of Fox would die in Toktong Pass, and die for nothing. Fox would fight it out right here.

As long as the sun lasted, Fox could get a little rest and prepare for the night. One young Marine noticed that the Chinese had come upon some empty Marine sleeping bags in the dark and bayoneted them to tatters, reaching for the lives of the men they thought still slept in them. And so he and his buddies filled with snow some bags belonging to now dead Marines, placing them just down the slope, in easy range. Other Marines improved their defensive positions, often barricading them with frozen Chinese corpses.

The Chinese came again after midnight that night, again amid a cacophony of whistles and bugles and whanging cymbals. Again they lost men in dozens, achieving only a small breakthrough of Barber's 3d Platoon, which soon patched the hole and exterminated the Chinese survivors with machine-gun fire. Marine howitzer rounds came streaking in from Hagaru, and Barber's mortars barked from their position down toward the road. And a group of Chinese died when they stopped to repeatedly shoot and bayonet those artfully arranged sleeping bags full of snow.

Fresh Chinese units struck the thin Marine line, but Barber's men held. Barber himself was hit, a single round that drove through both legs, as was Lieutenant McCarthy, commanding 3d Platoon. Lieutenant Petersen, 2d Platoon leader, was hit for the second time, but stayed grimly on with his men. There were twenty-nine other freshly hurt Americans, but many of them stayed in the fight. There was no place to fall back to—and after all, they were Marines.

And when the blessed daylight began to break, Fox had held again. Out in front lay at least two hundred more Chinese bodies, and as the sun rose Barber put in a counterattack that took back the ground lost on the first night. There wcrc two missing Marines, a machine-gun crew; their gun remained, its field of fire entirely blocked by Chinese corpses. There were also five more Marine dead, but Fox Hill still belonged to the Marine Corps.

An airdrop brought critical supplies during the morning, and a helicopter flew in with fresh radio batteries to keep alive the precious link with the Marine artillery at Hagaru. In the afternoon C-54 cargo aircraft made two more resupply drops to Fox: Both landed about five hundred yards west of the Marine perimeter. Lieutenant Peterson, disregarding his two wounds, led a party out to recover the supplies. They recovered some, but heavy fire drove them back into the perimeter.

After dark, however, under cover of the faithful 105s from Hagaru, Barber sent recovery parties west into the dark again. This time they were successful, returning unmolested with all the supplies, including immensely important hand grenades and illumination shells for the mortars. There were also plenty of blankets to keep the wounded alive.

Next morning the Chinese came again, again in the pitch-darkness, again in that terrible hour when a man's spirit is at its lowest ebb. This time they came in from south of the road, two companies of them, with little covering fire. Marine illumination rounds caught them in the open, and automatic weapons, mortars, and the Hagaru howitzers tore them apart. A few made it as far as the steep cut at the edge of the road, where the Marines rolled grenades down among them. The rest of the Chinese died there.

As the sun rose on November 30, Fox Company still firmly held its hill. There was hot coffee and heated rations, and the Chinese remained quiet. Barber was still firmly in command, although his leg wound had stiffened so badly that he had his legs splinted with boards to keep even a little mobility. He made a point of visiting his wounded. He had a message for his hurt Marines: "We're not pulling off this hill unless we all go together. And nobody stays unless we all stay together."

Later in the day his men began to take sniper fire from Rocky Ridge, the major Communist position to the north. Four Marine Corsairs rolled in to clobber the snipers with rockets, napalm, and five-hundred-pounders, and life on Fox Hill became a little more comfortable. The defenders of Fox

Hill were pros, young and old, the only way a Marine can be. They would have agreed with the First Division Marine to whom a *Life* magazine photographer addressed this question: "If I were God and could give you anything you wanted, what would you ask for?"

The Marine continued prying and chopping at a frozen can of ration beans: "Gimme tomorrow."

At nightfall parachutes blossomed over the valley, welcome packs of supplies swinging beneath them. This time they were half a mile off target, but Fox Marines recovered them anyway. And just behind the parachutes came darkness, and snow, and the twenty-below cold of the Korean night.

About one o'clock next morning, Fox came under fire from four Chinese machine guns on Rocky Ridge. Barber arranged for 105 fire from Hagaru, coordinated to arrive as his own mortars put illumination over the Ridge. As Hagaru reported "on the way," Barber's mortarmen bathed Rocky Ridge in brilliant light. They were ready with more illumination rounds, but they did not need to fire again.

For in one of the most astonishing pieces of shooting in this or any other war, the Hagaru guns put their first salvo on top of the Chinese machine guns. The forward observer reported tersely that there was no point in adjusting for further fire; the targets were destroyed. And the Hagaru gun pits were six miles away. After that, that night passed in relative peace.

So did the next one, the night of December 1–2. There was sniper fire, but no coordinated attack. And Barber learned that help was on the way. First Battalion, Seventh Marines, was on its way to Fox from Yudam-ni. Lieutenant Colonel Ray Davis was coming south like the Lone Ranger.

Davis had had a tough time getting started. He had fought hard for commanding high ground before he could even hit the road. Then, well after dark on December 1, his men pushed off into the frozen moonscape about two miles east of the road and turned south. Davis had left behind most of his heavy weapons, bringing only two 81-mm mortars and six heavy machine guns. He carried extra radios, as well; it was critical not to lose commo in that frozen hell east of the road.

His men were loaded. Some of them carried hundred-pound burdens. All carried extra ammunition, a mortar round, water, four days of canned rations, and their all-important sleeping bags. In a halt of any duration, a man without a bag might well freeze to death; without a bag, a wounded man carried on a litter would surely die of cold.

In temperatures sixteen below zero Davis' men scrambled up rock ridges and floundered through snowdrifts, steering by compass in the featureless night. The going was very tough, but for some hours there was no opposition. The first Chinese fire came from a hill called 1520, which Davis' men quickly overran, destroying a Chinese platoon caught stupid with sleep and cold.

Davis' men stormed and took three successive ridges, panting up steep, icy slopes, driving the Chinese before them. Davis was the spark, urging his tired men forward, personally leading groups of attacking Marines. Knocked down by a shell fragment that struck his helmet, he got up and led his men on into the fire and the appalling cold. His gallantry this grim night would win him the Congressional Medal of Honor.

But Colonel Davis' Marines were exhausted, swaying and falling in the snow as soon as the adrenaline of attack ran out. Thirty-seven-year-old Davis and his officers and NCOs kicked and cajoled and bullied, and got their men moving again. At last, about 3:00 A.M., Davis called a halt. As desperate as he was to move on, his men were zombies after twenty hours of heartbreaking marching and uphill assaults. His units were taking some fire, but his men had to rest.

And so they did, until dawn began to fight its way through the murk of a Korean winter morning. Then Davis got them on their feet and on the road south again, pushing on in spite of long-range Chinese fire from high ground around them. His H Company, bringing up the rear and covering the wounded, beat off one strong Chinese attack; otherwise, the Chinese seemed surprised and unready.

As Davis closed in on Fox Hill, his radioman called to him that Fox-Six was on the radio. At last he had contact with the redoubtable Barber, who supported 1st Battalion's advance with mortar-fire and called in air strikes on Chinese units in the battalion's path. And just before noon on the second of December, Davis's tired men crossed into Fox Company's perimeter. Their achievement was remarkable, a night march through a trackless waste under the worst possible weather conditions, and they were carrying twenty-two litter-cases.

They had made their marvelous march without having a single man killed. Tragically, their surgeon, a Navy doctor, was killed by a sniper soon after reaching the Fox perimeter. And two of Davis's Marines broke down completely; both collapsed physically, and so lost mental control that they had to be restrained. Neither man survived.

Fox was safe now, and Captain Barber took stock. Although morale was still high, it was high time his men had some help. He had started with 220 Marines. Now just 82 of them could still walk away. He had suffered a total of twenty-six killed, eighty-nine wounded, and three missing. Only one of Fox's seven officers was unwounded, and nearly everybody had frostbite and digestive difficulties. Barber himself would be evacuated, to spend a couple of months in a hospital in Japan. It had been, all in all, as fine a job of command against odds as anybody could remember.

The nation agreed. In August 1952 President Truman awarded the Congressional Medal of Honor to Major Bill Barber. With thousands of Marines depending on him, Barber had kept the faith. He had held his command together through the worst of times, and his men had left at least a thousand Chinese dead in the frozen waste around Fox Hill. The imprint on Barber's modest medal said simply, "Valor." There had been an enormous amount of it up and down that hideous path from Yudam to Hagaru. Of all the courageous men who braved the Chinese swarms and brain-numbing cold, nobody better exemplified the heart that makes a Marine than the quiet man who commanded on Fox Hill.

The dreadful breakout was not over. On the third, Lieutenant Colonel Davis' men attacked south of the road, driving a substantial Chinese force into the Marine spearhead from Yudam, and out under the guns and napalm of Marine fighter-bombers. By 10:00 A.M. they had destroyed a Chinese battalion.

Davis's battalion now took over the point of the "advance south," and the Marines pushed methodically on for Hagaru. There was still some fighting to do, and more Marines would die along the road, but the Yudam regiments would reach the Hagaru perimeter, intact and full of fight.

And as they passed under the cover of Marine tanks and

British Royal Marines, as they led the way into Puller's position, Davis' tattered men lifted their heads and fell into step. Some men climbed down from vehicles to hobble along, until the road was lined with marching Marines, in ranks and in step. "Look at those bastards," said a young Navy doctor. "Look at those *magnificent* bastards!"

The Marines had brought more than fifteen hundred casualties out with them, about a third of which were cases of frostbite. They would be quickly flown out to safety; the airfield had been completed two days before by engineers working around the clock, often under fire. And then the Marines would continue their advance to the sea, leaving Hagaru-ri aflame behind them on the seventh, leaving nothing of use to the enemy.

They would fight on doggedly south and southeast, and hordes of Chinese could not stop them. They marched and fought through Koto-ri, forced the dreadful gut of Funchilin Pass, and pushed on past Chinhŭng-ni. And then at last there was Hungnam and the welcoming sea. At Hungnam there was safety, a tight perimeter, and the guns of the Navy, which would pour thirty-five thousand rounds at the limping, listless Chinese pursuit.

So the Marines had come through, where General Sung had been sure they could not. Not only had they escaped the mouth of the Pit, but they had brought out their wounded and their weapons, and with few exceptions, their vehicles and their dead as well.

They had taken some seventy-five hundred casualties—about half from frostbite—and killed about forty thousand Chinese. Thousands more of Sung's men were down with wounds or frostbite. Heaps of Chinese corpses littered the frozen earth wherever they had fought the Americans. A myriad of little mounds of snow were the only monument to thousands more who had died of wounds, or simply frozen to death in the ghastly cold and Siberian wind.

General Sung's battered forces were too badly hurt to interfere with the evacuation of Hungnam. The Navy lifted off more than one-hundred thousand X Corps men, plus about the same number of desperate Korean civilians. The ships also took off 350,000 tons of supplies and over seventeen thousand vehicles. By Christmas eve it was all over. As

Hungnam burned to useless rubbish, a Navy admiral spoke for most Marines: "They never laid a glove on us!"

If the admiral's boast was a little overstated, it nevertheless summed up the way most Marines felt about their "advance" to the sea. They had whipped the best China had to offer, at terrible odds and in unbelievable weather. They had left Chinese 9th Army Group a wreck, and they themselves were still cohesive and prepared to fight.

If the magnificent bastards were a little cocky, they had every right to be.

THE MAN WHO PAID HIS DEBTS

Eliahu Itskovitz was a Rumanian Jew, and he had a long memory. He also believed that debts must be paid, no matter what the cost.

He was the last of his family. His parents and one brother had died in a World War II concentration camp; his other two brothers had been strangled. Only Eliahu had survived.

Young Eliahu knew exactly who had slaughtered his family. The criminal was a fellow Rumanian, a member of the Fascist Iron Guard called Stanescu. The boy Eliahu had been forced to watch as Stanescu personally strangled his brothers, and condemned the rest of the family to certain, lingering death in the camps.

But Eliahu had survived. He had been freed from the camp at sixteen, a walking corpse, and lost no time in calling at Stanescu's house. The Iron Guard sadist had fled, so Eliahu contented himself with stabbing Stanescu's son to death. It cost him five years of reform school, but at least it was part payment on the debt.

His sentence complete, he made his way to Israel. He grew

strong in his new country, and in time became a paratrooper in the new Israeli army. A whole new life lay before him: a new life and free air to breathe. He had come from the valley of death to a new land of unlimited opportunity. Here he could become anything he wished to be.

But Eliahu had something to do first.

He had never forgotten Stanescu, and never ceased questioning Eastern European Jews in Israel: Had anybody heard of Stanescu? Where had he gone? Was he still alive? And at last Eliahu had his answer: Yes, someone said, Stanescu had escaped; he had gotten into the French zone of occupation, and he might have joined the Foreign Legion. Eliahu made his plans.

First, he managed a transfer into the fledgling Israeli Navy. In time his ship called in Italy, and Eliahu applied for routine shore leave in Genoa. Once ashore, he simply caught a train, crossed the French frontier, and made his way to Marseilles and the Legion depot. In weeks he was in Algeria, grinding through tough Legion basic training at Sidi-Bel-Abbès. He then volunteered for Indochina, where much of the Legion was locked in vicious combat with the communist Vietminh. Stanescu was not near Bel-Abbès; maybe he was in the East.

In Haiphong Eliahu asked after Stanescu . . . and this time was rewarded. Yes, there was a big Rumanian corporal in the 3d Legion Regiment. He wasn't called Stanescu, but otherwise he sounded like the right man. And so Eliahu volunteered again, this time for the 3d, then on operations in the Red River delta.

And finally he had found his quarry. Stanescu did not recognize this tough, husky man as the skinny, scared kid he had brutalized a decade before. But Eliahu knew. He worked his way into Stanescu's section, soldiered well, and bided his time. His chance came near Bac Ninh, on Route Coloniale 18, when he found himself alone on patrol with the sadist who had murdered his whole family.

"Stanescu!"

The Iron Guard man whipped around, and Eliahu spoke in Rumanian. "You really are Stanescu, aren't you!"

As Stanescu sputtered and gaped, Eliahu raised his MAT-49 submachine gun. And said what he had waited all these years to say. "I'm one of the Jews of Chişinau!"

Eliahu dragged the bullet-torn body of his NCO back to the

rest of the squad; after all, the bastard was a Legionnaire, and you didn't abandon a comrade's body.

Too bad, said the other Legionnaires, another man killed by the Viets. He was a Rumanian, too, wasn't he?

Yes, said Eliahu. Yes. He was a Rumanian too.

After that, there remained the debt to the Legion. Eliahu soldiered on, serving out his five-year hitch faithfully.

And then, after his discharge, there was still another debt to pay. He walked into the Israeli embassy in Paris and asked to see an Israeli official. As that worthy gaped, Eliahu told the whole story. Ask the Legion, he said; they can confirm my history with them. But I'm still a deserter from the Israeli Navy.

No doubt the Navy court-martial was as astonished as everybody else who heard the young Legionnaire's story. No Jew could fail to be sympathetic, and the sentence was only a year. Finally, once Eliahu emerged from prison, there was one last installment on his obligation, and he returned to the Israeli Navy to serve out his enlistment.

And the last debt was paid.

DISASTER ON THE R.C. 4
THE BATTLE FOR DONG KHE

The Dien Bien Phu airhead fell to Vo Nguyen Giap's Russian-style divisions on May 7, 1954. Dien Bien Phu has been called the death knell of France in Indochina. It was that, indeed, but the passing bell had first rung back in the autumn of 1950. It had tolled clearly, for those with ears to hear, far away to the northeast, along the Chinese border on Route Coloniale 4, not far from a godforsaken place called Dong Khe.

The end of the war was foreordained after that, because

the French had lost control of the frontier. The embattled little posts along Route Coloniale 4 were gone, abandoned or reduced to ruins. And so, from that time forward, Giap's Vietminh had the sanctuary without which no modern insurrection succeeds. The door to high China was open, and would never be closed. And China was red.

Loss of the frontier meant simply that the Vietminh could never be stopped. It meant that the Communists, always rich in men, now had access to Kwangsi and Yunnan, a vast safe area in which to train, and an inexhaustible depot of modern arms and equipment. The Viets would be guerrillas no more; Giap would train them into a regular army, organized in regiments and divisions better armed than the outnumbered French. But nobody in high places realized at the time what loss of the border meant, or if they knew, was willing to admit it.

This is the story of the frontier battle that made possible Dien Bien Phu, and made inevitable French defeat in Indochina. It is the beginning of the American tragedy in Vietnam. It is the story of death on Route Coloniale 4.

The Chinese Communists had reached the northern frontier of Tonkin in 1949, and the border had been a running sore for the French all through 1950. The boil was worst inflamed between Lang Son, the major town of the eastern frontier, and Cao Bang, off to the west, a once peaceful provincial town, now heavily fortified and held by the Foreign Legion.

Cao Bang and the posts between—Dong Khe, That Khe, and the rest—had to be supplied, and throughout 1950 each convoy had become a major operation. Virtually nothing went through without heavy fighting, and much did not go through at all. One convoy, for example, lost 85 trucks out of 110. At bottlenecks like Luong Phai Pass, between That Khe and Dong Khe, large convoys might be held up for days on end, while French battalions went in again and again to open the way. Day in, day out, the R.C. 4 voraciously gobbled men and equipment; such wastage could not continue. The problem of the frontier had to be solved, one way or another.

In the end, the French command decided to abandon the border garrisons. First, the remote little posts west of Cao Bang were evacuated: Nguyen Binh, Backan, and the rest. And the French simply gave up trying to keep open the worst twenty-five miles of the R.C. 4, between Cao Bang and That Khe. But unaccountably the French high command held on to Cao Bang and Dong Khe, two little islands in a sea of hostile silence. They could be supplied only by air, and their garrisons were not strong enough to even try to close the border.

And so Giap's new divisions operated as they liked in the vastness of the Northwest. They and their Chinese friends had already built hard-surface roads up to the frontier, leading directly toward Cao Bang, Laokay, Monkay, and Lang Son. The new divisions had already operated and trained far up the valley of the Red, and snapped up Pho Lu and other isolated little posts during the spring of 1950. Giap was almost ready for the frontier.

For he possessed a fearsome weapon. His divisions were regulars, multiarmed organisms all responsive to a single will, every man driven by faith and revolutionary zeal, quite willing to die and press on regardless of losses. They had been well trained in China, and were well supplied. Gradually the new battalions and regiments would become full divisions. The 304th, 308th, 312th, 316th, and 320th Divisions would be ten-thousand man units, heavily armed with automatic weapons, mortars, bazookas, and recoilless rifles. Great convoys of Molotova trucks hauled their supplies to the border, and vast columns of coolies carried them farther.

The new Viet units were inflexible in many ways, bound tightly by political strictures and doctrine. And so sometimes they could not react to changed conditions as the French could; nor did they always take initiative as the French did. They lost men in thousands, and again and again French professionalism gained victories against the Viet numbers.

But in the end none of this mattered very much, because Giap had no end of men, and now he had all the arms he wanted. After each defeat the Viets criticized themselves, and refitted, and shared the lessons they had learned. And came again. And now, in the autumn of 1950, Giap was ready to finish the last French presence on the frontier. He began at Dong Khe.

Dong Khe was a small post on the R.C.4, a regular stopping place for the embattled convoys. Giap had overrun it at the end of May 1950, and his attack had been a small preview of what would happen at Dien Bien Phu.

For Dong Khe lay in a valley surrounded by the ubiquitous limestone hills of the north country, and the small garrison could not hold the high ground and the post too. So Giap's new army—elements of the formidable 308th Division— simply smashed the post for two days and nights with dozens of mortars and artillery pieces. When the bunkers were in ruins and the heavy weapons destroyed, they came at last, at night, in heavy waves, stoically taking casualties until they simply submerged the garrison. At 3:00 A.M. on the twenty-eighth of May it was over. Dong Khe's radio was silent.

Giap had chosen both time and place well. The clouds and rain of the monsoon had grounded the French aircraft that would have intervened in better weather. And there were no French forces of any size that could reach the tiny post in time. All the French command could do was sit by its radios and listen to Dong Khe die alone, out there in the black night.

But for a while, there had been cause for rejoicing. For a remnant of the garrison escaped, charging the Viets at last in the blackness and breaking out. And then, less than a day after the post had fallen, the French took it back. For while the Viets were relaxed, looting the post, the weather cleared, and thirty old Junkers trimotor transports appeared over Dong Khe. Before the Viets could react, the sky was full of parachutes. The 3d Colonial Para Battalion dropped on Dong Khe, and took the post back in ninety minutes of hand-to-hand fighting. The paras linked up with a relief force from That Khe, and the business of rebuilding the post began.

The Viets had been routed, leaving some three hundred dead and piles of arms. Among the booty was a commissar's notebook, which showed plainly that toward the end of September the 308th would be joined by other divisions, and the business of taking the entire frontier would begin. Sadly, nobody in high command paid much attention. Giap and his commanders would learn from Dong Khe, but the French leadership would not.

After the Dong Khe episode, the monsoon effectually brought a halt to any major fighting. The Viets continued to train, over across the vastness of the trackless frontier. They built a full-size replica of Dong Khe, and others of the fortifications of Cao Bang. On these they rehearsed endlessly. The pressure continued to tighten around Cao Bang, and everybody on the frontier knew Giap was coming. But still the French command dithered. Far from reinforcing the scattered frontier units, battalions were removed from Tonkin to faraway Cambodia and Laos, where they could not possibly intervene in time along the R.C. 4.

The last act of the disaster finally began one Saturday in September, and the curtain rose at Dong Khe. As before, the rebuilt post was battered flat by heavy weapons from the surrounding high ground. As long as it could, Dong Khe's artillery fought an unequal battle against Communist guns on the hills, just as the French gunners would fight later at Dien Bien Phu . . . and with the same result.

The Legion garrison fought on under the sheets of monsoon rain, reduced by sundown on Sunday to half their original number. And by dark Dong Khe's heavy weapons were silent. In the ruins the remains of the Legion garrison were fighting in the dark, small groups of tough infantry soldiers surrounded by swirling rivers of shouting little men. In the end, as the Viets flooded over the ruins of the post, an officer and a few men shot their way out in the darkness and confusion and escaped. In only sixty terrible hours, the post was gone for good.

There would be no retaking Dong Khe this time. Air reconnaissance, flying among the peaks at terrible risk through the monsoon, confirmed that the post was taken. And the Viets had learned their lesson well: They were waiting, alert, invisible below, hoping for a relief force.

Even at this stage, the final tragedy might have been averted, or at least delayed. For General Alessandri, a competent veteran, had prepared a comprehensive fifty-battalion operation, to close with the Viets in their jungles and destroy them. Alessandri was a leathered veteran of Indochina, a Legion man who knew the country and the enemy infinitely well. He had led a fighting retreat of a Legion unit all the way into China when the Japanese turned on the French garrisons in 1945.

Alessandri planned to plunge into the wild frontier country with his infantry, traveling light and closing with the Viets. He would destroy their dumps and their organization, and interdict the flow of Chinese supplies. In groups of five or six, his battalions would close with the Communists and destroy them. And his men would have help. Alessandri had the goodwill of the non-Vietnamese highlanders, the Meos and Mans and Nungs, ferocious fighting men who sold opium and hated Vietnamese.

Nobody knows whether Alessandri's plan would have succeeded. But at least it had a chance. At least it was better than dithering, waiting along the frontier for Giap to strike when and where he liked. But without explanation the operation was canceled by the supreme commander, Carpentier, far, far away in Saigon. Carpentier had no real conception of the terrain and conditions into which he sent men to fight and die. His decision was a death sentence for thousands of good fighting men.

The cancellation may have been the result of Carpentier's dislike and jealousy of Alessandri; it seemed to have no real military basis. Having refused to follow the only really feasible military remedy for the problem of the border, Carpentier now had to decide whether to reinforce the line of the R.C. 4, or to evacuate it entirely. In the event, he did neither, leaving the frontier garrisons terribly exposed.

His plan, such as it finally was, was grandiosely called the "Secret Personal Directive for the Defense of the Sino-Tonkinese Frontier." It envisioned suddenly evacuating Cao Bang, and moving its garrisons swiftly down the R.C. 4 to a benighted place called Namnang. There the Cao Bang garrison would meet a relief force moving west from Lang Son. There was also talk about fighting the Viets at the edge of the delta, although troops were moved at the same time to other parts of Vietnam. No really concrete plans were formed.

Orders were given in September for the evacuation of Cao Bang. To prepare for it and to deceive Giap, each day aircraft flew useless mouths out of Cao Bang, and flew in more troops. Everybody in the city industriously built up the fortifications, laid wire, and generally and obviously prepared for last-ditch defense.

A veteran Legion colonel, Charton, was sent in to command. He was a first-class soldier, and the move also got him out of Lang Son, where he was an embarrassing second-in-command. Charton made it plain that he thought the Lang Son commander, Constans, a favorite of Carpentier, was an idiot. He would turn out to be entirely correct.

The evacuation was supposed to catch the Viets by surprise, and would take place against the backdrop of a monstrous—and quite useless—operation at Thai Nguyen, down in the delta. The Thai Nguyen charade would in the event achieve nothing but headlines . . . and the removal of potential reinforcements beyond any hope of intervening in the tragedy about to unfold along the hellish terrain of the R.C. 4. At Thai Nguyen, the French would fire eighteen thousand artillery rounds against no opposition . . . On the R.C. 4, there was virtually no artillery support.

And Giap was not deceived at all. He lurked near Dong Khe with his new divisions, while the French operation began. From Cao Bang would come Colonel Charton, one of the legendary lions of the Legion. He would lead two fine regular units, a Legion battalion and a *tabor*—or battalion—of Moroccans. There was also a unit of local partisans, and a rag-tag column of civilians, the remains of the city's population, faithful supporters of the French for whom staying behind meant death or worse.

Charton would later be criticized for bringing with him truckloads of supplies and two artillery pieces. But Charton was a fine soldier, and he knew the R.C. 4 well. He was sure the Viets would be waiting, and was certain that he would need everything he had to cut through to safety. For Charton had no illusions about the retreat. He had wanted to go either down the R.C. 3, far to the southwest, or to fly more of the garrison out. But Hanoi would not hear of it. And so the Cao Bang garrison made ready, and waited.

At last the operation got under way. The Lang Son column set off up the R.C. 4, about the time Dong Khe fell for the second time. There were four battalions of Moroccans commanded by a Colonel LePage, a decent, indecisive man unfit for what promised to be a desperate venture, a gamble with fate that could only be won by daring, iron will, and speed. If the operation was to have a chance, its leader should have been one of the tigers, a para, a Legionnaire, or one of the *Groupe Mobile* types. First-class command was especially important, because these troops were tired, and their morale was low. They were not the cream of the crop.

And beyond belief, LePage and his two thousand men did not know why they were marching down the R.C. 4! LePage would not be told until he reached Dong Khe, and the real disaster began. Charton was also supposed to have been kept in the dark as to the purpose of the operation, but Alessandri, in an agony of conscience, had told him.

"It is madness," said Charton simply. Alessandri agreed, but could promise the tough Legion colonel only that he would be met at the twenty-eight-kilometer mark on the R.C. 4. Both veteran officers must have wondered whether anybody would be there to meet Charton. Neither could know the Lang Son column would fail as badly as it did.

Poor LePage was the wrong man in the wrong place. His men ran into moderate opposition early, and began to take casualties. They could not move their trucks and guns along the bridgeless, cratered road, so the heavy equipment was sent back. But they got through to That Khe in good order, and there exchanged one of the North African units for the most famous unit in the French army, the 1st BEP, the first battalion, Foreign Legion Paratroops. And still ahead were sixty miles of the worst country in the world, and Giap's brand-new regulars.

At last LePage pushed on northwest in clouds and rain, toward Cao Bang and Charton and the planned meeting point some twenty miles from Cao Bang. But along the way he had to take Dong Khe of ill omen, the grim, ruined fortress that controlled the road. His leading elements were unopposed as they passed bloody Luong Phai Pass, and as they approached Dong Khe's ghost-haunted valley, but the atmosphere was dismal. The North Africans were nervous and jumpy, LePage was uncertain, and the paras trusted neither their fellow soldiers, nor the force commander . . . with good reason, as it turned out.

Even so, they almost did it, against all hope. The leading detachment of paras got within a few hundred yards of the ruins of the post, but was too weak to carry it. Had LePage put in his whole force, hard, without delay, the column might have taken Dong Khe.

But he dithered and called for artillery by parachute, and the moment passed. On the next day, the second of October, LePage sent his troops in, but it was too late. The paras inflicted brutal casualties on a Viet force, and one French unit got to the edge of the airfield, but Dong Khe could not be taken. Air reconnaissance showed heavy Viet units moving on the basin in which the post lay, and the attack was broken off.

This was the time of final decision. Charton had not yet
started. He could still be ordered to get out via the R.C. 3,
and LePage's column to retreat as quickly as possible toward
That Khe. Alessandri tried one last time. He wired
Carpentier the plain truth: "Cancel everything. If you carry
on, it will be a crime."

But now Carpentier made the decision that sent thousands
of men to their deaths, against all reason, all military logic,
all good sense. He sent LePage into the horrible wilderness
south of Dong Khe, a trackless hell of limestone crags and
dense forest, waterless and uninhabited. Apparently
Carpentier had seen a wavy little line on a map, and the line
led through the badlands and came out again on the R.C. 4
close to Namnang, some twenty miles away. LePage could
simply march up the wavy little line to Namnang, avoiding
the Viets on the R.C. 4.

On the map it was all very simple. But as every soldier in
Southeast Asia knew, the jungle eats trails unless they are
constantly used. They simply disappear in the rioting vegeta-
tion. One year they are there; the next they are gone forever.
And so it would be with this line on the map, called the
Quangliet Track.

And so, by message air-dropped to him on the afternoon of
October 2, LePage finally learned what was expected of him
and his tired men. He obediently turned west, and his column almost immediately found itself in a trackless waste,
and the Viets were all around them in great numbers, stabbing at the column, and finally stalling it. And LePage called
for help.

But there was no help nearby, and none that could be sent
quickly from other areas . . . except Charton, now waiting at
the rendezvous point on the R.C. 4. He had reached
Namnang with the 3d Battalion of Legion infantry, the 3d Tabor of Moroccans, and some local partisans, followed by an
immense column of civilians. And so Charton was told to
leave the R.C. 4 and go down the thread on the Hanoi map,
the Quangliet Track, and the Legion colonel, good soldier
that he was, tried his best. He destroyed his guns and heavy
equipment, and cast about for guides who knew where the
Quangliet Track might be. But nobody knew, not even the
native partisans.

In the end they found a trace, something that might once

have been a real trail, and began to follow it. They had to move in single file, the soldiers carrying only water and ammunition, moving even so with terrible slowness through the dark, tangled wilderness. And tragically, the long line of civilians still followed, desperate to escape the Viets, hopeless but still clinging to life.

Bombarded with messages from Hanoi to hurry—messages from people who had not the slightest notion of the incredible difficulties Charton's men faced—the column pushed on. A screen of partisans led, followed by the Legion, the hard core of the column. The Moroccans came next, followed by the despairing mass of the civilians. And so they struggled on, a few miles a day, sensing the presence of the Viets all around them, and the weakest civilians began to fall behind, lost, to die in the wild trackless maze of limestone hills.

For a while the column was able to follow a stream bed, only about three yards across, and thick with vines and branches, which gave at least some sort of direction to the march. But then even that dried up, and they struggled on, uncertain even of the direction they should take. Charton repeatedly called for observation aircraft to help him find his way. But only one appeared, and that one simply dropped cigarettes and flew away.

Then at last Charton broke out into the valley of Quangliet, real open country, partly cultivated, where his men could see the sky. The column pushed hard down it, moving quickly, until they were stopped by machine-gun fire from the high ground on one side of the valley. At that point Charton did the only thing he could. He ordered his men onto the high ground, and they pushed on along a chain of limestone hills toward LePage, slipping and sliding on scree, clutched and tugged at by jungle. The column began to pull apart into small groups of men, and gaps began to appear.

But still they fought their way on, closer to LePage's remnant. And at last Charton could hear LePage's desperate radio messages, and pushed his tired men even harder to link up with LePage's exhausted column. Their desperate march had taken three days. Charton had made remarkable time through this miserable wilderness, but he was still too late. His exhausted men pushed on with their last strength, groping for the high ground near LePage's dying column.

For LePage was at the end of his rope. He had finally been

driven off the high ground by hordes of Viets, and had taken refuge in a dismal, waterless place called the Gorge of Coxha. And there the remains of the column huddled, fired upon from the higher ground all around them, thirsty and helpless.

But at last some hope dawned for them, for their radio-men could hear Charton's column, and talk to them, and the two commanders tried by radio to reach some sort of plan to retrieve the disaster. Charton could not see LePage's people, down in the bowels of the hideous Gorge of Coxha. But he could hear the firing all around the Gorge, and he knew their desperate situation.

The ultimate tragedy now unfolded. Charton had a moment in time in which to save his men. There was still a gap through which he could have pushed on hard for the R.C. 4, to link up with the 3d Colonial Paras, now advancing on the road under the shelter of That Khe's guns. He could have saved much of his battered, tired column, then reorganized and returned with the paras for anything that remained of LePage's desperate men. He radioed LePage, asking the senior officer's permission to do exactly that. But LePage, in extremis, would not agree.

So Charton's men, still trying to protect the wretched civilians, halted for the night on a series of hills. They pushed outposts out toward That Khe and toward Coxha, ready to link up with LePage. And then they fought off the Viets, hordes of them, leaving stacks of bodies littered down the sides of their positions. By full dark the French had held their high-ground positions, but they could see a myriad of little lights all around them, little dancing fireflies in the pitch blackness. They were the guides of Viet regiments moving in for a morning assault.

At about 3:00 A.M. LePage launched his attempt to break out of the dreadful Gorge of Coxha. Charton's people could hear the tremendous roar of firing, which went on and on until the first traces of dawn lightened the eastern sky. As always, the paras had led the way, climbing the almost sheer sides of the ravine under showers of grenades and automatic weapons fire, scrambling over the bodies of their comrades. Until finally the last few paras, against all hope, cleared the edge of the Gorge of Viets and opened a way out, out toward Charton's men waiting on their high ground. But most of the famous 1st BEP was dead in Coxha, and what was left of the column was mostly a rabble of Moroccans, crazy with fear, an undisciplined mob, many without weapons.

They would find no sanctuary. For the waves of Viets had driven Charton's column from part of the high ground. Here, too, the North Africans had panicked and run from two fine defensive positions, had run when the Viets were still hundreds of meters from them. The Legion went in ten times to try to regain the critical positions. One they recovered; the second they could not. On the tenth charge the battalion commander died, died scrambling up an almost sheer slope on an injured leg that made even walking painful.

And so the two columns met, a mass of hysterical, desperate men, bunched together on a long saddle between two peaks. Only the few survivors of the Legion kept their discipline. Even now the lion Charton tried to lead this awful mob out toward safety, out along the long ridge that led toward That Khe and the road. But he made only a mile.

For the Viets came again in masses, and Charton had nothing left to fight with, only the surviving handful of Legionnaires, and the few Moroccans who had not lost their heads entirely. For a little while they fought on, a little rock in a swirling river of Viets. Charton, already twice wounded, was hit twice again, and his orderly died valiantly taking a bullet intended for his colonel. Charton shot a Viet with his carbine, and then went down for good from still another wound. For a brief time there was hand-to-hand fighting, and then there was only silence.

The Communists carefully collected prisoners and such valuable booty as there was, and left the dead to bloat in the sun, all across the ridges and in the stinking gorge. Charton would survive, carefully saved, a valued prisoner, passing to a terrible captivity.

Some of the French broke out, to head through the wild country toward That Khe, little bands of men who would not quit. The remains of the BEP, about a hundred men, set out in five groups, led by the major commanding the battalion. Twenty-three would survive. The rest were gone: dead, captured, or just vanished, including the major, dying alone of a belly wound on the bank of a little stream.

Some won through to That Khe only to find the town full of Viets, for That Khe had been evacuated prematurely when

Hanoi lost its head entirely. Even the 3d Colonial Paras were gone, or what was left of them. And that fine battalion, already terribly understrength, would die trying to protect the retreat of still more panicked refugees to the east. They fought to the bitter end; only five men would struggle through to sanctuary at Lang Son.

The rest of the frontier went quickly, even Lang Son, the eastern anchor, shamefully abandoned by Constans without destroying its immense arsenals. Worse still, Lao Kay was evacuated, far up on the Yunnan border, commanding the mighty Song Coi, the Red River. Lao Kay's fall opened all the immense Northwest to the Viets, Lai Chau and the Thai country, Laos, and beyond. From this bloody autumn forward, the Viets' sanctuary was complete, and the way was open to the whole North and West. There was no longer a chance to hold more of Tonkin than the vital delta.

Almost four years later, when French paratroops jumped into the morning above Dien Bien Phu, it was as if nobody remembered the lessons of Dong Khe, or the power and organization of the Viet swarms that destroyed the columns on the saddle west of Coxha Gorge. Carpentier was gone by 1954, but his spirit lived on in the body of General Navarre, author of the colossal blunder at Dien Bien Phu. And once more the troops would pay the butcher's bill.

OMEN
The Fall of Pho Lu

About dawn on April 15, 1954, the second day of the Vietminh assault on the Dien Bien Phu perimeter, Colonel Piroth, the French artillery commander, lay down on his bunk in his dugout, pulled the pin from a grenade with his teeth, and held it to his chest. For Piroth, a one-armed veteran of much war, knew the airhead was doomed and blamed himself.

His gunner's eye saw clearly that his 105- and 155-mm howitzers, no matter how heroically served, could not hope to suppress the Communist artillery fire that crashed down into the valley from the high ground all around. For Piroth's pieces were badly outnumbered, and had to fire from open emplacements. They were desperately vulnerable to the Communist guns, tucked deep into tunnels in the surrounding hillsides, dug all the way through from the reverse slope.

Piroth took responsibility for the terrible miscalculation, but the fault was not entirely his. The achievement of Vo Nguyen Giap's Vietminh should have come as no surprise to the French high command, back in the air-conditioned comfort of the Hanoi Citadel. Piroth's superiors could have warned him, had they read and understood what lay within their own reports. For the entire tragedy had been played out at least once before, at a godforsaken place called Pho Lu.

Pho Lu lay far upstream on the Song Coi, the mighty Red River, some thirty kilometers downstream of Lao Kay, in the shadow of Yunnan. The Vietminh were in the area in great force, training and preparing the debut of Giap's new army: These were no longer guerrillas, content to hit, run, and hide, but real regular battalions, often better armed than their French counterparts. They were a strange, frightening new sort of force, what Bernard Fall aptly called the "insect armies," a swarm moved by revolutionary slogans and dialectic, responsive to a single will.

Pho Lu was a primitive little post made of logs, and stood beside a huge, still lake, deep in the great emptiness of the valley. All around lay the primeval forest and the limestone crags of the ancient hills, a desolate place brooding in the silence of countless ages. And it was here that Giap chose to try out his new weapon.

His tactics were simple enough. With immense effort his dedicated swarms manhandled heavy weapons onto the high ground overlooking Pho Lu. After that, he battered the tiny post into junk, and in the end the massed infantry submerged what was left.

The high command had reacted to Pho Lu's agony as best it could. A relief column set out from Lao Kay, but went astray in the almost trackless hills and never got close enough to help. A second force dropped in, a tiny, understrength company, 115 paras of the 3d Colonial Parachute Battalion. The little company survived only because they were dropped almost twenty miles away, on the other side of the Red River. They marched hard toward Pho Lu for hours, only to find themselves in the midst of two entire battalions of Vietminh that had been left on their side of the river.

The commander, Lieutenant Planey, did the only thing he could. The company turned back, destroying all equipment but a few radios, desperately fighting off the pursuing enemy, as other Vietminh crossed the Red to join in the chase. Planey finally made the terrible decision to abandon his dead, and got on a little faster. Burdened still with the wounded, he could not outdistance the pursuers, until in the evening six French fighters saw the paras' recognition panel, and caught the Viets in the open. The resulting carnage held up the leading elements of the 308th, and Planey and his survivors broke contact under cover of darkness.

Planey did well to get his battered little command to the safety of Lao Kay. His thanks was condemnation by the high command for leaving his dead. Some four years later, the caldron of Pho Lu was repeated on a much greater scale in the valley of Dien Bien Phu.

Giap did nothing he had not done many times before, beginning with Pho Lu: masses of coolies moving tons of ammunition and rice, and dug-in heavy weapons. He had learned how to counter the superlative courage, leadership, and fighting quality of the paras and the Legion.

The French high command had learned nothing. Giap did not, of course, knowingly rehearse at Pho Lu the capture of Dien Bien Phu. He probably never dreamed his enemy would hand him his chance for a massive victory, so far from support and air cover. But when the chance came, Giap had no doubt about his tactics.

He had done it all before.

DEATH IN THE MONSOON
The Siege of Dien Bien Phu

On May 31, 1954, Lieutenant Mako Makowiak, emaciated but still full of fight, stumbled onto a French patrol operating deep in northeastern Laos. He was one of only seventy-eight soldiers to escape the dreadful valley of Dien Bien Phu.

Many others had tried. They were dead, mostly killed by pursuing Vietminh or tribesmen greedy for the bounty the Viets offered, dead of exhaustion in the vastness west and south of the bloody valley. Some had simply vanished, gone forever in the great emptiness of the wild hill country.

Dien Bien Phu fell to General Vo Nguyen Giap's Russian-style divisions on May 7, 1954. French occupation of the little valley, Operation Castor, lasted only a little over six months. From its start on November 20, 1953, the operation was a monumental failure in intelligence and command. It was doomed by ignorant leaders, who gave orders from the comfort of a faraway headquarters while the elite of the Colonial Army bled to death almost three hundred kilometers away.

The first hard truth of war is that you do not fight a formidable enemy on his ground, where all his strengths may be used to the full, and yours may not. But that is precisely what the French command elected to do. The results were terribly predictable.

It took a superhuman effort just to find crews for the sixty-five C-47s and C-119s available in Tonkin. They flew out of Gia-Lam and Bach-Mai fields near Hanoi into the morning of November 20, 1953, carrying two of the finest battalions in the colonial forces. The operation was led by the hard core: the 6th BCP, the 6th Colonial Paras, under the fabulous Major Marcel Bigeard, and the II/1 RCP (2d Battalion, 1st Parachute Light Infantry), commanded by Major Jean Brechignac. Behind them were the 1st BCP, also an elite unit, and detachments of engineers and artillery.

The first sticks dropped into the valley at about 10:30 A.M., and caught the Vietminh by surprise. Dien Bien Phu—the name means, prosaically enough, "Seat of the Border Administration"—had been occupied by the Viets for about a year. The valley was inhabited by Thai tribesmen, the upper slopes by Meos. It was a valuable rice-producing area, and a collecting point for raw opium, for which nearly anything could be had on the black markets of Hong Kong and Bangkok. The village itself was a quiet place of perhaps a hundred houses, built near the winding Nam Yum River. It was tenuously connected to the delta by a long snake of a road, Route 41, which ended in the valley. A rugged trail called the Pavie Track led on through the wild country north of Lai Chau, the Thai capital.

The valley was headquarters for Vietminh Independent Regiment 148. Three of its battalions were along the Laotian border. But in the valley this peaceful Friday morning were Battalion 910 and three extra companies. In fact, as the sky began to fill with parachutes, most of the Viets were out training, their mortars and machine guns deployed all over one of the three drop zones the French had selected.

On this DZ, "Natasha," landed Bigeard's 6th BPC, about 650 men strong. Like most French units, it contained a substantial number of Vietnamese, which gave the 6th better fighting capacity than any all-Western unit. The Vietnamese fought very well, and their knowledge of local language and customs was invaluable.

The French took some casualties while they were still in the air, and one trooper smashed into the DZ beneath an undeployed chute. But the French were veterans, and they rallied quickly, moving down the line of the drop, collecting more friends. They then methodically pushed the Viets off the DZ and through the village, while Bigeard orchestrated the battle over several radios, calling in support from American-made B-26 medium bombers of the French air force. The paras fought house to house through the ruins, and the Viet defenders broke.

By the afternoon the French had put almost two thousand men on the DZs and driven out the enemy. Losses were light: eleven killed and fifty-two wounded to about one hundred Viet KIA and many WIA carried off by their comrades.

The next morning the commander of the whole operation parachuted in: forty-nine-year-old General Jean Gilles, his glass eye carefully buttoned into his pocket. With him was Lieutenant Colonel Pierre Langlais, hard-bitten commander of the airborne group: in French Army slang, "GAP 2." Langlais injured an ankle during the drop and had to be evacuated; but he would return, to lead the defense to the end.

Also on the ground were 653 men of the ubiquitous 1st BEP, the Legion paras, and two bulldozers, dropped from C-119 Flying Boxcars. One landed gracefully, and was promptly put to work filling holes in the old airstrip. The other descended less lightly, detaching itself from its canopy and burying itself ten feet into a rice paddy.

Every soldier not on security worked on the airstrip. The only paras who rested were those in a row of fresh graves near LZ Natasha, protected by a newly erected flagpole bearing the tricolor of France. These few were the first of many.

The last two para battalions were Major Pierre Tourret's 8th BPC (Parachute Assault Battalion) and the 5th BPVN, a Vietnamese battalion. With the 5th came veteran reporter Brigitte Friang, who already had made five combat jumps. Little gray-eyed Brigitte, in her early thirties, had survived Zwodau concentration camp and some of the most desperate fighting of the Indochinese war. This was just another assignment to her.

Some of the paras would gradually be replaced by North African troops and soldiers of the Legion. Artillery and tons of supplies arrived, as the airstrip was able to receive transport aircraft. Even a few light tanks were delivered in pieces, and assembled by French armor mechanics in the valley. More supporting personnel would arrive, and a hospital, until the valley held the equivalent of twelve battalions. In the practical French fashion, there would even be two BMCs (Bordel Mobile de Campagne—simply, a field brothel). The girls of one were Vietnamese. The other was staffed by girls of the Ouled Naïl, the North African tribe whose women by custom are prostitutes until they accumulate an appropriate dowry, marry, and settle down. In the bloody valley they would be nurses, too, and heroines, right to the bitter end.

The purpose of an airhead in this remote place has never been entirely clear. The operation was the child of General Henri Navarre, commander in chief in Indochina. He probably did not intend—at least at first—to fight it out at Dicn Bien Phu. The place was, after all, far away from any help. It was a long flight for air support, and could be reached on the ground only over many miles of the worst country in the world. And the monsoon was coming, which would badly impede fortification, movement, and aerial support.

But the French government had decided to defend northern Laos, and Navarre wrote afterward that he selected this remote valley as a base from which to do so. The idea seems to have been to operate from Dien Bien Phu into the hinterland, to break up any Viet offensive through the Thai country into Laos, and to cover the capital, Luang Prabang.

The fallacy was that this sprawling countryside lacked positions from which to block Giap's movements; there were no roads. The French could only grope through this vastness for Vietminh who could march anywhere, aided by armies of coolies.

Worse still, nobody in Hanoi seemed to appreciate that the valley was a trap. It was, as the soldiers said, "a chamber pot, and we are the material on its bottom." The area was the largest open place for many miles, but it was ringed by hills, hills overlooking the high ground on which the French defensive positions would be dug.

And those heavily wooded hills were within easy cannon range of the airfield. Flak pieces on them would sweep the path resupply aircraft must follow to drop supplies into the valley. All of those guns together could deny the French the use of the airstrip. And without the airstrip, Castor would surely die.

Navarre was not the only one who could not see the obvious. There were many visitors to the valley in the four months before the siege began, including American general "Iron Mike" O'Daniel, and an American mission that included antiaircraft experts. Apparently none of them saw the trap waiting in the valley.

General René Cogny, northern theater commander, initially opposed the operation. He told Navarre it could become a "battalion meat grinder," which was exactly what it turned into. But Cogny's opposition quickly became less strenuous, and planning went ahead routinely.

Virtually nobody could imagine how Viet commander Vo Nguyen Giap could move artillery and supplies across the terrible country surrounding the valley. They could not grasp the phenomenal power Giap had forged in what Bernard Fall aptly called the "insect armies."

In the last stages of planning, French intelligence discovered that Giap was shifting forces from the delta into the mountains of the Northwest. The bulk of his regular force were on the move: the 308th and 312th Infantry Divisions and the 351st Heavy Division. In time, they would be joined by two more divisions and an independent regiment.

The 351st was the key to Giap's plans. It was a Russian-style heavy-weapons division, whose establishment included twenty-four 105 howitzers, fifteen lighter guns, forty 82-mm mortars and twenty 120-mm heavies, 37-mm and .50-calibre AA guns, and twelve to sixteen Katyusha multiple rocket launchers. Adding regimental artillery and recoilless guns, Giap would have perhaps 175 artillery pieces in the valley before the battle's end.

By the twenty-eighth of November Navarre knew the major part of Giap's regulars were on their way toward the Thai country. Indeed, French intelligence estimated Giap's ultimate infantry strength within 10 percent of what it actually turned out to be. But the estimators missed badly on Giap's supply capability, concluding that he could amass perhaps twenty-five thousand artillery rounds at Dien Bien Phu. In fact, his guns would fire over one hundred thousand rounds into the airhead.

Giap's approach in great force changed nothing. The

French command was committed to Castor. Cogny suggested a diversionary operation against Giap's rear, to force him to fight in the delta with at least part of his forces. But he apparently did not flatly demand the valley be evacuated, the only real salvation. It might have been done then or, better still, after Giap had his troops trudging deep in the great wilderness of the Northwest.

Cogny's real feelings were impossible to reconstruct. While he later argued that he had warned Navarre, he did not consistently resist fighting. Indeed, as late as March 4, he is quoted as telling Navarre:

> We mustn't let the Viets change their minds. For the entrenched camp, this fight offers the prospect of a great defensive victory. It would be a catastrophe from the point of view of morale if the Viets failed to attack.

There were warning voices. Besides many unit officers, General Fay, chief of the air staff, saw danger clearly. On an inspection trip to the valley in mid-February, he put his fears plainly to René Plevcn, the armed forces minister, in Cogny's presence:

> I shall advise General Navarre to take advantage of the respite available to him and the fact that he can still use two airfields, to evacuate all the men he can, for he is done for.

Fay did see Navarre, and he did tell Navarre what he had told Pleven. He offered to stay in the valley and personally supervise the evacuation. But Navarre was not interested, and the garrison's last chance was dead.

There were errors made in the valley too. The garrison was not concentrated. The main complex of strongpoints was around the airfield, where most of the troops were dug in. But strong point Isabelle, seven kilometers off to the south, was too far away to be much help to the main complex. And it absorbed a quarter of the garrison, some 105-mm howitzers, and a platoon of M-24 light tanks.

And Castor's total strength was never great. Although seventeen French battalions fought in the valley at various times, there were never more than ten there at any one time. Their strength was diluted, during the battle, by at least three thousand men—mostly tribal partisans, North Africans, and Vietnamese—who deserted and lived like moles in holes along the Nam Yum River. The garrison faced an enemy consistently maintained at four divisions, heavily equipped with artillery and mortars.

And so the drama began. Giap was coming, in spite of grave misgivings among his staff about whether such a massive operation could be supplied so far away. But Giap, the little ex–history professor, was a natural commander. He knew, from Pho Lu and Dong Khe and other places, what his new army could do. He knew also what miracles could be accomplished with a supply corps of thousands of patient coolies. As he wrote afterward, he believed firmly in the ancient maxim of revolutionary war:

Strike to win, strike only when success is certain; if it is not, do not strike.

Giap, the self-taught soldier, saw the French danger far more clearly than did Navarre. And Giap prepared to strike.

The garrison dug in, laid wire, patrolled, and waited. On November 25 the first C-47 landed on the refurbished airstrip. Supplies poured in, and combat aircraft arrived to fly support sorties from the valley. And on December 12 the valley's new commander arrived, replacing Gilles, whose stout heart had failed him.

He was an aristocratic, flamboyant, womanizing, much-decorated cavalryman, a spahi, son of an ancient military family. He had commanded before in Indochina, and had the reputation of a *baroudeur,* a brawler who liked to fight. His name was Christian Marie Ferdinand de la Croix de Castries.

And the GAP 2 commander returned, the hard-nosed Breton Pierre Langlais, tough, profane, and hard-drinking, a Saint-Cyr man who had served his apprenticeship in the Sahara camel corps. He had seen much fighting in Indochina. His ankle had not fully healed, and he would get around for a while on a Thai pony.

The theory of offensive operation around Dien Bien Phu quickly proved unworkable. Several early sorties were successful, but on the morning of December 5 para units found Viet regulars on Route 41 only some three miles from Dien

Bien Phu. The French were victorious in a vicious short-range fight. But papers from the Viet dead revealed the unit was a battalion of Giap's 316th Division.

So Giap's regulars were coming in great numbers. De Castries had insulting leaflets dropped on them, urging them to attack. Giap was delighted. "They are staying," he said. "This time I have them."

Two strongpoints north of the main complex, Beatrice and Gabrielle, covered the direction from which the Viets would come. (Most of the other defenses were also given women's names. A rumor instantly appeared that all were named for de Castries's mistresses, a rumor never proved.)

Beatrice was garrisoned by a Legion infantry battalion. She commanded Route 41, and provided a spectacular view of the rest of the valley. No man could move, no shell could fall, anywhere in the French lines without observers on Beatrice knowing it.

The Legion would hold Beatrice if anybody could. It was still the old Legion, men from fifty nations serving the mystique of the Legion, a mystical professional bond that made superb fighting men. It is fashionable to assert that the Legion was largely German, full of Nazi war criminals and similar trash, and that Dien Bien Phu was largely a Legion battle. Both assertions are nonsense.

The French Expeditionary Force contained about 280,000 men. Of these, perhaps 20,000 were Legionnaires. Since the Legion limited to 25 percent of its strength any single national contingent, it could not have been more than, say, 35 percent German, including Germans who enlisted as Austrians or some other nationality. There were therefore perhaps seven thousand German Legionnaires in all Indochina. At Dien Bien Phu, including reinforcements, there were about four thousand Legionnaires. It is therefore unlikely that more than fourteen hundred Germans served there throughout the whole siege, although the myth persists.

Meanwhile, the French had evacuated Lai Chau, capital of the feudal Thai federation, the last French stronghold in the Northwest. The evacuation not only abandoned the loyal Thai tribesmen, but removed the last safe haven for French guerrilla groups operating against the Viet rear. The town could not be held against the entire 316th Division, already on its way.

The federation president and his entourage had been flown out, and so had several regular units, but the two thousand–odd men of the Thai partisan companies tried to reach Dien Bien Phu or Laos on foot, some with civilians trailing along behind them. The French command helped them with air drops when it could and talked to some of them by radio, but otherwise the small, light-armed units marched and fought alone. And died alone.

For they were pursued, and many of the little units were never heard from again. There sometimes was a final radio message, or a last glimpse of a French NCO and a handful of partisans leaving a clearing for the jungle. And then there would be only silence. The exhausted men who reached the Dien Bien Phu perimeter were incorporated into the garrison.

The evacuation of the Thai country again proved the valley would not be a "mooring point" for long-range offensive operations. For French columns had set out to meet the Thai companies, had become involved in full-scale firefights with Viet units, and had regained the valley only after heavy fighting and substantial casualties.

And on the last day of January Viet 105- and 75-mm pack howitzers began to fire on the airstrip, and on strongpoints Eliane and Dominique. Just as bad, flak began to reach out for French combat and supply aircraft over the valley. French aircraft struck back, and 105 and 155 counterbattery fire hammered the hills. But the Viet pieces were not on the reverse slope, where they should have been. They were *in* the mountain, in tunnels laboriously dug beneath the heavy vegetation, sometimes dug straight through the hill to the other side.

The French guns, in open pits, were plain as a gnat on a mirror to observers in the hills. The main complex had twelve 105s, four 155s, and twenty-four 120-mm mortars, plus four quadruple .50-calibre mounts and the battalion 82-mm mortars. Like most of the fighting bunkers, these weapons had little shelter from artillery fire. There had simply not been enough airlift capacity to fly in the required timber, pierced steel plate, and other supplies.

Major Sudrat, the harassed engineer, needed a further thirty-four thousand tons of engineer supplies. With the airlift capacity available, it would have taken five *months,* hauling nothing else, to fly in the required supplies. Sudrat could properly protect only the CP, the signal complex, and the X-ray room of the hospital.

Colonel Charles Piroth, the one-armed veteran artillery commander, was sure of three things. The Viets could not move guns all the way to the valley. Even if they somehow managed that superhuman feat, they could not keep them in ammunition. And French guns could crush any Viet artillery effort. He was tragically wrong in all three assumptions.

For Giap mounted a tremendous supply effort. By the end of February, he had stockpiled some forty-four thousand mortar and artillery rounds, and as many 37-mm flak shells. All of this ammunition, and hundreds of tons more in weeks to come, was coming in from the Chinese frontier, over five hundred miles of tortuous road. Most of the journey was made in Russian Molotova trucks under regular French air attack. But Viet camouflage was excellent, and the road was constantly repaired by thousands of coolies, army recruits, and three regiments of combat engineers. Thousands more coolies trudged along pushing ordinary Peugeot bicycles. Each carried up to five hundred pounds, frame and front fork strengthened with wood, bamboo extensions on the brake levers and one handlebar.

French air cut at Giap's logistic umbilical. So did the GCMAs (Groupement de Commandos Mixtes Aéroportés), guerrilla units armed and led by the French. The GCMAs bit so hard that by April at least ten Viet regular battalions were tied down guarding bridges and roads, trying to hunt down these elusive foes in the deep forest. But Giap could spare the men and take the casualties, and his vital arteries continued to flow.

Viet guns hammered the airstrip in February and March, destroying or driving off the aircraft there. And at last the storm broke on March 13. Artillery had fallen on the strip all day, and a crushing barrage struck Beatrice in late afternoon. Fire fell on Gabrielle as well, especially the heavy mortar battery that supported Beatrice. French artillery shot back, but quickly lost two 105s and a number of casualties.

As the night wore on, waves of Viet infantry came in on battered Beatrice, and one by one the Legion companies ceased to answer radio calls. By 10:30 P.M. all the Legion officers were down, but the remnants of the garrison fought on the darkness, cutting down the Viets in swaths, only to see new waves appear out of the night. Just after midnight the last radio message came from Beatrice, calling in artillery fire on top of the operator, who died under the French shells that killed his attackers. Only about 200 Legionnaires out of 750 had survived.

Late on the fourteenth the last of the spotter planes was destroyed, along with four inoperable Bearcat fighters and the radio beacon used to guide aircraft into the valley. There would be no more combat support from the airstrip. Night was falling, and everybody knew Gabrielle was next.

Gabrielle was held by the 5th Battalion, 7th Algerian Rifles, a fine unit of very high morale. The strongpoint was exceptionally well built, with a second defense line. But it was tiny, only five hundred by two hundred meters. Any artillery round that fell anywhere on it was liable to kill or wound.

The Viet fire began to come in about 6:00 P.M., a battalion of heavy mortars. Then 105s joined in, and the position began to crumble. Bunker after bunker was destroyed, and in the darkness the inevitable waves of Viet infantry began to penetrate. In the gloom the French counterattacked with grenades and submachineguns, and the hole was plugged. One such forlorn hope was headed by platoon leader Sergeant Rouzic, onetime getaway driver for France's most famous criminal, Pierrot-le-Fou (Crazy Pierre). Rouzic would be a rock for the French defense this wild night.

But the Viets came again and again, and about 4:00 A.M. a shell hit the CP, destroying its commo and badly wounding both the battalion commander and his replacement. The senior captain became hysterical, and a more junior officer, Captain Gendre, took command sometime around five o'clock. Help was coming, but it was too little and too late.

The tired Vietnamese paras counterattacked at five-thirty, led by a single company of the 1st BEP and a tank squadron. But as they forded the river, they were struck by accurate artillery fire and a battalion of Viets. The tanks, the Legion, and two and a half companies of BPVN went on. The rest did not, and the counterattack failed.

On Gabrielle, under sheets of monsoon rain, the French fought on, without hope. The remains of one company were forced to surrender, and marched off through minefields into captivity. As they approached one Viet, still alive, his guts tangled in the wire, a Viet officer commented: "You can step on him. He has done his duty for the People's Army."

Some of the French survivors shot their way out to meet the Vietnamese paras about eight-thirty. The handful who could not or would not leave the hill fought to the last cartridge in the ruins of their positions. Gabrielle was gone for good, and the battalion meat grinder had begun. On this day, too, one-armed Colonel Piroth realized that he could not fend off the Viet artillery. Weeping, he visited infantry command posts, trying pitifully to apologize for the failure of the guns. Then, in despair, he hugged a grenade to his chest, pulled the pin, and paid for his error in the only way he knew how. In Hanoi Cogny was already declaring that for months he had warned Navarre that the valley was "a mousetrap." The self-justification had begun.

On March 16 Bigeard's 6th Colonial Paras returned to the valley they took so long ago. Replacements dropped in too. But the flak was getting heavier, and resupply tougher and tougher.

Next day the French, by arrangement with the Viets, sent medical teams out to pick up eighty-six wounded survivors from Gabrielle. The Viets did little from compassion. They used the fact that Dr. Paul Grauwin's foul underground hospital was desperately crowded, for the Viets would neither accept their own wounded in French hands nor allow medevac aircraft to land.

The iron ring tightened. The listening posts (sonnettes—"doorbells") far out in front of the strongpoints reported more enemy activity. Dien Bien Phu was slowly strangling, and de Castries, the swaggering cavalryman, began to withdraw into himself and take little part in the defense. On March 24 Langlais acted. With his para commanders, he courteously told de Castries—whom he personally liked—they were taking command. Thereafter the "Paratroop Mafia" in fact led the garrison.

Air supply worsened. A C-47 was lost on March 26, and two more next day. The air force reluctantly raised the twenty-five-hundred-foot drop altitude to sixty-five hundred feet and later to eighty-five hundred, and more supplies fell outside the perimeter. Langlais resolved to do something about the flak to the west, and the job went to Bigeard.

He used the cream of the garrison, the paras and the Legion, and the tank squadron, led by quiet Captain Yves Hervouet, still in command with both arms in casts. The troops were confident, for Bigeard, their idol, was leading.

He is a winner [with] the innocence and toughness of a fanatic. Eight years of almost uninterrupted fighting have given him a mystical view of the army, of his comrades, of death. In a sort of flirtation with danger, he never carries any arms with him in combat, and constantly tells his men . . . "Learn to look death in the face. You are born to die. You are going where men go to die." His men love him, many of his companions find him unbearable, the enemy fears him.

They had reason to. The 6th BCP and the 8th Assault went in side by side under a fine artillery barrage, and the tanks struck the Viets in the flank. The Viets ran, leaving 350 dead, seventeen light flak runs, and hundreds of other weapons.

But the ground could not be held, and another C-47 ambulance plane, landing with great gallantry, was destroyed by artillery before it could take off with its load of wounded.

The crew and wounded survived, and the garrison was cheered by the addition to it of the aircraft's nurse, brown-eyed, smiling Genevieve de Galard-Terraube. She would serve on gallantly to the end, working endless hours next to Dr. Grauwin in the stinking underground hospital, where the mud was foul with maggots. She would win both the Croix de Guerre and the Knight's Cross of the Legion of Honor. When she returned to France, long after the valley had fallen, she had flown 149 medevac missions in Indochina: Forty of these were to Dien Bien Phu.

After that came the agony of strongpoints Eliane and Dominique, last-ditch defense and bitter counterattack, endless artillery churning up the tortured earth of the hills, waves of Viet infantry coming screaming out of the dark. The paras and the Legion held and held, taking back lost ground hand to hand in the dark. But the defenders were bleeding to death. There were too few replacements to fill the ranks, even though they were being dropped all over the perimeter, and untrained volunteers were making their first jump into the black night over the valley. The worn-out transport aircraft made more agonizingly slow runs across the airfield, but the replacements and the supplies came down everywhere in the nightmare wilderness of wire, craters, and equipment. And some landed outside the French perimeter; these would not be heard of again.

But the French persevered at Langlais's urging, and the next night most of the 2d Parachute Light Infantry (II/1 RCP) dropped into the valley. They made it with just two dead from enemy action and ten injuries, most of them minor hurts on landing. The casualties included the trousers of the battalion's hard-nosed commander, Major Brechignac, left in the barbed wire.

The valley also received reinforcements for the artillery and tank crews, and some of these were not trained as parachutists. These volunteers made their first jump, in the dark, into this hell of gunfire and jagged obstacles. Before the valley fell, about 4,300 replacements would jump into it. Of these, 681 were untrained volunteers. Surprisingly, their jump-injury rate was no higher than that of the trained men.

Now there was a brief lull, at least enough for Brechignac's paras to familiarize themselves with Eliane 10 and Dominique 3, which they would hold. Even the rain had ceased for a little while. On April 4 the Viets abandoned their foothold on E2, now a ravaged, shapeless mound of earth, stinking with almost 2,000 rotting bodies. The French parceled out their meager forces, trying to cover some ten kilometers of perimeter and guard about twenty-two hundred Viet PWs at the same time.

And on the night of April 5 began the agony of Huguette 6. It would pit a full four-battalion Viet regiment against the tiny garrison of eighty-eight Legionnaires and two lieutenants, plus a little scratch "intervention" company under Captain Viard. After midnight they were joined by the SAS company of the 8th Assault and two tanks. Just after 3:00 A.M., with the situation desperate, Captain Cledic of 2d Company 6, II/1 RCP, took his men on the dead run straight across the airstrip, and closed with the Viets hand to hand. In ferocious close-in fighting he drove them from H6, where twenty Frenchmen of the little garrison were still fighting on.

Bigeard led an attack through Cledic's people about six o'clock, his force no more than 160 men. They ran head-on into a Viet battalion counterattacking and miraculously held them, with the help of French artillery. And as the Viets fell back about eight o'clock, French aircraft caught them in the open and cut them down. When it was all over, there were some five hundred Viet dead inside H6; perhaps three hundred more lay in the wire outside, not counting wounded carried away in the retreat. French intelligence would soon report that Giap had called for more replacements.

But the hard core of the garrison, the paras and the Legion, had suffered also. Their casualties were far fewer than the Viets', but they could not be replaced except by the agony of airborne reinforcement. The five para battalions were reduced to some three hundred men each, except for II/1 RCP, which was a little stronger. The two Legion battalions had about the same number of effectives. For the rest, there were the remains of the North Africans and the Tais: perhaps twenty-five hundred shaky infantry.

Some reinforcements did come. On the ninth of April elements of the 2d BEP—the Legion paras—dropped into the valley. And at dawn on the tenth Bigeard put in one of his patented attacks to recover E1. He commanded from a hole full of radio sets, coordinating the guns, the mortars, and the attacking infantry, most of which came from his own 6th Colonial Paras. The paras were supported by virtually every gun in Dien Bien Phu, including direct fire from tank guns and the deadly hail of the quad-.50s. The air force arrived on time to cut off Viet reinforcements, and the paras went in in small groups, bypassing strongpoints and probing for weak spots.

E1 was French again, and the Viet battalion that had held it fell back toward the mountains in the east, to be hammered by the air force as they went. The two French companies had no time to enjoy their triumph. They were digging in, preparing for the inevitable counterattack. It came quickly, under heavy artillery preparation, a full regiment coming on out of the smoke and darkness and rain, regardless of casualties. The French automatic weapons piled the Viets up in heaps, but they could not kill fast enough. By 8:00 P.M. the French were holding only small pieces of the crest.

At the last moment some help arrived, two small companies of the 1st BEP, singing as they went in to die. Giap committed another battalion, and Bigeard put in his last reserve, two companies of the Vietnamese paras. The little men attacked singing the Marseillaise, and the Communists broke.

E1, a pile of torn earth and torn bodies, would remain in French hands for twenty days more, almost until the end. The Viets would try for Elaine again and again, and litter the slopes with their dead. But the paras would hold.

Viet morale sank. Prisoners said they had been driven to attack by the guns of their own people. Some units simply refused to advance. And so Giap modified his tactics. He would dig.

His trench line crept closer and closer, deeper and deeper. The French could hear the Viets digging underground, especially in the Five Hills area, where the Viets had a regiment raised in the coal-mining area of Dong Trieu. The artillery and mortar fire went on, too, and the casualty list got longer. There were pitifully few replacements dropped in, although plenty of soldiers were willing to go. In the delta, a complete Legion battalion volunteered en masse for Dien Bien Phu.

Over on the Huguettes the French were particularly hard-pressed as the tentacles of the trenches drew in tightly. By the fourteenth of April H1 and H6 were virtually cut off. If they fell, the Viets would be able to move flak in much closer to the center of the garrison, and resupply would become even tougher.

There were other problems. Supply was critical, not just ammunition, but food and medical supplies. On April 14 a massive fire destroyed most of the dump of rations. A few days before, the tobacco ration had burned, so that, as Langlais said, "all of Dien Bien Phu smelled as if it were smoking a gigantic pipe."

The French supply system shared some of the blame for shortages. For example, American flak vests were available to the French for the asking. Not until mid-April did anybody think of requesting them. The American depots in Japan produced them within five days, and still it took the French another eight days to drop the first installment into the valley. How many lives they might have saved had they been sent in months before.

By April 14 the Huguette defenders were in deep trouble. They were almost surrounded, and the Viets had driven a trench clear across the airstrip. Most of the 1st and 2d BEP was used to get water and ammunition in to the Huguette garrison. They made it, but the cost was fearful, both to the Legion and to the Viet prisoners who carried the supplies.

These Viets are worth mentioning. They were officially known as *prisonnier-interné militaire*, but no French soldier ever called them anything but PIMs. They were decently treated, and many worked willingly for the French. Some of them changed sides. When they did, the French indulged in a little charade in which a prisoner was reported to have escaped, and a new Vietnamese soldier was enlisted in one of the units.

The Viets had sworn to try as war criminals anybody supervising PIMs. It speaks well for French treatment of the PIMs, and the prisoners' sense of fairness, that when the fortress fell, the officers who commanded PIM detachments remained unidentified. One was even saluted by some of his PIMs as he was led off, a prisoner.

Resupply on April 15 reached almost 250 tons in spite of the flak, but there was disaster too. A fighter approached the valley, ready to drop a new set of aerial photographs and newly drawn maps to the French command. As the pilot made his run, canopy open, heavy flak opened on him and he took evasive action. The weighted pouch fell from the cockpit, and into Viet territory. It was a wonderful present for Giap: detailed information on the French positions, plus precise information on what the French knew about his own dispositions.

On the sixteenth another resupply operation was mounted: some sixty PIMs carrying ammunition and water, covered by paras. By the end of the day forty-two PIMs were casualties. The strongpoint had received enough water to give each man about a pint. It was better the next night. The trip was made with minor casualties, and for once there was plenty of water to drink.

But time had run out for H6. Langlais made the painful decision; holding the embattled outpost was not worth the endless drain in casualties. And so Bigeard orchestrated the evacuation: a breakthrough of small detachments of paras, supported by two of the four surviving tanks. This time it did not work. There were simply not enough men, and all their courage would not smash through the Viet trenches and mines.

So it was up to Captain Bizard, the tough commander of H6. He had earned the Officer's Cross of the legion of Honor on Huguette, and now showed how richly he had deserved it.

At 8:00 A.M. on the 18th he and his handful of Legionaires and paras struck the Viet trenches under the early morning fog, hurling grenades and covered by an automatic rifle fired by Legion Sergeant Ganzer. Wounded, Ganzer had volunteered to provide a base of fire. He would die quickly on H6, but his fire gave life to his friends.

For Bizard's little force struck the Viet trench by surprise, sprayed the defenders with their tommy guns, jumped the trench, and ran south into the fog. French mortars fired in support, and in bloody fighting the survivors won through to H2. Of sixteen officers who at various times had served on H6, only five still survived; enlisted losses were in proportion. The losses were of elite soldiers; they could not be made up.

The command's anger with Hanoi mounted. The lost aerial photos had not been replaced; they would have given the details of the trench system Bizard had attacked. Even trench periscopes would have given some accurate idea of the Viet dispositions. They had been asked for; Hanoi had not responded. Hanoi never would.

But things were not entirely one-sided. A deserter told the French that raw recruits made up much of the Viet forces, almost half of the 312th Division. Supplies were short, as the French Air Force pounded Route 41, and many Viet troops were discouraged. And the French could still strike hard. On the twentieth, raiders from the II/1 RCP struck Dominique 6 in the darkness, killing Viets and destroying bunkers. The next morning, a force from the 6th BCP struck a bunker on D5.

H1 fell on April 23. At about 2:30 A.M., Captain Chevalier reported that he was being overrun and asked for help. There was no time to reach him, for the Viets were simply inundating the position, appearing in small groups from some thirty approach trenches. No matter how many the Legion killed, there were always more. A few of the defenders reached friendly lines about daybreak. Chevalier was not among them; he and a little band of Legionnaires had fought it out, back to back on top of the command bunker, until they were submerged.

The decision was made to try to retake H1. And the decision was made by de Castries this time, for Langlais, and Bigeard as well, opposed the attempt because of the shortage of troops. Once the decision was taken, however, Bigeard devised his usual clockwork operation. However, exhausted as he was, he left the execution of it to Major Liesenfelt of the 2d BEP.

The result was tragedy. The operation began well as air support tore apart the Viets holding H1. However, the slim assault forces quickly became pinned down by torrents of enemy fire. But Liesenfelt, without a view of the battle, knew nothing of this, because his radio was turned to the wrong frequency. His battalion was dying as he sat placidly waiting for news. He only realized what had happened when de Castries' headquarters, monitoring the desperate calls for help, woke Bigeard.

Bigeard salvaged what he could. The attack was a failure, although elements of 2d BEP had gotten within fifty meters of H1. Although Bigeard got the men out, casualties had been heavy. One para officer, down in the open with serious wounds, shot himself to save his men, who were starting to crawl out to pull him in. Although the Viets had been badly hurt, the 2d BEP had lost some 160 men, and the valley had no reserve. The remaining men of the 2d BEP were now combined with what was left of 1st BEP to form a provisional unit, what the French call a *bataillon de marche*.

The need for replacements was now desperate. Another seventy-two volunteers jumped in on the night of April 24, but something more substantial had to be done. The supply situation was deteriorating. That the drops even approached the adequate was due in large measure to the chances taken by the American contract crews of the big C-119s, who bored in steadily to drop their loads within the perimeter, even though they were not required to fly in combat conditions.

The underground hospital now held almost nine hundred wounded, lying in conditions of nightmare horror, in mud crawling with fat white maggots. Down on Isabelle were more than one hundred more. And this did not count the seriously wounded men who simply stayed on duty and fought on. Even counting them, there were only about three thousand infantry remaining to hold the valley. They were outnumbered by at least ten to one, and massively outclassed in artillery. Their entrenchments were flooded, especially on the low ground, by the torrents of the monsoon. But still they held on.

And still the Viet trenches advanced, through the water and the muck, until in many places they were within grenade range. And because of the great flak danger, the American crews were at last pulled off the Dien Bien Phu run. The supply situation instantly worsened. The artillery was down to a single 155, its rifling so smooth that it was useless outside very short range. The remaining pieces were desperately short on ammunition. Pleas for periscopes and flak jackets still went unanswered.

Cogny and Navarre had by now descended to personal hatred, and barely spoke. Nevertheless, on the thirtieth Cogny pleaded for permission to again use the 119s. For now, in the heart of the monsoon, virtually no replacement and resupply was reaching the valley. The troops were on half rations. But the garrison still kept its guts and offensive spirit. Tiny raiding parties regularly struck the Viets, killing and taking prisoners. The paras and the Legion were perfectly willing to fight on, if they were given any help at all.

On April 30 the Legion celebrated Camerone Day, and incidentally the return of the American crews in their C-119s. April 30 was a holy day for the Legion, the traditional celebration of the gallant, long-ago stand of a Legion company against astronomical odds in Mexico. Traditionally it was—and is today—celebrated with blood sausage and much wine.

The Legionnaires in the valley did not so much mind the absence of blood sausage. What troubled them was the shortage of wine, aggravated when an airdrop of the foul Vinogel wine concentrate fell near Viet positions south of Eliane 2. At dark a patrol of Legion volunteers fell upon the Viets in the area, killing at least ten, wounding others, and returning with the precious Vinogel. Camerone Day was celebrated in style, and a few honorary Legionnaires were ceremoniously created. De Castries and Langlais became Legion corporals, and Bigeard and Genevieve de Galard were created PFCs.

On May 1 the Viets struck H5 hard, and established a foothold in the darkness of the monsoon. The paras counterattacked promptly at 2:30 A.M., and threw the enemy out in head-on fighting. But there was to be no rest for the exhausted troops. There was much activity all around the basin, much movement of Viet troops. The French veterans could sense another attack was brewing.

And they had little to meet it with. The effective infantry strength had fallen below three thousand. The artillery ammunition supply had improved, but there was barely enough for a single day of all-out fighting. And Langlais' Breton temper finally flared. His long message to Hanoi demanded the dropping of complete airborne units to reinforce his exhausted men, a measure that should have been taken long before. His message ended this way:

> We will win the battle without you and in spite of you. This message, copy of which I shall transmit to all airborne battalion commanders here, will be the last I shall address to you.

Langlais barely got the message off before a massive Viet artillery preparation fell on the valley. It went on and on, plowing up the tortured earth again, beating down the remains of the French wire, caving in the battered bunkers. Behind it came wave after wave of infantry, swarming up the slopes of Elaine and Dominique. Most of two divisions was attacking the two bastions, and this time there was no stopping the ocean of little green-clad men.

Dominique 3 died about 2:00 A.M. on the second of May, although its scratch garrison fought to the end. And on E1 the tiny para garrison also fought its last fight, hanging grimly on in the darkness as the ammunition ran out. By 2:10 it was gone too. Over on the Huguettes it was the same, a tiny, exhausted garrison drowning in a sea of Viets.

The Viets were taking horrible casualties also, and little groups of paras and Legionnaires were actually counterattacking, clashing hand to hand with the Viets in the dark, driving them back from the penetrations into E2, E4, and H4. By dawn the situation had stabilized in those positions, and the French still held.

But E1 and D3 were gone, and there was no reserve force left to counterattack. The Viets now overlooked the entire position. Nothing could move in the valley without the enemy seeing it. Without real reinforcements, the garrison was finished.

In Hanoi, Cogny had finally decided to commit the last battalion in the airborne reserve, the 1st BCP. But it would not reach the valley. Only its 2d Company was dropped, under Lieutenant Edme, a veteran of WWII service with British

SAS. He still wore their red beret. It was a welcome reinforcement, but only a drop in the bucket, for the company
was a little over one hundred strong, and the garrison would
lose over four hundred men on that day.

The garrison kept its courage. Every man who could fight
was on the line, as desperately wounded men dragged themselves back to their units to die with them. Captain Lucciani
commanded on H4, even though he had been thrice
wounded and had a bandaged hole where one eye should
have been. Aerial resupply had broken down again. To their
everlasting shame, French civilian pilots now refused to fly
into the valley. Some supplies reached the garrison, but not
nearly enough.

And on Eliane, the Legion had another worry. For weeks
they had heard the scraping and clanking of digging, far below their position. They listened in with a primitive sort of
geophone made of a stethoscope and an ordinary mess kit.
But now the sounds of digging had almost entirely stopped.
The Legionnaires could only wait and hope. They had their
hands full just staying alive, and shoring up their crumbling
bunkers against the roaring rains of the monsoon.

For the torrents of rain flooded everything, adding to the
agony of the wounded, washing away the meager fortifications on the fighting line. Under fire, the engineers crawled
at night onto the useless airfield to salvage pieces of pierced
steel plate. The PSP made useful roofs for the collapsing
bunkers.

On the night of May 4, another company of the 1st BCP
dropped into the valley, along with a small headquarters element. The company commander was Captain Pouget, who
until January had been aide to Navarre. Doubtless he could
have stayed in that soft position, but at last he had asked to
return to his unit. And now he was in the dying valley, perhaps to pay for his boss's mistakes.

Early in the morning Lucciani's turn came on H4. His
eighty-man garrison, a mixture of Legionaires and Moroccans, had been struck by a Viet force of more than three
thousand men. There was no help to send him, so Lucciani
fought on alone in the darkness and the rain. His men piled
up Viet bodies in the wire, hundreds of them, and were still
holding after two hours of endless assault.

But there were simply too many Viets, Lucciani went down

with a bad head wound, and the last little knot of defenders fought on until they were overwhelmed. The French head-quarters picked up a last message from H4 about 3:35 A.M., when a Moroccan platoon leader shouted into the radio that the Viets were in his trench. The helpless listeners heard him cry out when he was shot down. After that, Huguette 4 no longer answered.

About dawn, a tiny counterattack went in, a single tank and perhaps one hundred men, charging some two thousand Viets. The tiny forlorn hope fought its way from H3 all the way to the edge of H4 before the attack broke down. H4 would not be recovered.

On May 5 another seventy-odd men of 1st BCP dropped in, together with a meager resupply of ammunition. The bat-talion commander was with them, but was almost immedi-ately wounded. Pouget took command of the battalion, and took over the defense of Eliane 2. And over on Claudine that night, some Moroccan defenders deserted, cutting through the wire. They left a gap that could not be closed, even though several men of the Legion died trying to seal it.

So the handwriting was on the wall. And if anybody doubted that Dien Bien Phu was bleeding to death, a mes-sage from Cogny left no question. De Castries was encour-aged to hold on, to keep Viet pressure off other areas of the country. But he was authorized to break out, too, if he de-cided he could no longer resist.

Paradoxically, the airdrop on the sixth was very heavy, for the French civilian pilots had started flying again. And there were personnel reinforcements as well, ninety-one paras of the 1st BCP. They would be the last men into the dying for-tress. The airdrop went on into the morning, for the rain had stopped, and the French had mounted a major flak-suppression operation; over a hundred bombers and fight-ers hammered at the Viet AA guns, and the volume of antiaircraft fire slackened. Even so, this was the day the phe-nomenal luck of the American C-119 pilots ran out.

Gigantic, bearded James McGovern—nicknamed for Al Capp's Earthquake McGoon—was on his drop run, his forti-eth mission over the valley, when he took a hit in one engine. He feathered the milling prop, but then took a second hit and turned away, flying the airplane and its six tons of am-munition away from the valley. McGovern, his American co-pilot, and French crew died when the C-119 hammered into the ground and exploded.

There was still hope in the valley. If the Viet attack held off just a little while, long enough to gather some of the dropped artillery ammunition and drop the rest of 1st BCP into the valley, the garrison might beat off the assault and survive a little while more, while Giap readied another onslaught. But that morning Hanoi signaled information from a source very close to Ho Chi Minh himself: The Viets were coming that very night, to finish the garrison. So there would be no chance to resupply or reinforce. Castor would stand or fall on its present handful of soldiers and insufficient supply of ammo.

The stalwarts of the garrison made what preparations they could. Quiet Captain Hervouet, the armor commander, had Dr. Grauwin remove the casts from his arms. He would make his fight in the last operational tank. The commanders visited their pitifully thin lines, seeing to troop dispositions and warning the company officers and NCOs that the big one was coming. Langlais and Bigeard visited critical Eliane, where the paras, and bits and oddments of other units, dug and waited.

About noon a new affliction fell on the valley, the howling, screeching flight of Katyusha six-tube rockets, the same crude and terrifying weapon WWII German troops had called "Stalin Organs." Their effect on the fragile bunkers and exposed supply dumps was dramatic. Much of the remaining supply was destroyed, including nearly all the medical stores. Everywhere bunkers collapsed, and soldiers frantically dug their comrades out of the debris. At five-thirty artillery joined the attack, laying a heavy fire on E4 and E2, and about an hour later, as the light faded, thousands of Viets swarmed up the east face of E2.

These were men of the 102d Regiment, the crack outfit of Giap's whole army, and they were meant to strike the blow that would finish Dien Bien Phu. But the French artillery observer on E2 knew his business, and caught them with the massed fires of most of the operational howitzers and heavy mortars. The attack collapsed and recoiled, leaving hundreds of bodies in front of the French positions.

But Viet counterbattery fire crushed the pitiful remains of French artillery and battered the infantry bunkers. Claudine was also hard-pressed, and crucial C5 was lost. It was recovered by a wild counterattack led by the Legion sapper platoon, big, bearded men chosen for their size.

But there was no respite for the defenders. At ten o'clock the Viets began on E10 and E4. Wave after wave of Viets foamed in out of the dark, and broke on the rock of the French position. The para mortar gunners had fired their last round and were fighting as infantry. Langlais gambled, pulling two platoons of Legion paras under an officer named Lecour from the northern perimeter. They had some shelter as they moved through the underground tunnel system known as the "metro," but then had to brave the curtain of Viet fire across the Nam Yum all the way to the Elianes. Other tiny platoons were gathered from other units and sent to help. And Langlais made the heartbreaking command decision to abort the dropping of para reinforcements so that flares could be used to illuminate the battlefield.

But there was too little of everything, and by eleven the 6th BCP was cornered in three small bunker complexes. They fought on and on in the gloom until, by 3:00 A.M., Major Thomas and twenty men held only the commo bunker of E10. The rest of the strongpoint was gone. Most of the rest of the battalion was dead or dying out there in the dark, surrounded by piles of Viets. And that was not the worst of it.

For at 11:00 P.M. E2 simply exploded. The Viets had at last touched off their mine, and the results were catastrophic. Much of Edme's second company of the 1st BCP simply vanished in the geyser of earth, and other troops were injured or killed by flying debris. But when the Viet assault troops rushed in to follow up their advantage, they found themselves in a monstrous crater with sides of glutinous mud, and from the top the surviving paras methodically cut them down. The Viet infantry took horrible casualties, and their attack stalled. Three hours after the mine blew, Pouget actually counterattacked, driving his enemies farther into the crater.

Elsewhere in the wild night, small reinforcements from 8th Assault began to reach E10, thanks to a tiny group of paras from 6th BCP who repeatedly counterattacked to keep open the way from the Nam Yum to Eliane. The redoubtable Major Thomas was still clinging to his solitary bunker, and the French began to expand their foothold.

With Lecour's tiny reinforcement of Legion paras from the northern perimeter, Brechignac counterattacked on E4 and pushed the Viets out of the position. By first light, E4 was back in French hands. Lecour was still on his feet; so were his radioman and two paras. The rest were gone.

But at the same time, E2 was dying, for no reinforcements had reached the gutted hill. By 4:00 A.M. Captain Pouget was down to thirty-five men, and the Viets were pushing in all around him. Pouget asked permission to break out to E3. It was denied, with the curt reminder: "You're a paratrooper. You are there to get yourself killed." And so Pouget destroyed his radio and fought on, until a concussion grenade knocked him unconscious and he passed into captivity. It was just before five o'clock, and not long until dawn.

The new day brought no relief, for the ammo was running out on E4. At eight the Viets closed in again, and in half an hour it was over. Brechignac briefly said good-bye to Bigeard, the cries of the wounded and the shouts of fighting men clear in the background. He and Botella, commander of the Vietnamese paras, would remain on the hill with the doctor and the wounded. He had ordered the handful of able-bodied paras to break out. Only a few made it to the Nam Yum, where the bridge was held open by a pair of quad-.50s and two tanks, immobile but still firing. It was the end.

The eastern hills belonged to the Viets. And the northern strongpoints, denuded of troops, were crumbling. There would be no holding the valley. The only choices now were death, surrender, or breakout.

The breakout option was called "Albatross," a somewhat unfortunate choice in code names. The first proposal was to form two columns from the able-bodied troops. Their commanders would draw straws. The short straw meant a sacrificial attack, drawing the Viets to the natural escape route, to the south, where a French force called Condor was laboriously advancing toward the valley out of Laos. The other column would drive west into the mountains, catching the Viets by surprise. But newly dropped aerial photos killed the idea. The enemy had dug trenches across the last feasible escape route. A breakout would be a butchery, with little chance for anybody to leave the valley.

The option of fighting on was rejected also. It was all very well for the able-bodied. But there were all the thousands of helpless wounded. As one officer commented: "You can do Camerone with a hundred guys, not with ten thousand." There were no more options; surrender it would be.

And so, at about five o'clock on the afternoon of May 7, the firing died away. The French survivors prepared as best they could for what was coming, Bigeard, for instance, wrapping a silk escape map around his leg. The two hundred or so civilians were intent on trying to seep out to the south, including the native numbers of the intelligence detachment, who dared not become prisoners.

On Claudine and Dominique the girls of the field bordellos awaited the coming of the Viets. These women had been heroines, nursing and caring for the wounded. One came every day to feed a demented soldier who imagined he was a child again and had to be fed by his mother. Four of the Ouled Naïl girls had been killed during the siege. Nobody knows what happened to the Vietnamese prostitutes. They were never heard from again. At least some of the Algerian girls would survive; and one married an Algerian prisoner in Hanoi, and had a child by him.

The command bunker was occupied at five-thirty, and de Castries met his captors dressed in a clean uniform. Nobody is sure what was said, and it doesn't matter. The fighting simply stopped. The long, bloody siege ended in a matter-of-fact silence. In one of the last strongpoints to be occupied, Major Jean Nicolas faced a Viet soldier.

"C'est fini?" said the little man.

"Oui," said Nicholas. *"C'est fini."*

The valley was silent at last.

SILENCE IN THE VALLEY
... After Dien Bien Phu

There was never a breakout from the valley. A good many soldiers tried it, alone and by handfuls, but few succeeded. Most survivors passed into captivity, almost ten thousand of them, strictly segregated according to rank and nationality. The wounded were treated decently, at least at first. The Viet doctors sympathized with Grauwin and the other French medical personnel. Things would change within forty-eight hours, as the commissars took charge from the line soldiers. As pressure at home mounted to retrieve at least the most seriously wounded men, the French command sent a civilian doctor to negotiate with the Viets. At last, on the sixteenth, an agreement was reached under which the French might fly out 858 wounded, chosen strictly on medical grounds. The quid pro quo was French agreement not to bomb the roads leading away from the valley until the wounded were evacuated.

While the work of clearing the airfield crawled on, Viet commissars began to force reclassification of the wounded on political grounds, called "democratic urgency" in Communist jargon. This meant giving priority in treatment to non-European enlisted personnel, then other enlisted personnel, and dealing with officers and NCOs last. Two female commissars were assigned to pressure Genevieve Galard into signing a special appeal to Ho Chi Minh, to be used for international propaganda. Mme. Galard held out for ten days, but then signed, on Grauwin's order. Both feared continued resistance would only result in greater hardship for their wounded. Even then, promised that she would be sent home, the courageous nurse urged repatriation of all the medical personnel.

Mme. Galard was finally released on May 24. The other medical staff came out with the last of the wounded early in June. The United States opened its heart to many of the most seriously wounded, flying them into Westover Field, Massachusetts. And even the wounded had not lost their spunk. When badly wounded Sergeant Beres of the 1st BEP saw the captured colors of a Legion company lying unguarded in a Viet command post, he dragged himself in and snatched it, concealing it under his shirt. And when he was flown out to Laos on the twenty-fourth, the guidon came with him.

French casualties had been about nine thousand, including the seriously wounded flown out just after the siege ended. Almost seven thousand troops became prisoners, and were marched away. Many were wounded; all were exhausted. Tragically, many survivors of the bloody battle were now simply marched to death. They did their best, and carried many litter cases with them, but as they marched, they starved. For their rations were fourteen ounces of rice each day, and ten peanuts every tenth day. Even water was often scarce.

Men died each day, simply fell by the side of the road, unable to march further. Generally their comrades helped them as best they could, especially the paras, who carried their wounded and buried their dead with honor. There were some amazing stories of survival, like the Legion warrant officer who amputated his own gangrenous arm without anesthetic . . . and survived. And there was needless tragedy, such as the deaths of four men who contracted gangrene because their wrists were tied too tightly with wire. In the end, to the everlasting shame of the Vietminh, almost ten thousand men died on that dreadful march, or in the stark prison camps at its end. In three months.

Many of the bravest of the brave survived. Bigeard fought on in Algeria, as did many of the others. He, Langlais, and de Castries continued in the army, and rose to deservedly high rank. Brechignac, angry over French abandonment of Algeria, joined the 1961 military putsch, and was cashiered from the army. He later became a businessman. The same thing happened to Botella. Both Tourret and Pouget left the service in time, the first to enter business, the second to write. Genevieve Galard, whom the press nicknamed the "Angel of Dien Bien Phu," married an army officer and settled down.

Much ink has been spent arguing whether the French ever had a prayer of winning at Dien Bien Phu. Bigeard later told Bernard Fall, "If you had given me ten thousand SS troopers, we'd have held out." It is difficult to disagree with such a superb—and practical—soldier. The paras and the Legion carried the load in the valley. Had every man there been of their quality, had there been no unreliable units, no rats of the Nam Yum, the garrison might well have held on.

And it is also true that Giap had his own set of problems. His losses were enormous, especially among his trained infantry. Before the battle ended, he had committed many thousands of raw recruits. His supply line was stretched thin.

But even if the airhead had been held, it is difficult to picture any advantage to the French. The valley would have remained a battalion meat grinder, a chamber pot filled with France's best troops, far from the decisive area, the delta. Early operations in the valley proved conclusively that whatever else Castor might be, it was not a reasonable base for offensive operations. All it was good for was bait, bait to get Giap to move much of his regular force into the hinterland. Once he had done so, however, Hanoi made no real use of its chance to press him hard in the delta, to clear the vital rice bowl and hold it. And so the sacrifices in the valley of death were pointless in the end.

Today the valley is quiet. There is little to recall the ten thousand or so who died there, eight thousand of them Vietminh. There are, or were, a couple of monuments and a Viet cemetery. There is much salvage, of course, PSP, rusting wire, cartridge hulls beyond counting. Where the village was, military buildings were later constructed. The village itself was rebuilt a little farther south.

For the French who fell there, there was no memorial, except perhaps the monstrous crater on E2, which fills in a little with each year's rains. There may be some remembrance today, for in the early sixties Giap personally promised the French author Jules Roy that some sort of stone would be erected.

The monument to the French dead is in the hearts of men

at the French parachute school at Pau, at the Legion headquarters at Aubagne, just east of Marseilles, and wherever
good soldiers tell stories of other days. Whatever other
things the men of Dien Bien Phu lacked, they did not want
for courage.

Nor did their enemies. The little Viet soldiers gave of their
blood unstintingly, winning the admiration of the toughest of
the French. They fought with a puritan spirit, an unquestion-
ing revolutionary zeal, a childish innocence, that made them
run gladly into the lethal storm of French bullets. During the
siege some of them deserted to the French, and some complained and would not go forward. But the bulk of them
lived in a sort of patriotic trance, and thousands died that
way. They were absolutely positive of the rightness of their
cause, and certain of their victory.

In that summer of 1954 a peace agreement was reached,
and the prisoners were repatriated. The negotiations had
been going on even as men died miserably in the mud of the
valley. After it was all over, a veteran French correspondent
sat in the Normandy bar in Hanoi. Next to him sat several officers and Eurasian women, drinking champagne. One of the
soldiers was a well-known para officer, who had fought at
Dien Bien Phu. In what he told the correspondent lay the last
of the reasons the French lost at Dien Bien Phu, the reason
the French command understood least.

"It was all for nothing," said the para. "I let my men die for
nothing . . . The Viets told us they had won because they
were fighting for an ideal, and we were not. I told them about
my paras at Dien Bien Phu. I told them how they fought. And
they said, 'Heroism is no answer' . . . Dien Bien Phu was not
an accident of fate, it was a judgment."

TO DIE ALONE IN THE SILENCE
The Defense of Muong Chen

Sergeant Peyrol still carried his bottle of champagne. It bumped against his tired body as he plunged on through the dense forest toward the west and safety. Behind him in the thick gloom of midnight his Tai partisans followed him grimly, their weapons ready, their eyes watching their back trail. Ahead lay the Black River and safety. Behind them lay the smoking ruins of their post at Muong Chen and the bodies of their comrades. Also behind them, but very close, were hordes of Communist Vietminh . . . and death.

The bottle bumped against Peyrol again, but he would not leave it. For he had hoarded it to toast his little daughter's birthday, another world away in Verdun. If he lived, he would still drink it, warm or not, west of the Black in safety.

It was the fall of 1952, and only hours before, Peyrol's 284th Local Suppletive Company of Tai had been peacefully improving their little log post on Muong Chen hill. And then that evening, out of the east, came Major Marcelle Bigeard and his fabulous unit, the 6th Colonial Paratroops. They were tired, and carrying wounded. There was clearly much trouble behind them. Bigeard brought dreadful news.

The whole Tai country was overrun with Viets, and most of the whole 312th Division was chasing the paras. Bigeard's hopeless mission was to delay them long enough to give the little scattered garrisons a fighting chance to escape to the West. And for that he needed time. He faced Peyrol. "The Viets are about one hour behind us, and we need an additional three hours . . . You've got to last three hours at least, and we can make it."

The thirty-four-year-old master sergeant knew what that

meant. He had about eighty men, one log bunker, and another unfinished one. Against a division. But Peyrol was a good soldier, and understood the need. He answered simply: "Bien, mon Commandant."

Bigeard nodded. "Thank you. I knew you fellows wouldn't fail me."

And then he and his gaunt paras were gone, and Peyrol's men dug furiously in the little time they had left. The partisans knew what was coming, but they stayed.

Less than an hour after Bigeard's column had vanished into the west, the Viets struck Peyrol's little post. A curtain of mortar-fire fell around the bunkers, and behind it, out of the dusk, came the first wave of Viets, pushing into the wire and sharpened bamboo obstacles. They carried only grenades, to clear the way for their comrades, and they died in clusters. But more came, and still more, running over the bodies of their own dead and wounded.

But the Tais of Muong Chen were a tough bunch, and magically, three hours later, Peyrol found he and some of his men were still alive and still holding. By now most of the automatic weapons were empty or destroyed, and Viet corpses were heaped in front of the position. Peyrol decided. He had accomplished his mission, and it was high time to go.

And so in a roar of firing he and his surviving partisans broke out in the darkness and bolted up an obscure trail, breaking contact with the Viets in the gloom. They got away clean in the night, three Frenchmen and forty Tais, and the chase was on, sixteen days up and down the murderous limestone ridges, some of them eight thousand feet high.

They broke through one ambush, losing ten men in the process, and forged on, just ahead of the Viets. And then Peyrol's radio crackled, a message in French, giving the coordinates of a drop zone north of them. It could be a GMCA, a long-range commando unit . . . or it could be the Viets. Peyrol smelled a rat, and to his men's disgust, pressed on for the Black. Later he would learn that he had been right.

But at last, against all hope, starving and riddled with dysentery, Peyrol and fifteen men dragged themselves across the last ridge, and it was there: the broad torrent of the Black River, and across it lay safety. They were seen that evening by a French aircraft, and crossed the river that night, to fall into the arms of a French patrol sent to find them.

They still carried the flag from Muong Chen, and Peyrol still carried his bottle of champagne.

The country Peyrol had crossed—the northwest corner of Tonkin—contains some of the most godforsaken, desolate, brutal terrain on earth. It is a treacherous place of sharp limestone crags and ridges, covered with dense growth and monstrous forest, primeval, festering, dark and hostile. The trees and vines strangle and crush in a vicious struggle to survive, massed in armies of branches, thorns, and fallen timber, covered with rot and fungus. It also abounds with beauty: rhododendrons, strawberries, roses, and lilies.

This fever-haunted wilderness is paved with the bones of men, men dead of a dozen agonizing diseases, men dead quickly in the ecstasy of combat, men dead by inches, lost and starving. It is not a place for Westerners to live at all, let alone fight. But many did, and fought long and well. A tragic number are still there, sleeping in unmarked graves in the wilderness, dead in a lost cause, but wrapped in honor. This is their story.

Through this deadly land run eternally the great muddy rivers, rushing and twisting through grim gorges where the sun never shines, churning down from high China to the rice-rich delta and the South China Sea, bound for the vast pulsing hive of people and the vivid green patchwork of rice fields west and south of Hanoi.

Save for the rivers, the Northwest had no roads in the French days—indeed, there are precious few now. There were only narrow trails, slick, steep, heartbreaking paths running straight up the ridges, then plunging straight down the other side into the darkness of the gorges, then on again up the next exhausting climb.

People lived here then, and do still, many kinds of people. Some were absolutely primitive, like the shadowy naked Xas, who lived deep in the triple-canopy jungle and ate earth, a species of schist that apparently had at least a little nutritive value. Others, though more civilized, were still hard to understand and befriend, sunk deep in superstition, surrounded by any number of taboos, violation of any one of which might destroy the Frenchman's mission, if not the man himself.

In the far North lived the Meos, raisers of the opium poppy for aeons uncounted, harvesters of its thick, treacly juice, the raw material of heroin. Their product was of immense worth to those who transported, refined, and marketed the vile substance on its way to the outside world: Thai and Lao entrepreneurs, Burmese bandits, ex-nationalist Chinese soldiers, Vietminh Communists, and a host of others.

The Meos believe they are descended from the Great Holy Dog, a genealogy of which they are very proud. In fact, their distant ancestors originally came out of the very far North; they are said to have some racial kinship to the Eskimos. They live on the mountaintops, where they burn and slash off the thick vegetation to clear fields for their lovely, brilliant, deadly poppies. They are an attractive, smiling people. They are also first-class fighting men at need.

Farther down the slopes of the northern mountains live the Man highlanders, many subtribes of them. They are also formidable soldiers, whose primary loyalties lay with the French, and whose attachment to their native hills was more compelling than life.

In the valleys, in some of the clearer areas, live the delightful Tai, blood cousins to the Siamese far to the south. They are graceful, handsome people, and are raisers of rice. Their subtribes are distinguished one from the other by the color of their women's blouses, the Black Tai, the White Tai, and so on.

Friends to the French, these people charmed every Westerner who knew them, especially their beautiful women, who wear long black skirts reaching to their ankles, and close their blouses with silver clasps. Some of their towns were quite considerable places, clean and well laid out. They are a warm, honest, hospitable, independent people . . . or were. God knows what they have become today.

And there are others, tribes known to the Vietnamese collectively—and contemptuously—as *Moi:* "wild people." These tribes, dozens of them, are generally of that racial strain known to the French as Montagnards. They are closely related to the Montagnards of the South, well known to Americans who served in Vietnam.

"Moi" is a pejorative word, a term of contempt. The Montagnards, for their part, cordially detested the Vietnamese. Forced to choose, most of them adhered to the French, who at least treated them fairly, as the Americans would treat their kinsmen later on.

The Red River, mother of the North, rushes down out of China and into the jungle of Tonkin. Where it leaves the high ground stands the Tai town of Lao Kay, and at that place there is a bridge. In the French days, there was no other bridge for almost two hundred miles downriver, so that Lao Kay was a crossroads, the gateway to all the vast empty spaces. It was a center of smuggling and trade—which often amounted to the same thing in the North. It was also a clearinghouse for information and a market for guns and opium. It was the door to high China, the hills and plateaus of Yunnan, the way on to Tibet and the Himalayas.

On occasion regular French units manned garrisons across the frightful emptiness beyond Lao Kay, up against China. They were resupplied by river usually, and sometimes by parachute. Much of the local security, however, was provided by tribal partisan formations led by one or two Frenchmen. And in the farthest reaches of this frightening land, the war was carried on by the men of the GCMAs, *Groupements de Commandos Mixtes Aéroportés:* the Airborne Composite Commando Groups. In the twilight of the war the unit would be called GMI, *Groupement Mixte d'Intervention,* and would take control of all operations behind Viet lines, airborne or not.

Neither the local partisan leaders nor the GCMAs have monuments. Many lack so much as a grave marker. They did not make good press, because they went where correspondents did not, and fought an ugly, twilight war that provided no headlines. They were not raiders, but rather guerrilla leaders. They went out into the silence not for a mission, or a tour, but "for the duration." They stayed with their tribal partisans, often deep inside Viet territory, until they died or broke down or were terribly wounded, or simply disappeared without trace.

A wounded man stood some slim chance of survival if he had the right kind of wound and tremendous luck. But a hurt man had to be carried to safety by his partisans, often for days over the dreadful tracks of the wilderness. Often undernourished and ill already, the man often died slowly of the pain and the terrible jolting of the trip, and was buried somewhere in the vastness of the jungle.

Even after the wracking strain of the carrying, the wounded man still had to face days on the river, his men paddling by night and hiding by day, unless the party could find an airstrip. Then he might be flown out in relative comfort, if there was an aircraft available, if the monsoon rain or *crachin* mist lifted, if the Vietminh did not close in on the strip. If.

In those grim days, there were no more than ten operational helicopters in all Vietnam at any one time. Extraction by helicopter, so routine in the American days, was almost unknown to the French. Many men of the partisan groups and the GCMAs still sleep in the silence of the North, men who would certainly have lived with any sort of timely medevac. Serious wounds were therefore deeply feared, especially a head wound, or any abdominal wound at all. Such hurts were a virtual death warrant.

At their peak the GCMAs controlled some fifteen thousand guerrillas, scattered for hundreds of miles across the North and the wild country of the central highlands. They were organized in tribal groups of up to four hundred men, led by a handful of French NCOs, sometimes with an officer in command. Sometimes the French leader, officer or NCO, operated entirely alone, the only European in a thousand square miles of primeval wilderness. He could call on no artillery, no air strikes, not even a *Luciole,* a "firefly" to drop flares at night.

He had to learn the local dialect, usually unwritten, and all the customs and taboos of the tribe. He had always to carry himself as the warrior without peer, even when he staggered with exhaustion and shook with malaria, the endemic scourge of the whole country. He depended utterly on his tribesmen and their women, for his only contact with his leaders was a tiny, tinny voice on his radio set, a French outpost God only knew how many impassable miles away. As long as his batteries or hand-crank generator lasted.

He ate what his tribesmen ate, slept and lived as they did, sometimes took a wife—or more than one—from his tribal allies. He was resupplied by air, when he was resupplied at all. He participated by invitation, when he was successful, in the tribe's festivals and religious ceremonies. At these times he had to stomach eating, and being smeared with, blood and all manner of other vile concoctions. Of necessity he drank immense quantities of chum, the crude rice wine that was the essential stuff of ceremony and celebration.

And through all his days in this silent vastness, he always remembered that *he* was France, the personified image of his country. His only satisfaction was that he knew he and his warriors tied down many thousands of Vietminh, who otherwise would be thrown in against the French regular forces, down in the vital delta and over against the Chinese border.

And time and again the GCMAs were called on to cover and protect regular forces *in extremis*. Partisans of the GCMAs helped to safety the handful of hardy souls who escaped the fallen fortress of Dien Bien Phu, more than seventy soldiers who would not have made it out without the aid of the partisans.

Their weapons were French, grenades, rifles, and submachineguns, the occasional machinegun or light mortar, parachuted to them in tiny clearings or Meo poppy fields, kicked out the doors of C-47s and ancient trimotored Junkers. With these they struck at Viet communications, at tribal villages loyal to the enemy, at isolated patrols. And always they hit Viet units searching for them, covering their partisans' villages and families in the endless, silent pavanne of war in the empty spaces.

They traveled light, stripped to bare essentials: weapons, ammunition, water, a few emergency rations, a sack or a hollow bamboo carrying cooked rice, salt, perhaps some dried fish. When they had it, they carried quinine against the endemic malaria, and pills of codeine terpene to hold back the cough or sneeze that could mean death to an ambush party.

One typical partisan action was fought north and east of Kontum, in the murderous jungle-covered granite ridges of the Annamese Cordillera. The raiders were Hue Montagnards, led by two Frenchmen, a lieutenant and an NCO. They had marched for two days, moving in the wild country away from villages and fields, passing close to inhabited areas only in darkness.

Now they had lain in ambush for thirty-six hours, keeping absolute silence, munching iron rations of chocolate, biscuit, and sweets laced with vitamins. Below them lay rice fields, a shimmering patchwork of green rippling in the breeze, a stream, a trail, and a bridge. There had been no human movement, only the turtledoves in the trees, and deer coming down in the dusk to drink at the stream.

But then, as darkness began to gather on the second evening of the ambush, there were no deer, and the ambush party knew that there was something, someone, out there under the tall trees. And at last they came into the open: first three ordinary-looking tribesmen, who sat casually on the little bridge and washed their feet in the stream beneath. After a time, satisfied, these scouts called up to the woods, and a little column of Vietminh appeared. They were lowlanders in gray uniforms, relaxed and secure, their weapons slung, chattering and laughing together.

The French commander held his fire until the Viets reached the bridge, and some began drinking from the stream. Then the fire struck them in the open without protection, dropping them thrashing on the path and in the mud and water of the paddies beyond. Only a few escaped, running desperately back into the bush, chased by mortar fire. As suddenly as it had begun, the storm of fire ended, and the ageless silence returned. The partisans collected their enemy's weapons and a few wounded prisoners, and were gone into the gathering dusk.

And then all that remained by the little bridge were the scattered cartridge hulls, the motionless lumps that had been men, and a single badly wounded Viet, his wound dressed, left with a note asking that the favor might one day be returned. And soon the darkness descended, and at last, in the night, the shy deer came down to water.

The twilight war was raid and ambush, lying in wait along a track in absolute silence, sometimes for days, in the hope that the enemy would choose this way, and would suspect nothing. And if the group's intelligence was accurate, and the enemy did not suspect, and saw and heard and smelled nothing, the ambush would be sprung in a ferocious, terrifying, merciless blast of gunfire and grenades. Then the dead would be quickly stripped of useful weapons and gear, the bodies left for the ants and kites and other creatures. It never took the wilderness long to clean her skin; the remains of men were soon gone, and the primordial silence returned.

The war in the vast empty places was largely pitiless, with little feeling or mercy expected or given. The Vietminh cared only for the cause, for their consuming ideology. People were not very important, not as people anyway. They were only resources, like rice or bullets, and not nearly as important as either of those.

Captured French partisans were often left at the side of the trail, horribly mutilated as a warning to their fellows not to oppose the inevitable march of the people's paradise. Most horrible of all, some partisans were found standing, stiff and dead, staring at nothing, held erect by stakes driven up through the anus, far up toward the breastbone. And the tribal partisans responded in kind, in hatred and ruthless anger.

Everything—life itself—depended on remaining unseen and undetected. Any sign of man, even tiny scraps of food, was buried or thrown far off the trail. Even the grass was smoothed down to erase any sign of the partisans' passing.

Danger lay everywhere in the wild country. It was the enemy, seeking, probing, setting his own ambushes. And it was the malaria, the leeches and the snakes, the occasional tiger or angry buffalo. And it was the enormous swarms of ants, rivers of voracious insects flowing across the jungle floor with a sound like sand sliding down a chute—it was death to stand in that path.

And it was the man-traps: pits lined with bamboo stakes; deadfalls that would crush a man beneath a falling tree; bows made of bent branches, rigged to drive a bamboo arrow into the belly of a man who brushed its trip wire; great balls studded with spikes set to swing down a trail, impaling a man. And there was danger of a more subtle kind, the awful sense of being entirely alone, always stalked, never secure, that sometimes drove men to senseless violence, or to see things that were not there.

Fierce loyalties grew up between the French leaders and their partisans. To hold that allegiance, the officers and NCOs had to show that they could protect the villages, the rice fields, the women and livestock and opium of their soldiers. And so they trained their recruits: scouts and watchers to cover the trails into their tribal territory; fighting detachments under dependable native leaders, trained to react swiftly and professionally to Viet intruders; propaganda agents to spread the news of Communist atrocities and bring more villages to the side of France.

Without breaking, the best of the French leaders stood the awful isolation, the loneliness, and the fear, and the primordial silence. They grew in stature, in leadership. They cast long shadows in the wild country: "Father," some were called, and a profound affection grew between them and their men. And in the end, when the tricolor was gone from the far country forever, a few of the French leaders elected to stay behind, even though they were near enough to French forces to escape the triumphant Vietminh.

It was death to stay behind, death soon or death later. But these men would not share the abandonment of the partisans by France. They would die, but at least they would die with their honor intact. And so this handful of Frenchmen remained, returning in the dark days of defeat the dedication their tribesmen had given them in better times.

There is no serious question about the efficacy of the GCMAs. At the time of Dien Bien Phu, in the spring of 1954, some five thousand partisans operated in the far country of northwestern Tonkin and northeastern Laos. Much of their operations was against the supply route serving Vo Nguyen Giap's regiments besieging the French airhead.

These five thousand partisans were supported on some two hundred tons of supplies each month, air-dropped into remote clearings. Inside the airhead, the fifteen-thousand-man garrison used up some two hundred tons per *day*, also air-dropped. It is estimated that the garrison tied down some thirty-eight Viet battalions. By May, the same estimate suggested, the GCMAs occupied as many as fourteen battalions. So one third the men, at one thirtieth the price in supplies and airlift capacity, tied down almost one half as many enemy troops.

Certainly there are other factors in the equation of effectiveness. For example, the Dien Bien Phu garrison inflicted many more casualties on the Viets than did the partisans—as well as suffering more. But on balance, in terms of occupying enemy troops who would otherwise be used in the critical delta, the impact of the French-led partisans was enormous.

It is not an indictment of the GCMAs that they failed to cut the main Viet supply route into the valley of Dien Bien Phu, some eight hundred kilometers of track leading all the way from Lang Son on the Chinese frontier. There were simply not enough of them to close it. In any case, their function was to hit and run, not fight pitched battles to hold a stretch of road. What they did, they did well. The fault for the disaster at Dien Bien Phu lies neither with the hard core of the garrison, the paras and the Legion, nor with the GCMAs, but with the incompetent French command who conceived the whole foolish venture.

The end came suddenly for the men of the GCMAs. After Dien Bien Phu, France and the Vietminh came quickly to agreement, and the French colonial army went home, or to Algeria. Uneasy peace came to the northern deltas, to the rich rice country along the feet of the Annamese Cordillera, and to Cochin China in the South.

But there was no peace in the great empty spaces of the North, or in the wild highlands. Although the French command did what it could to timely order the GCMAs out, many were never heard from again. If they were not near either French-held country or a primitive airstrip, they could not be extracted. Those whose batteries or generator were gone could no longer talk or hear. And most of the rest were much too far away, deep in hostile territory, to contact by other means.

When she could, France saved not only her soldiers of the GCMAs, but the native partisans who fought with them. Those who were close to French-held territory, in particular some of the Muong and Nung, were moved south to the mountain country around Dalat, and resettled there. But most of the partisans either could not or would not leave their distant homelands.

After a while nothing more was heard of them, or of the Frenchmen who had stayed with them. Only one man, a captain, is known to have gotten clear from a GCMA operations area deep in the interior. He was a veteran who spoke several tribal dialects, and made a monumental five-hundred-mile march to safety through some of the worst going on earth. The others did not make it. They were simply gone, vanished, disappeared forever in what the French called *la guerre des grandes vides:* the war of the vast empty spaces.

As late as 1959, and perhaps later, remnants of the GCMAs still fought on in their mountain fastness in the far North. But one by one these tiny flickering lights went out. In time the last groups were hunted down or betrayed.

But before the GCMAs passed into history, there was one horrible death rattle. Almost two years after the fighting had ended, French officers heard one last, chilling desperate call from somewhere in the vastness of the North. Nobody knows who the caller was, or where, but he was certainly French. This is what he said:

> You sons of bitches, help us! Help us! Parachute us at least some ammunition, so that we can die fighting instead of being slaughtered like animals!

And after that there was only silence.

FIRE BASE IN THE FISHHOOK
WHEN CHARLIE ROGERS WORRIED ABOUT HIS MEN

Charlie Rogers was in a lot of pain when I first met him. He was lying in a hospital bed in the 97th General Hospital in Frankfurt, Germany, where the surgeons had just taken another load of North Vietnamese mortar fragments out of his small battered body.

Although he was hurting, his family back in the States needed a power of attorney for something or other—I forget what—and he had asked for some legal help. The call came to my office in the evening, after duty hours; I was alone, and took it myself.

Colonel, said a voice from the 97th, we have a patient who needs a power of attorney. Can you send one of your folks?

No, said I. Everybody's gone home, but I'll come myself. Who is it?

Major General Rogers, said the voice, the new corps deputy commander.

I'll be there, said I, got my field jacket, and walked out to find my ancient VW beetle.

I'd heard of General Rogers, and liked what I heard.

Helluva guy, said the grapevine, tough, effective, very caring indeed. Since I was the Corps Staff Judge Advocate, its head lawyer, I'd work with the general, so I looked forward to the meeting.

The man in the hospital bed was black, small and husky, soft-spoken and courteous. Here he was, in considerable pain, a major general who could command services when he needed them, and his chief concern was whether I'd be a few minutes late getting home to my family on the edge of Frankfurt. I thought he was the most genuine, open person I'd ever met.

I was right. In later days, after General Rogers healed and took up his duties at corps headquarters, I saw him virtually every day. And the first time I saw him in uniform, I glanced at his ribbons, as soldiers do on first meeting. You can tell at a glance where a man has been, and make some shrewd guesses about what he's done.

And the first thing I noticed was the little light blue ribbon with tiny white stars, perched atop the rest of his ribbons. It was the Congressional Medal of Honor, something you don't see every day. And as I got to know the general better, and to like him more and more, I made it my business to find out how he won it.

It happened on a fire base in the Fishhook, an area of Vietnam close to the Cambodian border, in November of 1968. A fire base was a position, usually on a hill, on which American troops set up a defensive perimeter. Out of it infantry companies went forth to beat the bushes for the enemy. From it, artillery and mortars fired in support of the infantry effort.

Charlie Rogers was a lieutenant colonel in those days, commanding the 1st Battalion of the 5th Artillery, some of whose howitzers were on the fire base.

In that darkness of early morning, the fire base was struck by a torrent of enemy mortar and rocket-fire, followed by a wave of Communist infantry pouring through gaps blown in the American wire. Rogers rallied his men, got his howitzers firing point-blank at the attackers, and led a counterattack against a group of enemy who had broken through his perimeter. Twice painfully wounded, he killed several of the attackers and drove the rest out of the fire base.

Bleeding badly, he then led a second counterattack against

another human-wave assault, stopping it cold and cleaning the fire base of its survivors. He moved through the gloom, through the din and the scarlet and yellow shell-bursts, as if he were on peacetime maneuvers, calling to his men, ordering, encouraging, supporting.

Just about dawn the enemy came again, dozens of little men running in through the darkness, crying out and firing as they came, and again Rogers ran to the threatened area. He found a gun whose crew was down, grabbed any man he could reach to rally a scratch gun crew, poured point-blank fire into the wave of assaulting infantry.

And then he himself was scythed from his feet by a heavy mortar round that burst on the parapet of his gun position. Terribly hurt, even Charlie Rogers could not get up this time. But if his legs would not work, his heart and brain never quit. Though he could not rise, he stayed in command, calling to his men, still their heart and soul. And as the dawn broke, so did the enemy, leaving heaps of dead inside the fire base and strewn across the ground outside.

Many years on, General Rogers talked about that night on the fire base in the Fishhook. He was asked by a television interviewer whether he knew fear during those desperate hours. The little general's brow knit and he hesitated a little. "No," he said at last. "No. I was too busy worrying about my men." It was the absolute truth. Charlie Rogers spent his life worrying about other people. That wonderful faculty is what won him his Medal of Honor and his stars . . . and a world of friends.

After he retired, he settled in Germany, and he became an ordained minister. He spent a lot of time with American soldiers still, and the youngsters loved him. That care and concern and faith simply emanated from him, touching everybody around him.

He's dead now, dead long before his time, dead at only sixty-one. I hadn't seen him in a decade, but I felt terribly diminished when I heard he was gone. Nobody who knew him ever wondered how he held the line that terrible night in the Fishhook, way back in '68. To meet him was to know.

LZ X-RAY

———————— ∿ ————————

Brigadier General Chu Huy Man had decided to attack the Americans. Thus far his part of the 1965 Tay Nguyen Campaign—the Western Plateau Operation—had not gone well, and he was hungry for victory. He had sustained serious losses without a real success, but he still commanded the equivalent of a regular army division, heavily armed and powerfully motivated.

When General Man's "field front" of three regiments had first arrived in the highlands west of Pleiku, he had had high hopes. Each of his regiments was authorized twenty-two hundred men, organized in three battalions of four companies each. His men had suffered casualties from illness on the way south, but they were trained and ready. They carried the Russian AK-47 assault rifle, the excellent RPD light machine gun, and a shoulder-fired rocket launcher that would propel a deadly 82-mm warhead out to about 150 meters. They were supported by mortars and antiaircraft machine guns, and they had the advantage of the Cambodian sanctuary, where they could wait and rehearse until the time came to strike.

But the offensive had sputtered. First, in July, had come a thrust at the Special Forces camp at Duc Co, a benighted place west of Pleiku, held by a handful of Green Berets and about four hundred Montagnard and Nung tribesmen. It had been a nasty surprise, for the tribesmen were well led and well dug in, and the Vietnamese relief column had fought well enough to avoid annihilation. So the North Vietnamese 32d Regiment had pulled back after taking about a hundred casualties. Next time they would bring more firepower.

Then, in mid-October, there had been the night attack on the Special Forces camp at Plei Me. Man's 33d Regiment had surrounded the camp, defended by a couple of hundred poorly armed Jarai highlanders and a handful of American Special Forces soldiers. Man's regiment had the muscle to overrun the camp with one maximum effort, but instead the attacks were only strong enough to press the defenders hard. The idea was to induce a relief column to plunge out toward the camp, and then to use other NVA units to ambush and destroy it. Only afterward would the camp die.

Plei Me had proved a tough nettle to grasp, and the fire of the defenders piled up Man's soldiers in heaps on the defensive wire. And then had come the C-130 flare ship and the lumbering Skyraider fighter-bombers with their bombs and the terrible napalm. When the South Vietnamese army in Pleiku finally reacted, their armored column drove into the ambush east of Plei Me all right, but then it turned out to be tougher than expected. It stopped short of Plei Me, but it neither ran nor disintegrated, and before long those dreadful fighter-bombers were overhead again, and Man's casualties mounted.

Meanwhile, although Man did not know it, his attack had attracted a new and terrible enemy. The pressure on Plei Me and the relief force had induced the movement of elements of the 1st Cavalry Division westward into the Pleiku area. Thus far they were there to support the sputtering South Vietnamese effort, but before long they would take the offensive themselves.

When they did, they would make military history. For the Cav was the first truly airmobile division of the world, the highly professional harbinger of the helicopter war. They had begun life as the 11th Air Assault Division, and had exhaustively tested the whole concept of large-scale airmobility, developing the doctrine and many of the tools and techniques.

The division commander, Major General Harry Kinnard, had put the Cav elements around Pleiku under the command of Brigadier General Richard T. Knowles. Kinnard could not have picked a better man. Knowles was a born fighting man, careful of his men but always intent on closing with the enemy. His chance would come, but slowly, for when the ARVN request for help finally came, it was too late to fix and fight the attackers of Plei Me. They were gone, leaving a stinking moonscape of shell and bomb craters, and the nauseating sweet smell of death.

The Vietnamese were content to lick their wounds. Knowles was just getting started. He would push west, into the wild country toward Cambodia, and he would give the North Vietnamese army no rest. He would move as no large unit had ever moved before, by great leaps and bounds, covering his helicopter-borne combat assaults with fighter-bombers and gunships and surprise, and the fire of howitzers lifted into hastily prepared fire bases.

The 1st Brigade of the division was selected for the task, beefed up by an extra rifle battalion and two lift companies of the 227th Assault Helicopter Battalion. Each company had four platoons of four "slicks," HU-1D troop-carrying helicopters, each with an attached "hog," or gunship, packing four machine guns and two rocket pods. In addition to its regular attached tube artillery battalion, the brigade had a battery of ARA —aerial rocket artillery—Hueys heavily loaded with rockets, able for brief periods to drench the enemy with high explosive.

The leapfrog tactics of the Cav bore immediate fruit. In repeated contacts with the North Vietnamese the brigade's troopers killed and wounded dozens of the enemy at light cost to themselves, and captured substantial numbers of weapons, grenades, and ammunition. On one occasion, in November, they captured an entire regimental field hospital, including some patients. An NVA battalion that tried to counterattack got itself badly mauled by the Americans, and fell back to the west.

This new kind of war was very hard for Man's troops to handle, well trained as they were. For the Americans were never anywhere very long, and nobody could tell where they would next appear. And when they did, they came without warning, and with murderous firepower. And this new enemy was lean and mean, well trained and eager. He carried little more than ammunition and water, and he moved very fast.

As the Cav worked west, their commander's attention was more and more often drawn to a dominant terrain feature over against the Cambodian border. It was a massif called the Chu Pong, and below it ran a river known as the Ia Drang. There were hostiles there; that was clear. Recon choppers had seen at least two heavily used trails, one of them very clear and well worn. The American command did not know it yet, but this densely forested place was the assembly area for General Man's lacerated command. In it was the whole NVA Front, what remained of the 32d and 33d Regiments, and the brand-new 66th, just down the Ho Chi Minh Trail from the north.

Now, the Ia Drang flows down out of the highlands from the northeast, ultimately joining the great Mekong far to the west. It passes the base of the Chu Pong to the north, and other rivers flow on to the south of the high ground. At one point the Ia Drang flows north and south for a little way, and it was here, on the night of November 3, that the Americans caught an NVA force in a fierce ambush with grenades and M-79 grenade launchers and Claymore mines.

A violent firefight followed at the American patrol base as Cav gunships raked the NVA and reinforced the beleaguered patrol in the dark. When dawn came, the Cav had killed some hundred NVA soldiers for one KIA of their own. It was a bravura demonstration of airmobility. The force had been inserted unknown to the North Vietnamese, who attributed the helicopter noises to the everlasting American reconnaissance. Man's troops had been well and truly suckered, and then whipped into the bargain. General Man was eager to get some back.

And so General Man made his daring decision. He would attack the Americans, moving all the way east to battered Plei Me. He would destroy the whole camp this time, and then push on toward vital Pleiku. And he would take the whole Front with him. The tattered 33d Regiment was directed to form a provisional battalion out of what battered soldiers remained. The still viable 32d would go, and the fresh 66th. And Man would use a battalion of 120-mm mortars and one of 14.5-mm twin antiaircraft machine guns.

But Man got his fight much sooner than he expected. His opponent would be the 3d Brigade of the Cav, even now relieving the 1st Brigade below the Chu Pong Massif. There would be two battalions of the 7th Cavalry, now airmobile infantry, lineal descendants of the men who died with Custer along the Little Big Horn. They were joined by the 2d Battalion of the 5th Cavalry, attached from the 2d Brigade, a battalion of tube artillery, the usual ARA and lift helicopters.

The 3d Brigade would search out the enemy and destroy him, and it would look for him in the Chu Pong.

There were not many places suitable for landing zones. An ideal LZ needed to be at least reasonably clear of obstacles, within range of artillery support if possible, and above all capable of taking as many birds as possible at once. Of the three that the Cav recon spotted, only two were feasible. One, called Yankee, was usable but tough; there were tall tree stumps on it. So it would be the other, LZ X-Ray. It could handle as many as ten Huey slicks at once, and near it the scouts had seen a trail and telephone wire. The enemy was there, or nearby.

The enemy was indeed there, and in force, for X-Ray was almost on top of the North Vietnamese concentration. The Cav would insert a battalion into X-Ray, feeding in the companies as quickly as possible—it would be the 1st Battalion of the famous 7th Cavalry, who greeted one another with "Garry Owen," the title of the regiment's ancient horse cavalry marching song. They were highly trained and ready, and they were wonderfully led. They would need all their courage and ability in the charnel house clearing called LZ X-Ray.

For General Man now changed his plans. Plei Me would have to wait, for the Americans were here, on his turf, where he could bring to bear his whole force, and in favorable terrain. Here he would win his victory over the Americans. Here his men would have their revenge for the defeats and casualties thus far.

It was a typical Cav operation. First there were dummy artillery preparatory fires on two other potential LZs, including Yankee. Then the fire shifted to X-Ray and the terrain around it, twenty minutes of steel supplemented toward the end by ARA helicopters. Right behind them would come the troop-carrying slicks, their own door gunners and the accompanying gunships flooding the edges of the LZ with fire as the slicks flared to land.

The 1st of the 7th came in with a rush, Captain John Herren's B Company leading, the battalion commander right along with them. This was Lieutenant Colonel Hal Moore, a tough, experienced West Pointer who had seen much hard fighting in Korea. Moore set up his CP in the center of the LZ, where a monstrous anthill loomed ten feet above the grass.

B Company secured the LZ until Captain Tony Nadal's A Company was on the ground, and the slicks had departed for the forty-minute round trip to collect Charlie Company. Now Moore turned Herren loose to push out from the LZ, probing for the enemy. It was still quiet, but Moore was sure the enemy was nearby. He got confirmation quickly, as B company spooked and tackled a frightened North Vietnamese regular soldier. He was a deserter, he said, and had been living on bananas for days. But he also said there were three NVA battalions up on the Chu Pong, hungry for a fight.

They had to be found. And so, just past noon, Herren began to push out farther, moving up a finger of high ground poking down toward the LZ from the Chu Pong. Two platoons abreast, his men crossed a dry creek bed below the LZ, and warily moved about 150 meters uphill.

They ran head-on into their quarry, and the fight for X-Ray was on. Herren's second platoon, commanded by Second Lieutenant Henry T. Herrick, was very soon cut off under a hail of fire. Young Herrick pulled his men into a tight perimeter and fought fire with fire. He was taking heavy casualties, and one machine-gun team had been wiped out, its weapon turned on the platoon by the NVA. But Herrick held on, calling his company commander to ask for help.

By this time, elements of Charlie Company were sprinting from choppers on the LZ, artillery fire was striking the lower slopes of the Chu Pong, and air force Skyraiders were hammering those same slopes with five-hundred-pound bombs. Adjustment of these fires was difficult, because observation was not easy through the smoke, dust, and vegetation. But a little at a time, the forward observers managed to work the ordnance down toward the LZ where it was needed. About two-thirty one Skyraider took fire from NVA 12.5 antiaircraft machine guns and bored into the ground. Its pilot did not get out, but the other fighter-bombers kept coming. Shortly afterward, two helicopters were disabled by hostile fire, although the crews of both birds were unhurt.

The NVA, "hugging" the American units tightly to avoid the artillery and air strikes, put in attack after attack on the thin American lines, especially on Herrick's embattled platoon and the troops hanging on to the ground around the creek bed. The lift helicopters were still taking fire as well, but they bored on in, bringing the last of Charlie Company and the first elements of Delta. The company commander's radio operator was killed on the helicopter as it settled into the LZ, and within a few minutes the captain's arm was shattered by an NVA bullet.

Some of the lift ships were also taking out the worst of the wounded from the aid station on the LZ. The battalion surgeon was there working with several aidmen, but some of the hurt troopers needed more help than the doctor could give on X-Ray.

By four o'clock Hal Moore had his understrength battalion together, and the situation was beginning to stabilize a little. His chief concern was Lieutenant Herrick's platoon, still cut off up the mountainside, still surrounded and under very heavy pressure. The ground was too hard to permit digging in under heavy fire, so the platoon simply hugged the ground and took it, returning the fire when it had a target. But by the middle of the afternoon, young Lieutenant Herrick was dying, struck by a bullet that passed transversely through his body.

The young officer had still kept his head and remained in command as long as he could function, ordering his platoon sergeant to call in defensive artillery and redistribute the ammunition among the surviving platoon members. But finally the youngster slipped away, and the platoon sergeant was killed almost immediately after taking command.

The sergeant commanding one squad, and the mortar forward observer, were both killed in the next few minutes, and the artillery forward observer was already disabled. The little platoon was in extremis. It had landed twenty-nine strong. Nine men were dead and thirteen more wounded, and now a remarkable man took command.

Staff Sergeant Clyde Savage commanded the third squad of the platoon, and he was a professional. He had begun the fight by neatly extricating his squad from the initial violent contact on the hillside. He is known to have killed at least a dozen enemy soldiers with his M-16. Now he immediately pulled the artillery FO's radio to him and began to adjust artillery fire, closer and closer to the platoon's position. Savage's position was under attack by at least one company, probably two, but his artful use of artillery kept the enemy at bay and caused them terrible casualties. His cool leadership would win him the Distinguished Service Cross.

About five o'clock Moore tried again to rescue his isolated platoon, sending both A and B companies in to the attack. They ran into a hail of fire, pushing ahead for a while against NVA soldiers firing from holes and trees. Lieutenant Joe Marm ran gallantly across open ground to destroy an enemy machine gun with grenades and M-16, but courage was not enough. Marm's action would earn him a bullet in the jaw and the Medal of Honor, but the attack could go no further. All of Tony Nadal's platoon leaders were down, dead or wounded, and it was clear that the two companies would bleed to death trying to reach Herrick's platoon.

Moore wisely withdrew his battered companies into a night perimeter. As they fell back in the gathering dusk, reinforcements arrived in a cloud of dust and *whop-whop* of rotors, Bravo Company of Moore's sister battalion, the 2d of the 7th. Its commander, Captain Myron Diduryk, fed his men into the perimeter and prepared for the night.

During the hours of darkness the helicopters kept coming, working their way into X-Ray guided by the flashlights of the pathfinder detail. They brought desperately needed resupply: ammunition, morphine and dressings, water. Up on the Chu Pong little lights were moving, the lights of NVA units moving down to renew the battle. The next day would be another tough one.

It was not an easy night, either. The NVA probed the perimeter all through the darkness, but without any serious penetration. All through the night air support was overhead, including flare-droppers and Puff the Magic Dragon, the Gatling gun aircraft. Meanwhile, more support for X-Ray was forming up, including a full fresh battalion, the 2d of the 5th Infantry, due to start for Moore's men overland at daylight. Another company of 2d Battalion, 7th Infantry would be lifted in by helicopter early in the morning.

Up on the hillside, Sergeant Savage's little band repulsed three attacks, calling in artillery within a hundred feet of their positions. They could hear the NVA calling to one another in the pitch darkness, and dragging away their dead and wounded after each assault. The wounded platoon medic, Specialist Five Charles Lose, still tended to his wounded in the darkness, using C-ration toilet paper when his dressings ran out. The platoon savaged their attackers repeatedly, and miraculously lost not a single man more during the long night.

At first light Moore pushed patrols outside his main perimeter, and they immediately ran into heavy NVA fire. The enemy followed with heavy attacks on the American defenders, attacks the Cav troopers drove back with murderous close-range fire and grenades. Now all supporting fires were being coordinated from Moore's CP inside the X-Ray perimeter, the rounds working in within fifty yards of the perimeter.

Brigade added more artillery to the screen falling around X-Ray, and Air Force fighter-bombers continued to drop their ordnance almost on top of the American defenders. One American died as napalm splashed into the perimeter, but miraculously that was the only "short round" the Air Force dropped during the fight.

By noon the NVA fire had slackened substantially, and 2d of the 5th pushed panting into the perimeter from the south. Its commander, Lieutenant Colonel Bob Tully, conferred quickly with Moore. Both men were most concerned about the lost platoon, still hanging on up on the slope of the Chu Pong. And so Tully's fresh troopers and weary Bravo Company, 1st of the 7th, pushed on through the creek bed and up into the scrub, and came at last to Sergeant Savage's battlefield.

Savage's people had not suffered a fatal casualty since he had taken command, and the evidence was everywhere of the terrible destruction they had brought down on the NVA. The relief force found the lost machine gun and its crew, and with them the bodies of successive NVA crews who had tried to use the gun against the Americans. Farthest uphill they found the body of the first man killed in Herrick's platoon, a .45 pistol still clutched in his hand. NVA dead were scattered everywhere.

Meanwhile, Moore's men had pushed out from X-Ray in all directions. They found desolation. Hundreds of North Vietnamese corpses littered the ground. Some were stacked in heaps behind the anthills, and bloody bandages and blood trails covered the entire area. And there were American dead as well: One soldier lay with his hands locked on the throat of a dead Communist infantryman. An American lieutenant lay dead, five NVA corpses around him.

There was still sporadic hostile fire, but the NVA had shot their bolt. American artillery and air searched for them, and away to the west B-52 bombers put in an "arc light," a massive carpet of bombs that ripped and shredded the forest and the earth.

That night four more attacks came in on X-Ray, to be repulsed with great slaughter. By dawn the NVA fire had slackened, though the Cav greeted the new day with a "mad minute," a torrent of fire in which every man hosed down the ground and trees before him. And with that it was almost over. The Americans swept the ground in front again, Diduryk's men taking some wounded in a brisk firefight that cost the enemy twenty-seven more dead. And then, behind more artillery, the sweep was completed and evacuation began. Every American who had come into X-Ray had been accounted for—they would all leave the desolation of the LZ, both the living and the dead.

The Cav had covered itself with glory. Hard-nosed Colonel Moore said it for everybody, tears running down his face: "I've got men in body bags today that had less than a week to go in the army. These men fought all the way; they never gave an inch."

So the Cav left X-Ray, amid the carping of some of the media who didn't understand that real estate meant nothing in the long haul, only the need to bring the enemy to battle and whip him.

And whipped the North Vietnamese army certainly was. A total of 634 bodies were counted on the ground, and the NVA penchant for hiding its losses meant that at least another 500 had been carried away. Add to those the severely wounded who would die in spite of primitive medical treatment, and it is fair to place the enemy's dead at a minimum of 1,500. Their abandoned equipment included over two hundred rifles and carbines, twenty-one machine guns—including four water-cooled heavy Maxims—five rocket launchers, and two mortar tubes, plus ammunition beyond counting. American losses were 79 killed and 121 wounded.

In later times there were those who tried to ridicule the estimate of NVA casualties. Many of these were people with a political ax to grind, and virtually none of them had more than a rudimentary idea of what combat and fighting men are like. Their whining to the contrary notwithstanding, the

American victory at X-Ray was clear and convincing. One Vietnamese survivor of the fight said later that his battalion of the 66th Regiment could muster fewer than one hundred soldiers after X-Ray, and many of these were wounded.

Hal Moore, who would finish a distinguished career as a three-star general, never tired of stating and restating one immutable truth. The American soldiers who fought in Vietnam had no superiors, and very few peers. Regulars or draftees, they were tough, professional, and willing.

The shame of it all was that neither the political leadership of their country, nor many of the citizens at home, were worthy of them.

IN FEW WORDS

Just after the United States announced her intention to intervene against Iraq, my wife and I visited our captain son, serving with the 101st Airborne Division (Air Assault) at Fort Campbell, Kentucky.

The whole post was seething with purposeful activity, as equipment was made ready and columns of vehicles loaded up and moved out for ports of embarkation. In spite of any number of bittersweet farewells—we got to see our son for about two hours—the atmosphere at Campbell was all immense determination and high professionalism.

As we left Fort Campbell, we followed a column of the 101st's vehicles for a while. The tailgate of the last truck sported a big sign—black paint on a piece of cardboard. It was written simply in imperishable GI language and said all there was to say, for the 101st and for America:

GONE TO KICK ASS!

And so it was to be.

BIBLIOGRAPHY

For readers who would like to read more about the engagements this book describes, following are some short bibliographies of the major sources used, set out by chapter. Where I consider a book an exceptionally fine piece of work, I have said so. For example, the chapter on 77 Brigade at Mogaung relied in part on what I consider to be the finest book ever written on men at war: Brigadier John Masters' *The Road Past Mandalay*.

For general information, I can recommend some excellent sources. The West Point Atlases are uniformly excellent for all of America's wars. As to our Civil War, anything by Douglas Southall Freeman or Bruce Catton is both dependable and excellent. For the old British and British Indian Army, the wellspring is Sir John Fortescue's multi-volume *History of the British Army*.

THE GENTLE WATERS OF AVON

Beamish, Tufton. *Battle Royal*. London: Muller, 1965.

Costain, Thomas. *The Magnificent Century*. Doubleday, 1959.

Halliwell, Phillips. *Rishanger's Chronicle of the Barons' War*. London: Camden Society, 1940.

Hutton, William. *Simon de Montfort and His Cause*. Putnam's, 1888.

Knowles, C. *Simon de Montfort*. London: Hist. Assoc., 1965.

Murray, Jane. *The Kings and Queens of England.* Scribner's, 1974.

McDonald, John. *Great Battlefields of the World.* Macmillan, 1984.

Prestwich, Michael. *Edward I.* U. California Press, 1988.

Prothero, G.W. *Life of Simon de Montfort.* Longman's Green, London, 1877.

Smurthwaite, David. *Battlefields of Britain.* Webb & Bower, Exeter, Eng. 1984.

Treharne, R.F. *Simon de Montfort and Baronial Reform.* Hambledon Press, London, 1986.

THE END OF A THOUSAND YEARS

Barber, Noel. *The Sultans.* Simon & Schuster, 1973.

Maclagan, Michael. *The City of Constantinople.* Praeger, 1968.

Melegari, Vezio. *The Great Military Sieges.* Thomas Crowell, 1972.

Oman, Sir Charles. *The Byzantine Empire.* Putnam's, 1892.

Ostrogorsky, Georgije. *History of the Byzantine State.* Rutgers, New Brunswick NJ, 1969.

Runciman, Sir Steven. *The Fall of Constantinople, 1453.* Cambridge, 1965.

Vasiliev, Alexander. *History of the Byzantine Empire.* Wisconsin Press, 1952.

NO SURRENDER

Arber, Edward. *The Last Fight of the Revenge At Sea.* Constable & Co., Westminster, 1901.

Bell. *Elizabethan Seamen.* Lippincott, nd.

Cheyney, Edward. II *A History of England.* Longmans, Green, New York, 1926.

Corbett, Julian. II *Drake and the Tudor Navy.* London: Longmans, Green, 1917.

Housman. *War Letters of Fallen Englishmen.* Gollancz, London, ca 1930.

Miller, Amos. *Sir Richard Grenville of the Civil War.* London: Phillmore, 1979.

Raleigh, Walter. *A Report of the Truth of the Fight About the Isles of the Azores This Last Summer.* London: Ponsonbie, 1591. reprinted in Arber, op. cit.

Rowse, A.L. *Sir Richard Grenville of the Revenge.* Houghton Mifflin, 1937.

A TRIAL OF SOULS

American Heritage. *The Revolution.*

Dwyer, William. *The Day Is Ours!* Viking, 1983.

Katcher, Phillip. *Encyclopedia of British, Provincial & German Army Units, 1775–1783.* Stackpole, 1973.

Ketchum, Richard. *The Winter Soldiers.* Doubleday, 1973.

Leckie, Robert. I *The Wars of America.* Harper & Row, 1968.

Lesser, Charles. *The Sinews of Independence.* U. of Chicago Press, 1976.

Montross, Lynn. *Rag Tag and Bobtail.* Harper, 1952.

Natkiel, Richard. *Atlas of American Wars.* Bison Books, 1986.

Pearson, Michael. *Those Damned Rebels.* Putnam's, 1972.

Stryker, William. *The Battles of Trenton and Princeton.* Houghton Mifflin, 1898.

PIERRE'S HOLE

Billington, Ray. *The Far Western Frontier.* Harper, 1956.

DeVoto, Bernard. *Across The Wide Missouri.* Houghton Mifflin, 1947.

Time-Life Books. *The Trailblazers.* Time-Life, 1973.

Gilbert, Bil. *Westering Man, The Life of Joseph Walker.* Atheneum, 1983.

Leonard, Zenas. *The Adventures of Zenas Leonard.* Oklahoma Press, 1959.

Patterson, Bradley. "The Pierre's Hole Fight," in Potomac Corral of the Westerners' *Great Indian Fights.* Nebraska Press, 1966.

Sunder, John. *Bill Sublette, Mountain Man.* Oklahoma Press, 1959.

Vestal, Stanley. *Mountain Men.* Houghton Mifflin, 1937.

DIE HARD

Barnes, R.M. *Regiments and Uniforms of the British Army.* London: Seeley Service, 1950.

Fortescue, John. *History of the British Army.* London: Macmillan, 1910–1930.

ANABASIS

Connor, Seymour. *North America Divided.* Oxford, 1971.

Davis, Julia. *Ride With The Eagle.* Harcourt, Brace, 1962.

Dufour, Charles. *The Mexican War.* Hawthorn, 1968.

Faulk, Odie. *The Mexican War, Changing Interpretations.* Swallow Press, 1973.

Hughes, John. *Doniphan's Expedition.* Bryant & Douglas, 1907.

Robinson, Jacob. *A Journal of the Santa Fe Expedition Under Colonel Doniphan.* Princeton, 1932.

Singletary, Otis. *The Mexican War.* U. of Chicago Press, 1960.

Smith, Justin. I *The War With Mexico.* Macmillan, 1919.

Twitchell, Ralph. *The Military Occupation of New Mexico, 1846–51.* Privately published, 1909.

WHEN OLD ROCK BENNING
HELD THE BRIDGE

Bradford, Ned (ed.). *Battles and Leaders of the Civil War.* Appelton-Century-Crofts, 1956.

Catton, Bruce. *Mr. Lincoln's Army.* Doubleday, 1951.

Clark. "A Hard Day For Mother," *Yankee.* July 1979.

Commager, Henry. *The Blue and the Gray.* Bobbs-Merrill, 1950.

Frassanito, William. *Antietam, The Photographic Legacy of America's Bloodiest Day.* Scribner's, 1978.

Freeman, Douglas. II and III *Lee's Lieutenants.* Scribner's, 1943.

Freeman, Douglas. II *R.E. Lee.* Scribner's, 1934.

Luvaas, Jay, & Nelson, Harold. *The Battle of Antietam.* South

Mountain Press, 1987. [A United States Army War College Staff Ride—excellent.]

Murfin, James. *The Gleam of Bayonets*. Yoseloff, 1965.

Palfrey, Francis. *The Antietam and Fredericksburg*. Scribner's, 1882.

Schildt, Stephen. *Drums Along The Antietam*. McClain, 1972.

Sears, Stephen. *Landscape Turned Red*. Warner, 1985.

Sears, Stephen. *Bloodiest Day: The Battle of Antietam*. Eastern Acorn Press, 1990.

Tilberg, Frederick. *Antietam*. National Park Service Handbook 31, 1960, rev. 1961.

BAYONET!

Catton, Bruce. *Glory Road*. Doubleday, 1952.

Catton, Bruce. *This Hallowed Ground*. Doubleday, 1955.

Coddington, Edwin. *The Gettysburg Campaign*. Scribner's, 1968.

Commager, Henry. *The Blue and the Gray*. Bobbs-Merrill, 1950.

Dowdey, Clifford. *Death of a Nation*. Knopf, 1958.

Haskell, Franklin. *The Battle of Gettysburg*. Wisconsin History Commission, 1908.

Persico, Joseph. *My Enemy, My Brother*. Viking, 1977.

Pfanz, Harry. *Gettysburg, The Second Day*. North Carolina Press, 1987.

Pullen, John. *The Twentieth Maine*. Lippincott, 1957. [*Excellent.*]

Tilberg, Frederick. *Gettysburg*. National Park Service Handbook 9, 1954.

Wheeler, Richard. *Witness to Gettysburg*. Harper, 1987.

TRIPLE CANISTER

Catton, Bruce. *Glory Road*. Doubleday, 1952.

Downey, Fairfax. *The Guns At Gettysburg*. McKay, 1958.

Freeman, Douglas. III *Lee's Lieutenants*. Scribner's, 1944.

Haight, Theron. *Three Wisconsin Cushings*. Wisconsin History Commission, 1910.

Hancock, Mrs. W.S. *Reminiscenses of W.S. Hancock.* Webster, 1887.

Haskell, Franklin. "High-Water Mark, The Battle of Gettysburg," in Webb (ed.) *Crucial Moments of the Civil War.* Fountainhead, 1968.

Hollingsworth, Alan. *The Third Day At Gettysburg, Pickett's Charge.* Holt, 1959.

Junkin, David. *Life of Hancock.* Appleton, New York, 1880.

Montgomery, James. *The Shaping of a Battle: Gettysburg.* Chilton, 1959.

Naisawald, Louis. *Grape and Canister.* Oxford, 1960.

Stewart, George. *Pickett's Charge.* Houghton Mifflin, 1959.

Tucker, Glenn. *High Tide At Gettysburg.* Bobbs-Merrill, 1958.

TWELVE TO ONE

Brady, Cyrus. *Indian Fights and Fighters.* Doubleday, 1909.

Hutchins, James. "The Fight At Beecher Island," in Potomac Corral of the Westerners' *Great Western Indian Fights.* Nebraska Press, 1966.

Leckie, Robert. *Military Conquest of the Southern Plains.* Oklahoma Press, 1963.

Utley, Robert. *Frontier Regulars.* MacMillan, 1973.

THE BIGGEST FIGHT OF ALL

Carter, Harvey. *Dear Old Kit.* Oklahoma Press, 1968.

Coggins, Jack. *Arms and Equipment of the Civil War.* Wilmington, NC: Broadfoot, 1989.

Compton, Lawrence. "The First Battle of Adobe Walls," in Potomac Corral of the Westerners' *Great Western Indian Fights.* Nebraska Press, 1966.

Dykes, J.C. "The Second Battle of Adobe Walls," in *Great Western Indian Fights.*

Estergreen, M. Morgan. *Kit Carson.* Oklahoma Press, 1962.

Guild, Thelma. *Kit Carson.* Nebraska Press, 1984.

Pettis, George. *Kit Carson's Fight With The Comanche and Kiowa*

Indians At The Adobe Walls, On the Canadian River. Rider, Providence, 1878.

Sabin, Edward. *Kit Carson Days.* Chicago: McClurg, 1914.

Thomas, Dean. *Cannons, An Introduction To Civil War Artillery.* Thomas, Gettysburg, 1985.

THE HAND OF CAPTAIN DANJOU

Geraghty, Tony. *March Or Die.* New York: Facts On File, 1986.

McLeave, Hugh. *The Damned Die Hard.* New York: Saturday Review, 1973.

O'Ballance, Edgar. *The Story of the French Foreign Legion.* London: Faber, 1961.

Porch, Douglas. *The French Foreign Legion.* Harper Collins, 1991.

PLEVNA

Barber, Noel. *The Sultans.* Simon & Schuster, 1973.

Elegari, Vezio. *The Great Military Sieges.* Crowell, 1972.

Furneaux, Rupert. *The Siege of Plevna.* London: Anthony Blond, 1958.

Greene, Francis. *The Russian Army And Its Campaigns In Turkey, 1877–78.* Appleton, New York, 1908.

Montagu, Irving. *Camp & Studio.* London: W.H. Allen, 1892.

Pears, Edwin. *Life of Abdul Hamid.* Holt, 1917.

Smith, Joseph. *Smallarms of the World.* Stackpole, 1969.

Walker, Dale. *Januarius MacGahan, The Life and Campaigns of an American War Correspondent.* Ohio University Press, 1988.

FATE AND GLORY

Barnes, R.M. *Regiments and Uniforms of the British Army.* London: Seeley Service, 1950.

Batchelor, John and Hogg, Ian. *Artillery.* Scribner's, 1972.

Brown, Ashley and Reed, Jonathan (eds). *The Special Forces.* National Historical Society, 1989.

Buchan, John. *History of the Great War.* Houghton Mifflin, 1923.

Corbett-Smith, Arthur. *The Retreat From Mons.* London: Cassell, 1916.

Dunn, J.C. *The War The Infantry Knew, 1914–1918.* Cardinal, 1989.

Dupuy, Trevor. *The Battles In The West.* Watts, 1967.

Gordon, George. *Mons And The Retreat.* London: Constable, 1918.

Maurice, Frederick. *Forty Days in 1914.* Doran, 1919.

Terraine, John. *Mons, The Retreat To Victory.* London: Batsford, 1960.

SAINT GEORGE'S DAY

Bell, John. *The Zeebrugge Affair.* Doran, 1918.

Carpenter, A.F.B.. *The Blocking of Zeebrugge.* Boston & New York: Houghton Mifflin, 1922.

Keyes, Roger. *Naval Memoirs.* Dutton, 1935.

Newbolt, Henry. V *Naval Operations.* [Admiralty official history, WW I] London: Longmans, Green, 1931.

Pitt, Barrie. *Zeebrugge.* New York: Ballantine, 1966.

Stock, James. *Zeebrugge.* New York: Ballantine, 1974.

WHEN THE BUTTERFLY
WHIPPED THE EAGLE

Gibbons, Floyd. *The Red Knight of Germany.* Doubleday, 1927.

Munson, Kenneth. *Fighters 1914–18.* MacMillan, 1969.

Nowarra, Heinz. *Richthofen and the Flying Circus.* Los Angeles: Aero Publishers, 1958.

Reynolds, Quentin. *They Fought for the Sky.* Bantam, 1958.

Schurmacher, Emile. *Richthofen, The Red Baron.* Warner, 1970.

Titler, Dale. *The Day The Red Baron Died.* Walker, 1970.

GOODBYE, MY SON

Jellinek, Frank. *The Civil War In Spain*. London: Gollancz, 1938.

Matthews, Herbert. *The Yoke and the Arrows*. Braziller, 1961.

Payne, Robert. *The Civil War In Spain*. Putnam's, 1962.

Thomas, Hugh. *The Spanish Civil War*. Harper, 1961.

THE NAVY'S HERE

Bennett, Geoffrey. *Battle of the River Plate*. U.S. Naval Institute, 1972.

Campbell, Archibald. *The Battle of the Plate*. London: Jenkins, 1940.

Churchill, Winston. *The Gathering Storm*. Houghton Mifflin, 1948.

Frischauer, Willi and Jackson, Robert. *The Altmark Affair*. MacMillan, 1955.

H.M. Admiralty. *Battle of the River Plate*. London: H.M.S.O., 1943.

Pope, Dudley. *Battle of the River Plate*. Putnam's 1969.

Rasenack, Friedrich. *Panzershiff Admiral Graf Spee*. West Germany: Koehlers Verlagsgellschaft, Herford, 1957.

Roskill. I *The War At Sea, 1939–1945*. London: H.M.S.O., 1976.

Vian, Sir Philip. *Action This Day*. London: Muller, 1960.

Von der Porten, Edward. *The German Navy in World War II*. Galahad, 1969.

IN THE WITCH'S KETTLE

Carrell, Paul. *Hitler Moves East*. Bantam, 1967.

Craig, William. *Enemy At The Gates, The Battle For Stalingrad*. Ballantine, 1968.

von Melinthin, F.W. *German Generals of World War II*. Oklahoma Press, 1977.

WHEN MAD MIKE CALVERT
TOOK UMBRAGE

Allen, Louis. *Burma, The Longest War*. St. Martin's Press, 1984.

Bidwell, Shelford. *The Chindit War*. MacMillan, 1980.

Calvert, Michael. *Prisoners of Hope*. Corgi, 1973.

Carew, Tim. *The Longest Retreat*. Hamish Hamilton, 1969.

Fellowes-Gordon, Ian. *The Magic War*. Scribner's, 1971.

James, Harold and Sheil-Small, Denis. *The Gurkhas*. Stackpole, 1966.

Masters, John. *The Road Past Mandalay*. Harper, 1969 [The *best* book about war ever written, for my money].

Ogburn, Richard. *The Marauders*. Harper, 1959.

Slim, W.S. *Defeat Into Victory*. Cassell, 1956.

Swinson, Arthur. *The Battle of Kohima*. Stein & Day, 1967.

FOR VALOR

Appleman, Roy. *Escaping the Trap*. Texas A&M Press, 1990.

Blair, Clay. *The Forgotten War*. Times Books, 1987.

Congressional Medal of Honor. Sharp & Dunnigan, 1984.

Hammel, Eric. *Chosin*. Vanguard Press, 1981.

Hopkins, William. *One Bugle, No Drums*. Algonquin Books, 1986.

Leckie, Robert. II *The Wars of America*. Harper & Row, 1968.

Leckie, Robert. *The March To Glory*. Bantam, 1961.

Montross, Lynn. *U.S. Marine Operations in Korea: Vol. III Chosin Reservoir Campaign*. USMC, 1957.

Spurr, Russell. *Enter The Dragon*. Newmarket Press, 1988.

DISASTER ON THE R.C. 4

Bodard, Lucien. *The Quicksand War*. Atlantic—Little, Brown, 1967 [fascinating book by a French correspondent and old Asia hand—fine insight into the early part of the French war and the Byzantine politics of Vietnam].

Davidson, Phillip. *Vietnam At War*. Presidio, 1988 [*excellent general history*].

Fall, Bernard. *Street Without Joy*. Stackpole, 1967 [the all-around best book about the French days in Vietnam].

DEATH IN THE MONSOON

Davidson, Phillip. *Vietnam At War*. Presidio, 1988.

Fall, Bernard. *Hell In A Very Small Place*. Vintage, 1968 [the best book I know about Dien Bien Phu].

Fall, Bernard. *Street Without Joy*. Stackpole, 1967.

Leary, William. "CAT At Dien Bien Phu," *Aerospace Historian*, Sept. 1984.

Roy, Jules. *The Battle of Dien Bien Phu*. Pyramid, 1966.

TO DIE ALONE IN THE SILENCE

Fall, Bernard. *Street Without Joy*. Stackpole, 1967.

Riessen, Rene. *Jungle Mission*. Crowell, 1957.

LZ X-RAY

Cash, John. "Fight At Ia Drang," in *Seven Firefights in Vietnam*. US Army, 1970.

Coleman, J.D.. *Pleiku*. St. Martin's Press, 1988.

Davidson, Phillip. *Vietnam At War*. Presidio, 1988.

Moore, Harold and Galloway, Joseph. *We Were Soldiers Once . . . And Young*. Random House, 1992 [the best book I know about the American time in Vietnam and one of the best ever about men at war].

INDEX